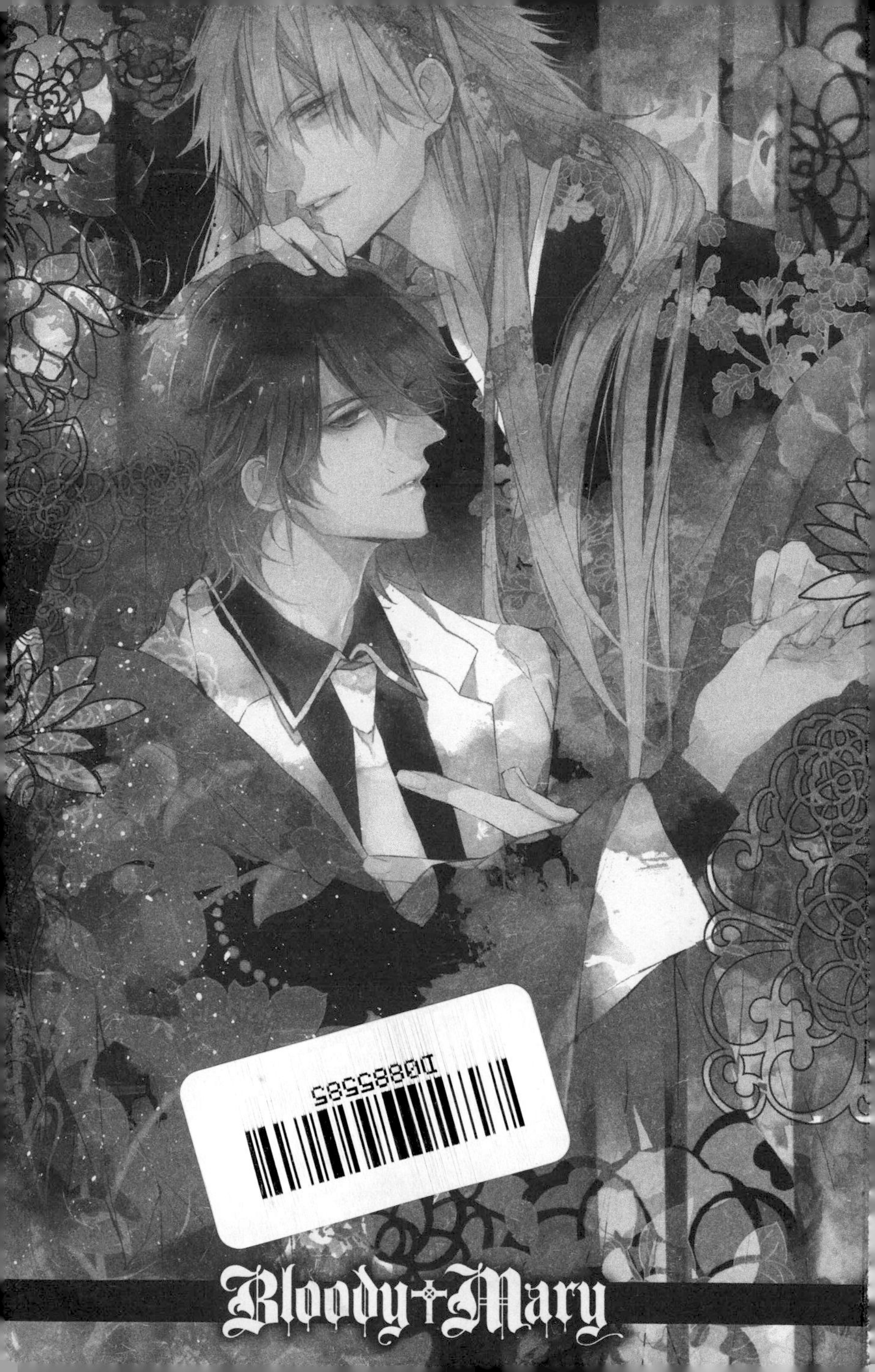
Bloody+Mary

Bloody✝Mary

③ contents

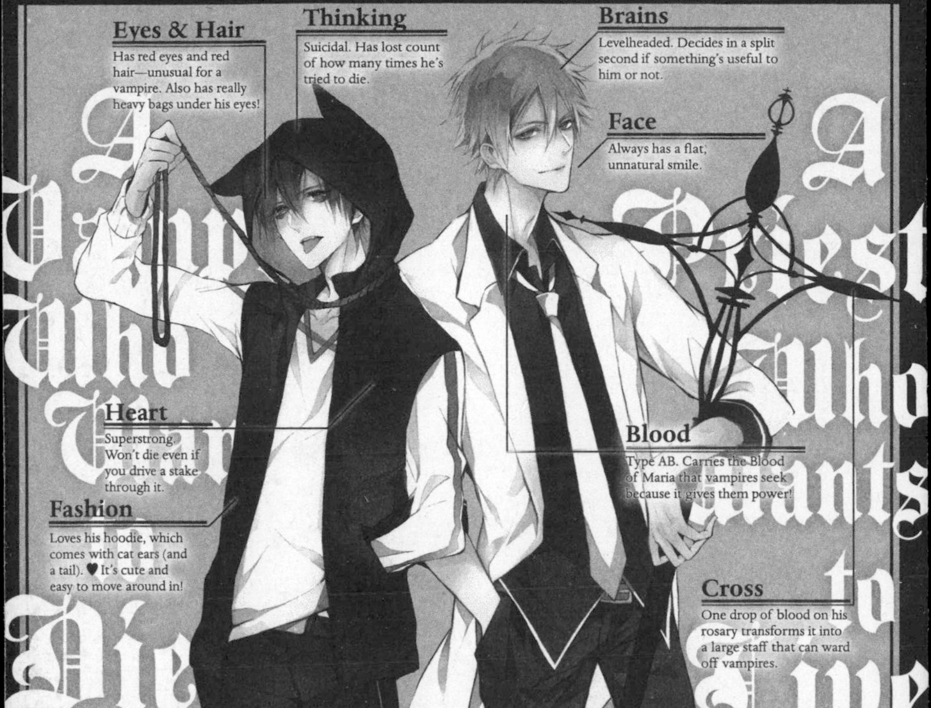
Eyes & Hair
Has red eyes and red hair—unusual for a vampire. Also has really heavy bags under his eyes!
Thinking
Suicidal. Has lost count of how many times he's tried to die.
Brains
Levelheaded. Decides in a split second if something's useful to him or not.
Face
Always has a flat, unnatural smile.
Heart
Superstrong. Won't die even if you drive a stake through it.
Blood
Type AB. Carries the Blood of Maria that vampires seek because it gives them power!
Fashion
Loves his hoodie, which comes with cat ears (and a tail). ♥ It's cute and easy to move around in!
Cross
One drop of blood on his rosary transforms it into a large staff that can ward off vampires.
Die
Live
BLOODY MARY
Legs
His height—179 cm—makes him good at fleeing the scene.
ICHIRO ROSARIO DI MARIA
Legs
Has an amazing ability to jump. Enjoys sitting atop his favorite lamppost at Bashamichi.

An immortal vampire who wants nothing more than to die. He has long searched for Maria, who is supposed to possess the Power of Exorcism that can kill him, but so long as that power is sealed within and is therefore inaccessible to Maria (for now), Mary won't get his wish of death.

After sneaking into the Sakuraba estate with Maria, Mary is now being held captive by Yzak, who he'd been searching for! Convinced that Mary is the vampire who killed his son Yusei, Yzak tortures Mary in order to learn how he did it. But when Mary laughs off his efforts with a boastful "I can take the pain!" Yzak decides to try a different approach...

A high school student and priest who lives in Yokohama. He came to hate vampires after his father, Yusei, was murdered by one.

While searching for the Power of Exorcism that he should possess, he discovers that the Sakuraba family has kept information hidden from him, thus causing him to lose all faith in the Sakurabas. Together with Mary, he trespasses onto the Sakuraba estate and comes across disturbing old photographs of himself hooked up to what looks like equipment for an experiment. Seeing the photos stirs up memories of the night he saw a vampire standing over his dead father. The vampire looked strikingly similar to Mary.

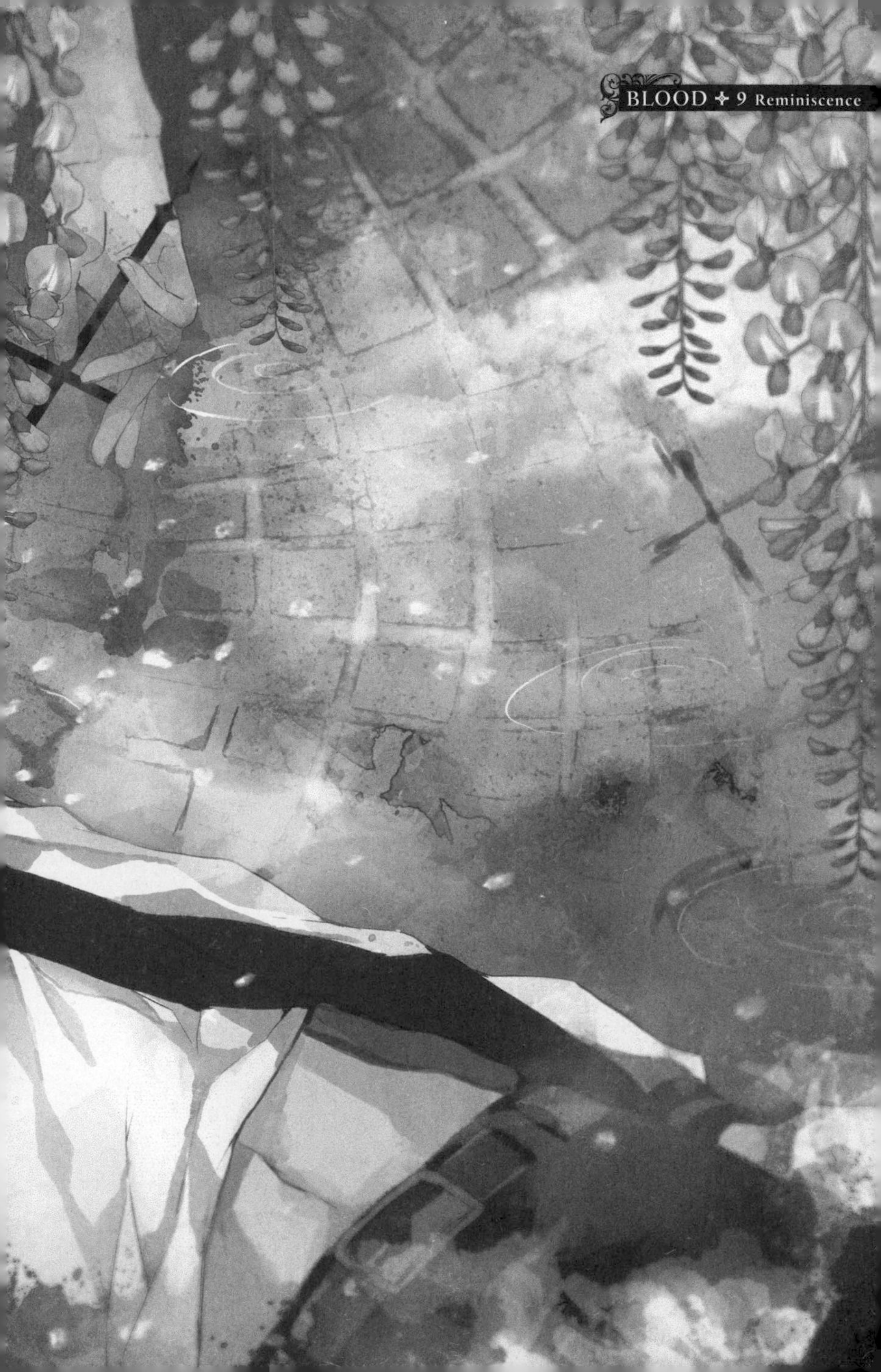
BLOOD ✦ 9 Reminiscence

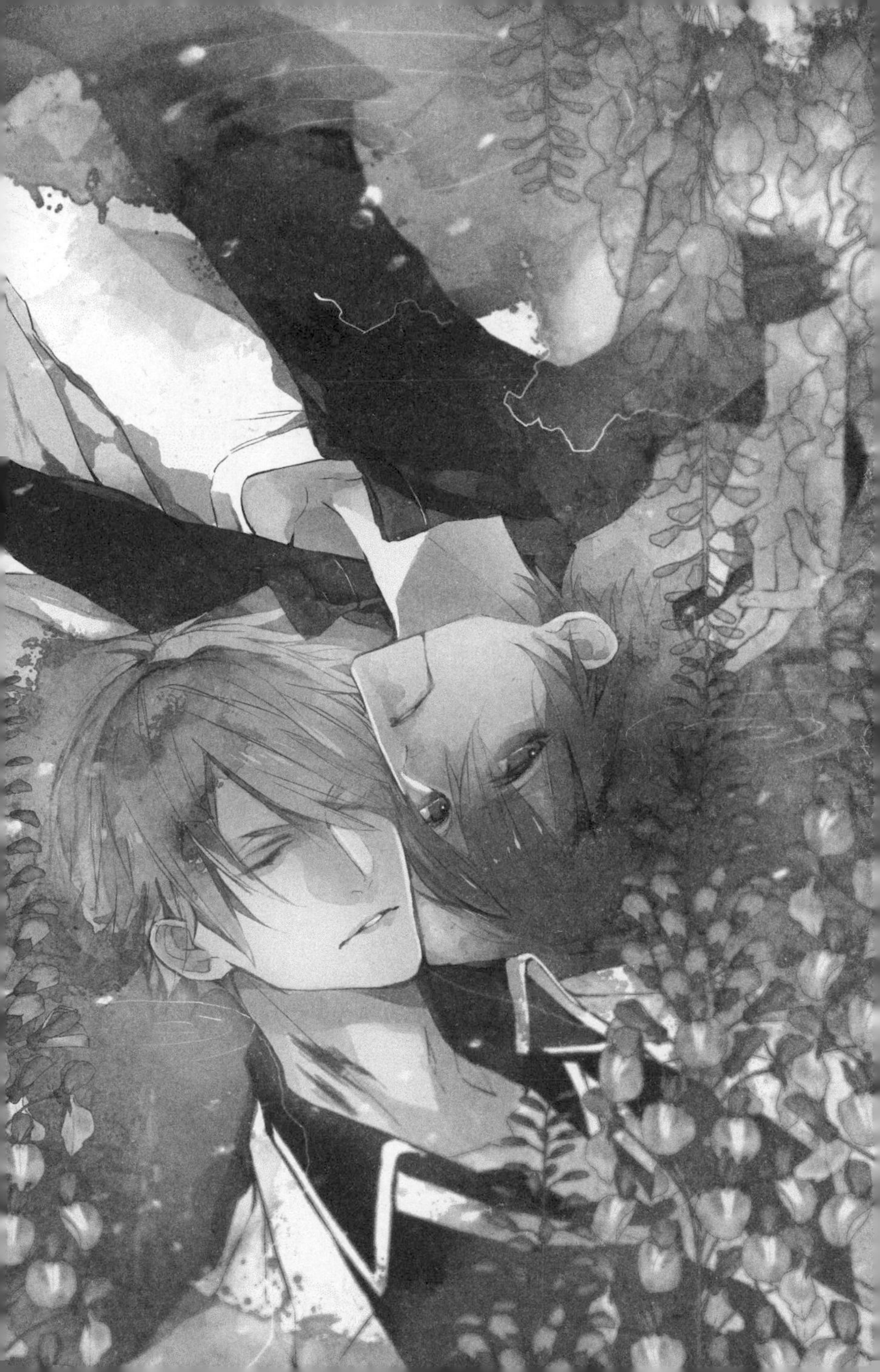

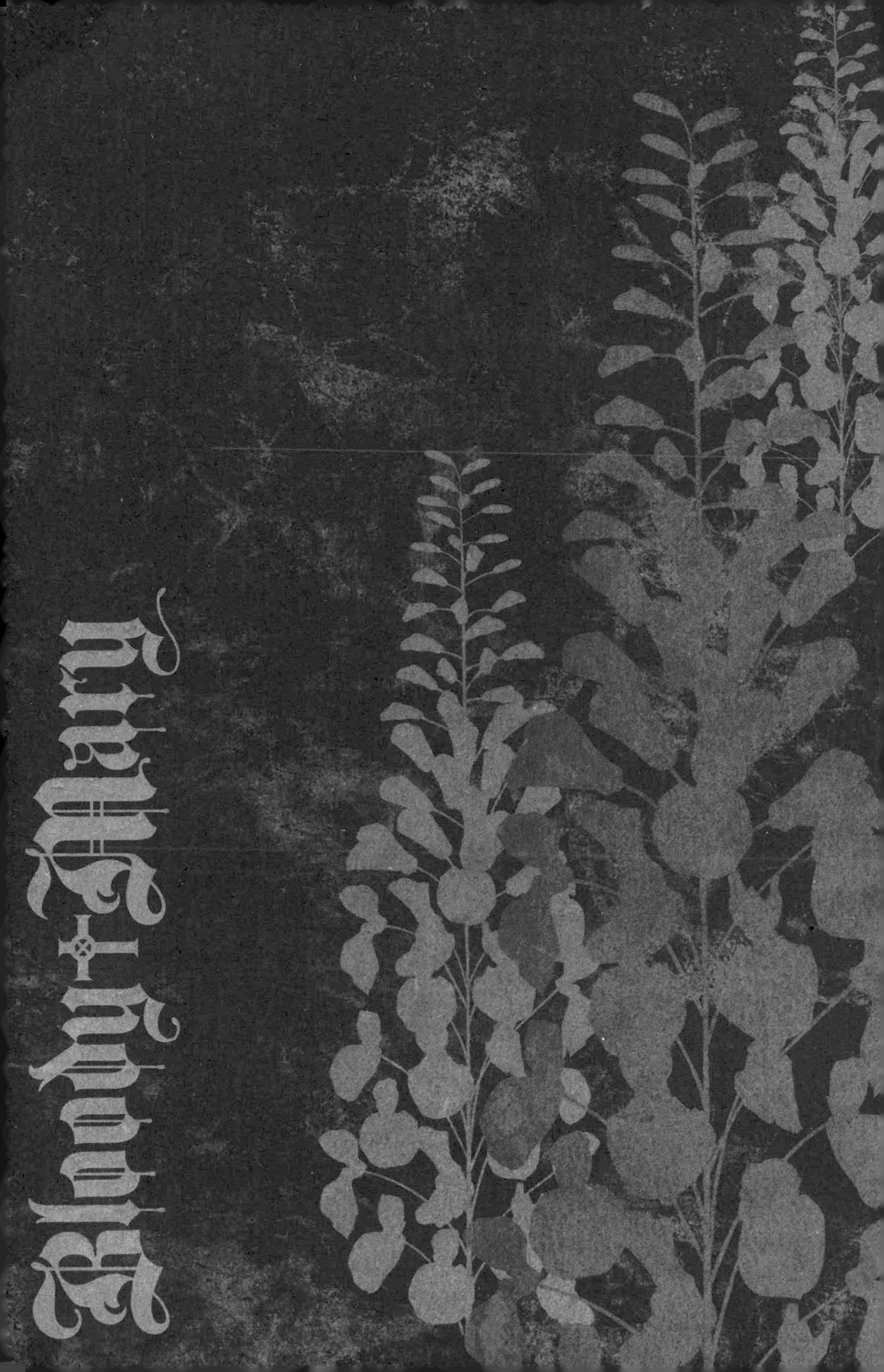
Bloody Mary

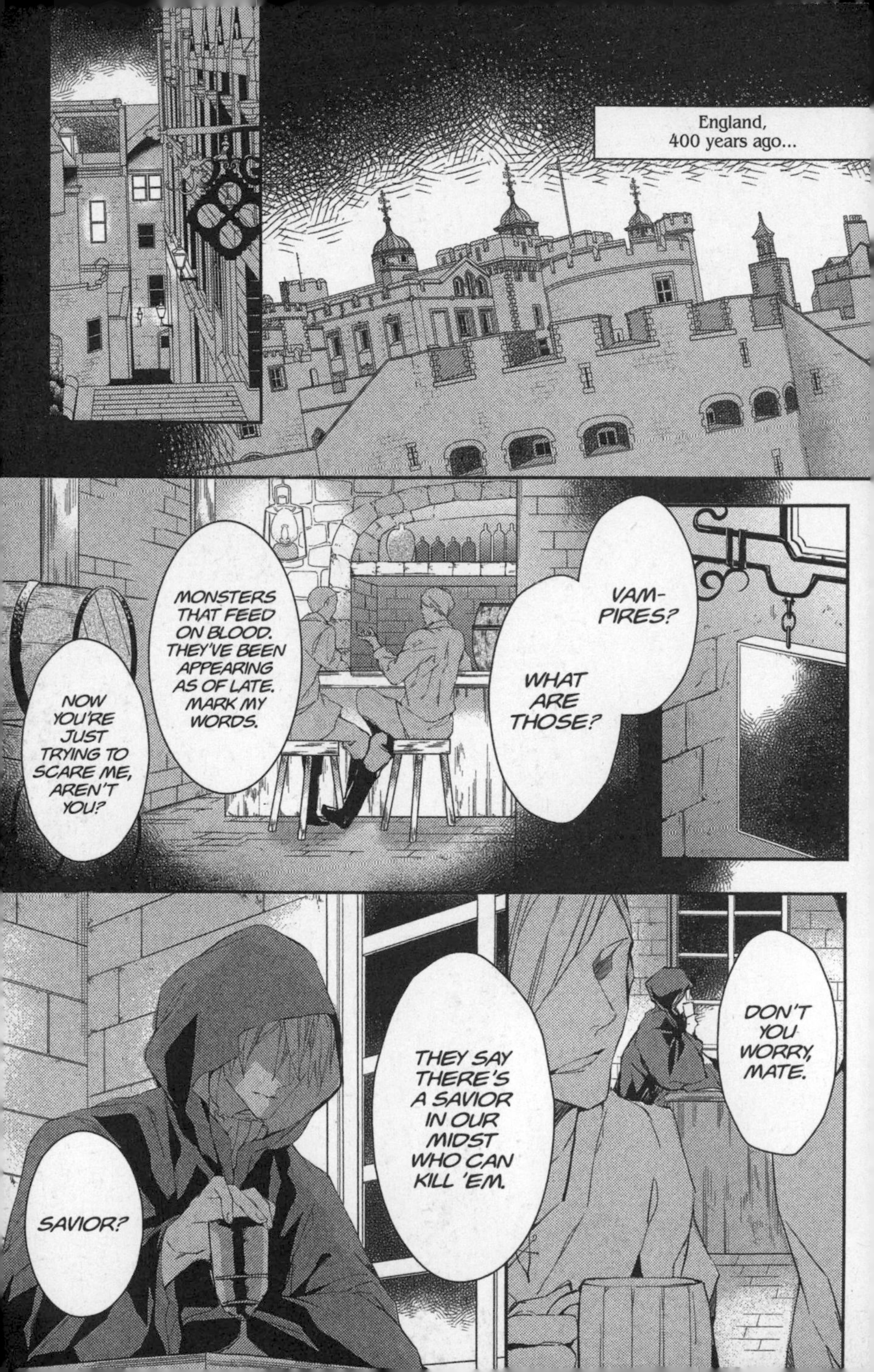
England,
400 years ago...
VAM-PIRES?
WHAT ARE THOSE?
MONSTERS THAT FEED ON BLOOD. THEY'VE BEEN APPEARING AS OF LATE. MARK MY WORDS.
NOW YOU'RE JUST TRYING TO SCARE ME, AREN'T YOU?
DON'T YOU WORRY, MATE.
THEY SAY THERE'S A SAVIOR IN OUR MIDST WHO CAN KILL 'EM.
SAVIOR?

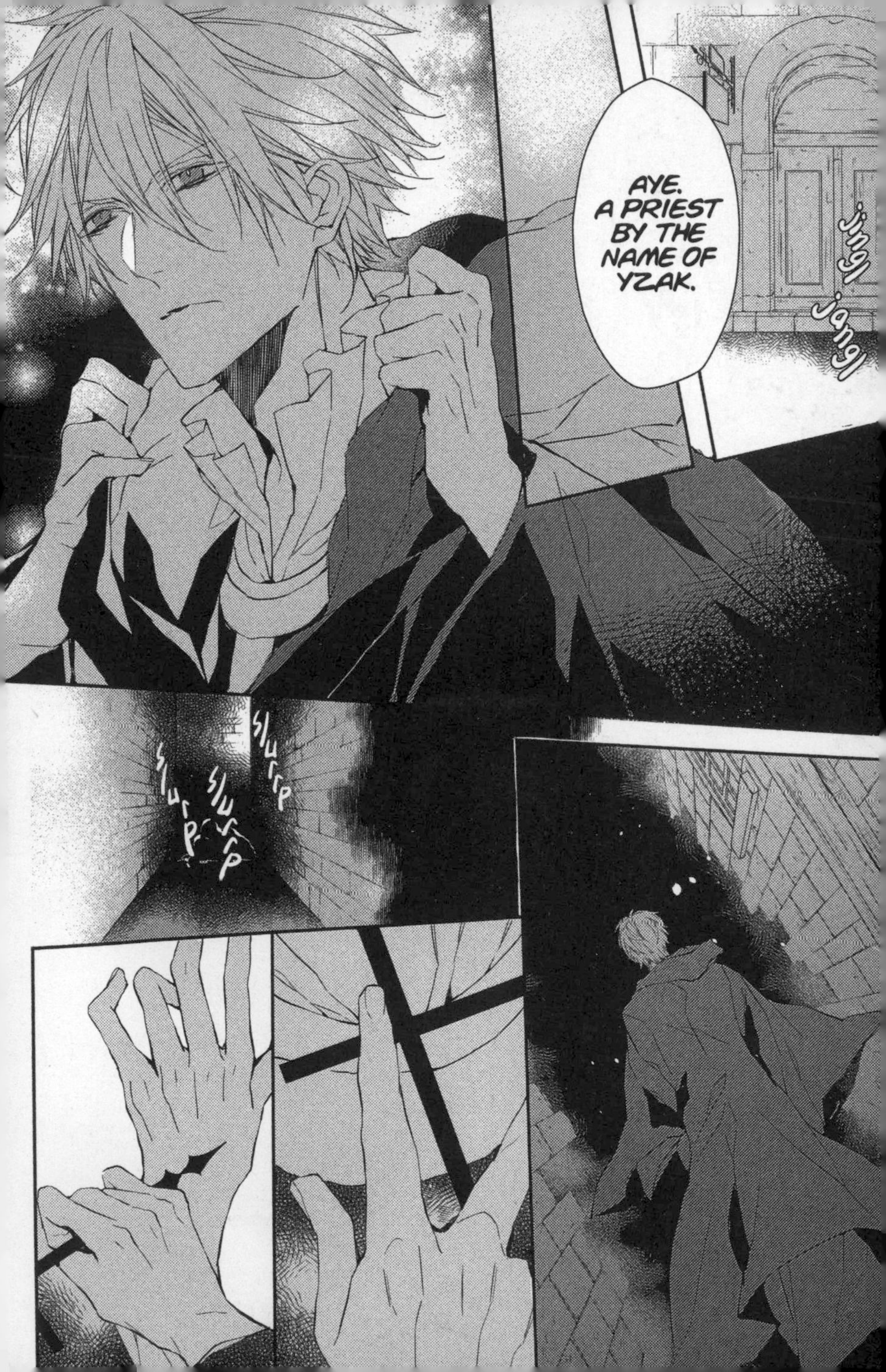
jingl jangl
AYE. A PRIEST BY THE NAME OF YZAK.
slurrp
slurrp
slurp

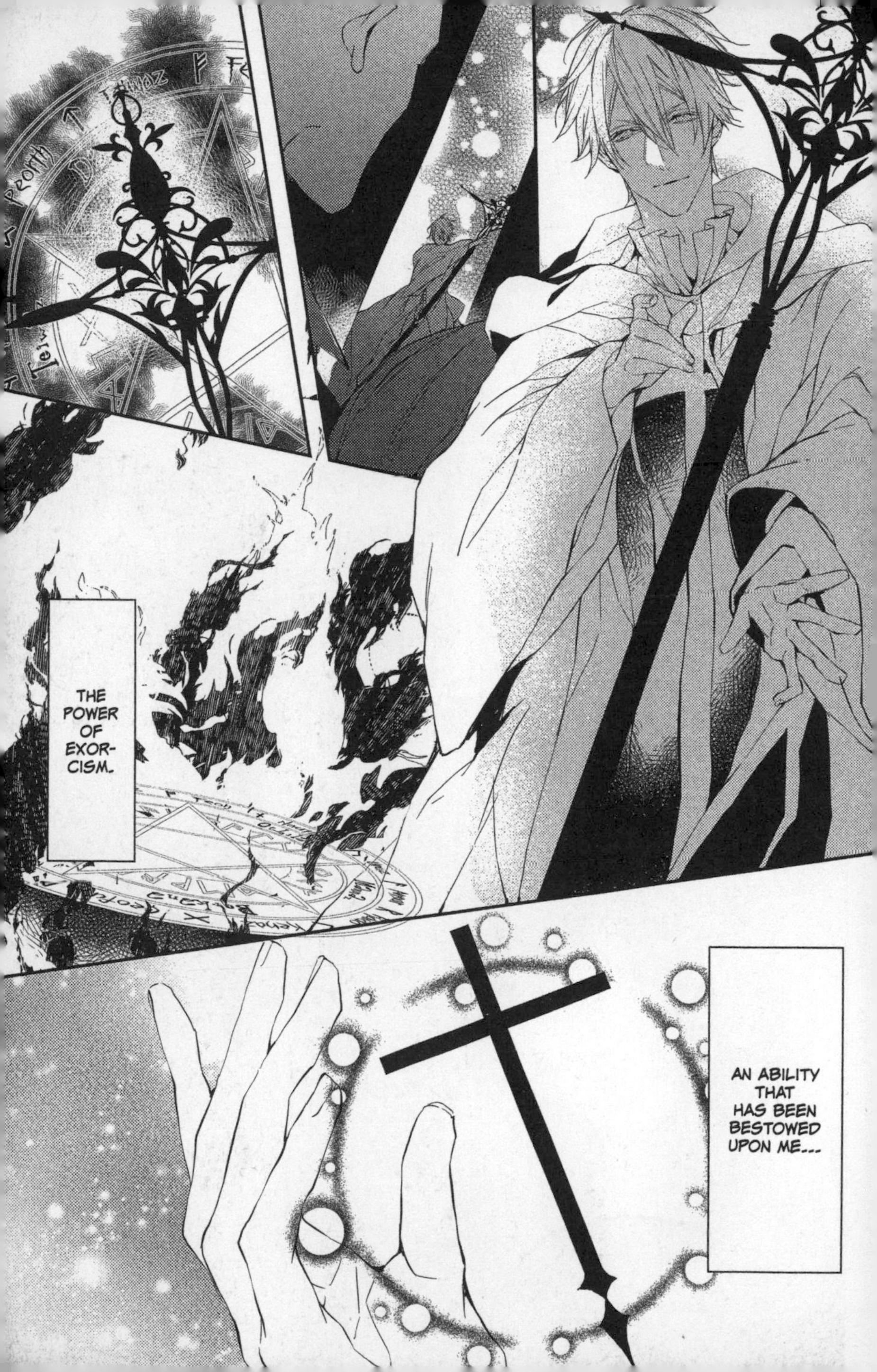
THE POWER OF EXOR-CISM.
AN ABILITY THAT HAS BEEN BESTOWED UPON ME...

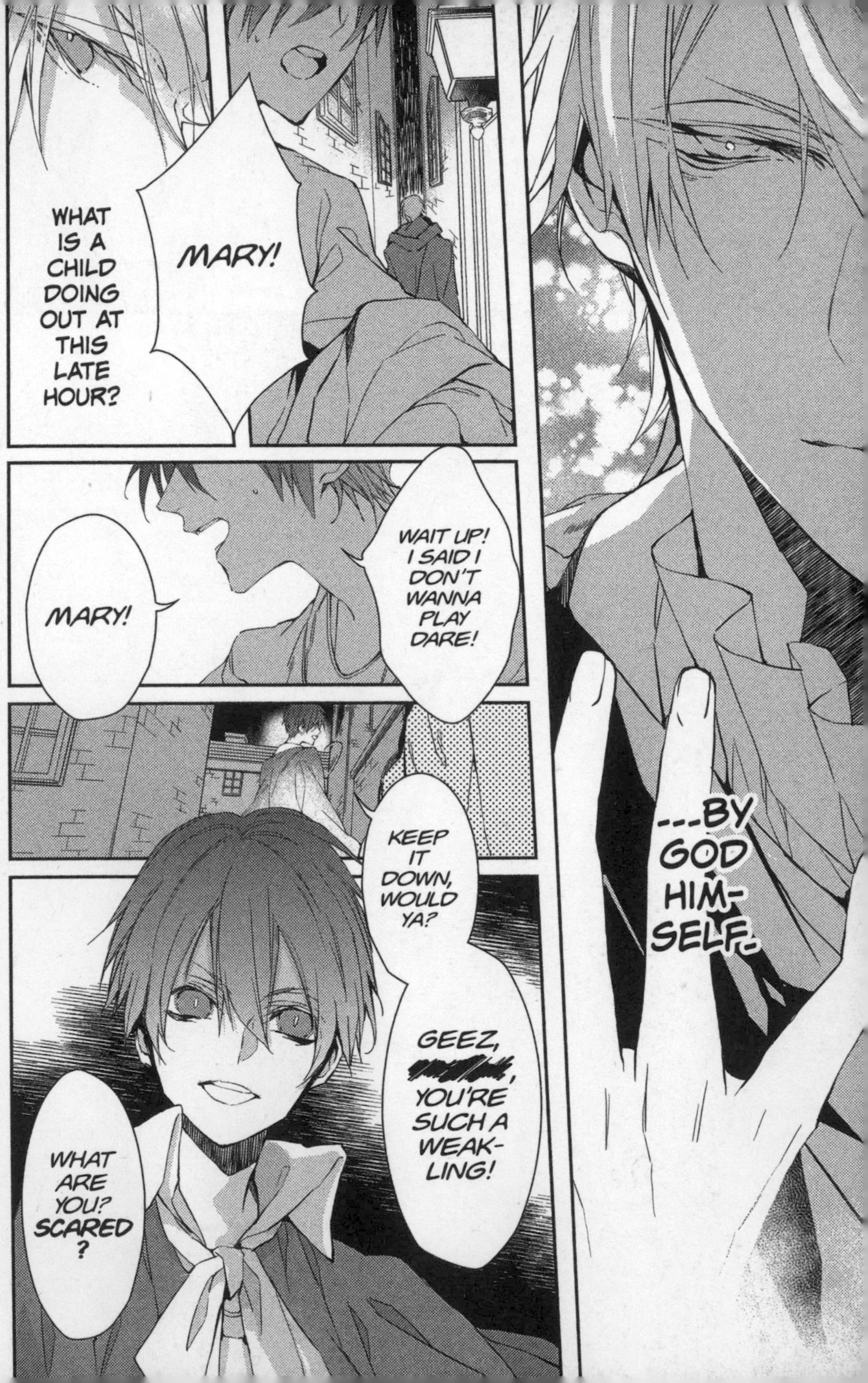
---BY GOD HIMSELF.
MARY!
WHAT IS A CHILD DOING OUT AT THIS LATE HOUR?
WAIT UP! I SAID I DON'T WANNA PLAY DARE!
MARY!
KEEP IT DOWN, WOULD YA?
GEEZ, [redacted], YOU'RE SUCH A WEAKLING!
WHAT ARE YOU? SCARED?

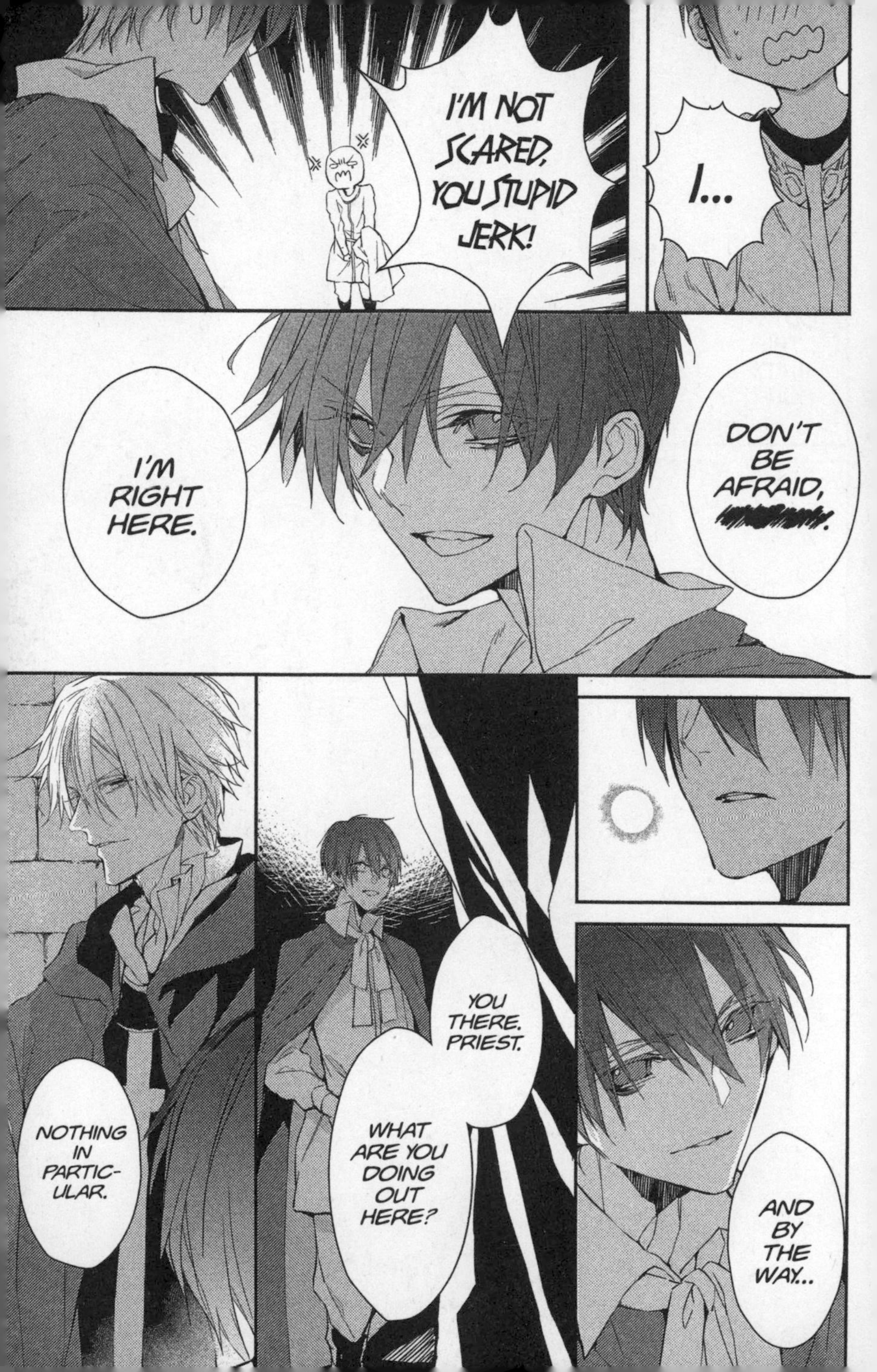
I...
I'M NOT SCARED, YOU STUPID JERK!
DON'T BE AFRAID, [redacted].
I'M RIGHT HERE.
AND BY THE WAY...
YOU THERE. PRIEST.
WHAT ARE YOU DOING OUT HERE?
NOTHING IN PARTIC-ULAR.

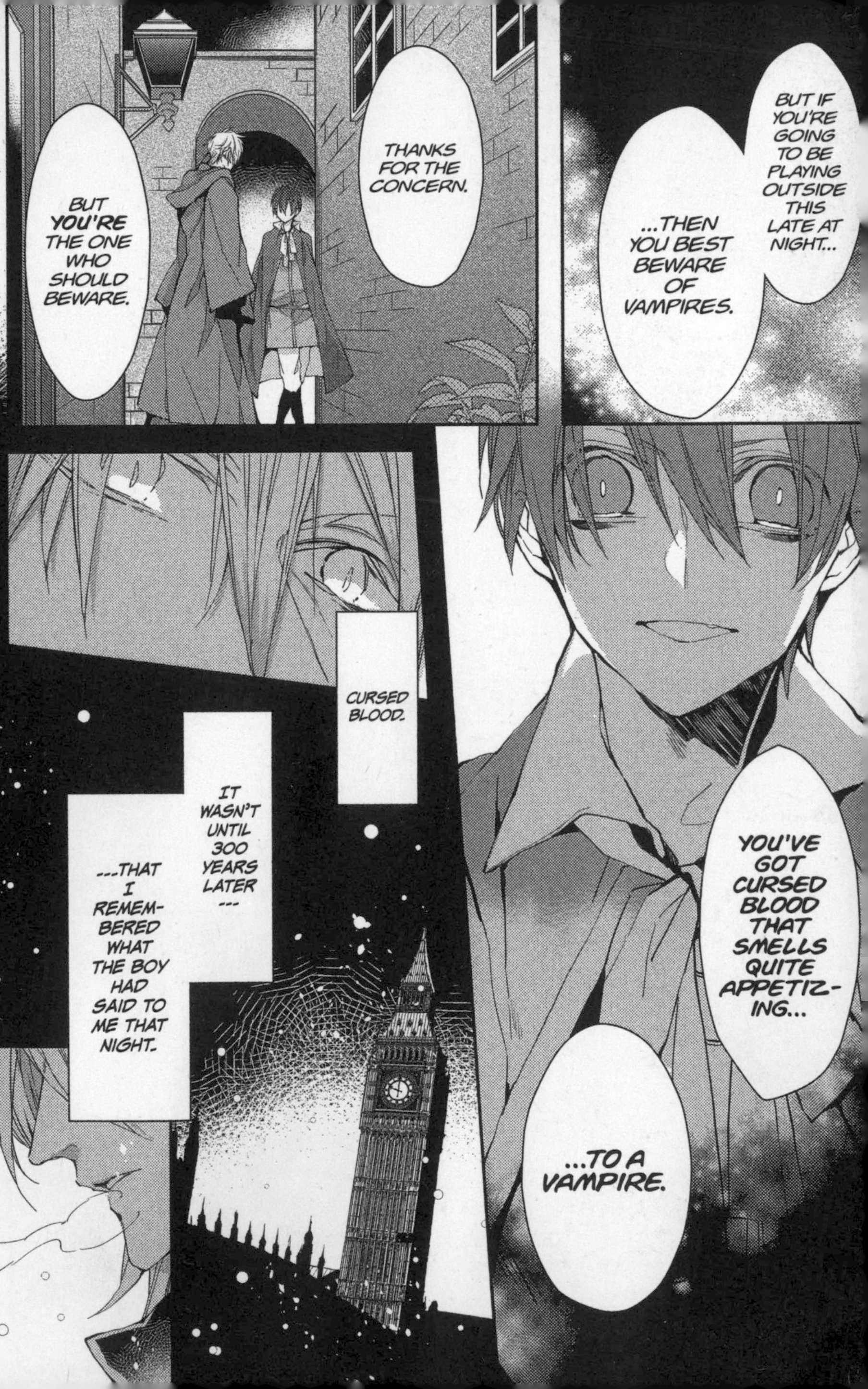
BUT IF YOU'RE GOING TO BE PLAYING OUTSIDE THIS LATE AT NIGHT...
...THEN YOU BEST BEWARE OF VAMPIRES.
THANKS FOR THE CONCERN.
BUT **YOU'RE** THE ONE WHO SHOULD BEWARE.
YOU'VE GOT CURSED BLOOD THAT SMELLS QUITE APPETIZ-ING...
...TO A VAMPIRE.
CURSED BLOOD.
IT WASN'T UNTIL 300 YEARS LATER ---
---THAT I REMEM-BERED WHAT THE BOY HAD SAID TO ME THAT NIGHT.

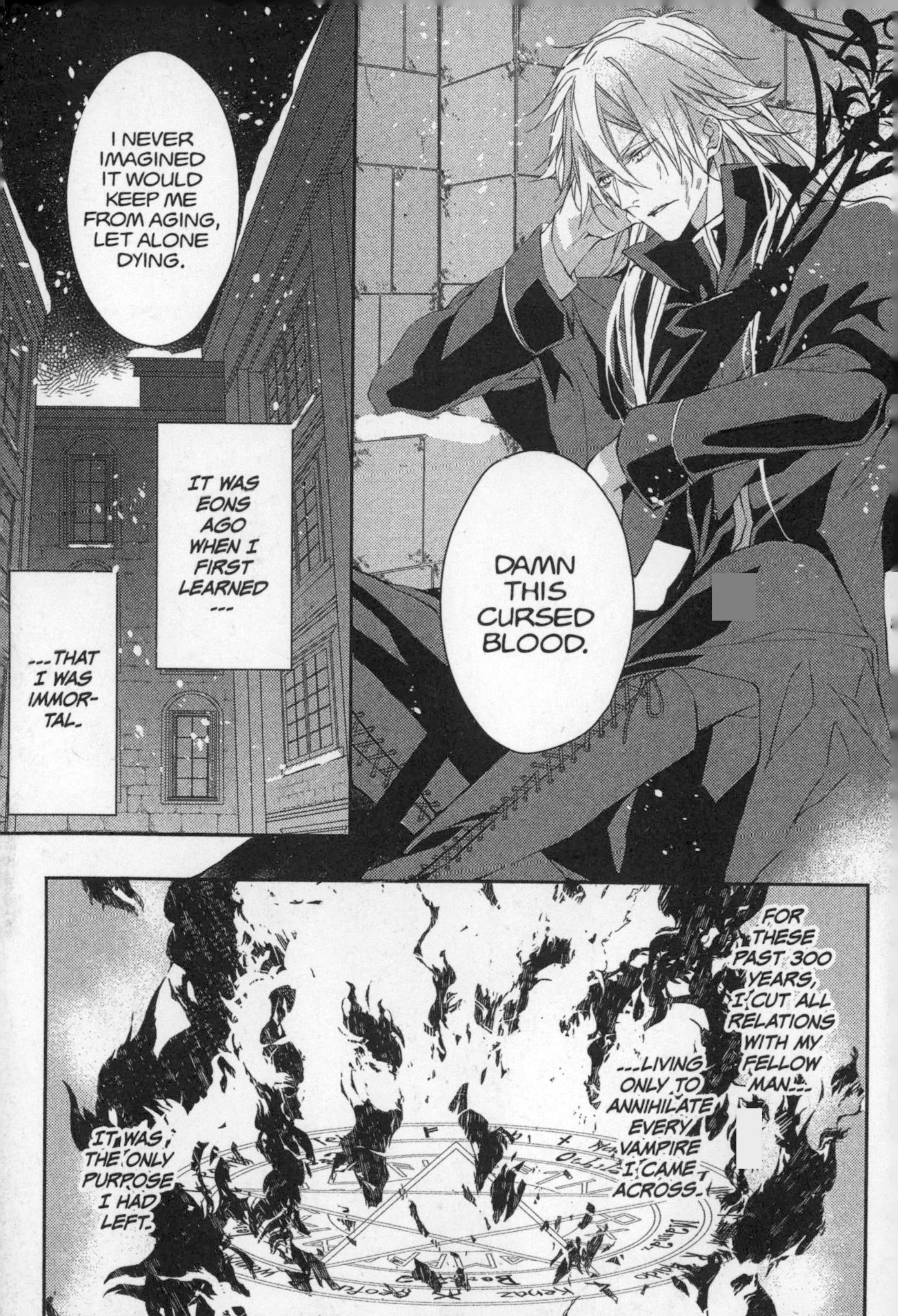
DAMN THIS CURSED BLOOD.
I NEVER IMAGINED IT WOULD KEEP ME FROM AGING, LET ALONE DYING.
IT WAS EONS AGO WHEN I FIRST LEARNED ---
---THAT I WAS IMMORTAL.
FOR THESE PAST 300 YEARS, I CUT ALL RELATIONS WITH MY FELLOW MAN---
---LIVING ONLY TO ANNIHILATE EVERY VAMPIRE I CAME ACROSS.
IT WAS THE ONLY PURPOSE I HAD LEFT.

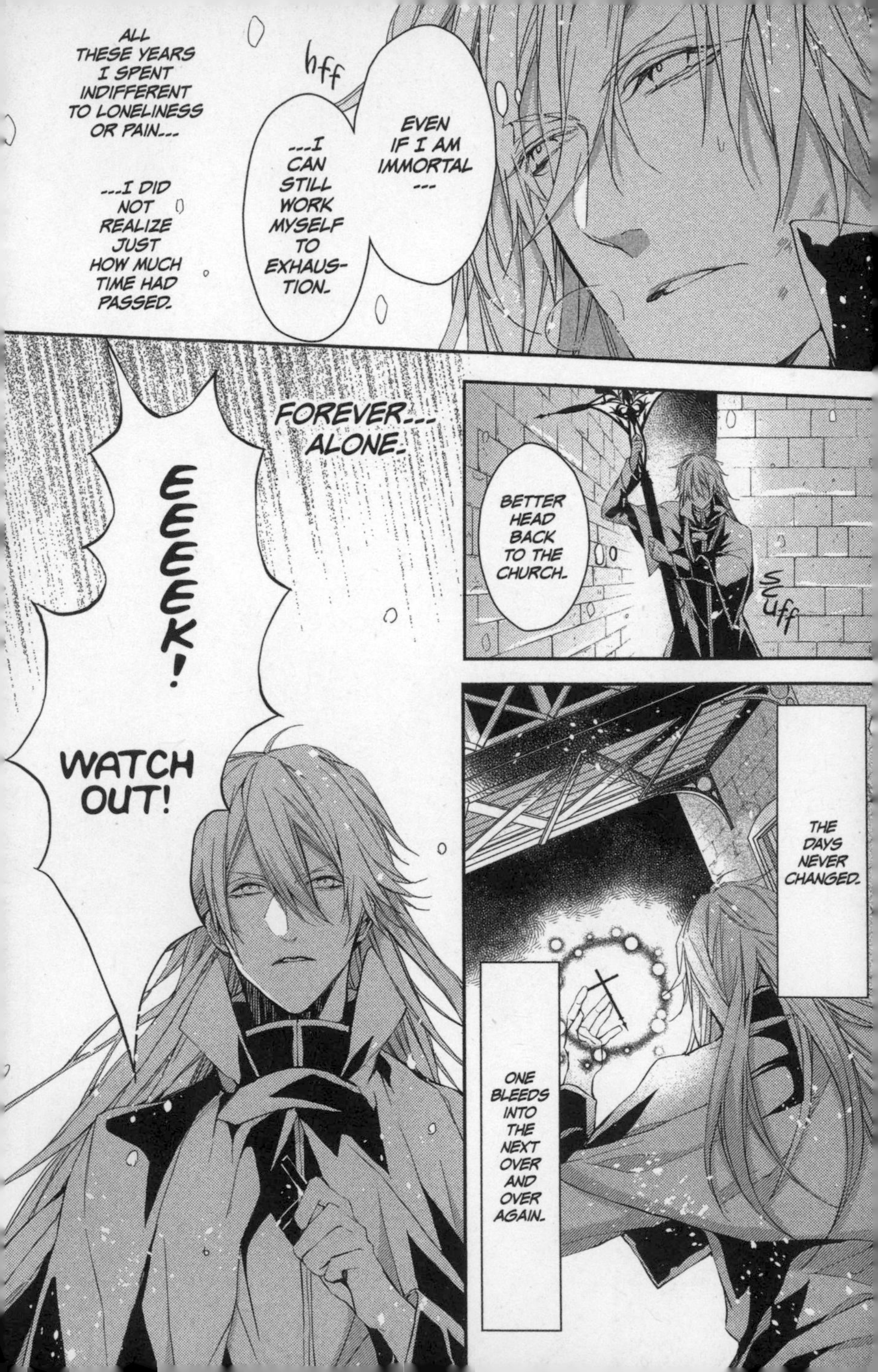
EVEN IF I AM IMMORTAL ---
---I CAN STILL WORK MYSELF TO EXHAUSTION.
hff
ALL THESE YEARS I SPENT INDIFFERENT TO LONELINESS OR PAIN---
---I DID NOT REALIZE JUST HOW MUCH TIME HAD PASSED.
BETTER HEAD BACK TO THE CHURCH.
scuff
THE DAYS NEVER CHANGED.
ONE BLEEDS INTO THE NEXT OVER AND OVER AGAIN.
FOREVER--- ALONE.
EEEEK!
WATCH OUT!

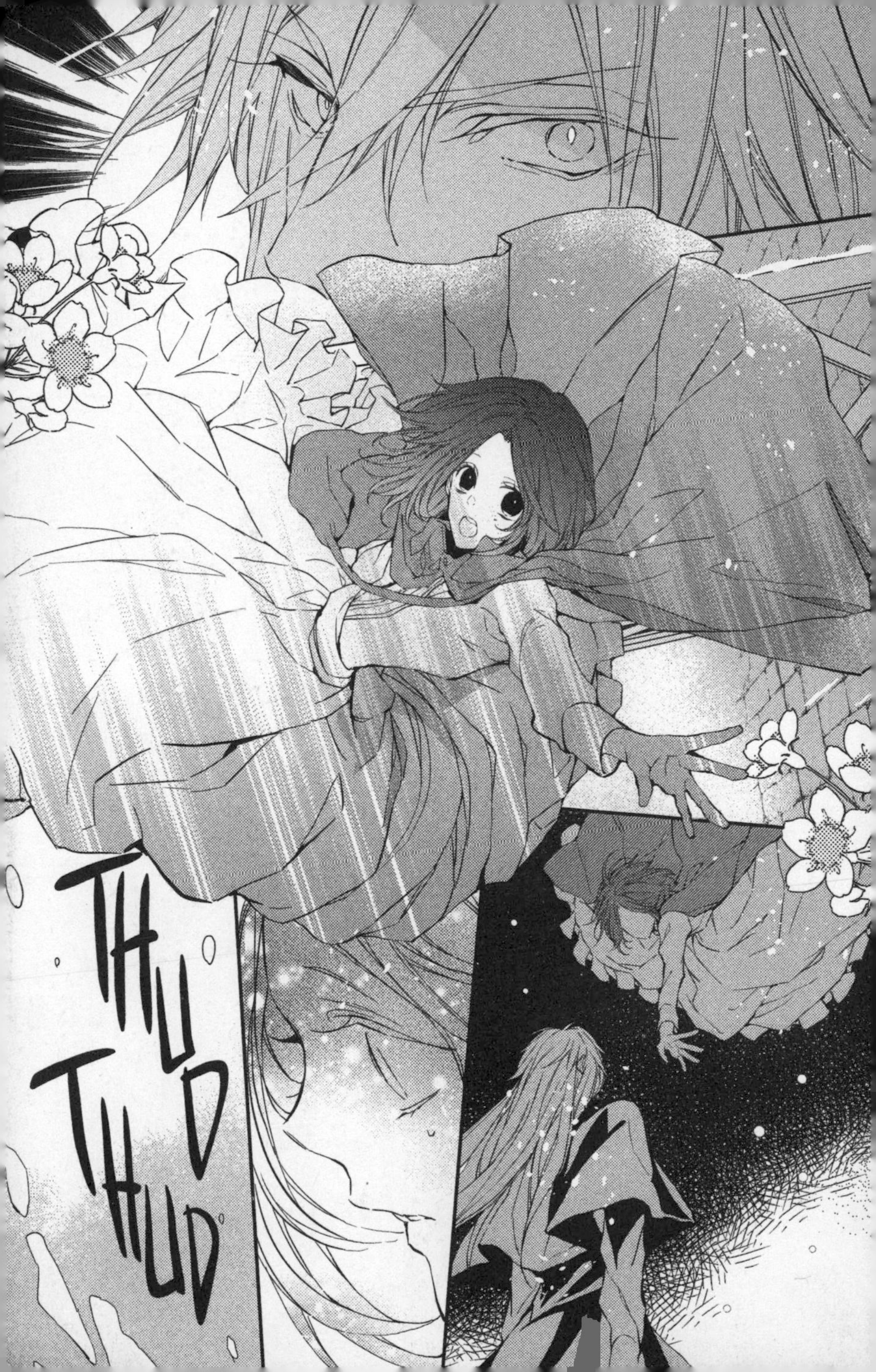
THUD THUD

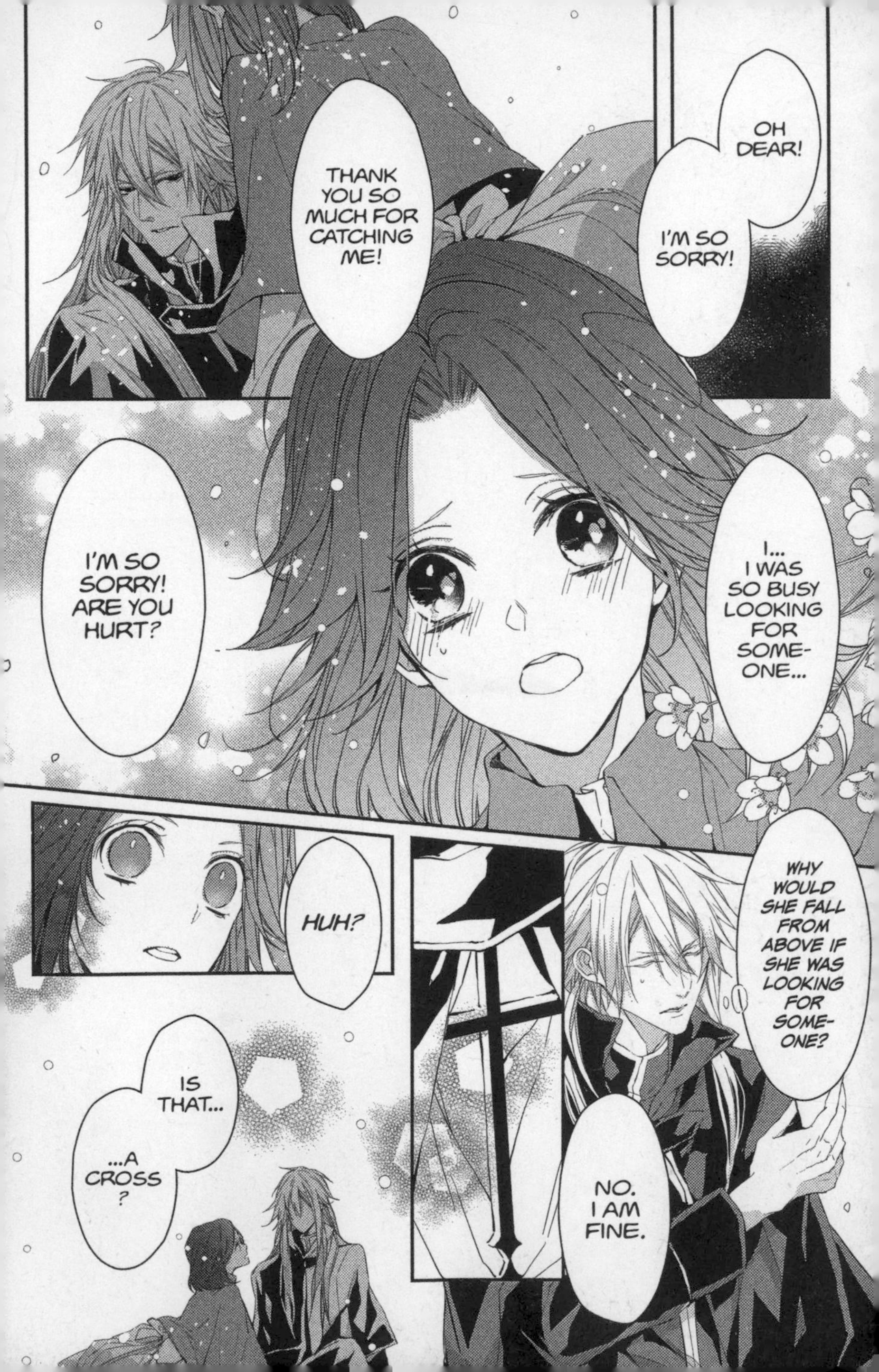
OH DEAR!
I'M SO SORRY!
THANK YOU SO MUCH FOR CATCHING ME!
I... I WAS SO BUSY LOOKING FOR SOME-ONE...
I'M SO SORRY! ARE YOU HURT?
WHY WOULD SHE FALL FROM ABOVE IF SHE WAS LOOKING FOR SOME-ONE?
NO. I AM FINE.
HUH?
IS THAT...
...A CROSS?

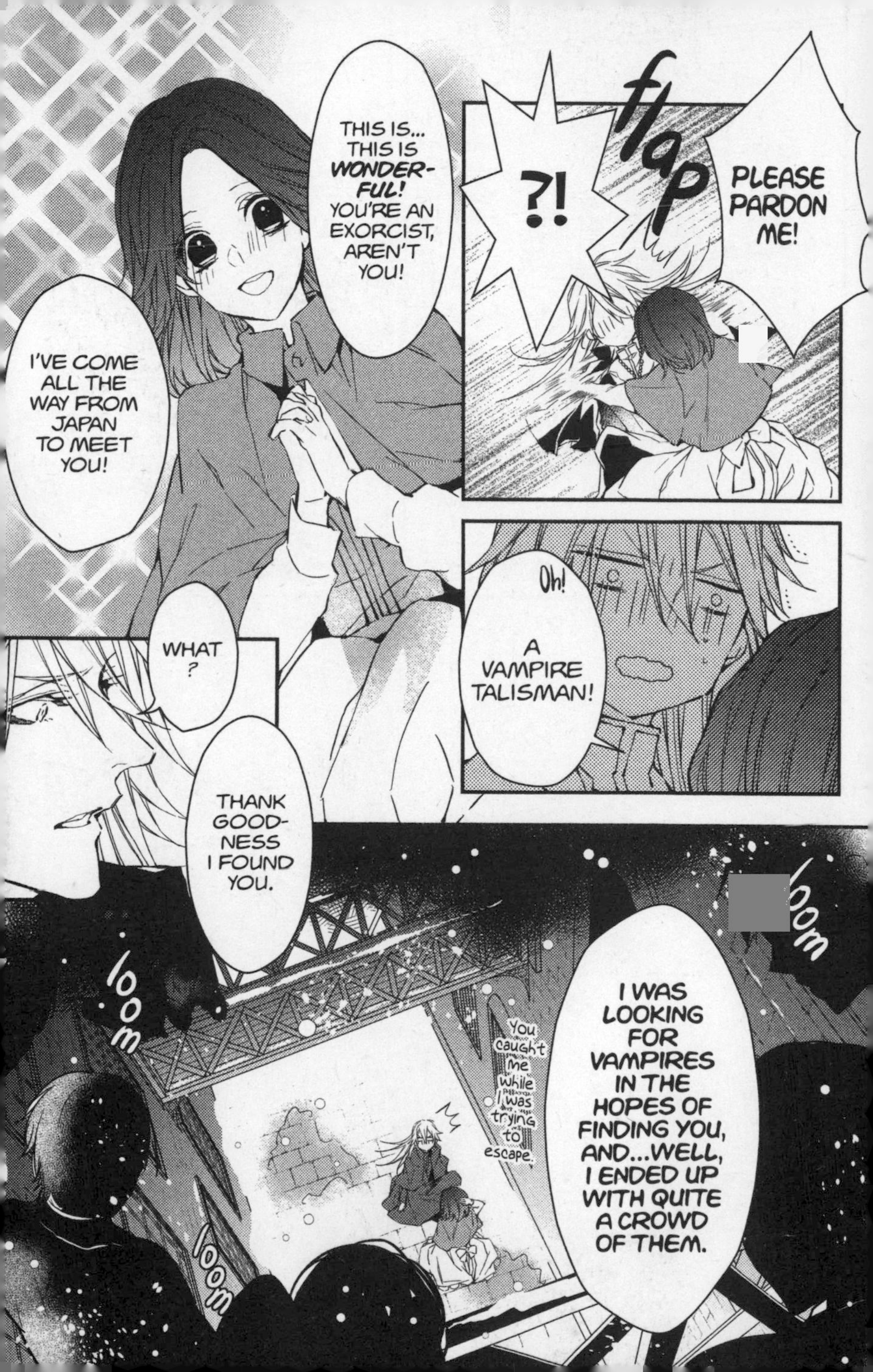
PLEASE PARDON ME!
flap
?!
Oh!
A VAMPIRE TALISMAN!
THIS IS... THIS IS WONDERFUL! YOU'RE AN EXORCIST, AREN'T YOU!
I'VE COME ALL THE WAY FROM JAPAN TO MEET YOU!
WHAT?
THANK GOODNESS I FOUND YOU.
loom
I WAS LOOKING FOR VAMPIRES IN THE HOPES OF FINDING YOU, AND...WELL, I ENDED UP WITH QUITE A CROWD OF THEM.
You caught me while I was trying to escape.
loom
loom

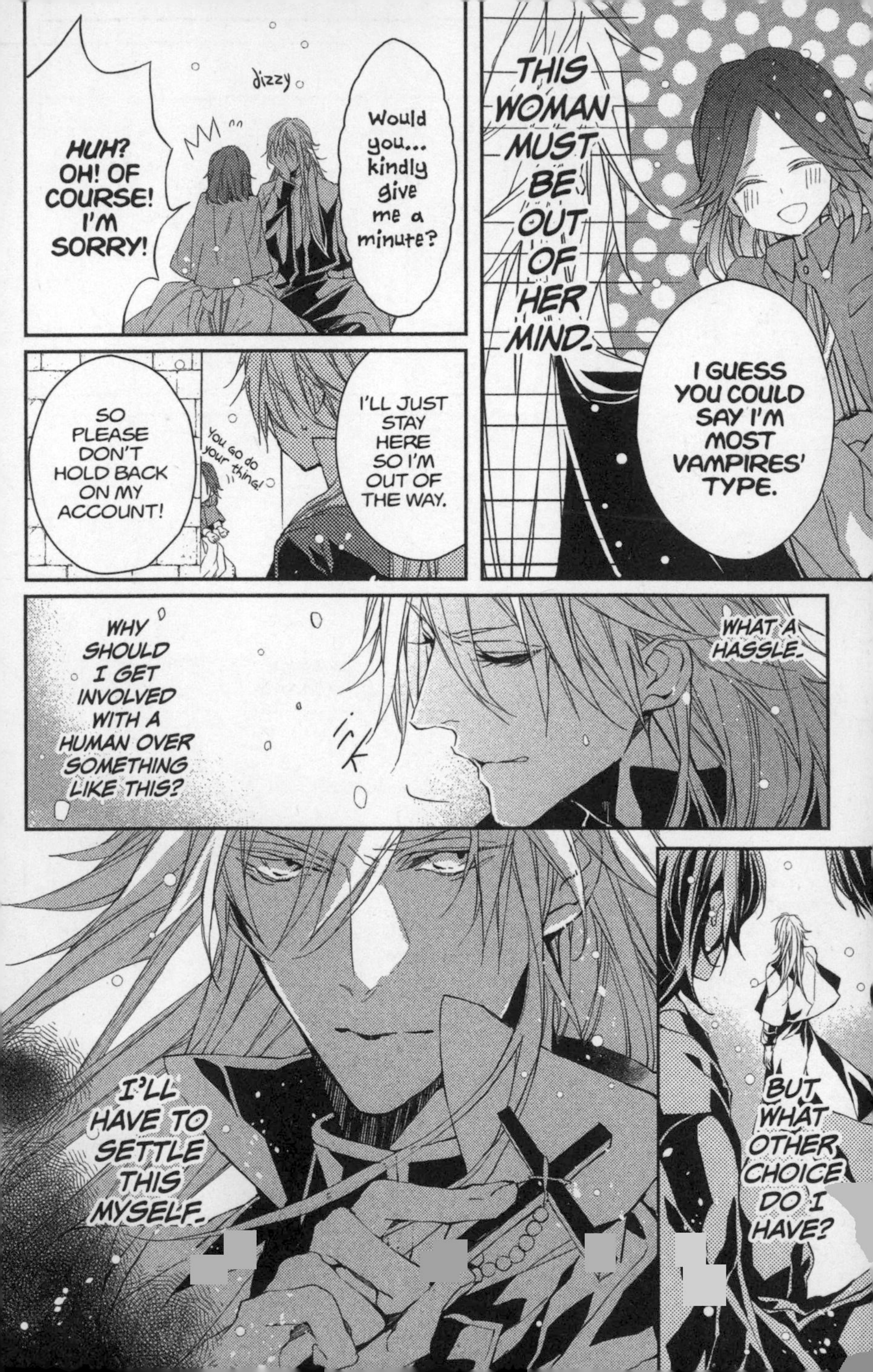
I GUESS YOU COULD SAY I'M MOST VAMPIRES' TYPE.
THIS WOMAN MUST BE OUT OF HER MIND.
Would you... kindly give me a minute?
dizzy
HUH? OH! OF COURSE! I'M SORRY!
I'LL JUST STAY HERE SO I'M OUT OF THE WAY.
You go do your thing!
SO PLEASE DON'T HOLD BACK ON MY ACCOUNT!
WHAT A HASSLE.
irk
WHY SHOULD I GET INVOLVED WITH A HUMAN OVER SOMETHING LIKE THIS?
BUT WHAT OTHER CHOICE DO I HAVE?
I'LL HAVE TO SETTLE THIS MYSELF.

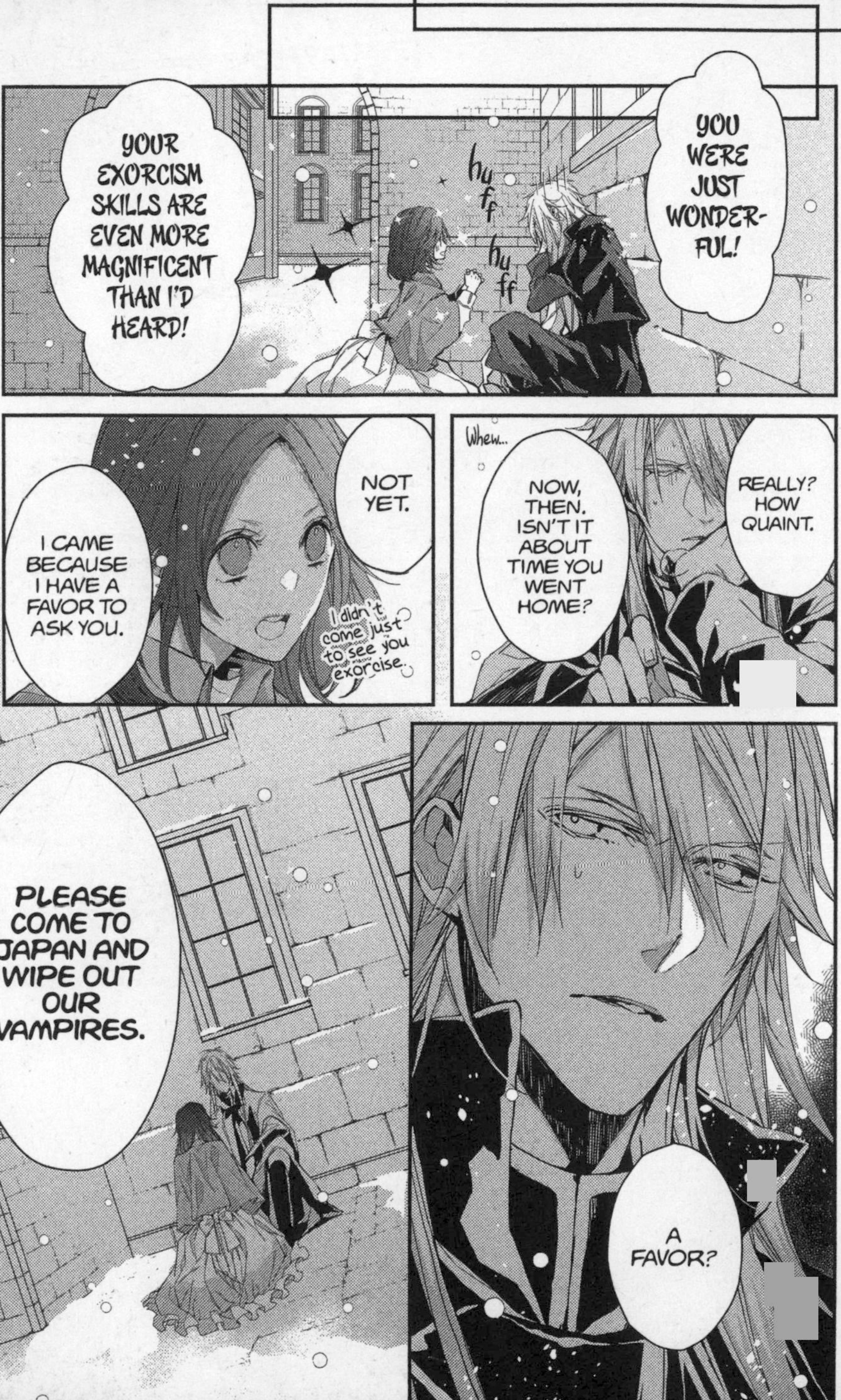
YOU WERE JUST WONDER-FUL!
huff
huff
YOUR EXORCISM SKILLS ARE EVEN MORE MAGNIFICENT THAN I'D HEARD!
REALLY? HOW QUAINT.
Whew...
NOW, THEN. ISN'T IT ABOUT TIME YOU WENT HOME?
NOT YET.
I CAME BECAUSE I HAVE A FAVOR TO ASK YOU.
I didn't come just to see you exorcise.
A FAVOR?
PLEASE COME TO JAPAN AND WIPE OUT OUR VAMPIRES.

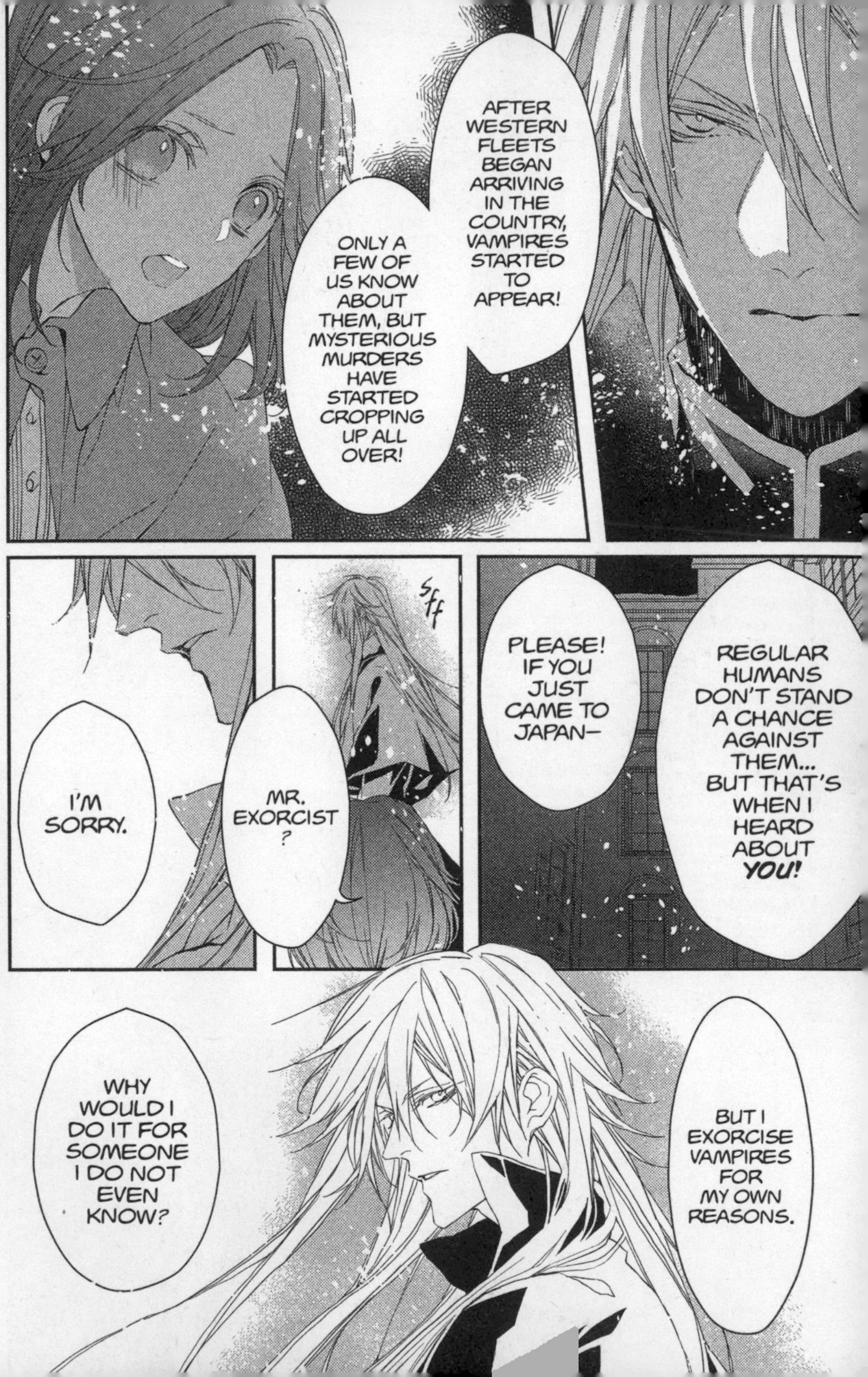
AFTER WESTERN FLEETS BEGAN ARRIVING IN THE COUNTRY, VAMPIRES STARTED TO APPEAR!
ONLY A FEW OF US KNOW ABOUT THEM, BUT MYSTERIOUS MURDERS HAVE STARTED CROPPING UP ALL OVER!
REGULAR HUMANS DON'T STAND A CHANCE AGAINST THEM... BUT THAT'S WHEN I HEARD ABOUT **YOU!**
PLEASE! IF YOU JUST CAME TO JAPAN—
SFF
MR. EXORCIST?
I'M SORRY.
BUT I EXORCISE VAMPIRES FOR MY OWN REASONS.
WHY WOULD I DO IT FOR SOMEONE I DO NOT EVEN KNOW?

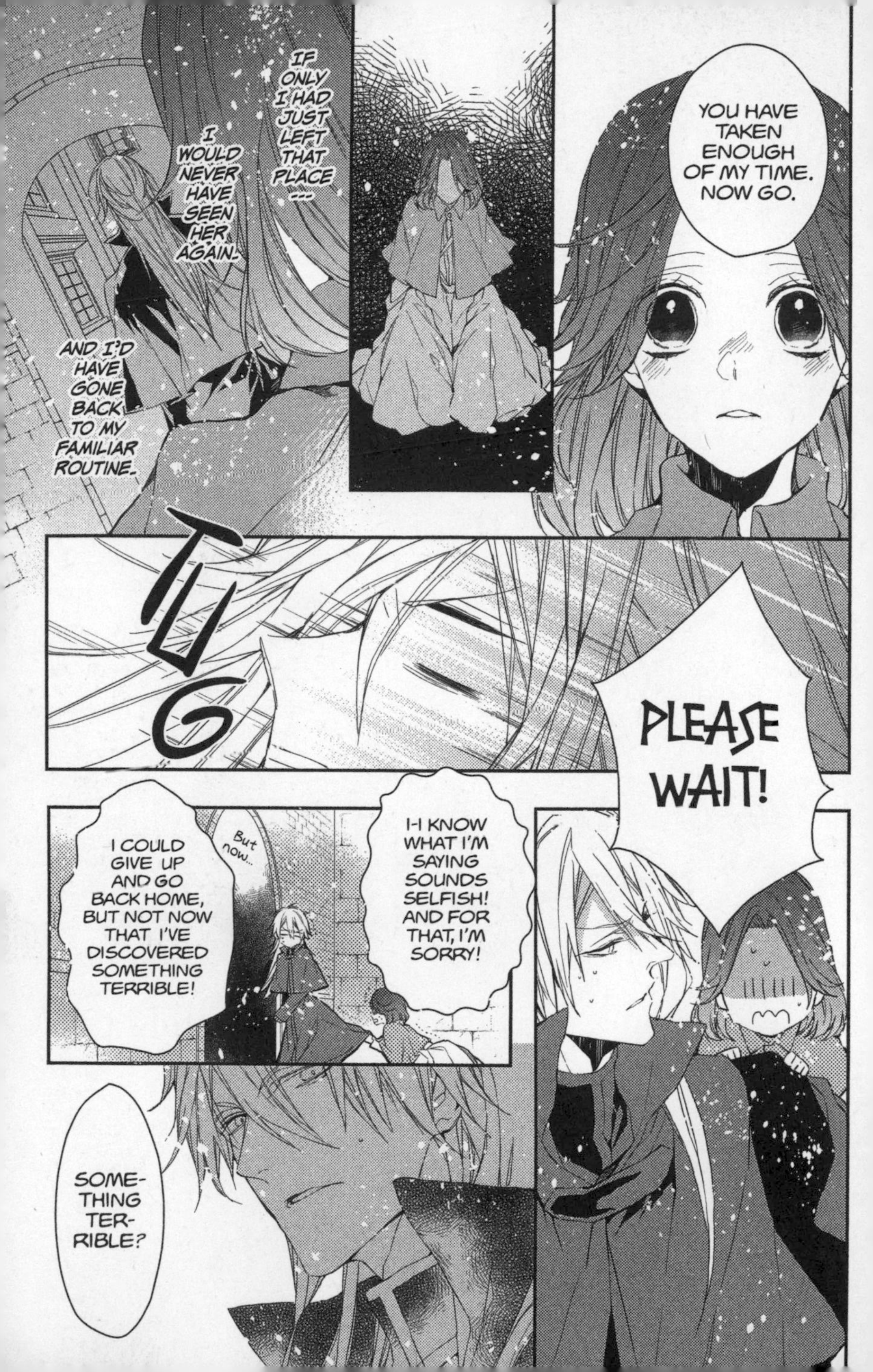
YOU HAVE TAKEN ENOUGH OF MY TIME. NOW GO.
IF ONLY I HAD JUST LEFT THAT PLACE ---
I WOULD NEVER HAVE SEEN HER AGAIN.
AND I'D HAVE GONE BACK TO MY FAMILIAR ROUTINE.
TUG
PLEASE WAIT!
I-I KNOW WHAT I'M SAYING SOUNDS SELFISH! AND FOR THAT, I'M SORRY!
But now...
I COULD GIVE UP AND GO BACK HOME, BUT NOT NOW THAT I'VE DISCOVERED SOMETHING TERRIBLE!
SOME-THING TER-RIBLE?

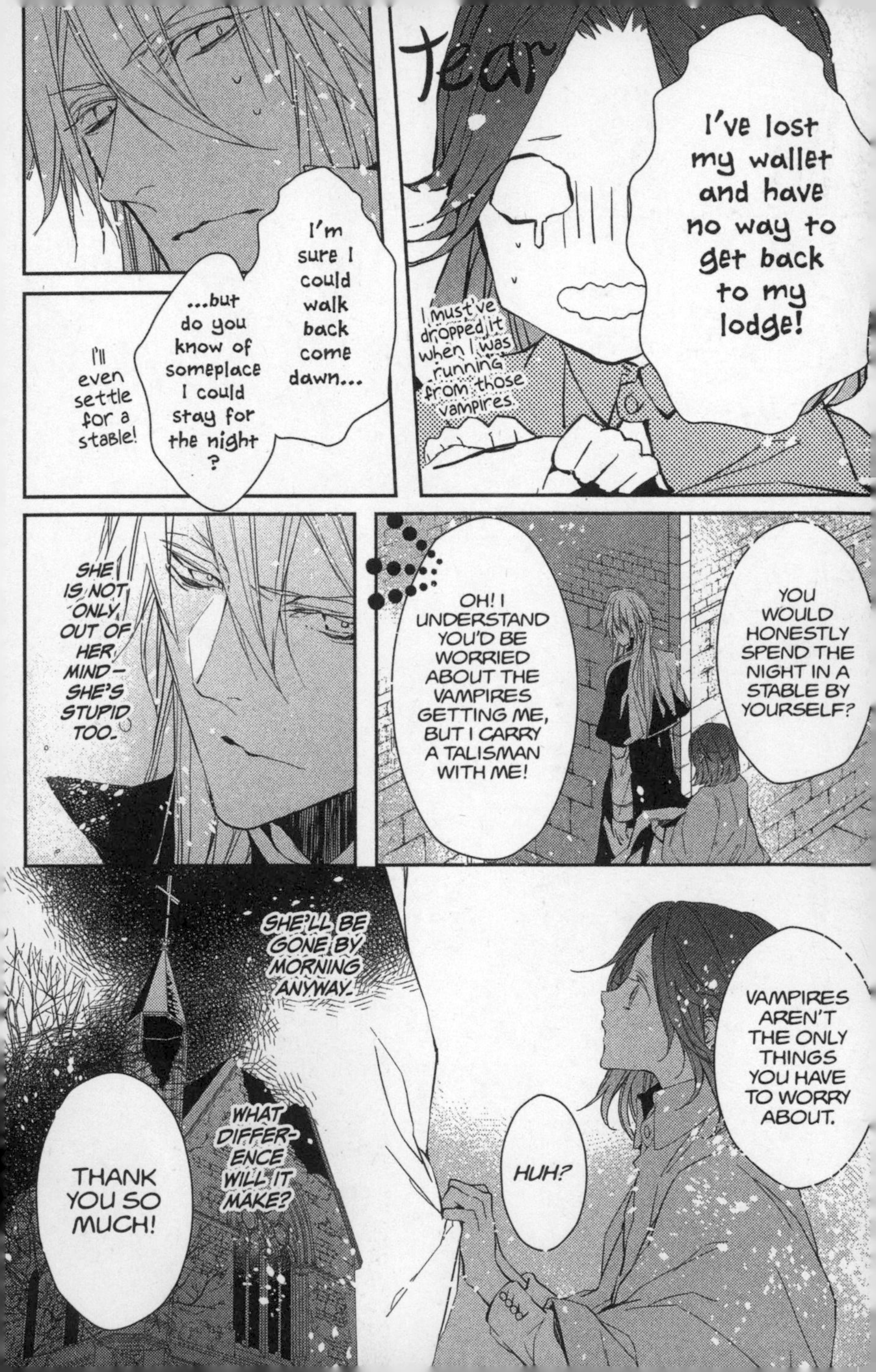
tear
I've lost my wallet and have no way to get back to my lodge!
I must've dropped it when I was running from those vampires.
I'm sure I could walk back come dawn...
...but do you know of someplace I could stay for the night?
I'll even settle for a stable!
YOU WOULD HONESTLY SPEND THE NIGHT IN A STABLE BY YOURSELF?
OH! I UNDERSTAND YOU'D BE WORRIED ABOUT THE VAMPIRES GETTING ME, BUT I CARRY A TALISMAN WITH ME!
SHE IS NOT ONLY OUT OF HER MIND—SHE'S STUPID TOO.
VAMPIRES AREN'T THE ONLY THINGS YOU HAVE TO WORRY ABOUT.
HUH?
SHE'LL BE GONE BY MORNING ANYWAY.
WHAT DIFFERENCE WILL IT MAKE?
THANK YOU SO MUCH!

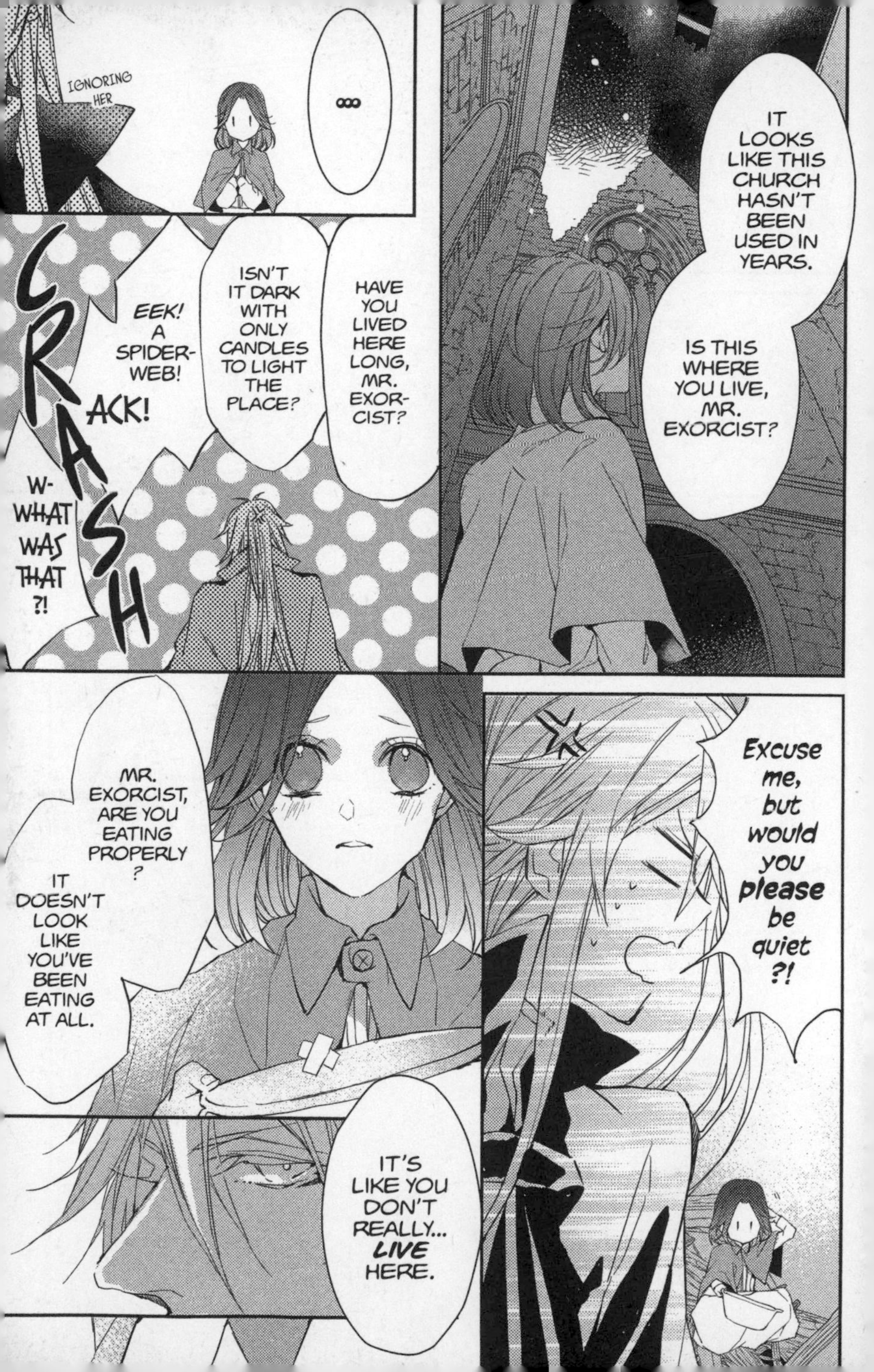
IT LOOKS LIKE THIS CHURCH HASN'T BEEN USED IN YEARS.
IS THIS WHERE YOU LIVE, MR. EXORCIST?
...
IGNORING HER
HAVE YOU LIVED HERE LONG, MR. EXOR-CIST?
ISN'T IT DARK WITH ONLY CANDLES TO LIGHT THE PLACE?
EEK! A SPIDER-WEB!
CRASH
ACK!
W-WHAT WAS THAT ?!
Excuse me, but would you please be quiet ?!
MR. EXORCIST, ARE YOU EATING PROPERLY ?
IT DOESN'T LOOK LIKE YOU'VE BEEN EATING AT ALL.
IT'S LIKE YOU DON'T REALLY... LIVE HERE.

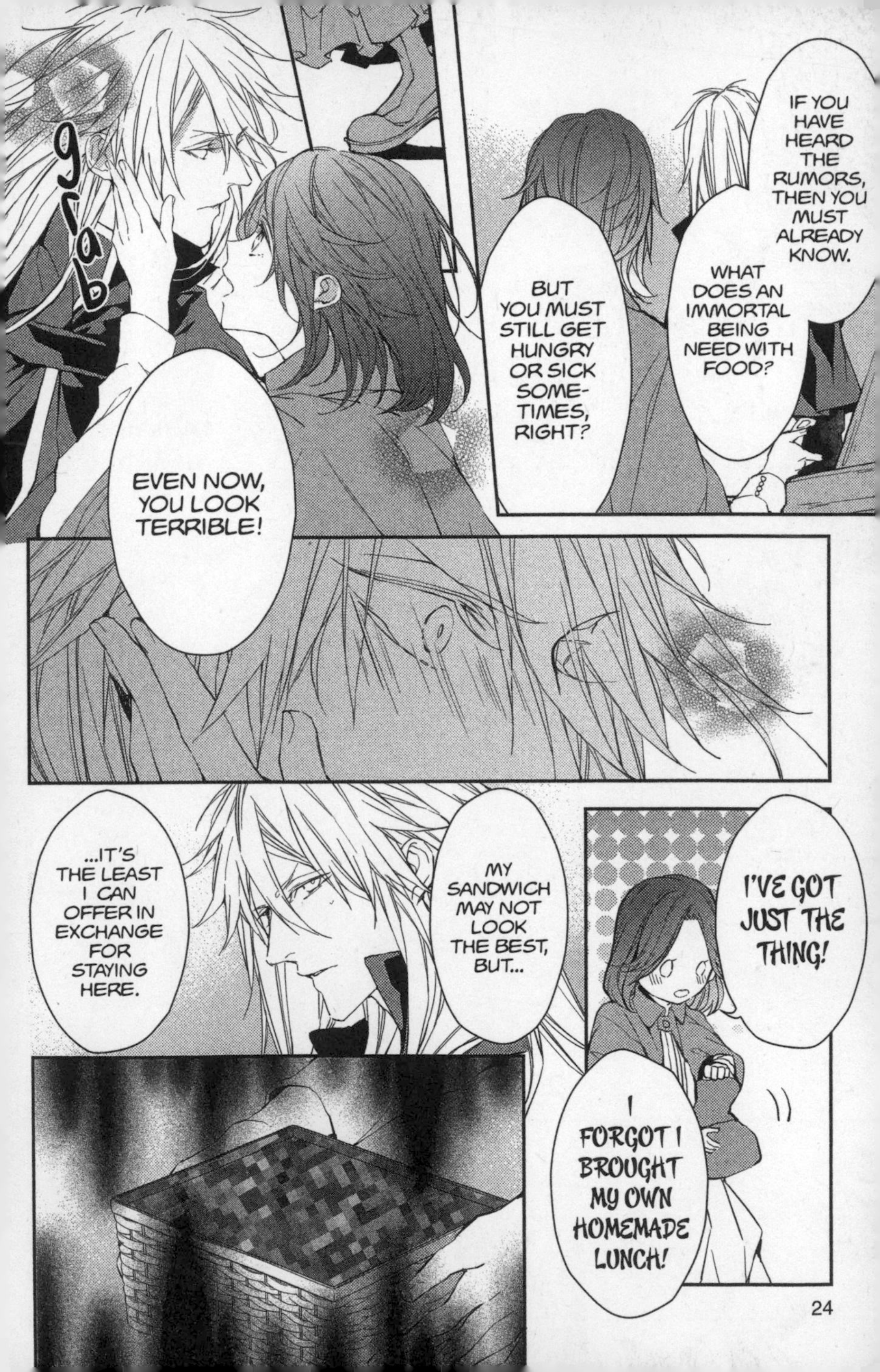
IF YOU HAVE HEARD THE RUMORS, THEN YOU MUST ALREADY KNOW.
WHAT DOES AN IMMORTAL BEING NEED WITH FOOD?
BUT YOU MUST STILL GET HUNGRY OR SICK SOME-TIMES, RIGHT?
grab
EVEN NOW, YOU LOOK TERRIBLE!
I'VE GOT JUST THE THING!
I FORGOT I BROUGHT MY OWN HOMEMADE LUNCH!
MY SANDWICH MAY NOT LOOK THE BEST, BUT...
...IT'S THE LEAST I CAN OFFER IN EXCHANGE FOR STAYING HERE.

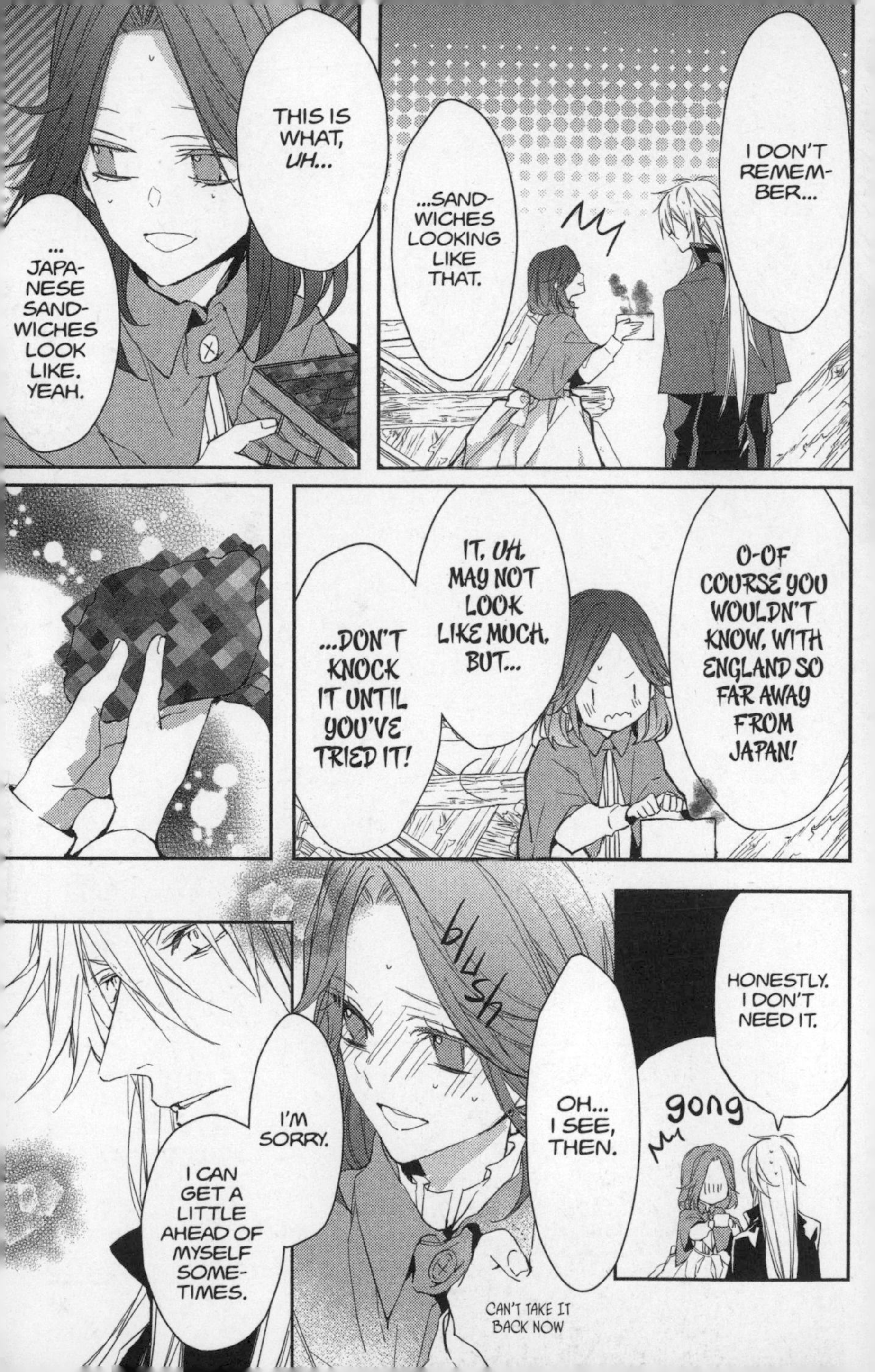
I DON'T REMEMBER...
...SANDWICHES LOOKING LIKE THAT.
THIS IS WHAT, UH...
...JAPANESE SANDWICHES LOOK LIKE. YEAH.
O-OF COURSE YOU WOULDN'T KNOW, WITH ENGLAND SO FAR AWAY FROM JAPAN!
IT, UH, MAY NOT LOOK LIKE MUCH, BUT...
...DON'T KNOCK IT UNTIL YOU'VE TRIED IT!
HONESTLY. I DON'T NEED IT.
gong
OH... I SEE, THEN.
blush
I'M SORRY.
I CAN GET A LITTLE AHEAD OF MYSELF SOMETIMES.
CAN'T TAKE IT BACK NOW

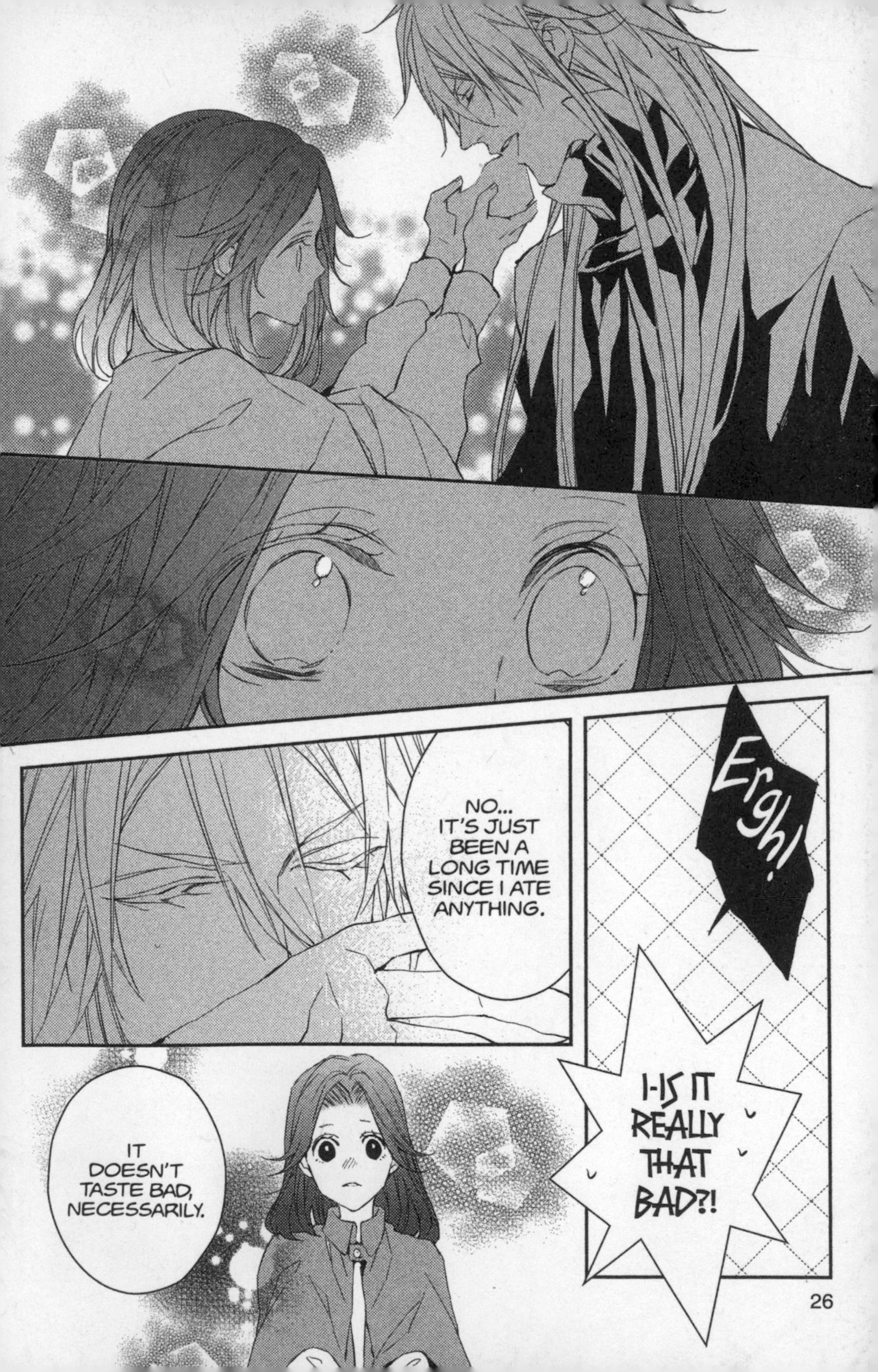
Ergh!
I-IS IT REALLY THAT BAD?!
NO... IT'S JUST BEEN A LONG TIME SINCE I ATE ANYTHING.
IT DOESN'T TASTE BAD, NECESSARILY.

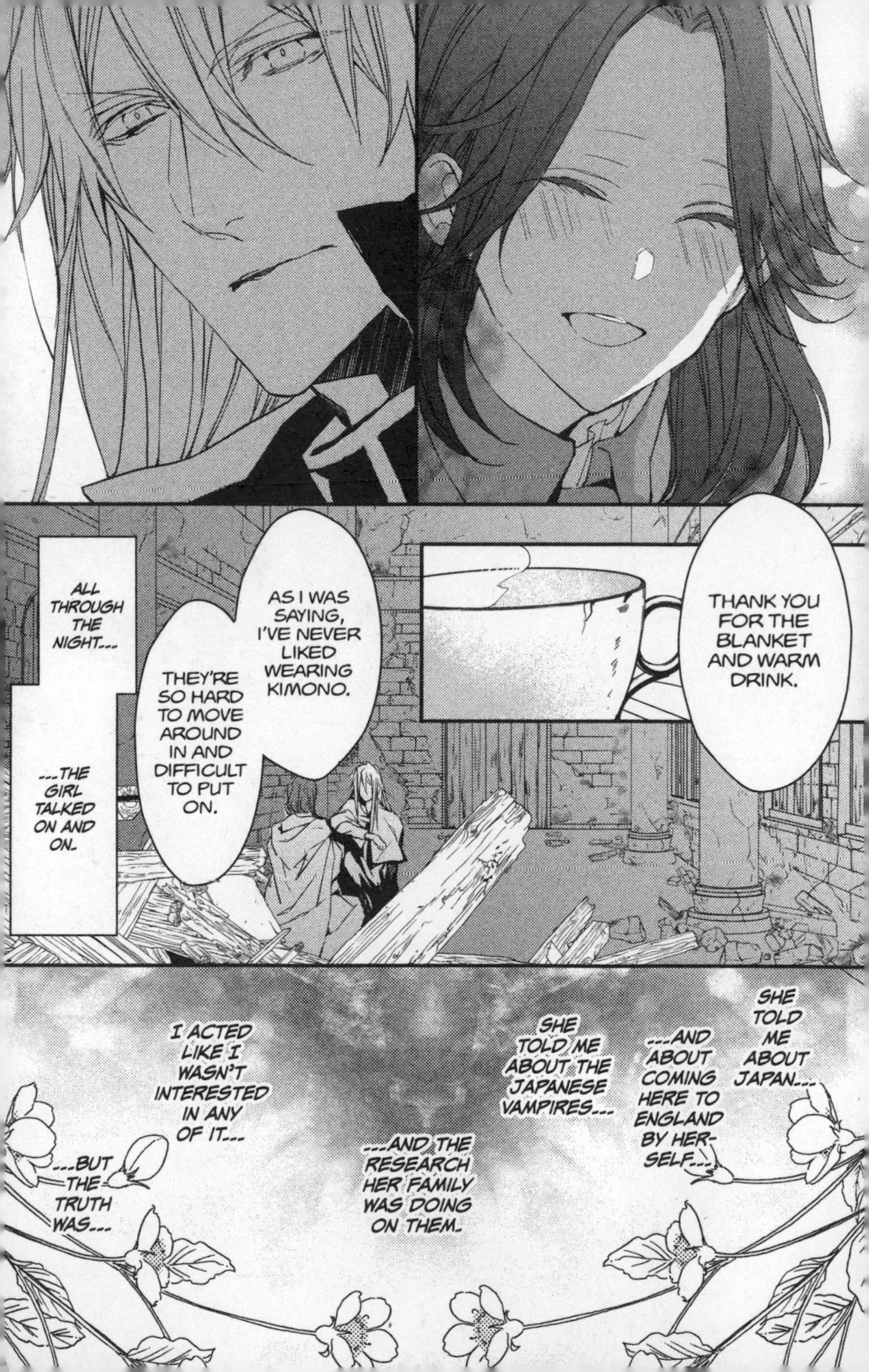
THANK YOU FOR THE BLANKET AND WARM DRINK.
AS I WAS SAYING, I'VE NEVER LIKED WEARING KIMONO.
THEY'RE SO HARD TO MOVE AROUND IN AND DIFFICULT TO PUT ON.
ALL THROUGH THE NIGHT...
...THE GIRL TALKED ON AND ON.
SHE TOLD ME ABOUT JAPAN...
...AND ABOUT COMING HERE TO ENGLAND BY HER-SELF...
SHE TOLD ME ABOUT THE JAPANESE VAMPIRES...
...AND THE RESEARCH HER FAMILY WAS DOING ON THEM.
I ACTED LIKE I WASN'T INTERESTED IN ANY OF IT...
...BUT THE TRUTH WAS...

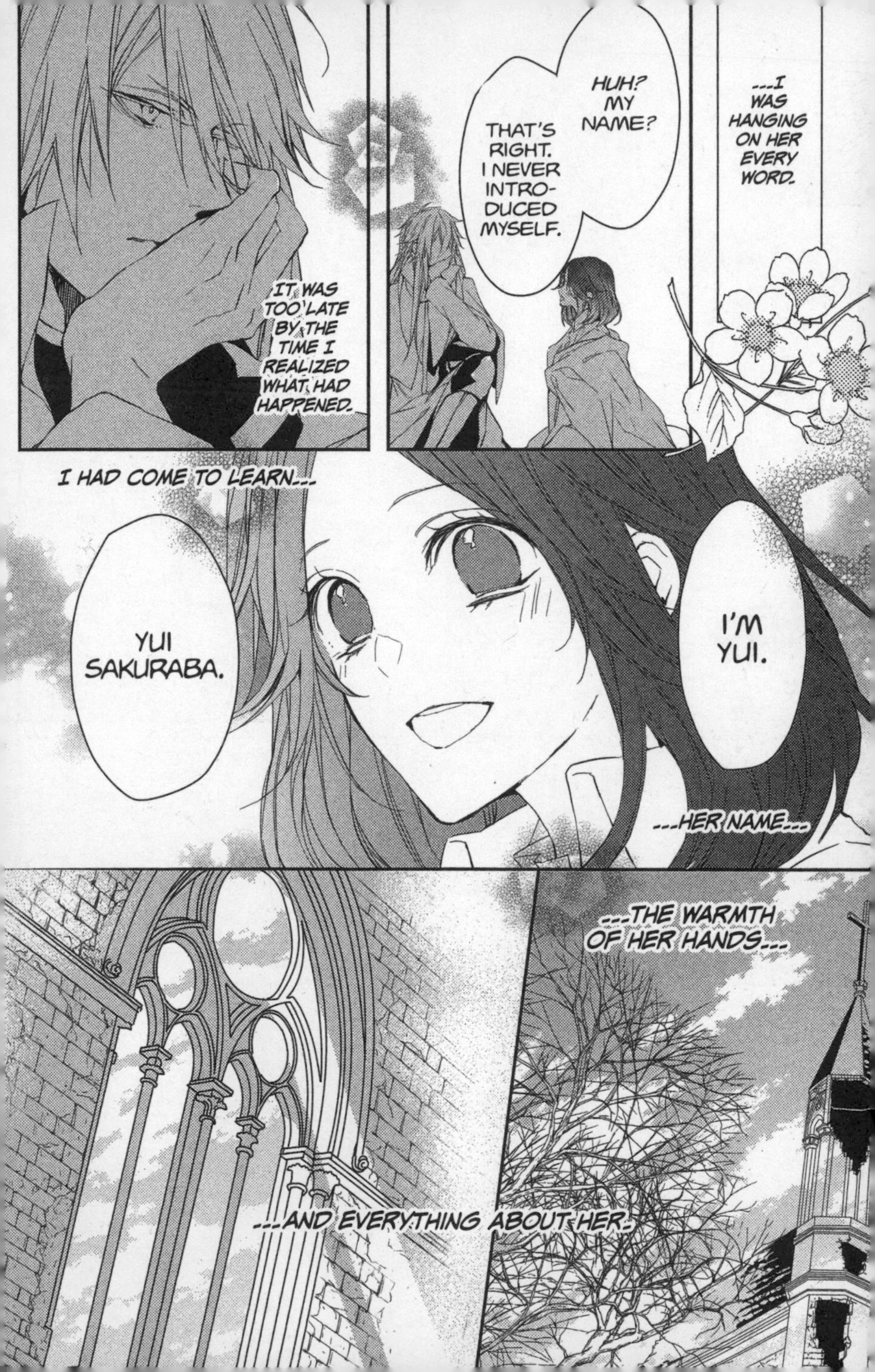
---I WAS HANGING ON HER EVERY WORD.
HUH? MY NAME?
THAT'S RIGHT. I NEVER INTRO-DUCED MYSELF.
IT WAS TOO LATE BY THE TIME I REALIZED WHAT HAD HAPPENED.
I HAD COME TO LEARN---
I'M YUI.
YUI SAKURABA.
---HER NAME---
---THE WARMTH OF HER HANDS---
---AND EVERYTHING ABOUT HER.

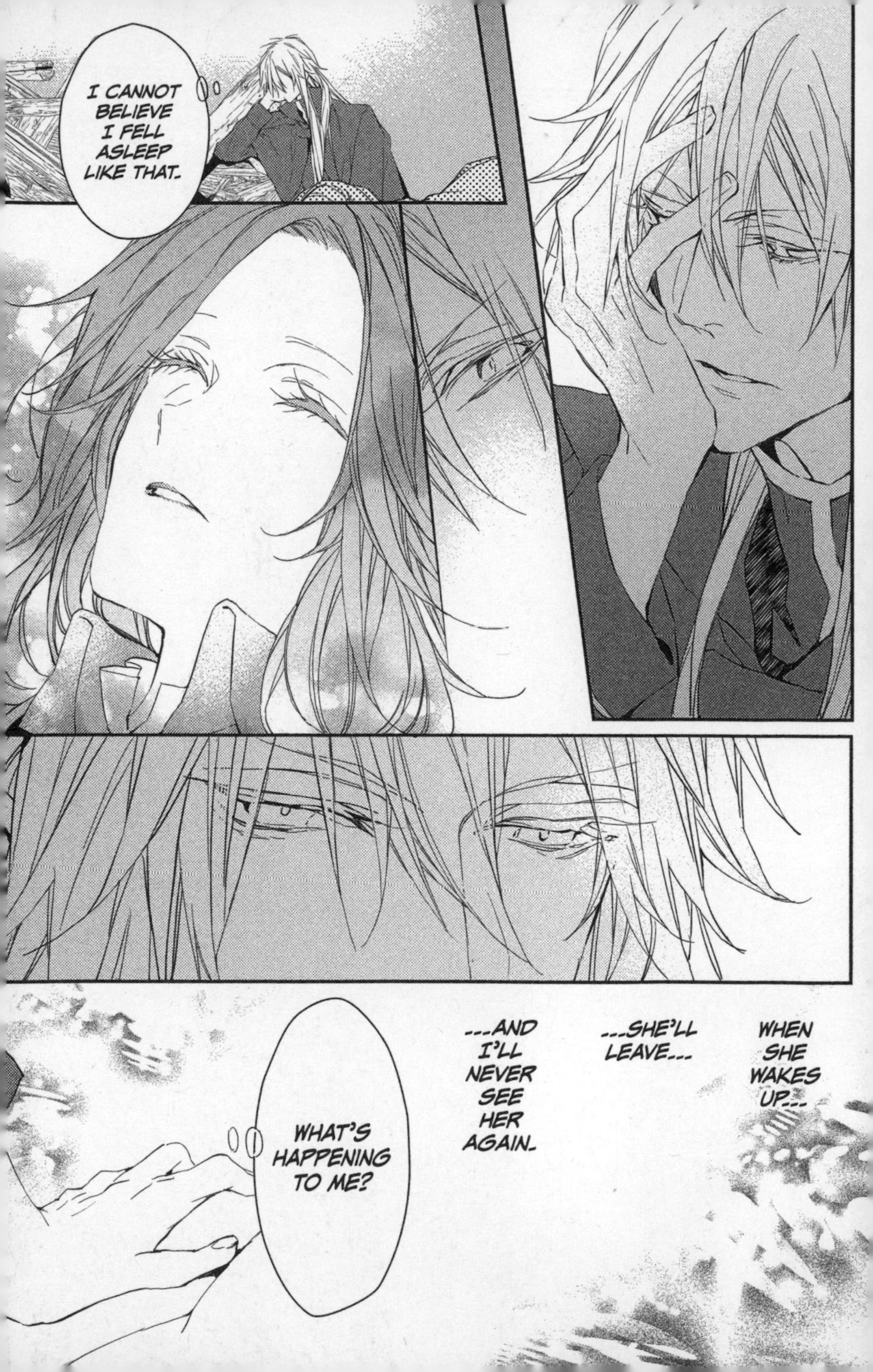
I CANNOT BELIEVE I FELL ASLEEP LIKE THAT.
WHEN SHE WAKES UP...
...SHE'LL LEAVE...
...AND I'LL NEVER SEE HER AGAIN.
WHAT'S HAPPENING TO ME?

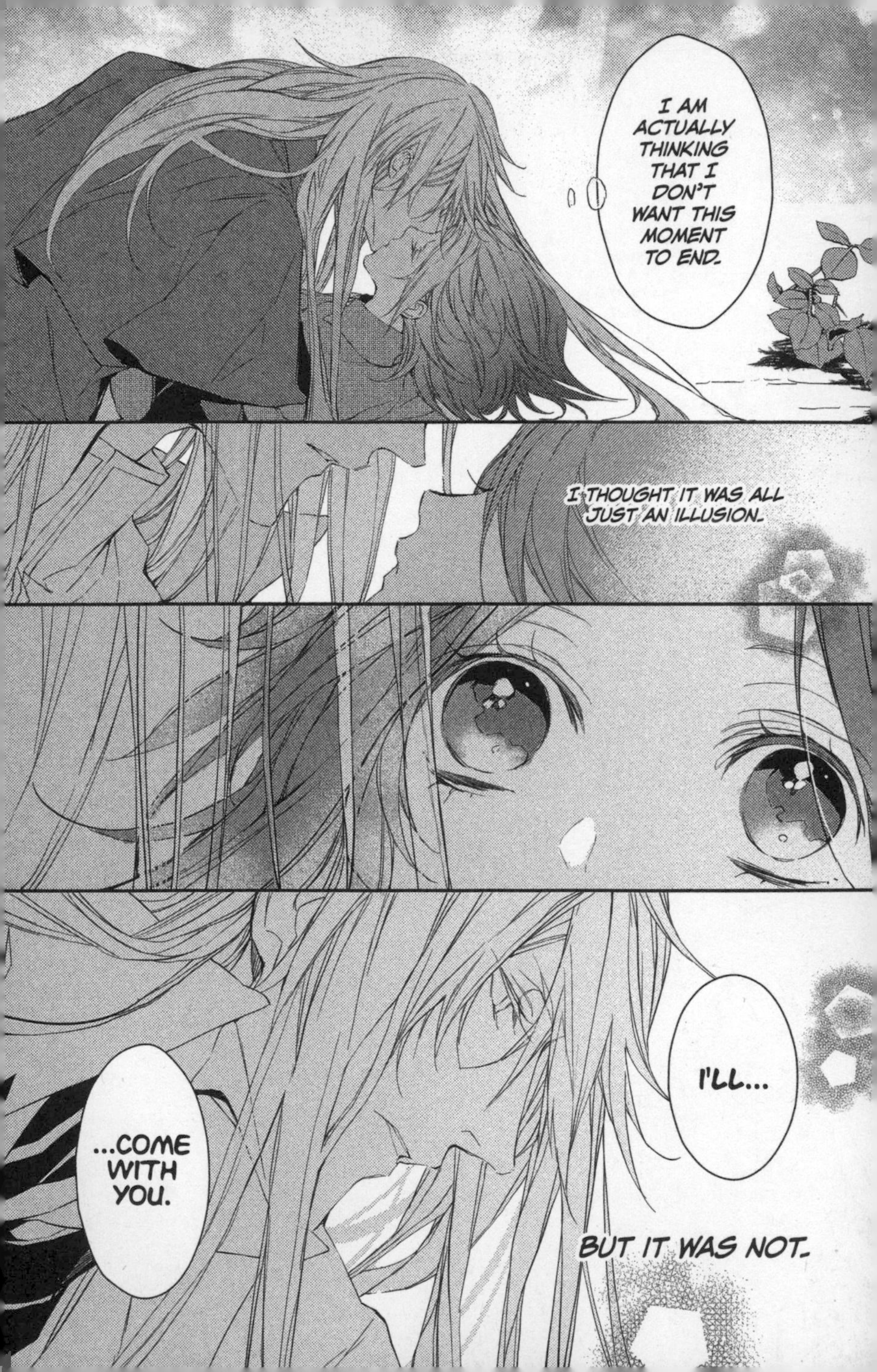
I AM ACTUALLY THINKING THAT I DON'T WANT THIS MOMENT TO END.
I THOUGHT IT WAS ALL JUST AN ILLUSION.
I'LL...
...COME WITH YOU.
BUT IT WAS NOT.

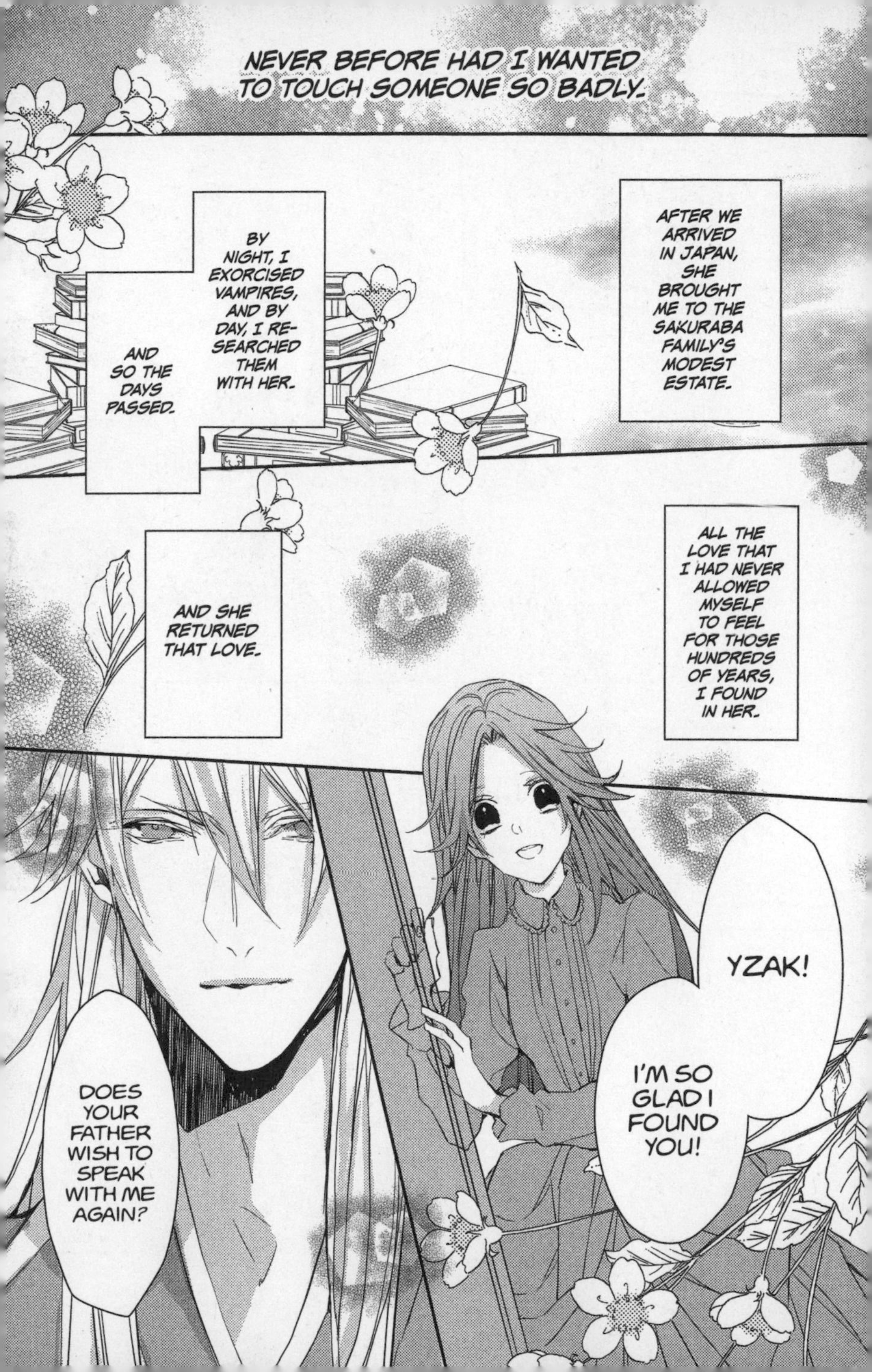
NEVER BEFORE HAD I WANTED TO TOUCH SOMEONE SO BADLY.
AFTER WE ARRIVED IN JAPAN, SHE BROUGHT ME TO THE SAKURABA FAMILY'S MODEST ESTATE.
BY NIGHT, I EXORCISED VAMPIRES, AND BY DAY, I RE-SEARCHED THEM WITH HER.
AND SO THE DAYS PASSED.
ALL THE LOVE THAT I HAD NEVER ALLOWED MYSELF TO FEEL FOR THOSE HUNDREDS OF YEARS, I FOUND IN HER.
AND SHE RETURNED THAT LOVE.
YZAK!
I'M SO GLAD I FOUND YOU!
DOES YOUR FATHER WISH TO SPEAK WITH ME AGAIN?

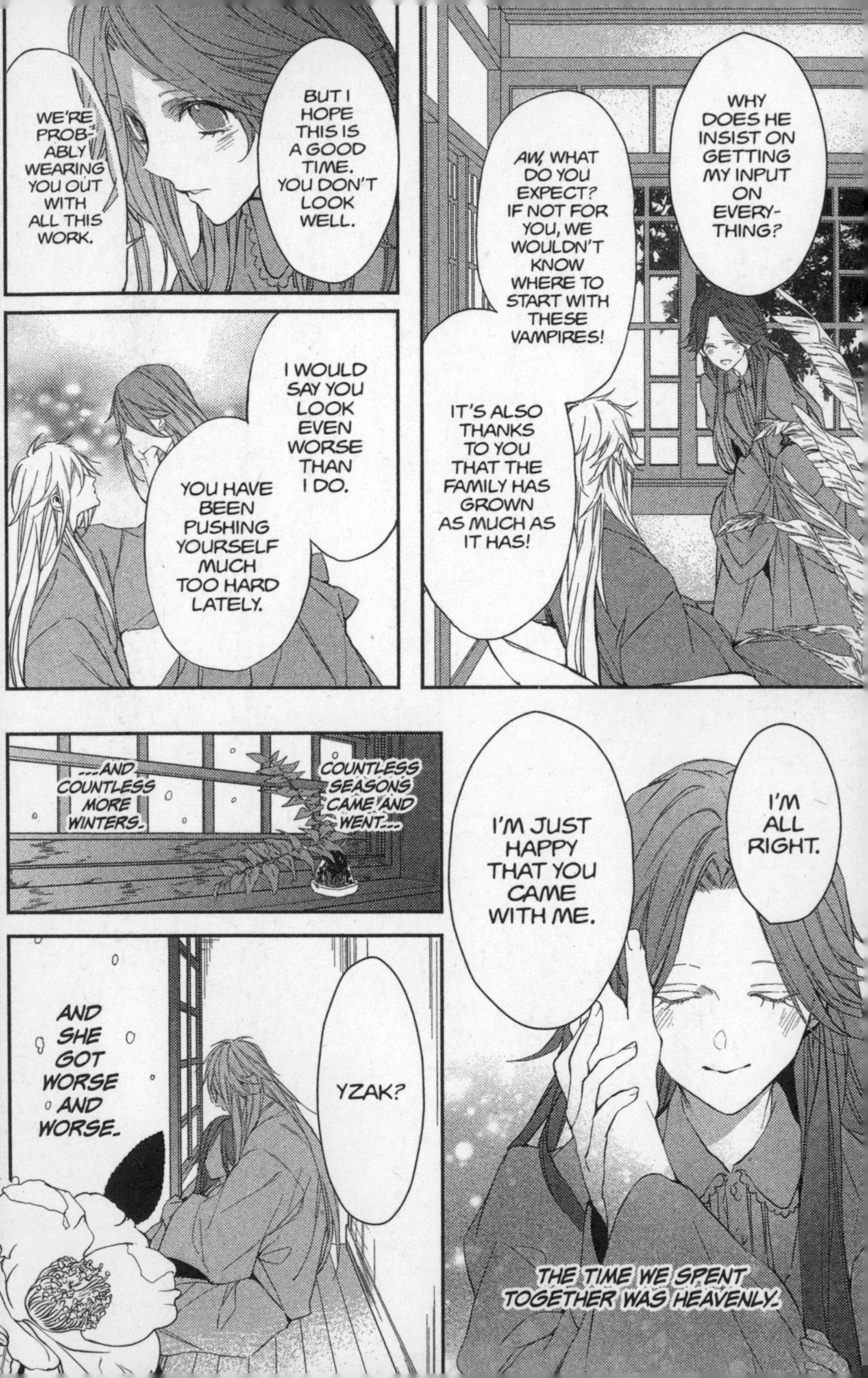
WHY DOES HE INSIST ON GETTING MY INPUT ON EVERY-THING?
AW, WHAT DO YOU EXPECT? IF NOT FOR YOU, WE WOULDN'T KNOW WHERE TO START WITH THESE VAMPIRES!
IT'S ALSO THANKS TO YOU THAT THE FAMILY HAS GROWN AS MUCH AS IT HAS!
BUT I HOPE THIS IS A GOOD TIME. YOU DON'T LOOK WELL.
WE'RE PROB-ABLY WEARING YOU OUT WITH ALL THIS WORK.
I WOULD SAY YOU LOOK EVEN WORSE THAN I DO.
YOU HAVE BEEN PUSHING YOURSELF MUCH TOO HARD LATELY.
I'M ALL RIGHT.
I'M JUST HAPPY THAT YOU CAME WITH ME.
THE TIME WE SPENT TOGETHER WAS HEAVENLY.
COUNTLESS SEASONS CAME AND WENT...
...AND COUNTLESS MORE WINTERS...
YZAK?
AND SHE GOT WORSE AND WORSE...

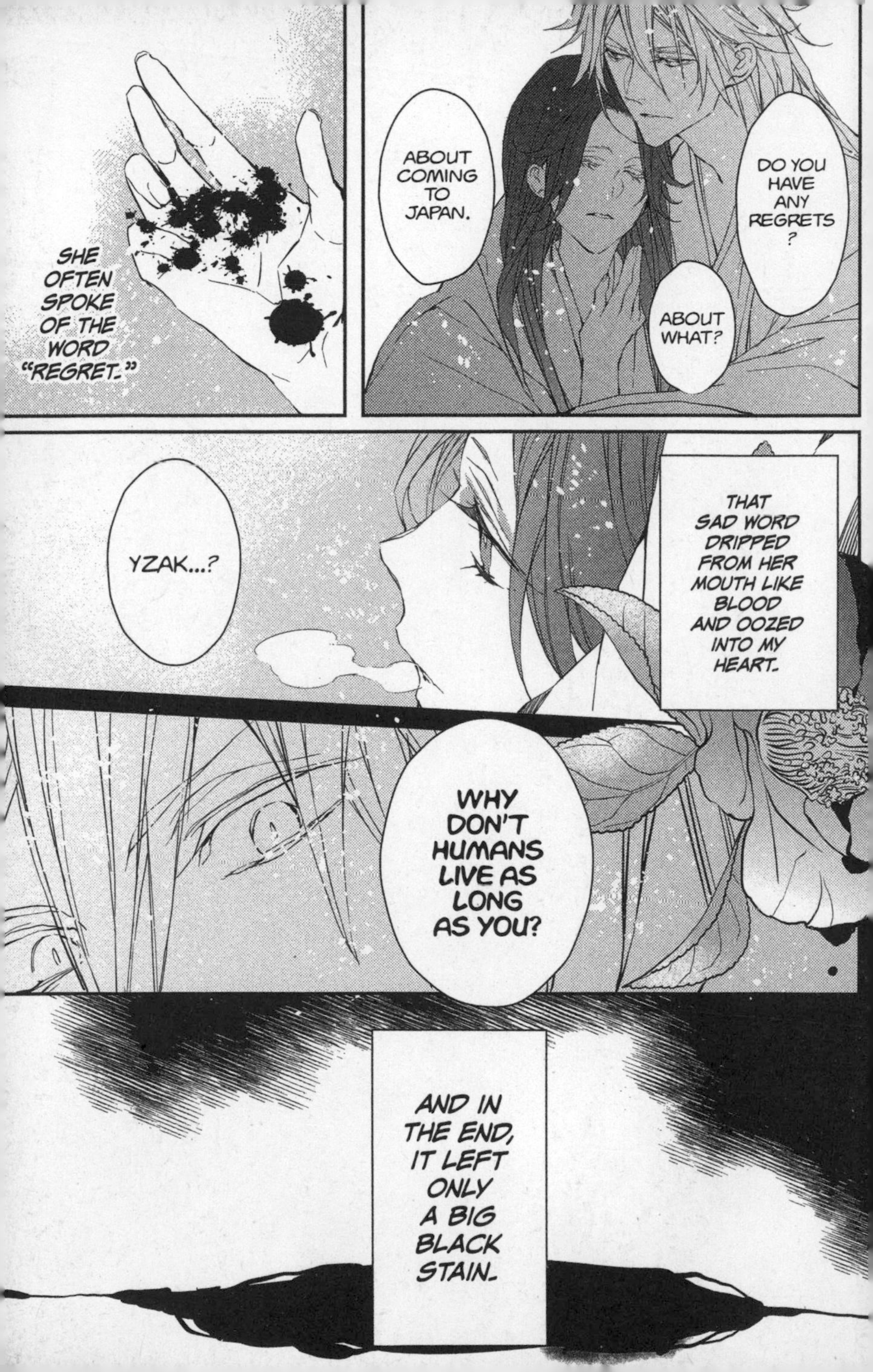
DO YOU HAVE ANY REGRETS?
ABOUT WHAT?
ABOUT COMING TO JAPAN.
SHE OFTEN SPOKE OF THE WORD "REGRET."
THAT SAD WORD DRIPPED FROM HER MOUTH LIKE BLOOD AND OOZED INTO MY HEART.
YZAK...?
WHY DON'T HUMANS LIVE AS LONG AS YOU?
AND IN THE END, IT LEFT ONLY A BIG BLACK STAIN.

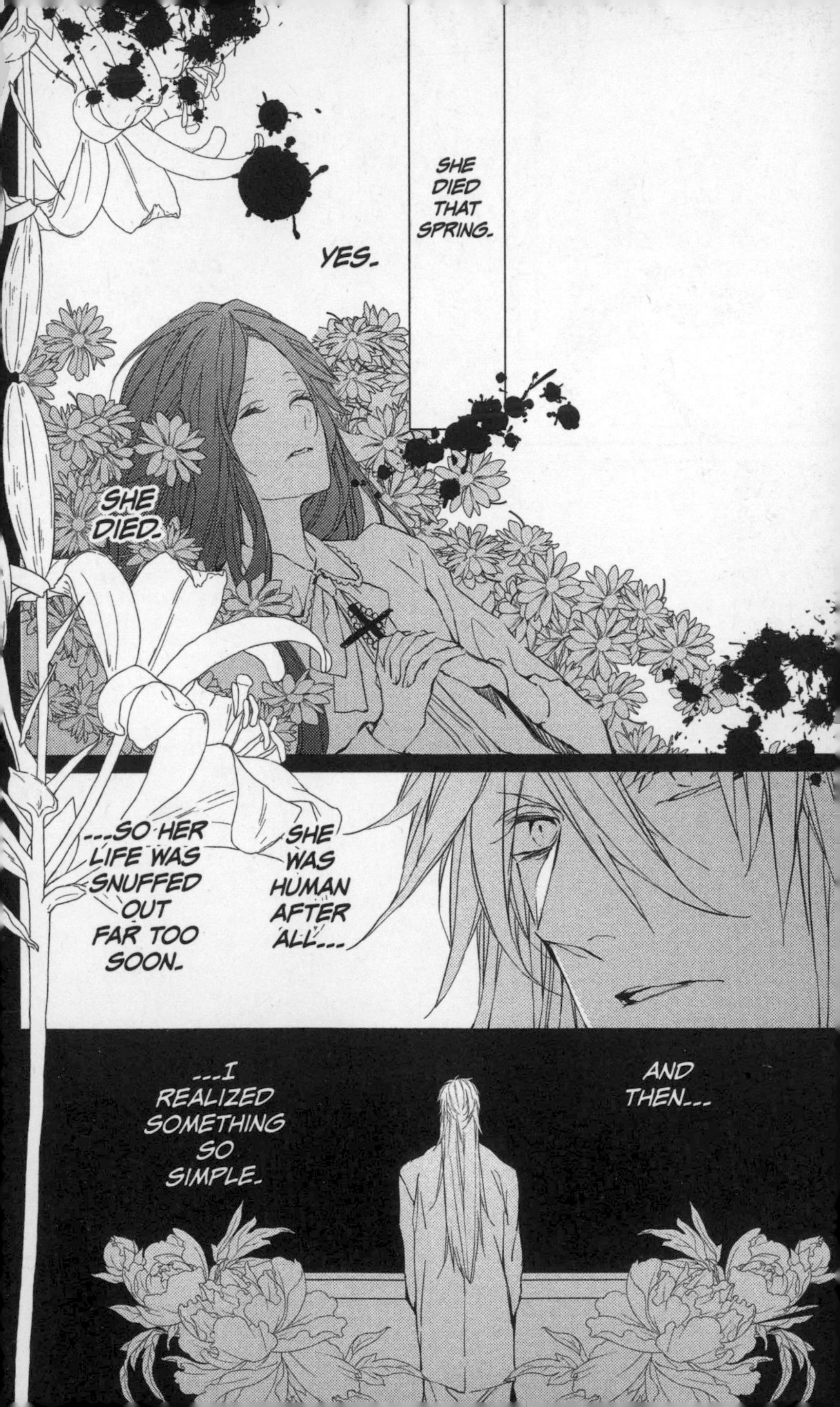
SHE DIED THAT SPRING.
YES.
SHE DIED.
SHE WAS HUMAN AFTER ALL...
...SO HER LIFE WAS SNUFFED OUT FAR TOO SOON.
AND THEN...
...I REALIZED SOMETHING SO SIMPLE.

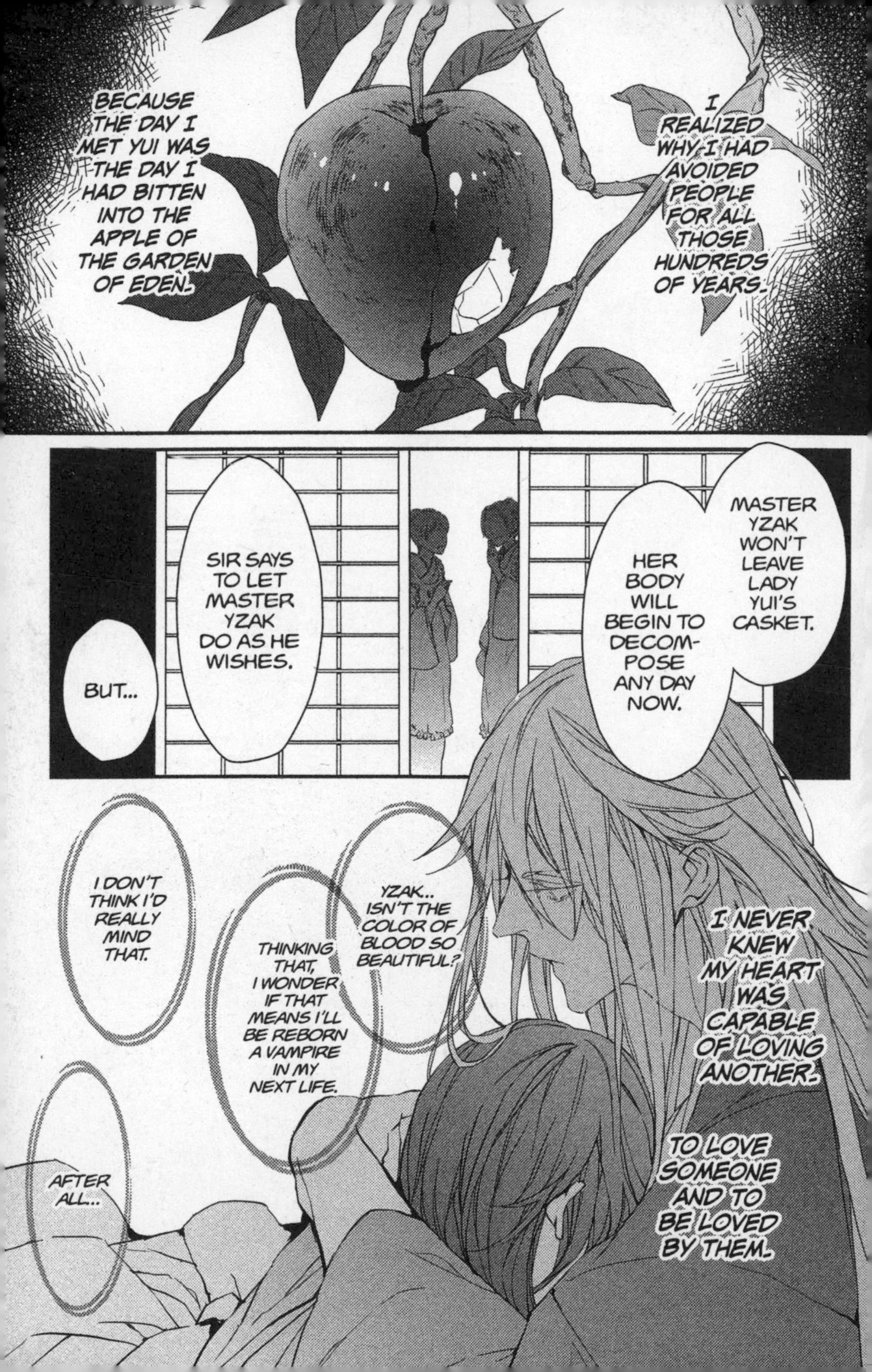
I REALIZED WHY I HAD AVOIDED PEOPLE FOR ALL THOSE HUNDREDS OF YEARS.
BECAUSE THE DAY I MET YUI WAS THE DAY I HAD BITTEN INTO THE APPLE OF THE GARDEN OF EDEN.
MASTER YZAK WON'T LEAVE LADY YUI'S CASKET.
HER BODY WILL BEGIN TO DECOM-POSE ANY DAY NOW.
SIR SAYS TO LET MASTER YZAK DO AS HE WISHES.
BUT...
I NEVER KNEW MY HEART WAS CAPABLE OF LOVING ANOTHER.
TO LOVE SOMEONE AND TO BE LOVED BY THEM.
YZAK... ISN'T THE COLOR OF BLOOD SO BEAUTIFUL?
THINKING THAT, I WONDER IF THAT MEANS I'LL BE REBORN A VAMPIRE IN MY NEXT LIFE.
I DON'T THINK I'D REALLY MIND THAT.
AFTER ALL...

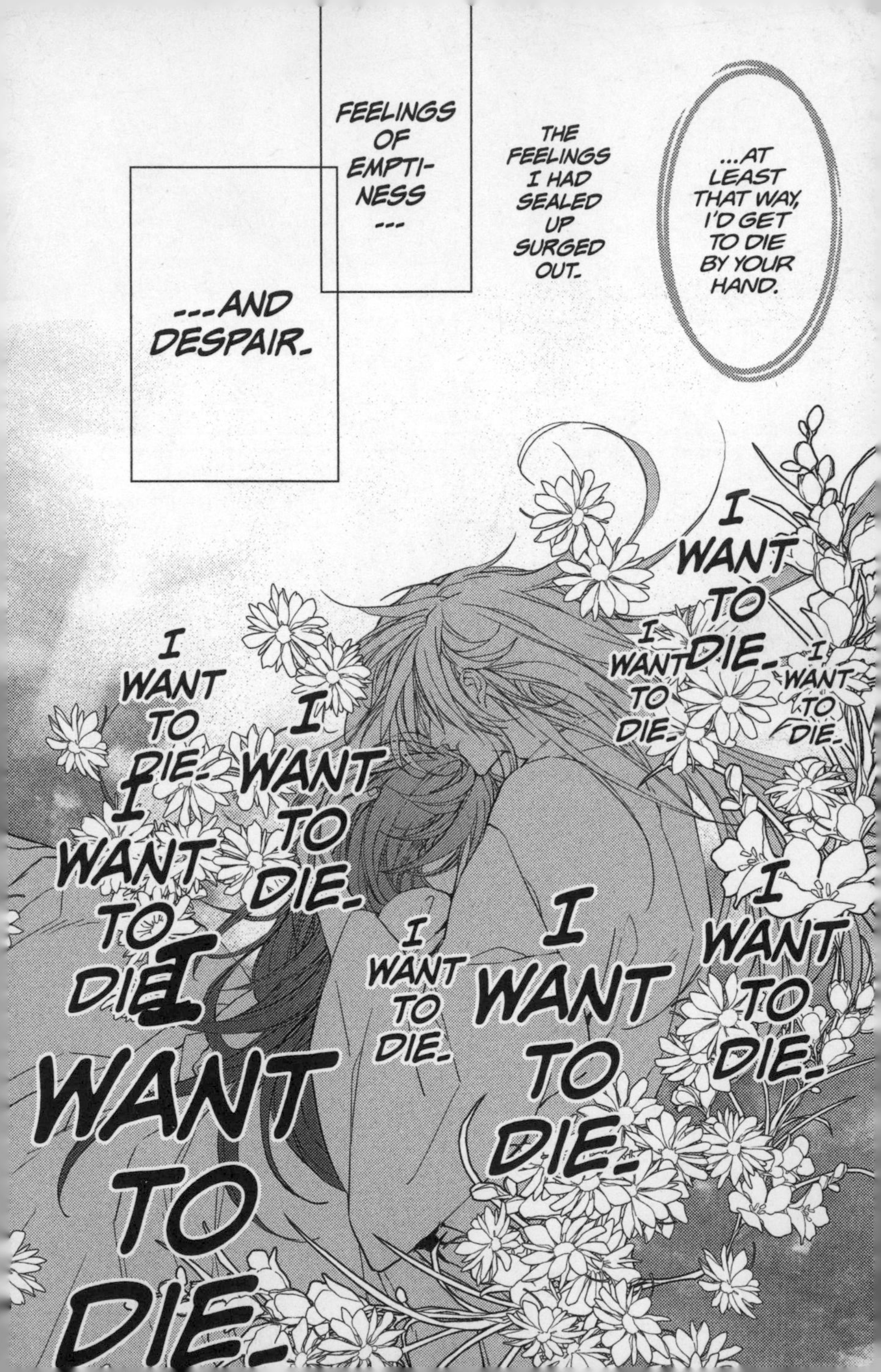
...AT LEAST THAT WAY, I'D GET TO DIE BY YOUR HAND.
THE FEELINGS I HAD SEALED UP SURGED OUT.
FEELINGS OF EMPTINESS---
---AND DESPAIR.
I WANT TO DIE.
I WANT TO DIE.
I WANT TO DIE.
I WANT TO DIE.
I WANT TO DIE.
I WANT TO DIE.
I WANT TO DIE.
I WANT TO DIE.
I WANT TO DIE.
I WANT TO DIE.

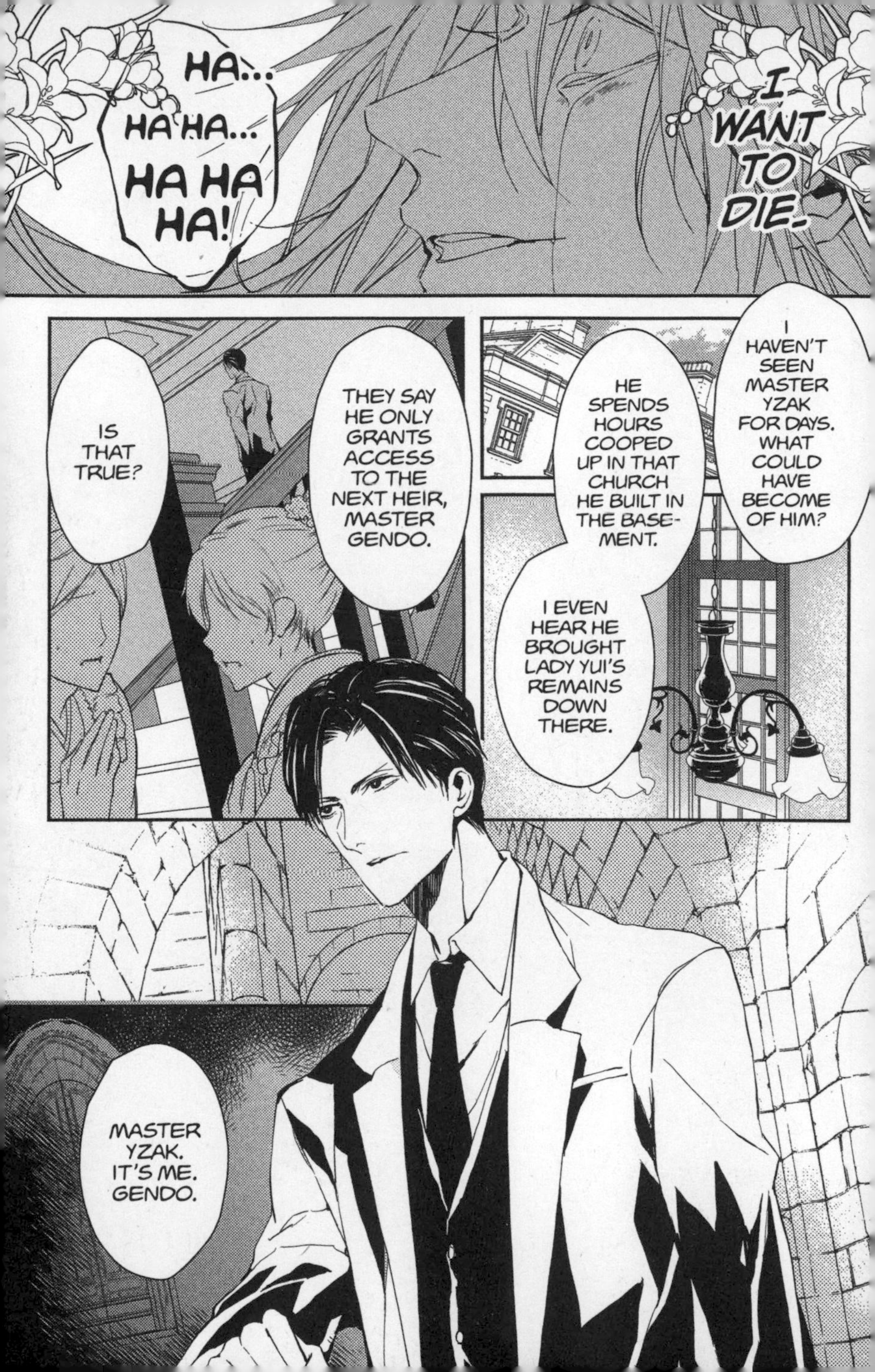
I WANT TO DIE_
HA... HA HA... HA HA HA!
I HAVEN'T SEEN MASTER YZAK FOR DAYS. WHAT COULD HAVE BECOME OF HIM?
HE SPENDS HOURS COOPED UP IN THAT CHURCH HE BUILT IN THE BASE-MENT.
I EVEN HEAR HE BROUGHT LADY YUI'S REMAINS DOWN THERE.
THEY SAY HE ONLY GRANTS ACCESS TO THE NEXT HEIR, MASTER GENDO.
IS THAT TRUE?
MASTER YZAK. IT'S ME. GENDO.

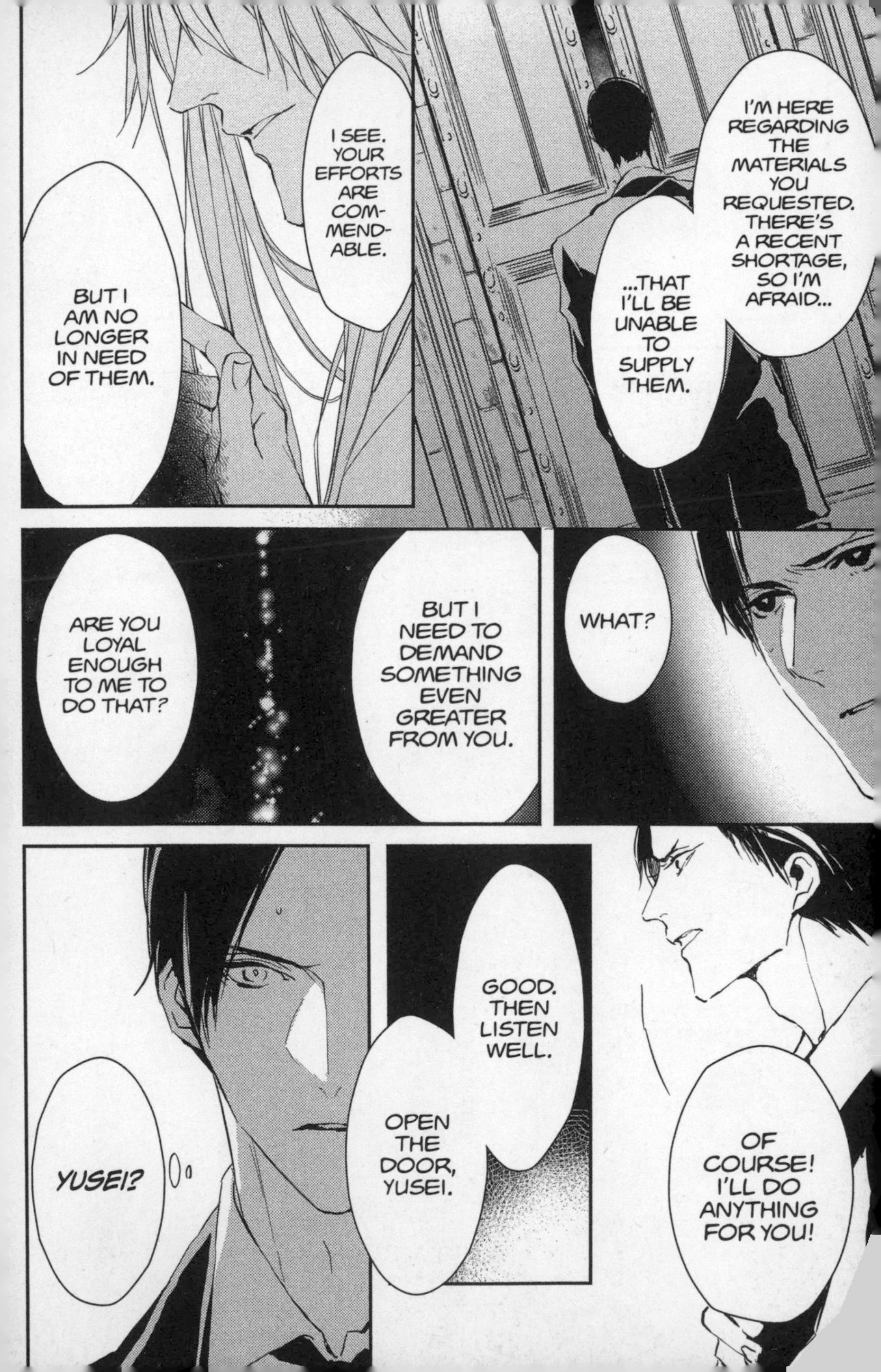
I'M HERE REGARDING THE MATERIALS YOU REQUESTED. THERE'S A RECENT SHORTAGE, SO I'M AFRAID...
...THAT I'LL BE UNABLE TO SUPPLY THEM.
I SEE. YOUR EFFORTS ARE COM-MEND-ABLE.
BUT I AM NO LONGER IN NEED OF THEM.
WHAT?
BUT I NEED TO DEMAND SOMETHING EVEN GREATER FROM YOU.
ARE YOU LOYAL ENOUGH TO ME TO DO THAT?
OF COURSE! I'LL DO ANYTHING FOR YOU!
GOOD. THEN LISTEN WELL.
OPEN THE DOOR, YUSEI.
YUSEI?

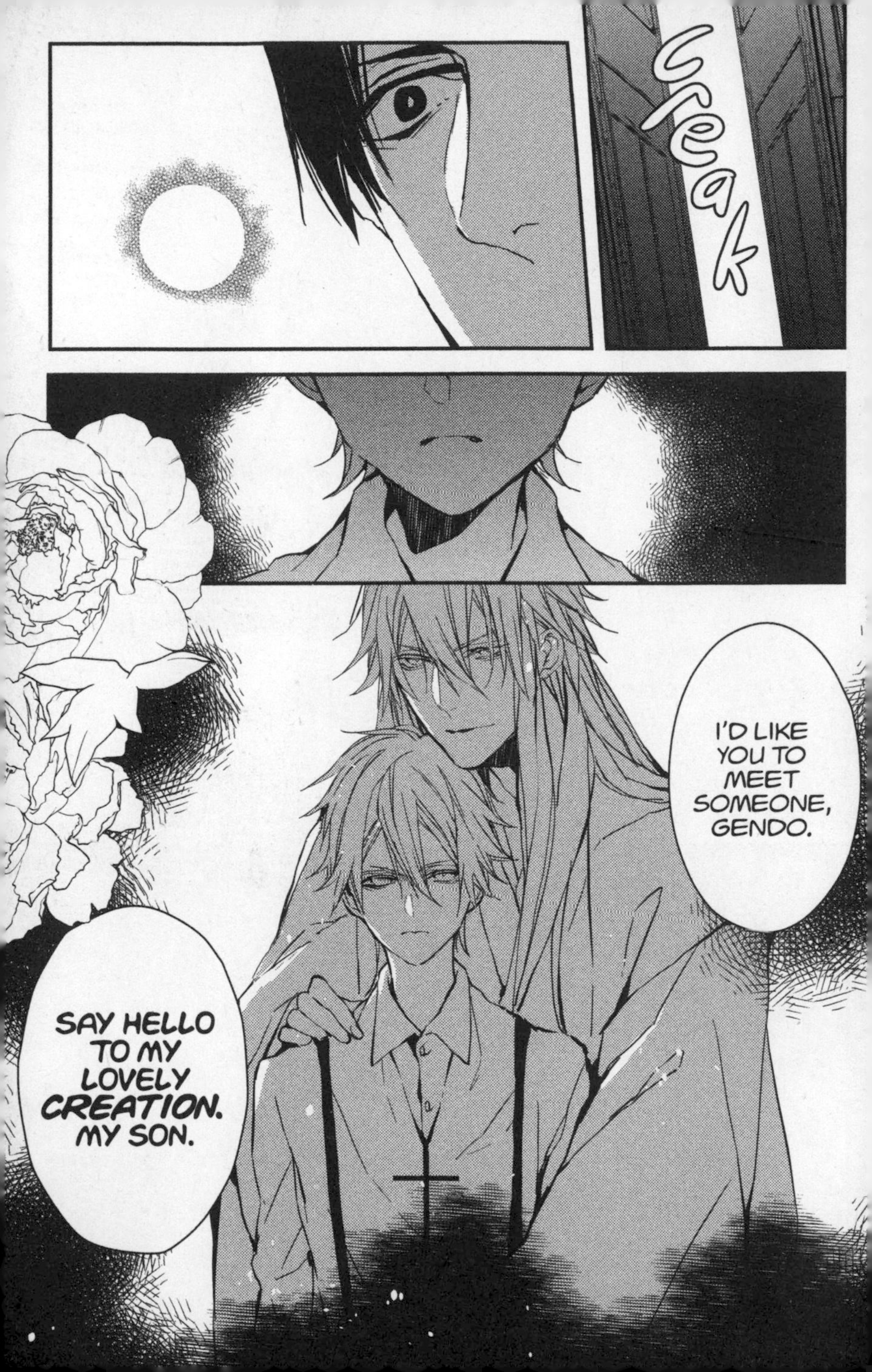
creak
I'D LIKE YOU TO MEET SOMEONE, GENDO.
SAY HELLO TO MY LOVELY *CREATION.* MY SON.

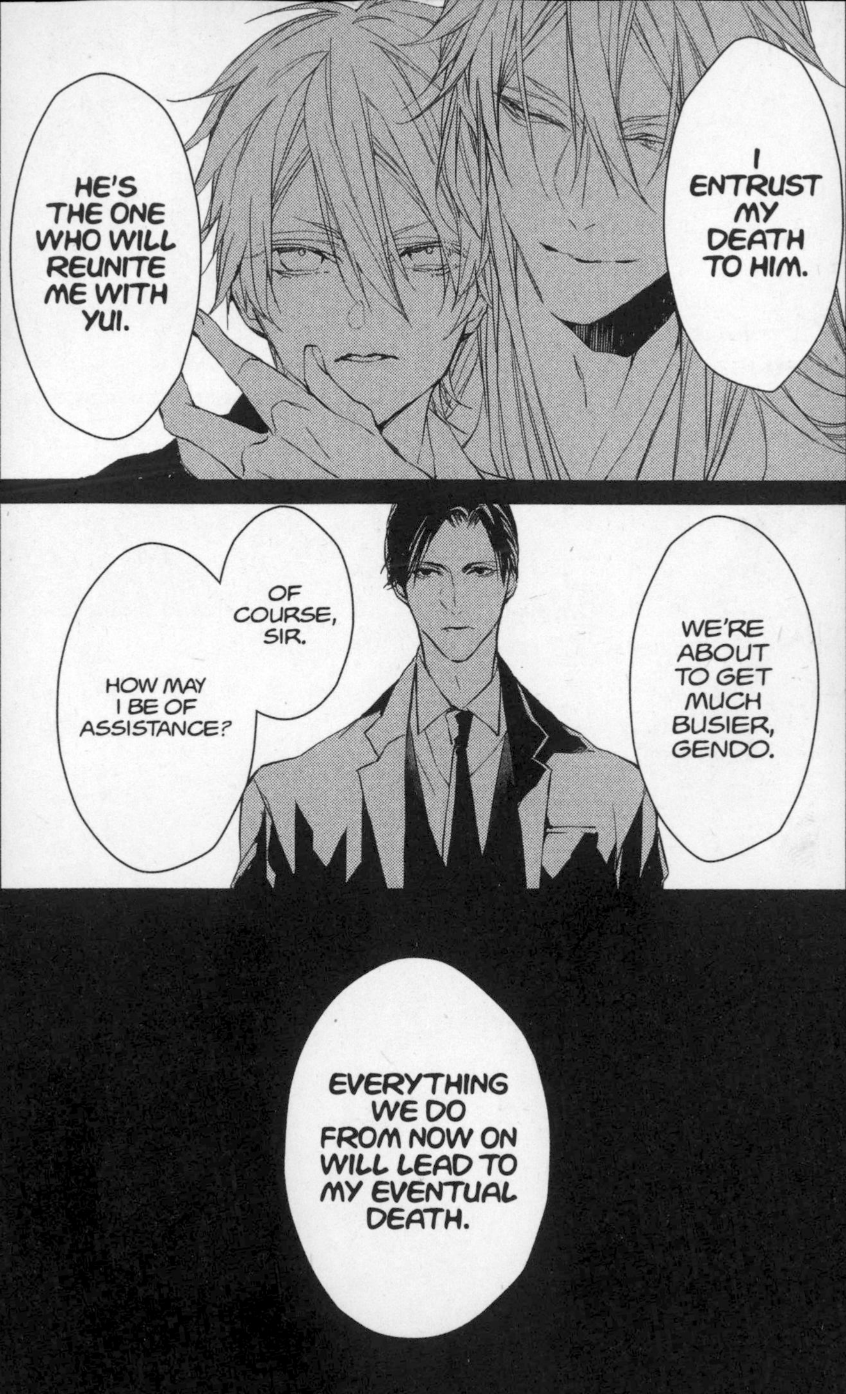
I ENTRUST MY DEATH TO HIM.
HE'S THE ONE WHO WILL REUNITE ME WITH YUI.
WE'RE ABOUT TO GET MUCH BUSIER, GENDO.
OF COURSE, SIR.
HOW MAY I BE OF ASSISTANCE?
EVERYTHING WE DO FROM NOW ON WILL LEAD TO MY EVENTUAL DEATH.

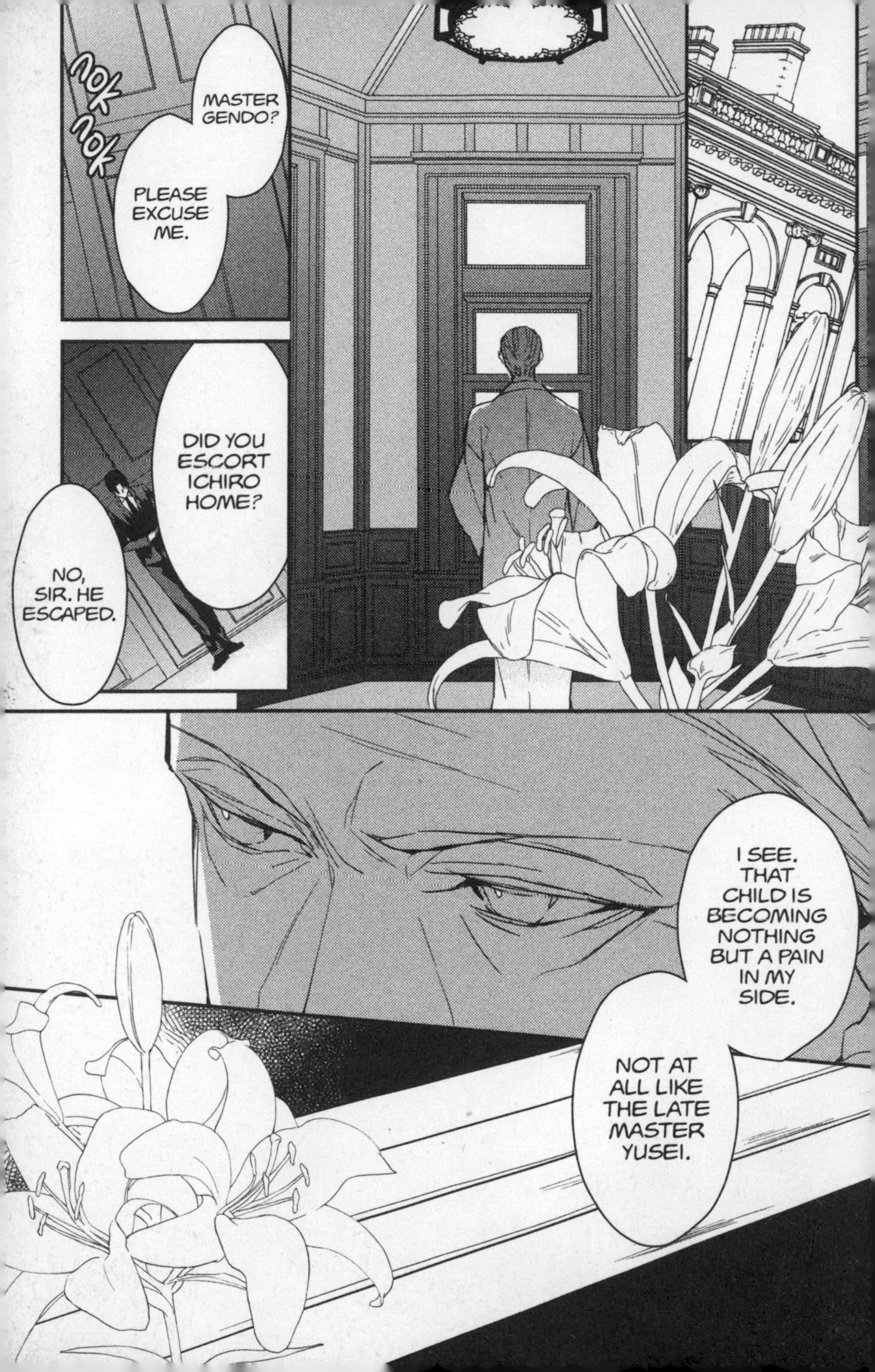
NOK NOK
MASTER GENDO?
PLEASE EXCUSE ME.
DID YOU ESCORT ICHIRO HOME?
NO, SIR. HE ESCAPED.
I SEE. THAT CHILD IS BECOMING NOTHING BUT A PAIN IN MY SIDE.
NOT AT ALL LIKE THE LATE MASTER YUSEI.

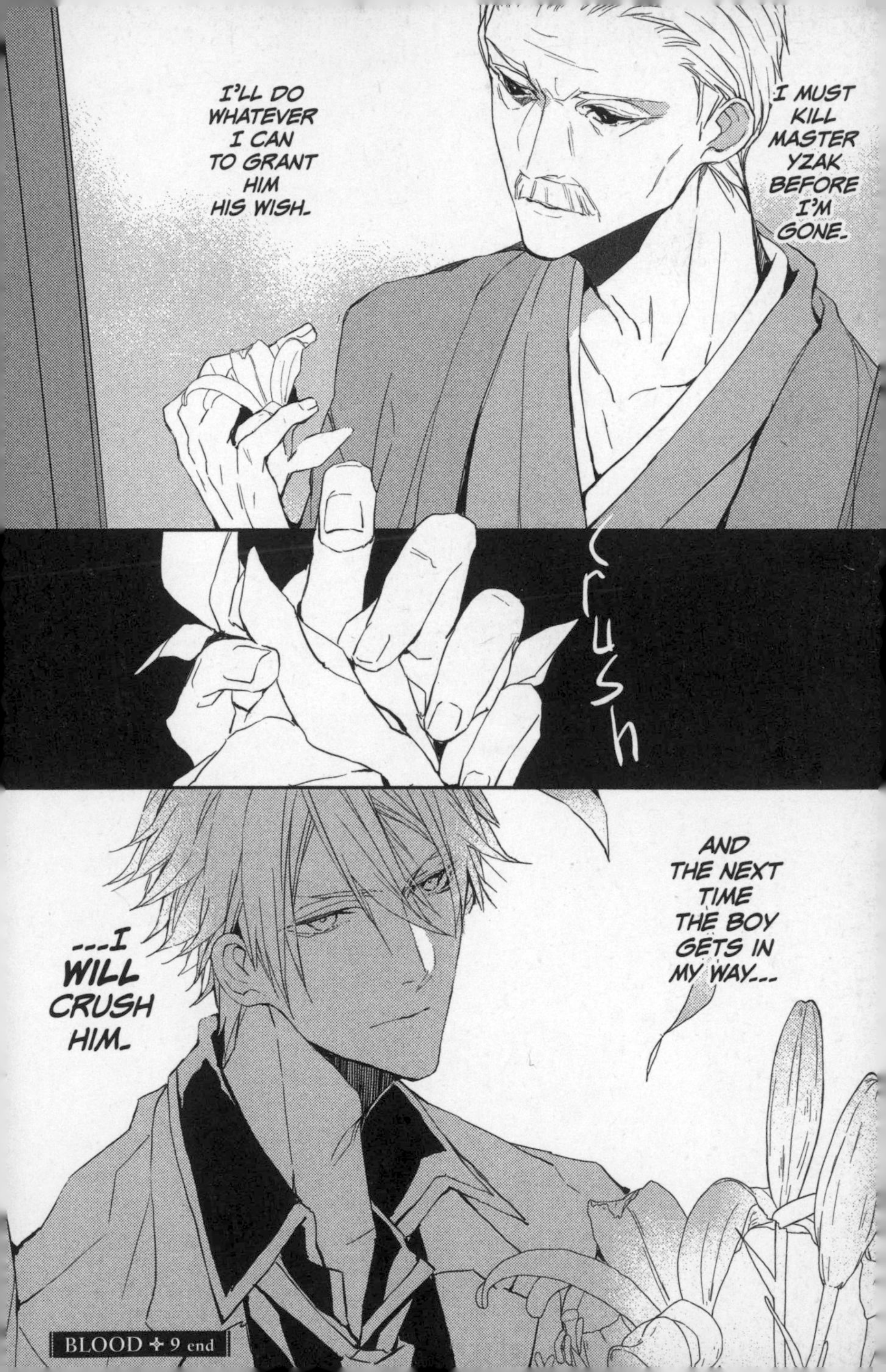
I MUST KILL MASTER YZAK BEFORE I'M GONE...
I'LL DO WHATEVER I CAN TO GRANT HIM HIS WISH...
crush
AND THE NEXT TIME THE BOY GETS IN MY WAY...
...I WILL CRUSH HIM...

BLOOD ✣ 9 end

Bloody+Mary

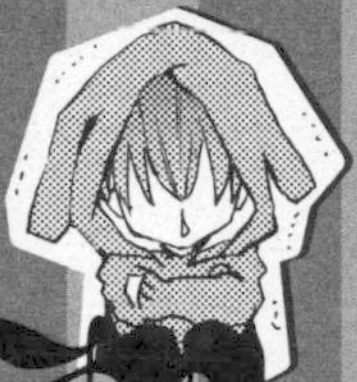

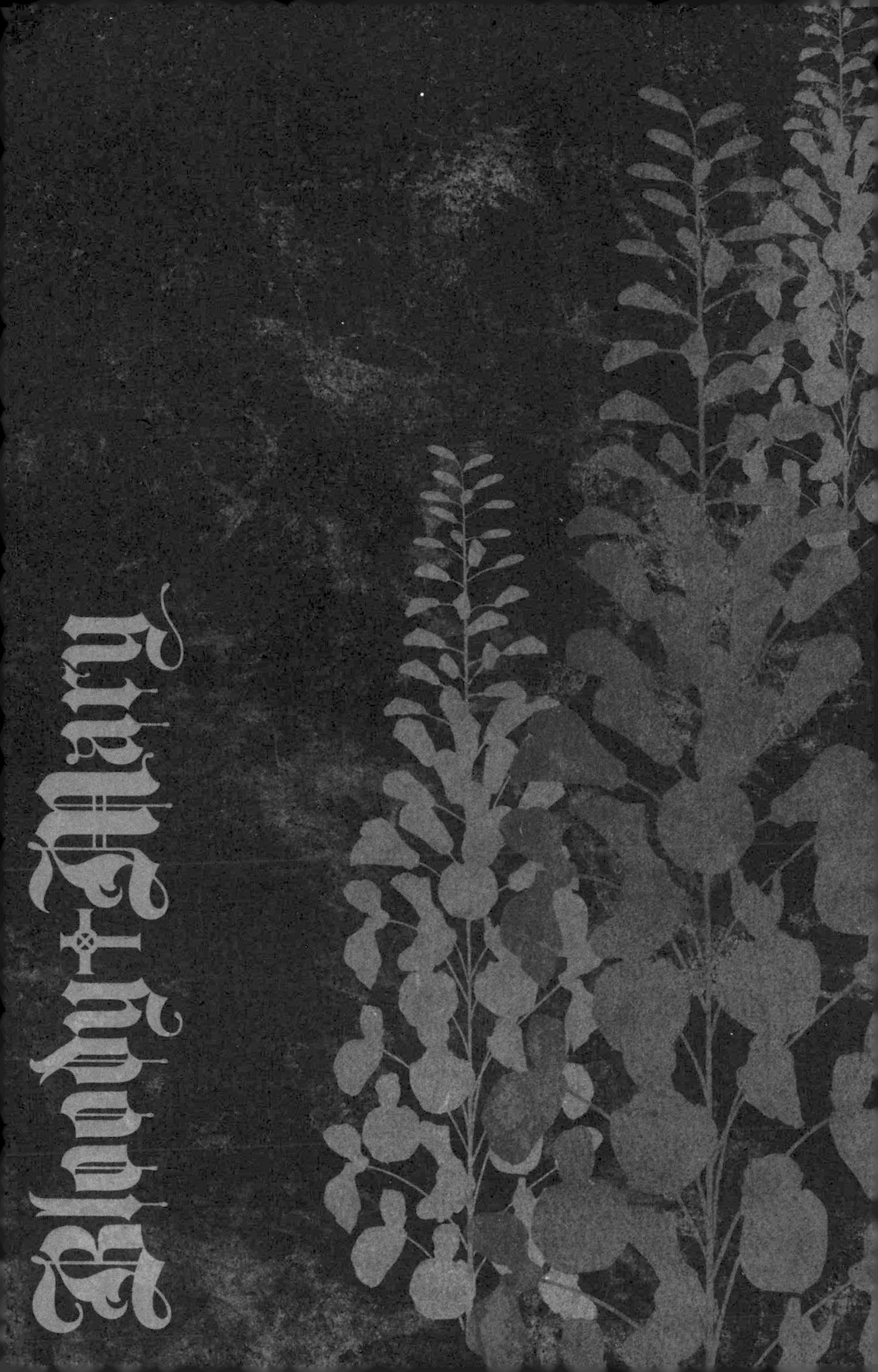
Bloody Mary

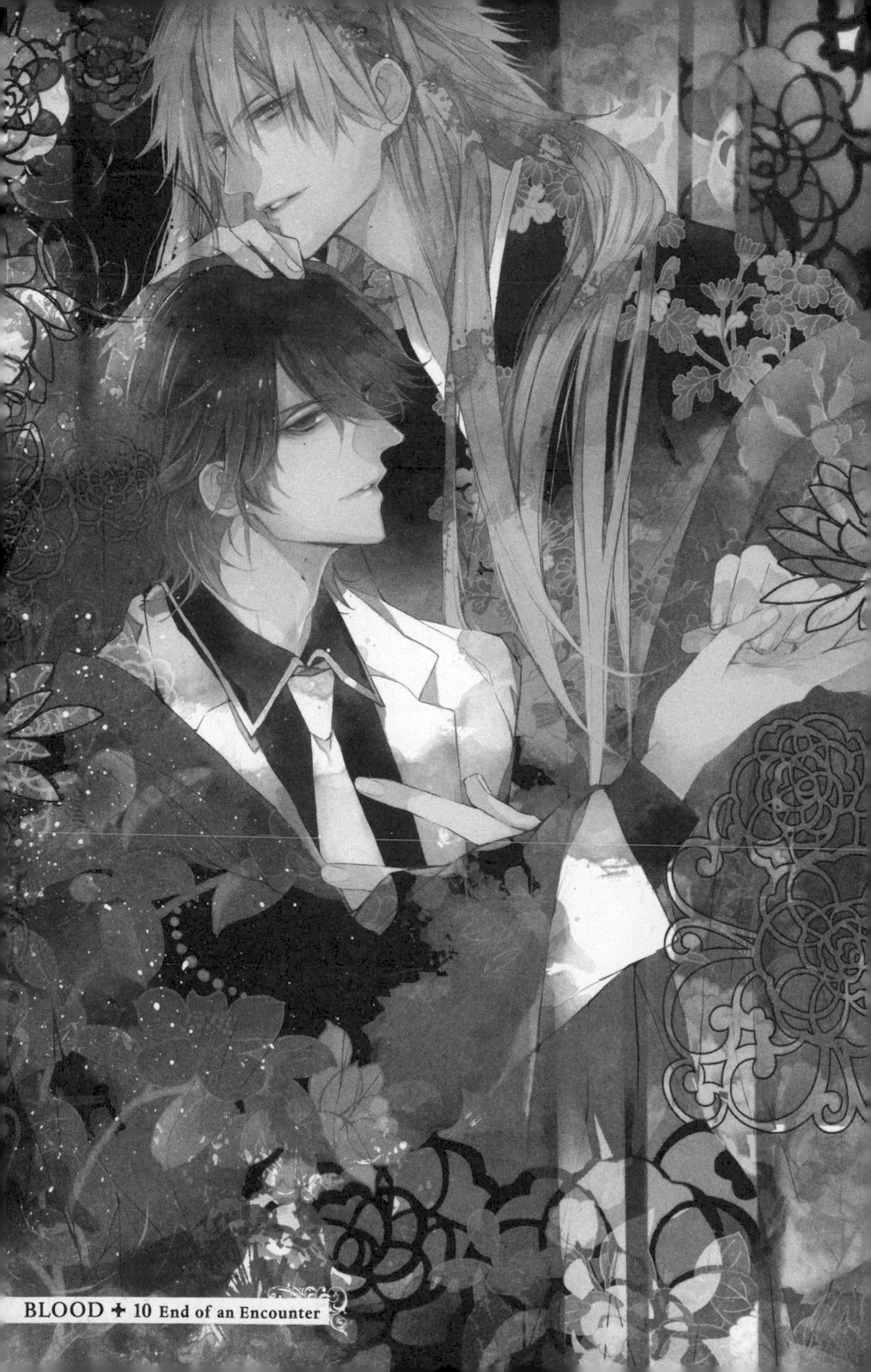
BLOOD ✦ 10 End of an Encounter

Bloody Mary

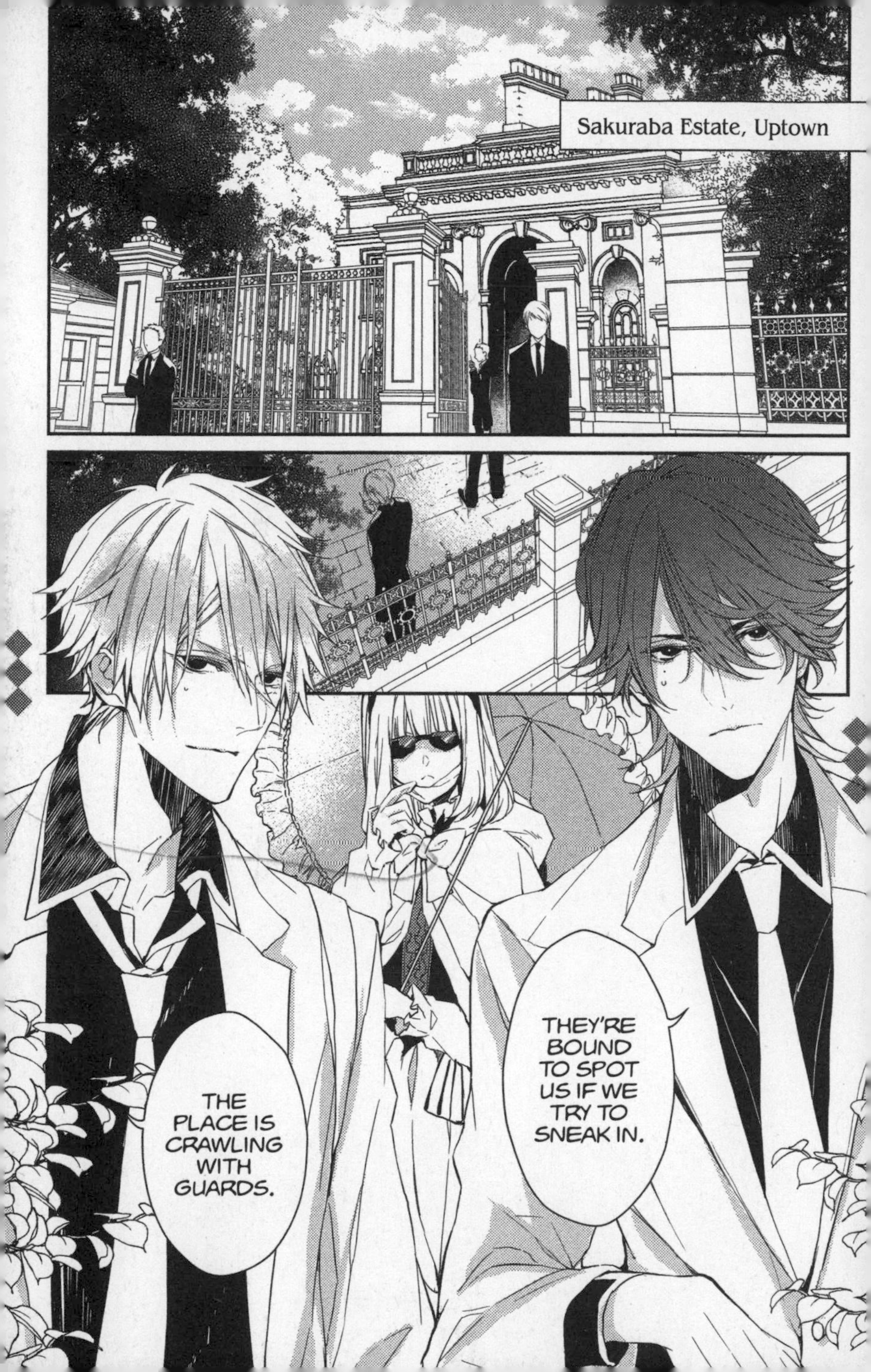
Sakuraba Estate, Uptown
THEY'RE BOUND TO SPOT US IF WE TRY TO SNEAK IN.
THE PLACE IS CRAWLING WITH GUARDS.

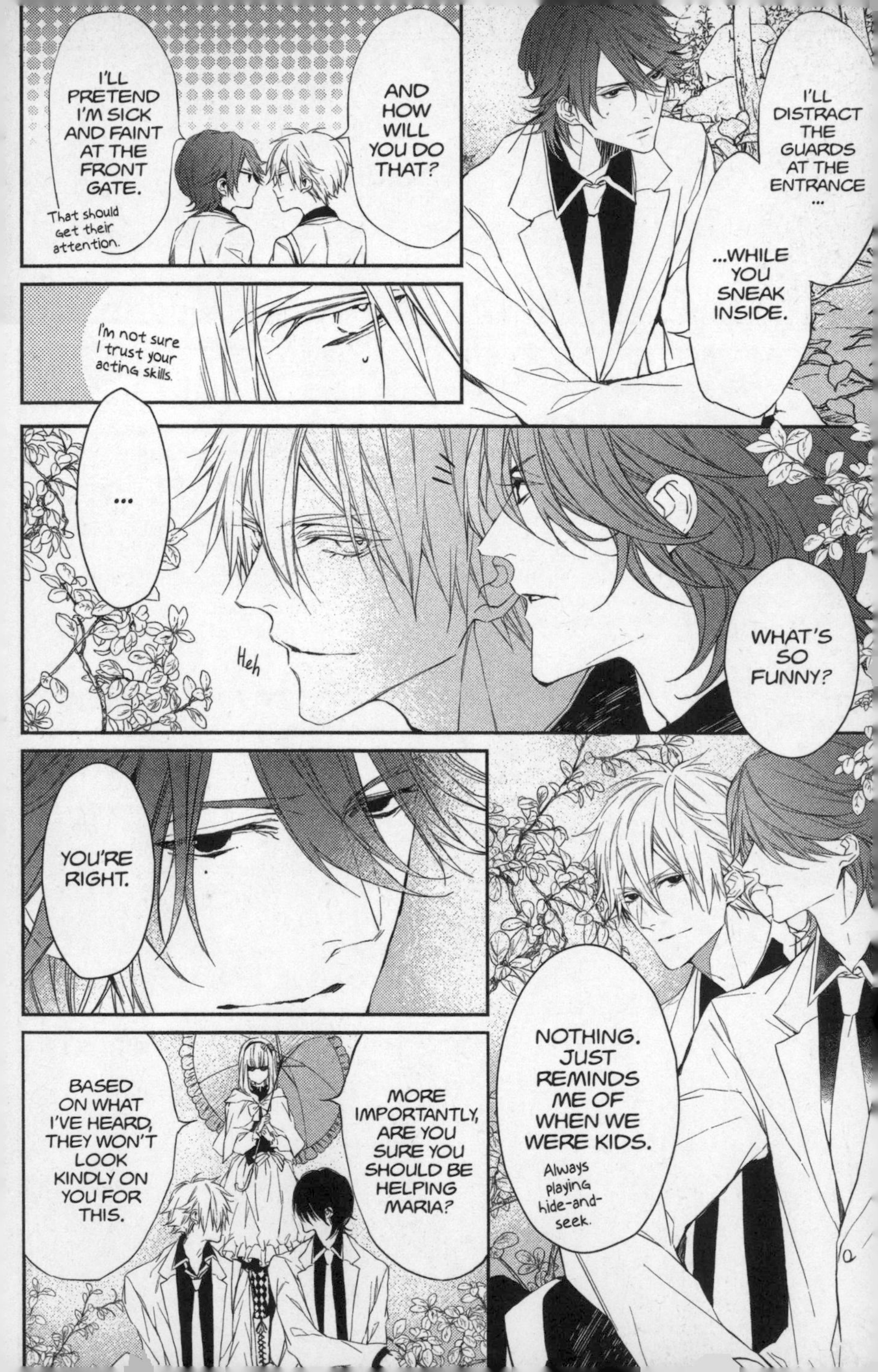
I'LL DISTRACT THE GUARDS AT THE ENTRANCE ...
...WHILE YOU SNEAK INSIDE.
AND HOW WILL YOU DO THAT?
I'LL PRETEND I'M SICK AND FAINT AT THE FRONT GATE.
That should get their attention.
I'm not sure I trust your acting skills.
WHAT'S SO FUNNY?
Heh
...
NOTHING. JUST REMINDS ME OF WHEN WE WERE KIDS.
Always playing hide-and-seek.
YOU'RE RIGHT.
MORE IMPORTANTLY, ARE YOU SURE YOU SHOULD BE HELPING MARIA?
BASED ON WHAT I'VE HEARD, THEY WON'T LOOK KINDLY ON YOU FOR THIS.

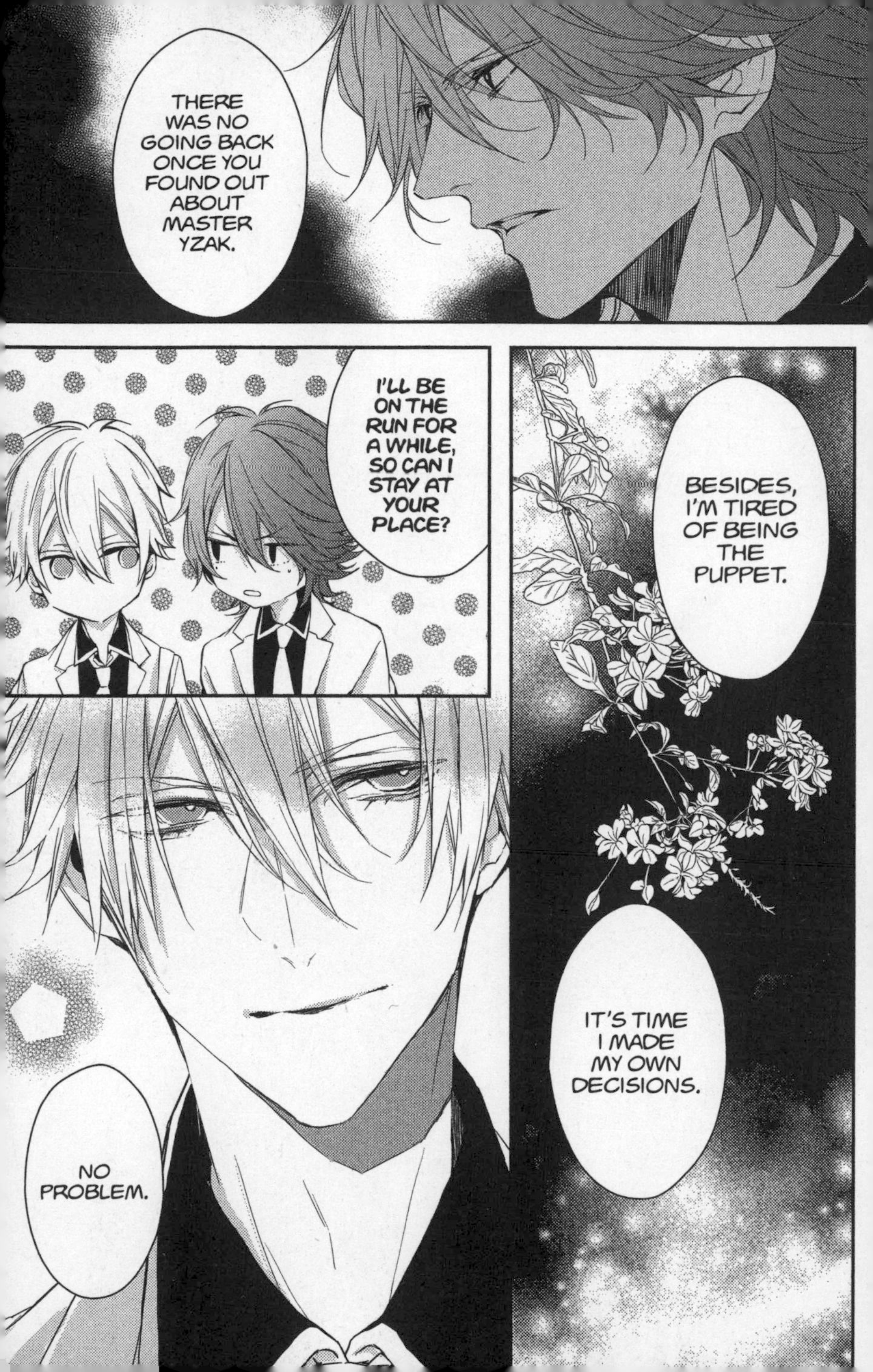
THERE WAS NO GOING BACK ONCE YOU FOUND OUT ABOUT MASTER YZAK.
BESIDES, I'M TIRED OF BEING THE PUPPET.
IT'S TIME I MADE MY OWN DECISIONS.
I'LL BE ON THE RUN FOR A WHILE, SO CAN I STAY AT YOUR PLACE?
NO PROBLEM.

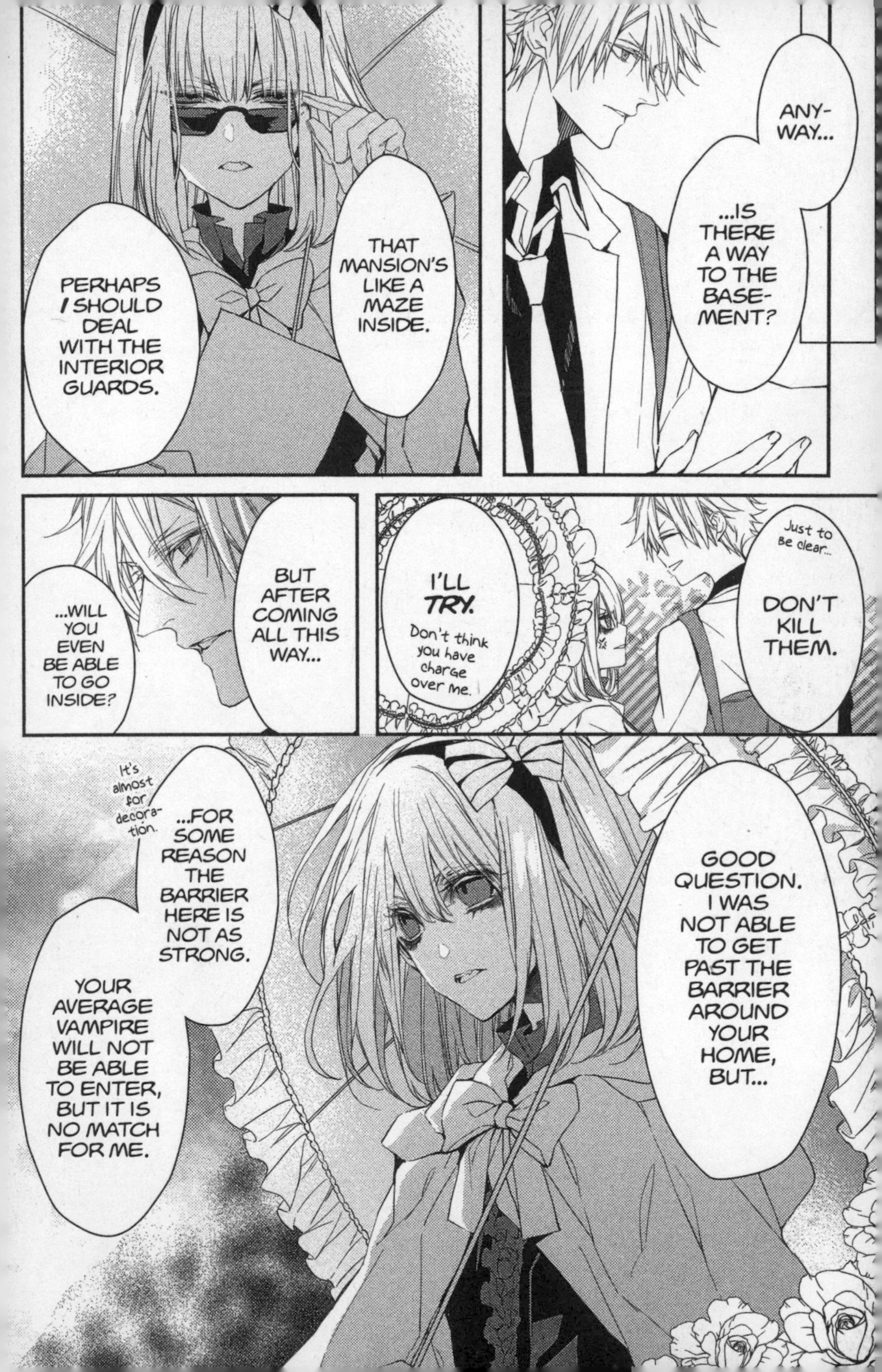
ANY-WAY...
...IS THERE A WAY TO THE BASE-MENT?
THAT MANSION'S LIKE A MAZE INSIDE.
PERHAPS *I* SHOULD DEAL WITH THE INTERIOR GUARDS.
Just to be clear...
DON'T KILL THEM.
I'LL *TRY*.
Don't think you have charge over me.
BUT AFTER COMING ALL THIS WAY...
...WILL YOU EVEN BE ABLE TO GO INSIDE?
GOOD QUESTION. I WAS NOT ABLE TO GET PAST THE BARRIER AROUND YOUR HOME, BUT...
...FOR SOME REASON THE BARRIER HERE IS NOT AS STRONG.
It's almost for decora-tion.
YOUR AVERAGE VAMPIRE WILL NOT BE ABLE TO ENTER, BUT IT IS NO MATCH FOR ME.

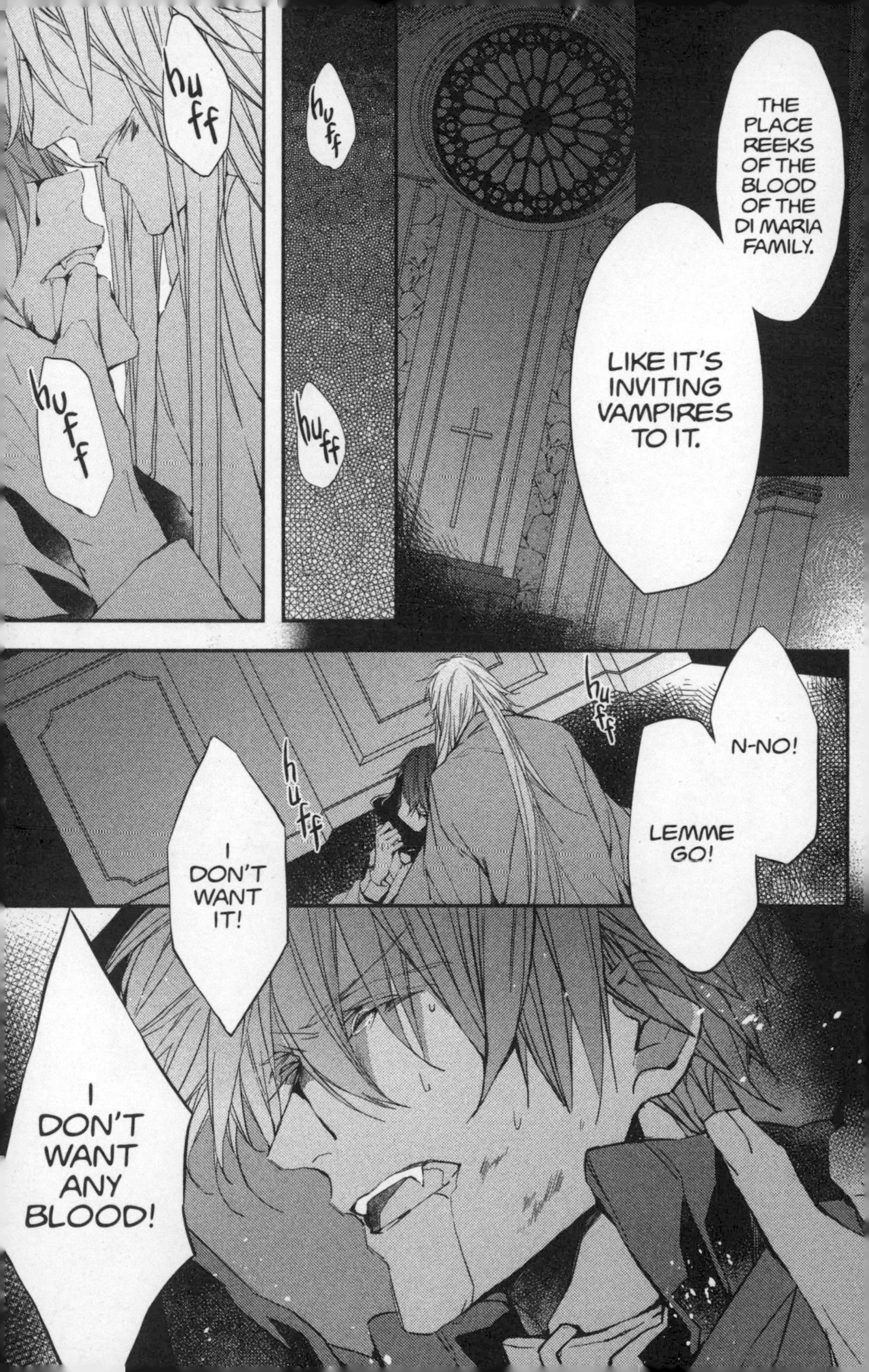
THE PLACE REEKS OF THE BLOOD OF THE DI MARIA FAMILY.
LIKE IT'S INVITING VAMPIRES TO IT.
huff
huff
huff
huff
N-NO!
LEMME GO!
huff
huff
I DON'T WANT IT!
I DON'T WANT ANY BLOOD!

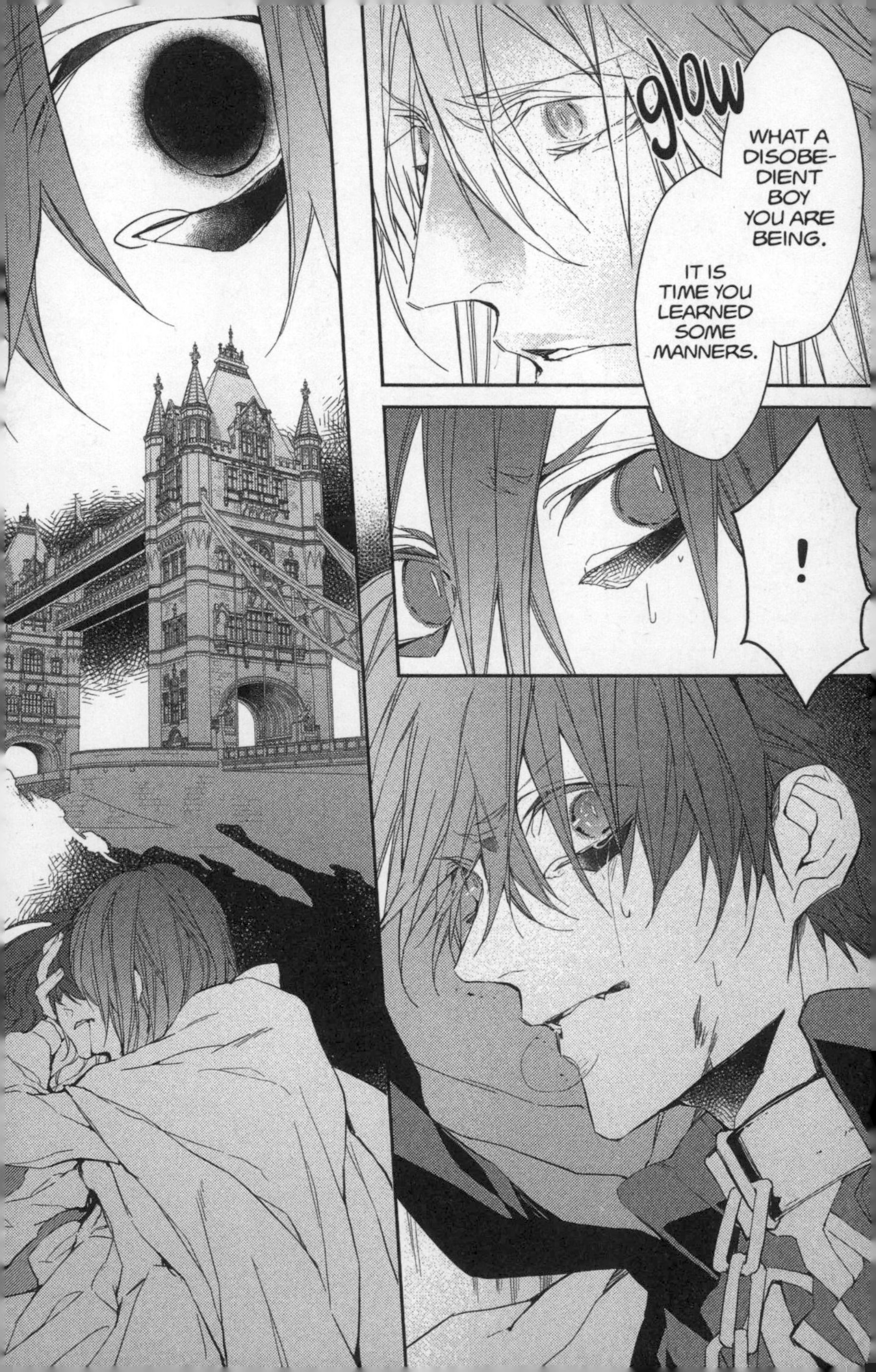
glow
WHAT A DISOBE-DIENT BOY YOU ARE BEING.
IT IS TIME YOU LEARNED SOME MANNERS.
!

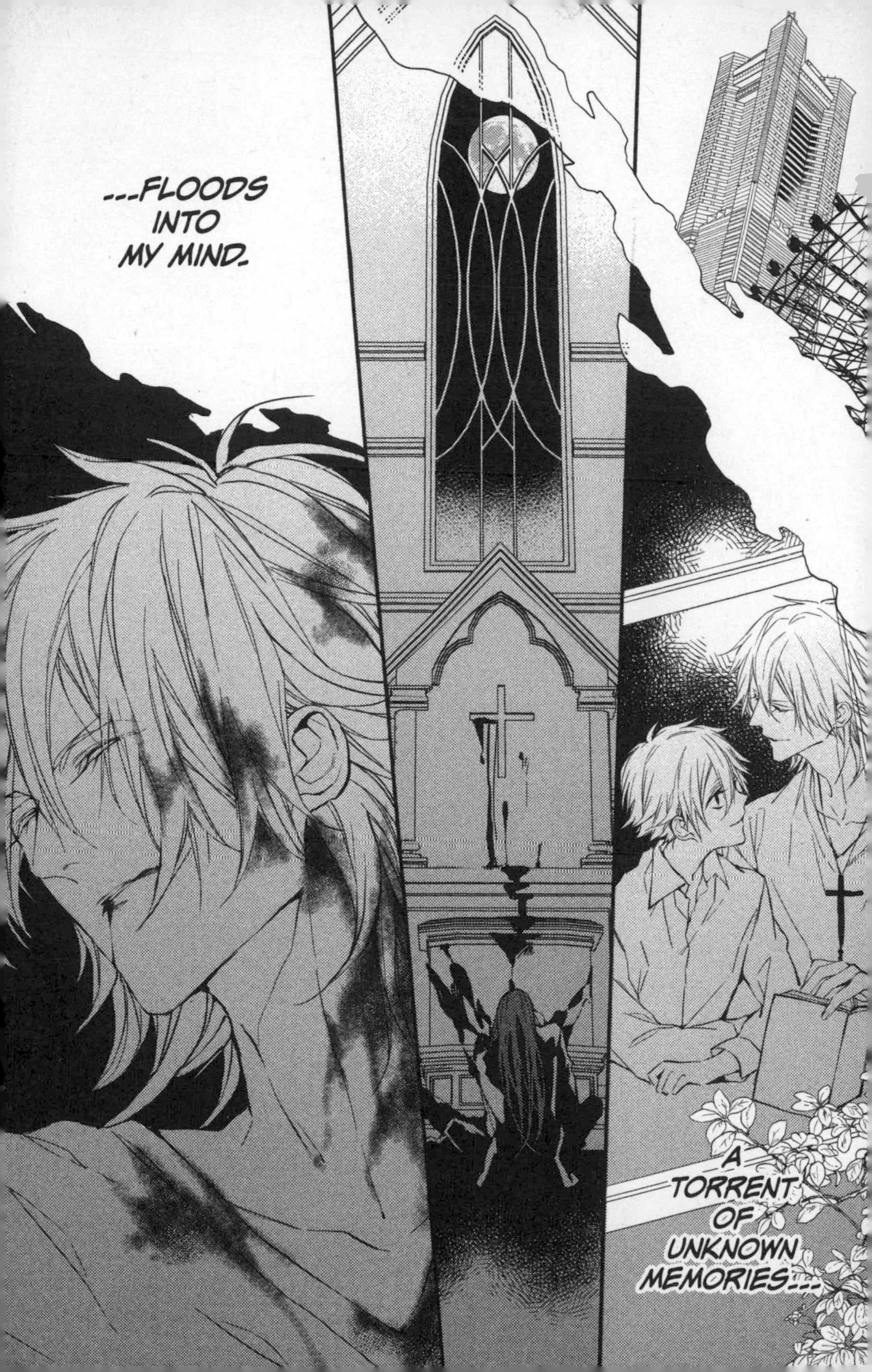
A TORRENT OF UNKNOWN MEMORIES...
...FLOODS INTO MY MIND.

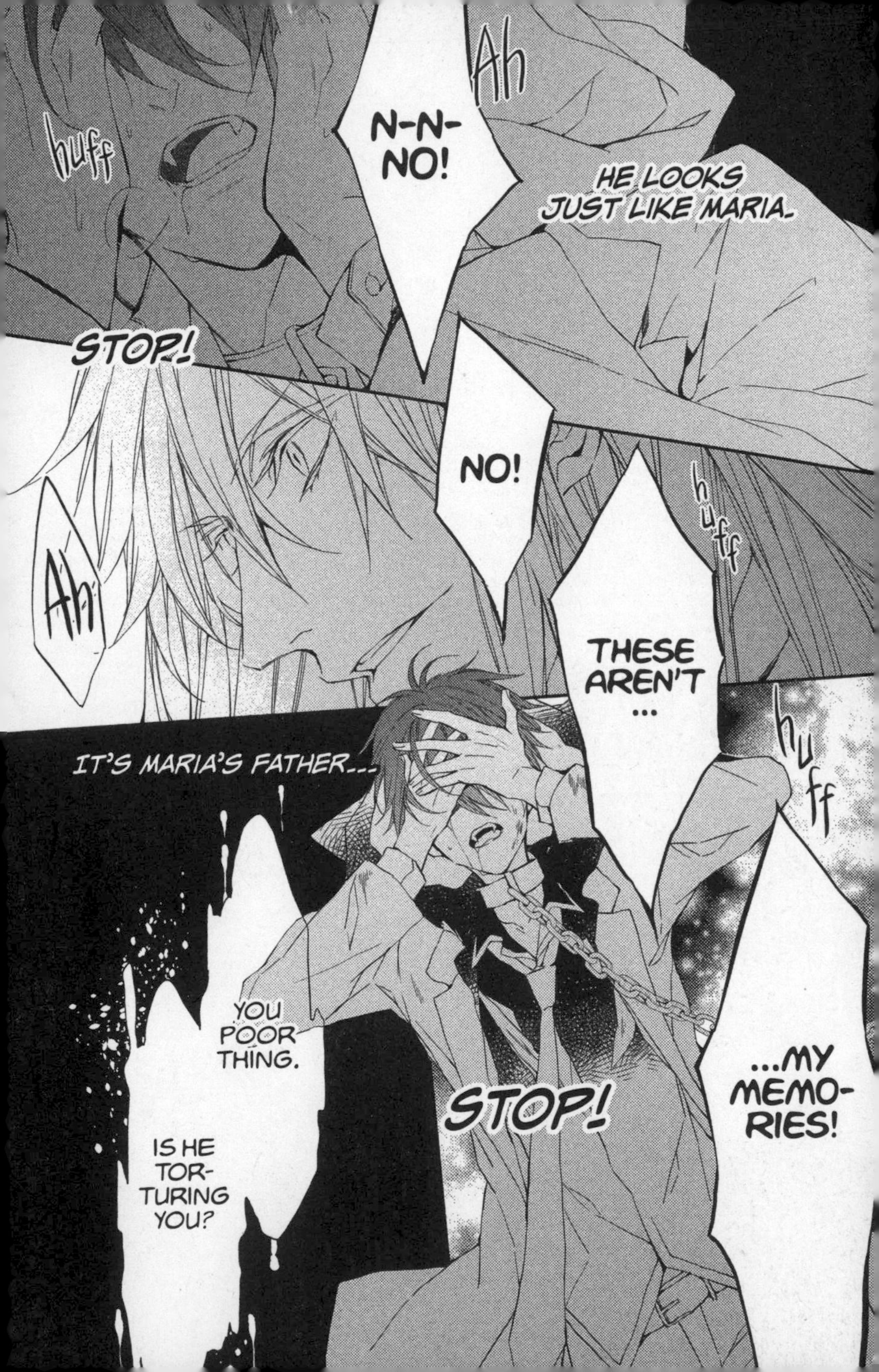
HE LOOKS JUST LIKE MARIA.
Ah
N-N-NO!
huff
STOP!
huff
NO!
Ah
THESE AREN'T ...
huff
...MY MEMO-RIES!
STOP!
IT'S MARIA'S FATHER...
YOU POOR THING.
IS HE TOR-TURING YOU?

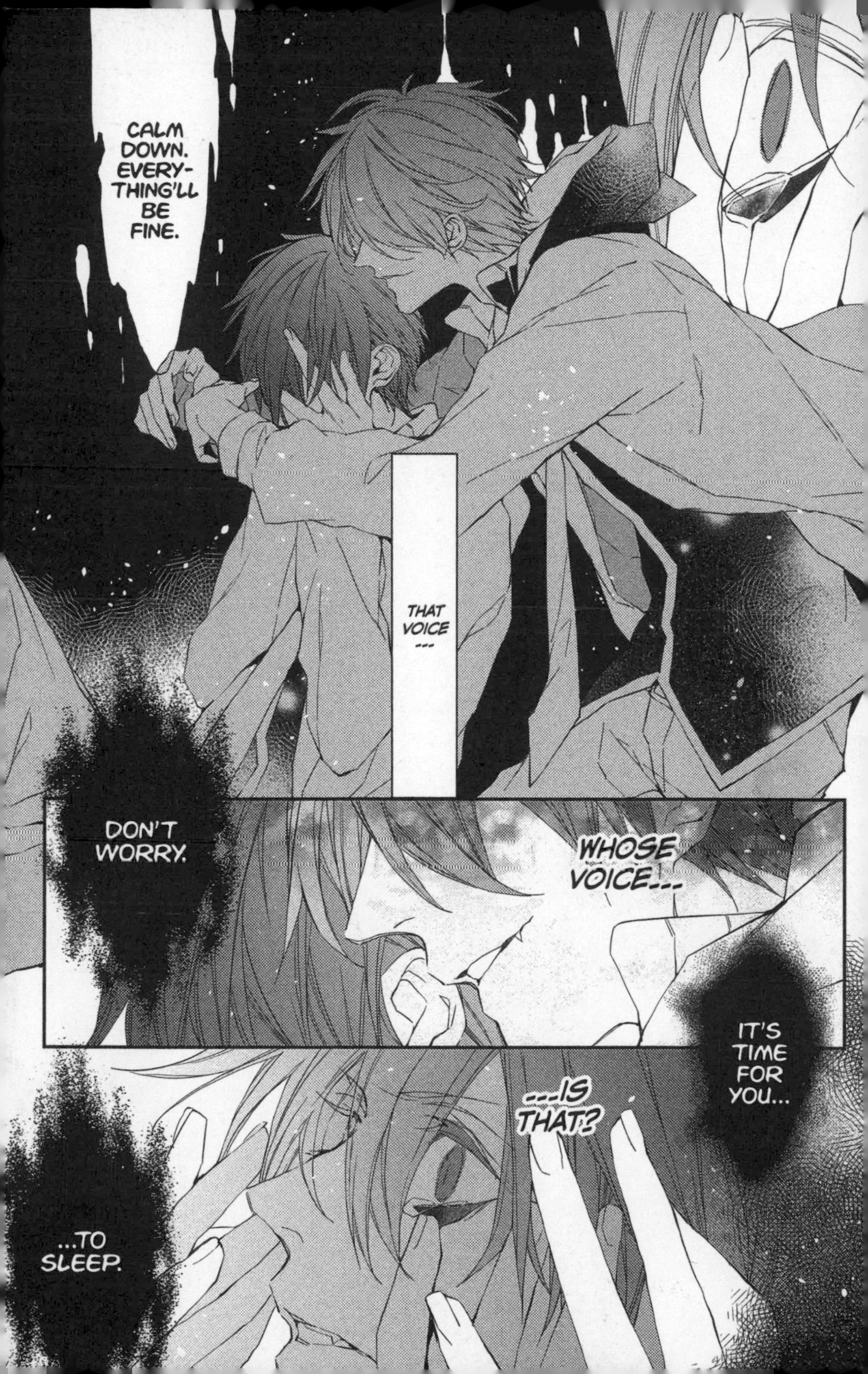
CALM DOWN. EVERY-THING'LL BE FINE.
THAT VOICE ---
WHOSE VOICE---
DON'T WORRY.
IT'S TIME FOR YOU...
---IS THAT?
...TO SLEEP.

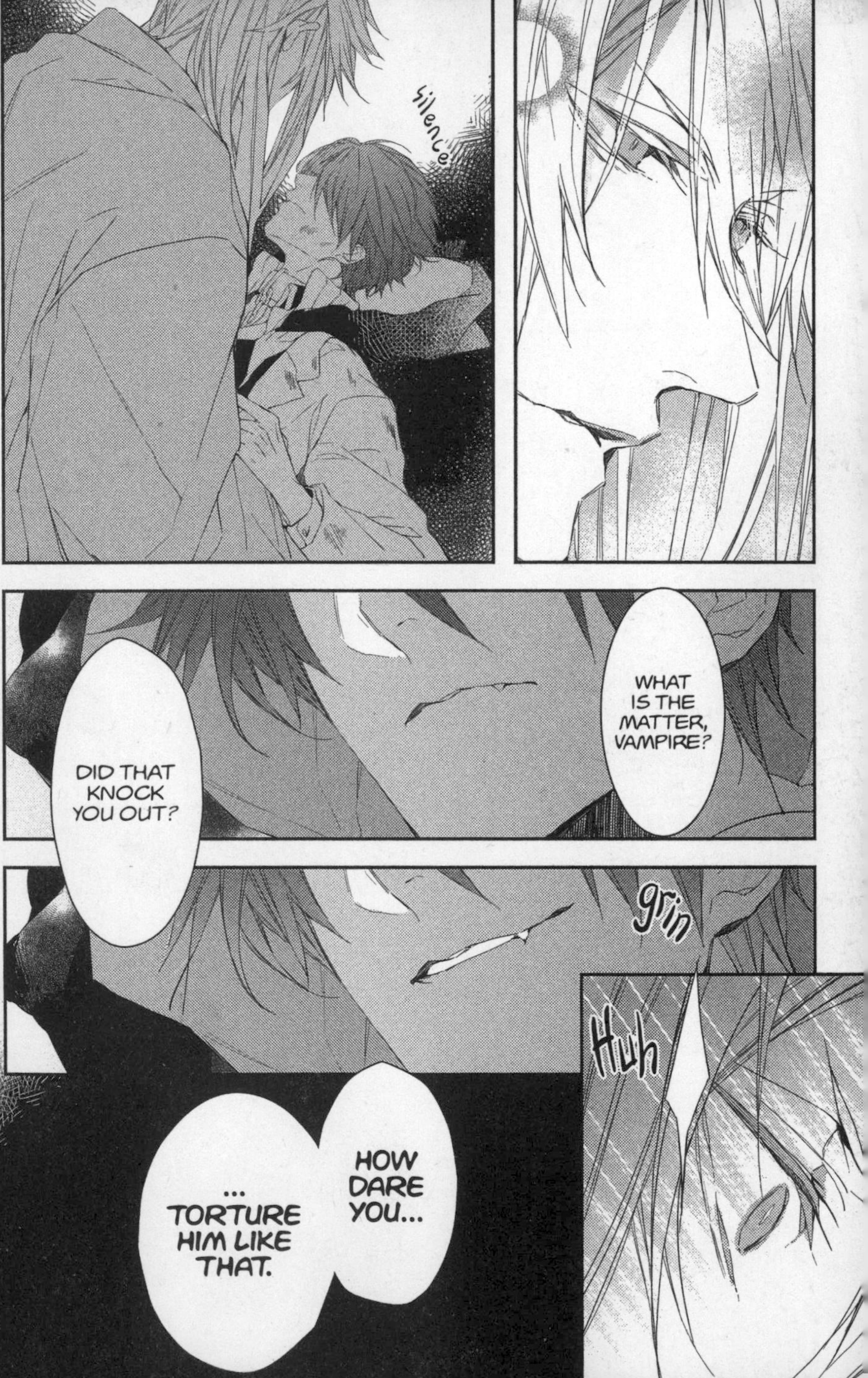
silence
WHAT IS THE MATTER, VAMPIRE?
DID THAT KNOCK YOU OUT?
grin
Huh
HOW DARE YOU...
...TORTURE HIM LIKE THAT.

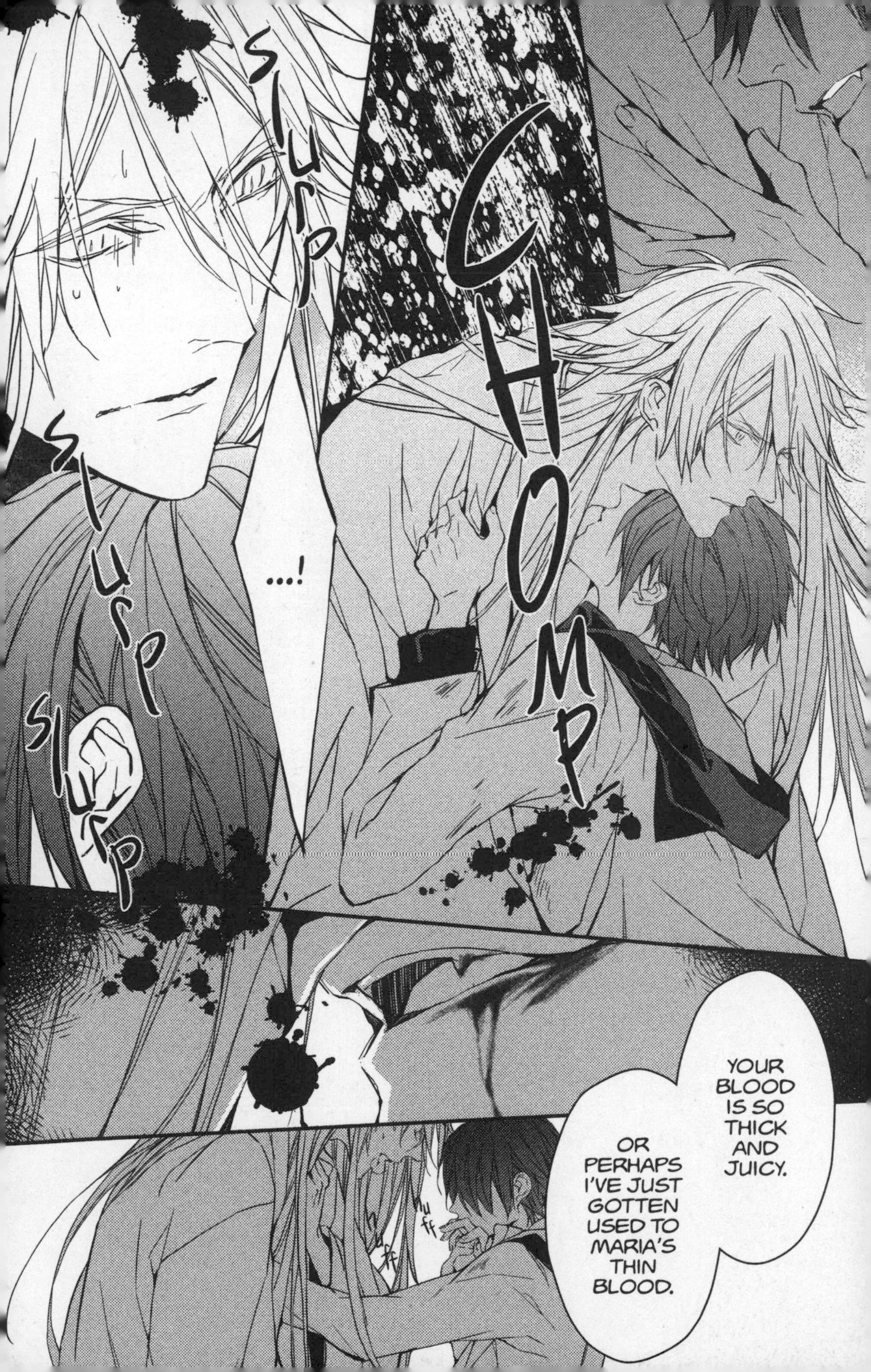
CHOMP!
SLURP
SLURP
SLURP
...!
YOUR BLOOD IS SO THICK AND JUICY.
OR PERHAPS I'VE JUST GOTTEN USED TO MARIA'S THIN BLOOD.
huff

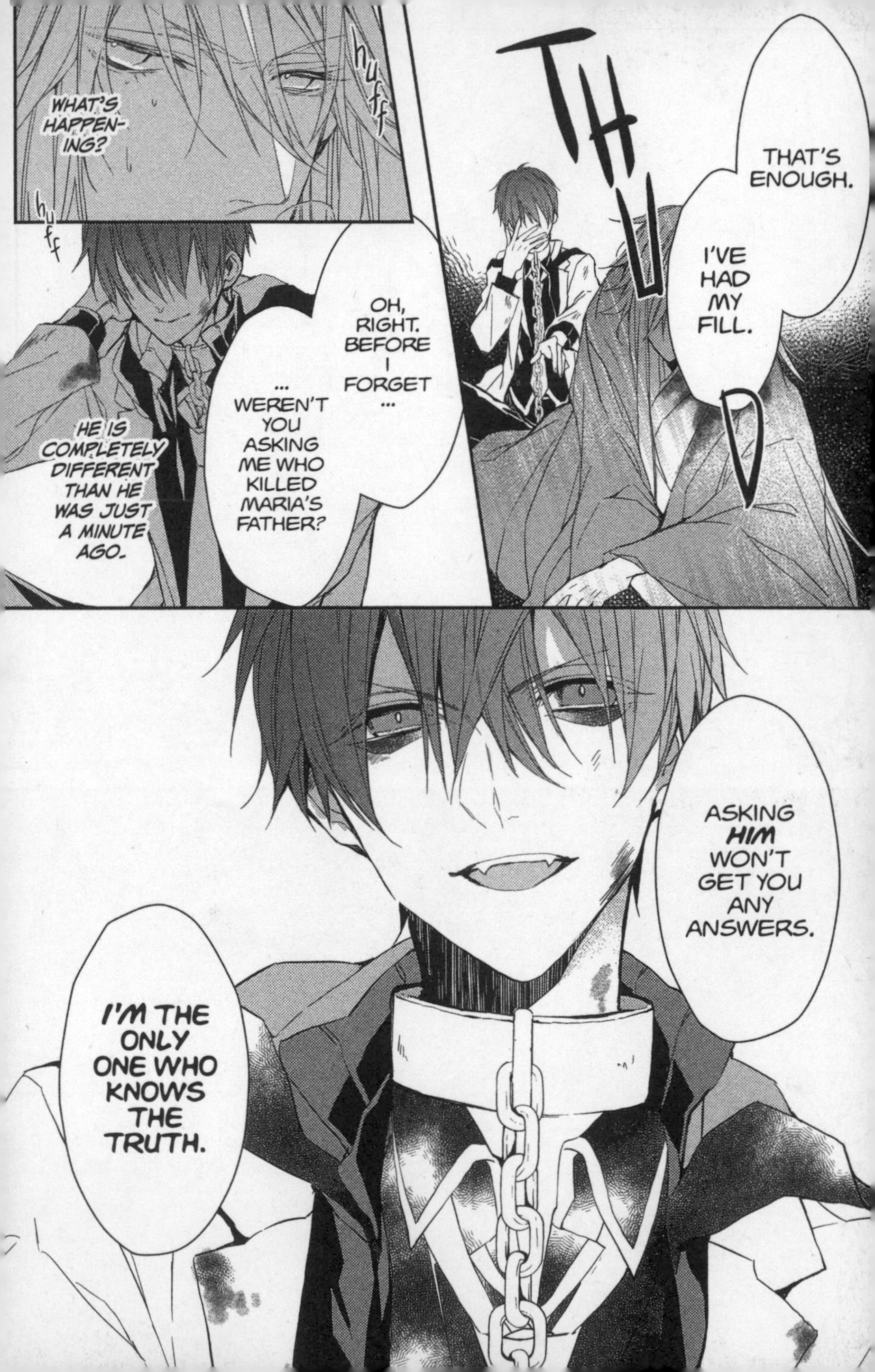
THUD
THAT'S ENOUGH.
I'VE HAD MY FILL.
WHAT'S HAPPEN-ING?
huff
huff
OH, RIGHT. BEFORE I FORGET ...
... WEREN'T YOU ASKING ME WHO KILLED MARIA'S FATHER?
HE IS COMPLETELY DIFFERENT THAN HE WAS JUST A MINUTE AGO.
ASKING HIM WON'T GET YOU ANY ANSWERS.
I'M THE ONLY ONE WHO KNOWS THE TRUTH.

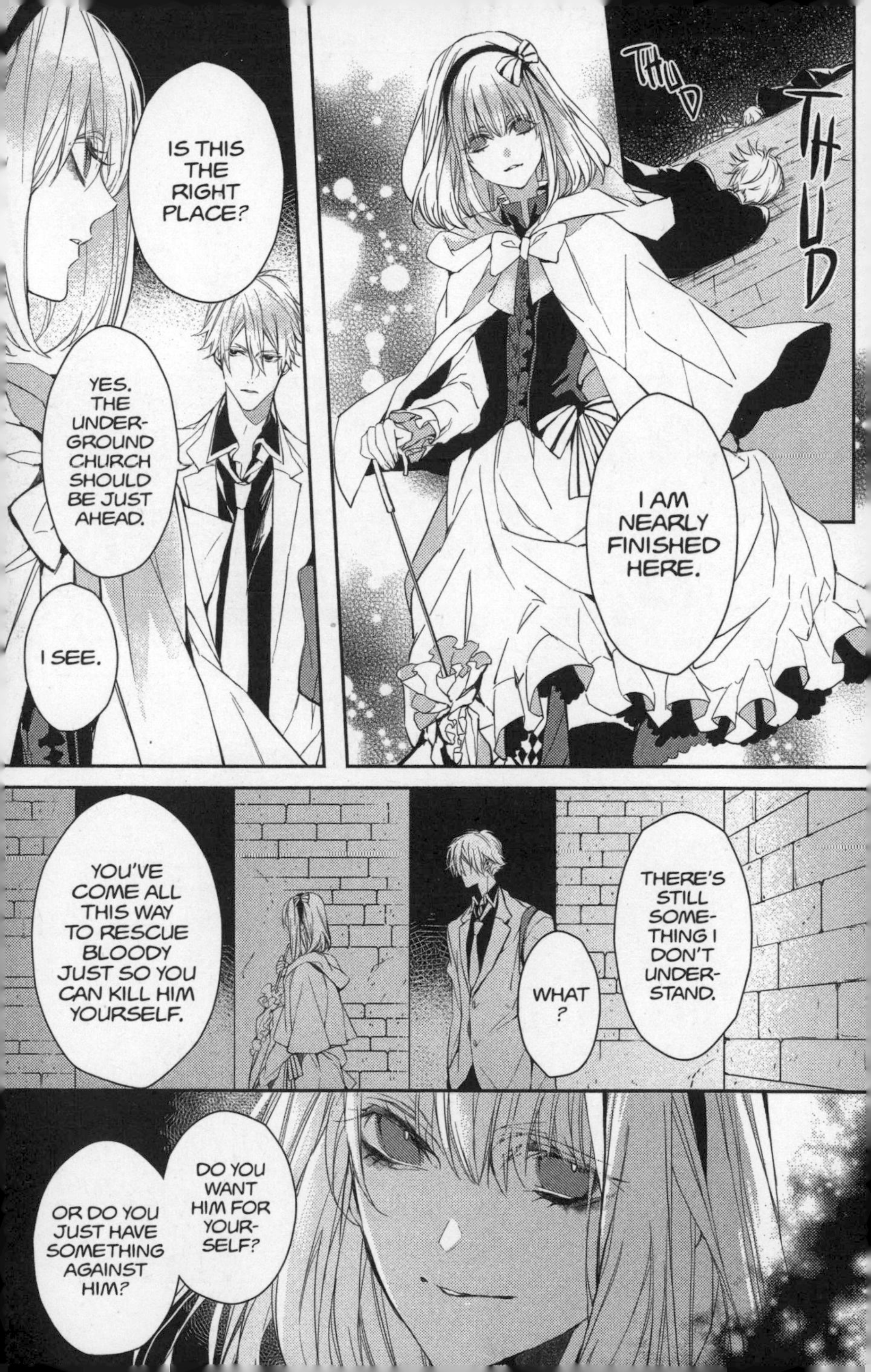
THUD
THUD
I AM NEARLY FINISHED HERE.
IS THIS THE RIGHT PLACE?
YES. THE UNDERGROUND CHURCH SHOULD BE JUST AHEAD.
I SEE.
THERE'S STILL SOMETHING I DON'T UNDERSTAND.
WHAT?
YOU'VE COME ALL THIS WAY TO RESCUE BLOODY JUST SO YOU CAN KILL HIM YOURSELF.
DO YOU WANT HIM FOR YOURSELF?
OR DO YOU JUST HAVE SOMETHING AGAINST HIM?

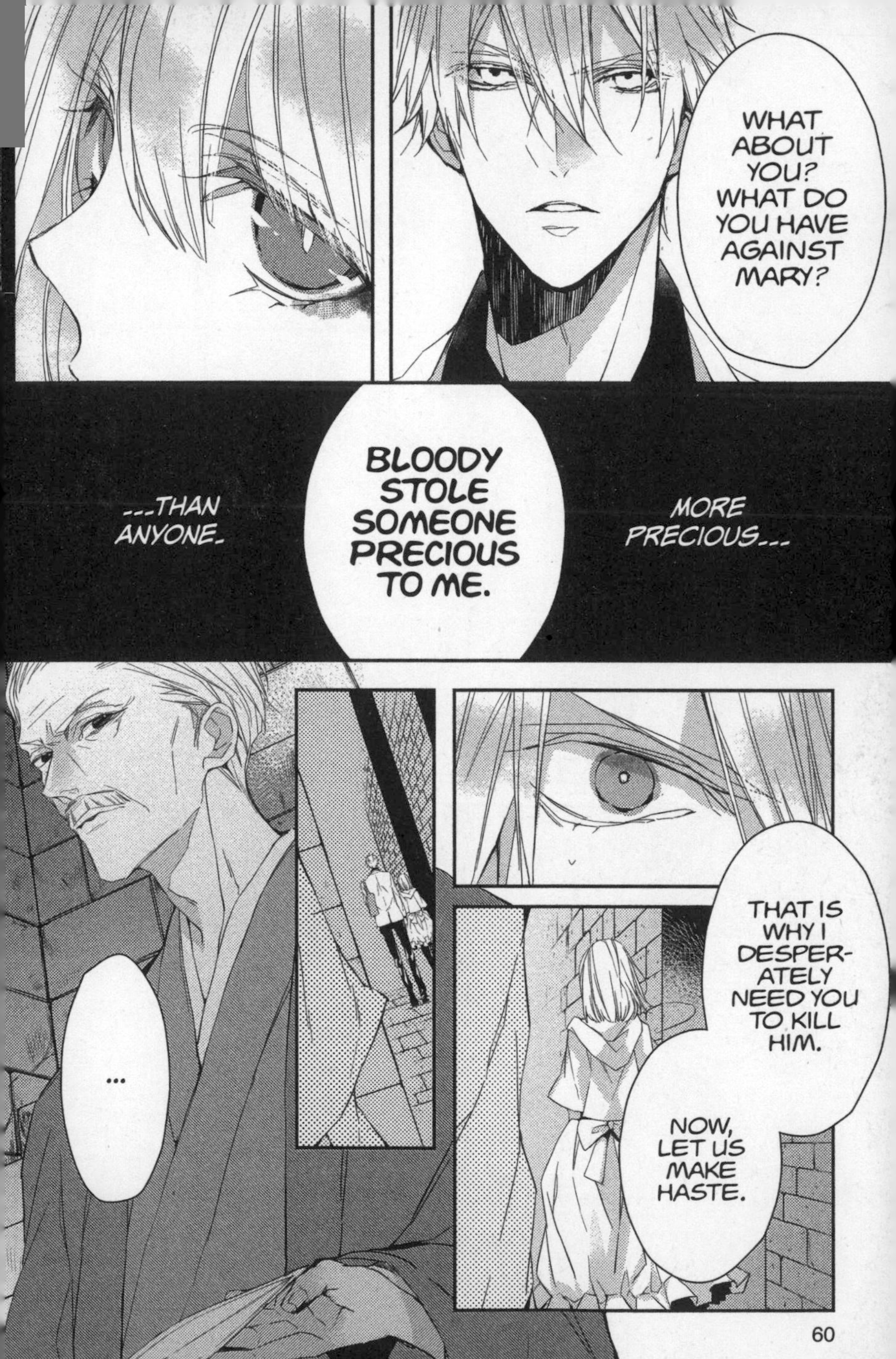
WHAT ABOUT YOU? WHAT DO YOU HAVE AGAINST MARY?
MORE PRECIOUS...
BLOODY STOLE SOMEONE PRECIOUS TO ME.
...THAN ANYONE.
THAT IS WHY I DESPERATELY NEED YOU TO KILL HIM.
NOW, LET US MAKE HASTE.
...

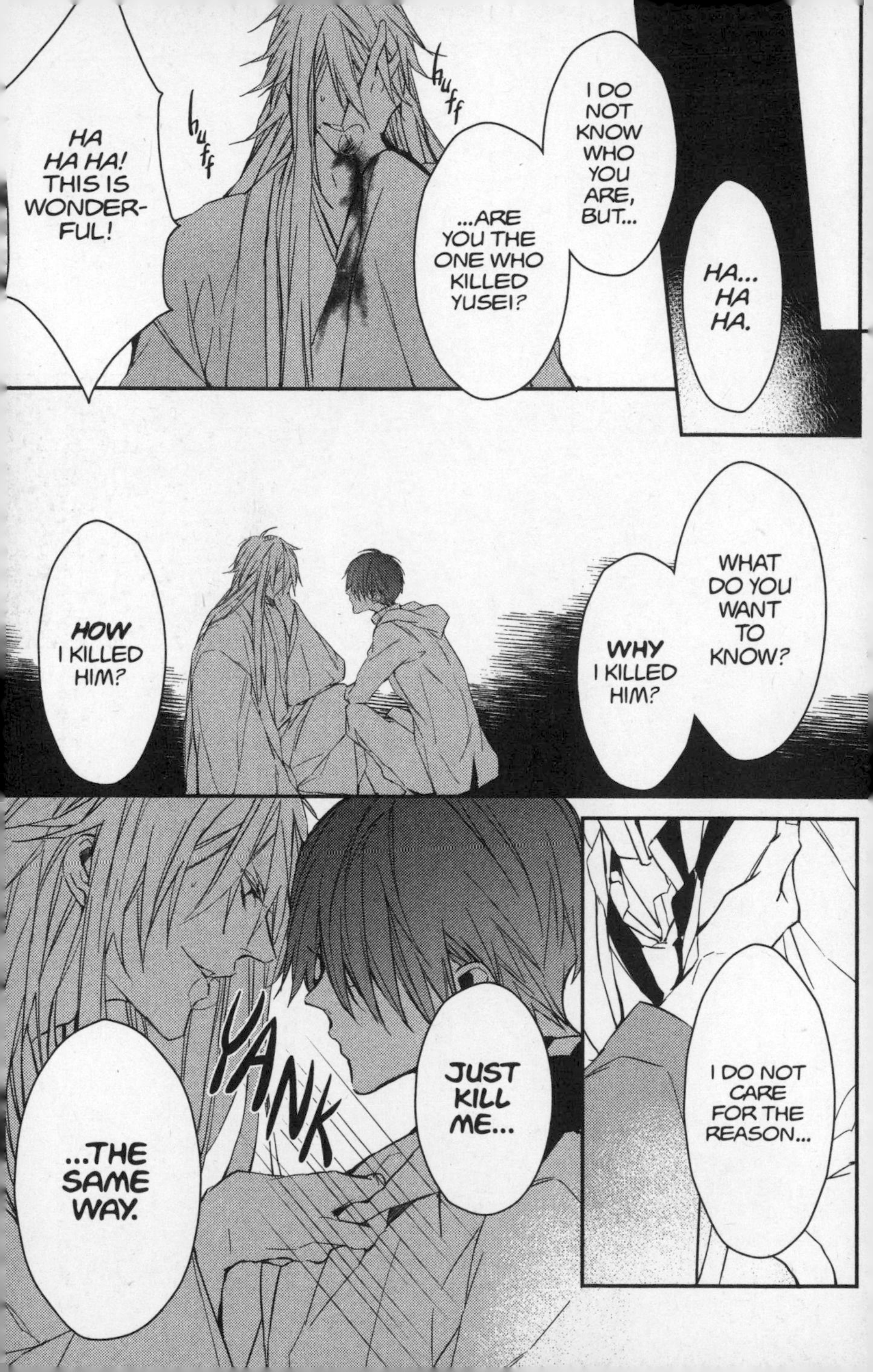
HA... HA HA.
I DO NOT KNOW WHO YOU ARE, BUT...
...ARE YOU THE ONE WHO KILLED YUSEI?
huff
huff
HA HA HA! THIS IS WONDER-FUL!
WHAT DO YOU WANT TO KNOW?
WHY I KILLED HIM?
HOW I KILLED HIM?
I DO NOT CARE FOR THE REASON...
JUST KILL ME...
YANK
...THE SAME WAY.

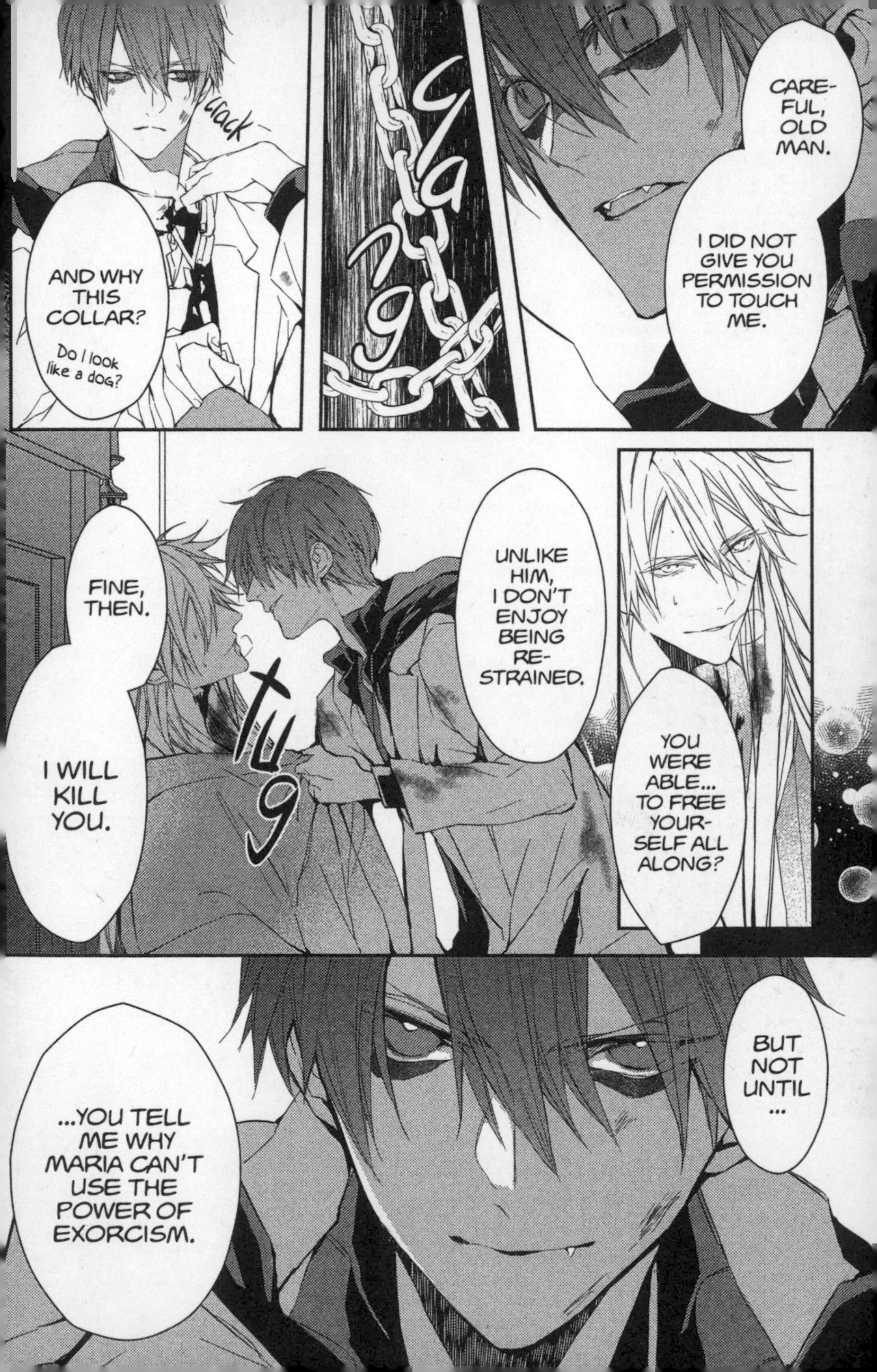
CARE-FUL, OLD MAN.
I DID NOT GIVE YOU PERMISSION TO TOUCH ME.
clang
crack
AND WHY THIS COLLAR?
Do I look like a dog?
YOU WERE ABLE... TO FREE YOUR-SELF ALL ALONG?
UNLIKE HIM, I DON'T ENJOY BEING RE-STRAINED.
FINE, THEN.
tug
I WILL KILL YOU.
BUT NOT UNTIL ...
...YOU TELL ME WHY MARIA CAN'T USE THE POWER OF EXORCISM.

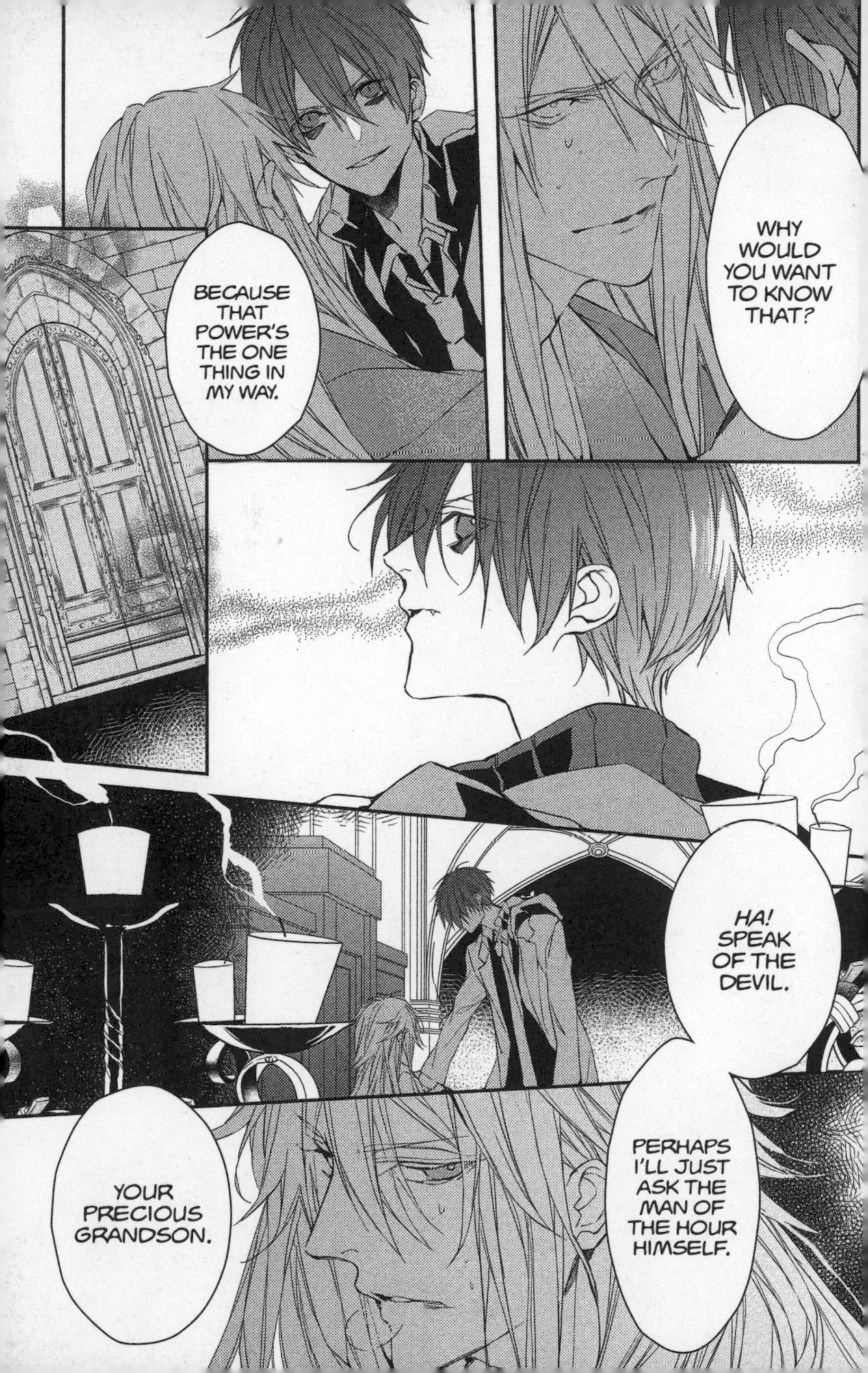
WHY WOULD YOU WANT TO KNOW THAT?
BECAUSE THAT POWER'S THE ONE THING IN MY WAY.
HA! SPEAK OF THE DEVIL.
PERHAPS I'LL JUST ASK THE MAN OF THE HOUR HIMSELF.
YOUR PRECIOUS GRANDSON.

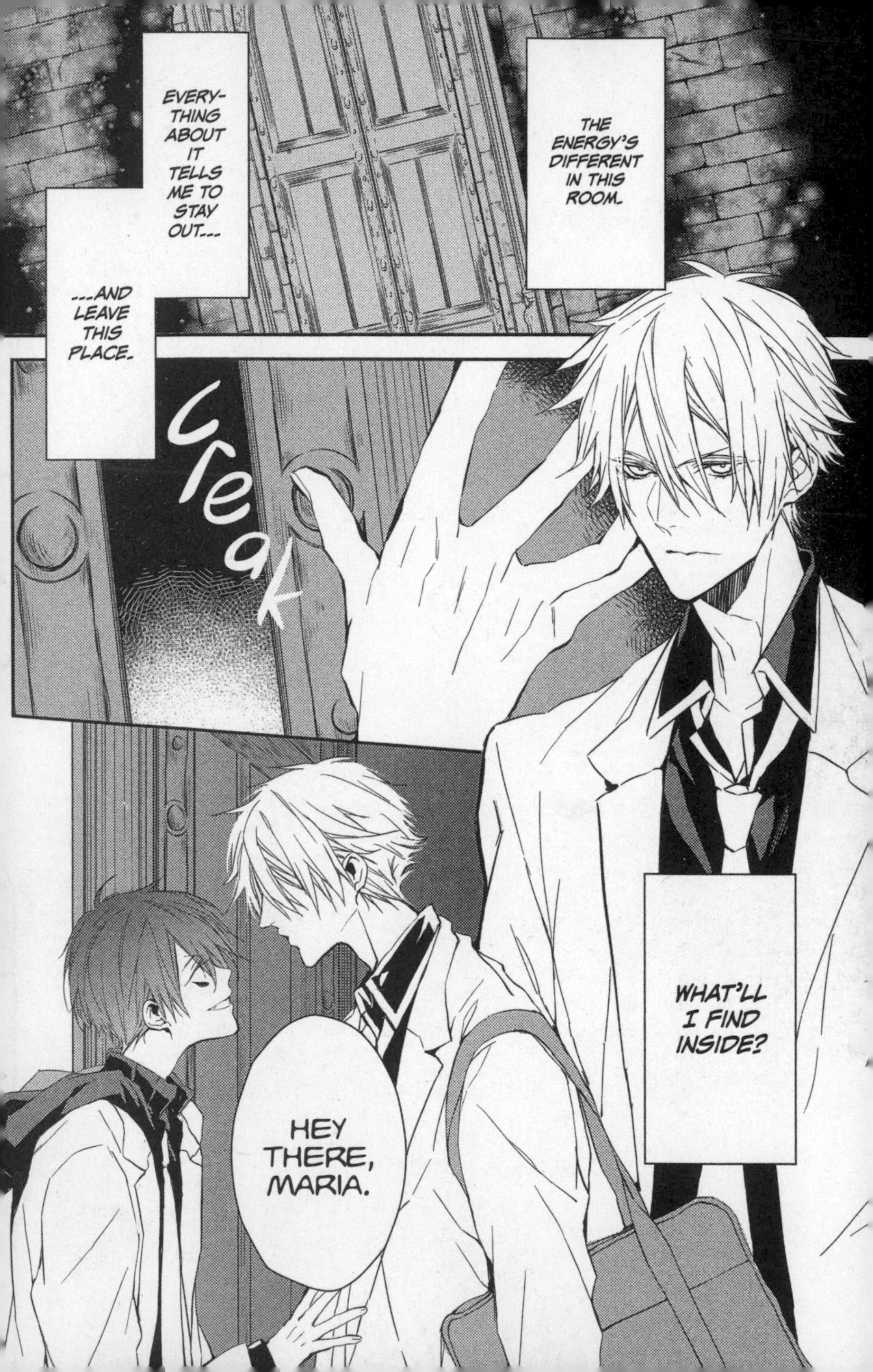
THE ENERGY'S DIFFERENT IN THIS ROOM.
EVERYTHING ABOUT IT TELLS ME TO STAY OUT...
...AND LEAVE THIS PLACE.
creak
WHAT'LL I FIND INSIDE?
HEY THERE, MARIA.

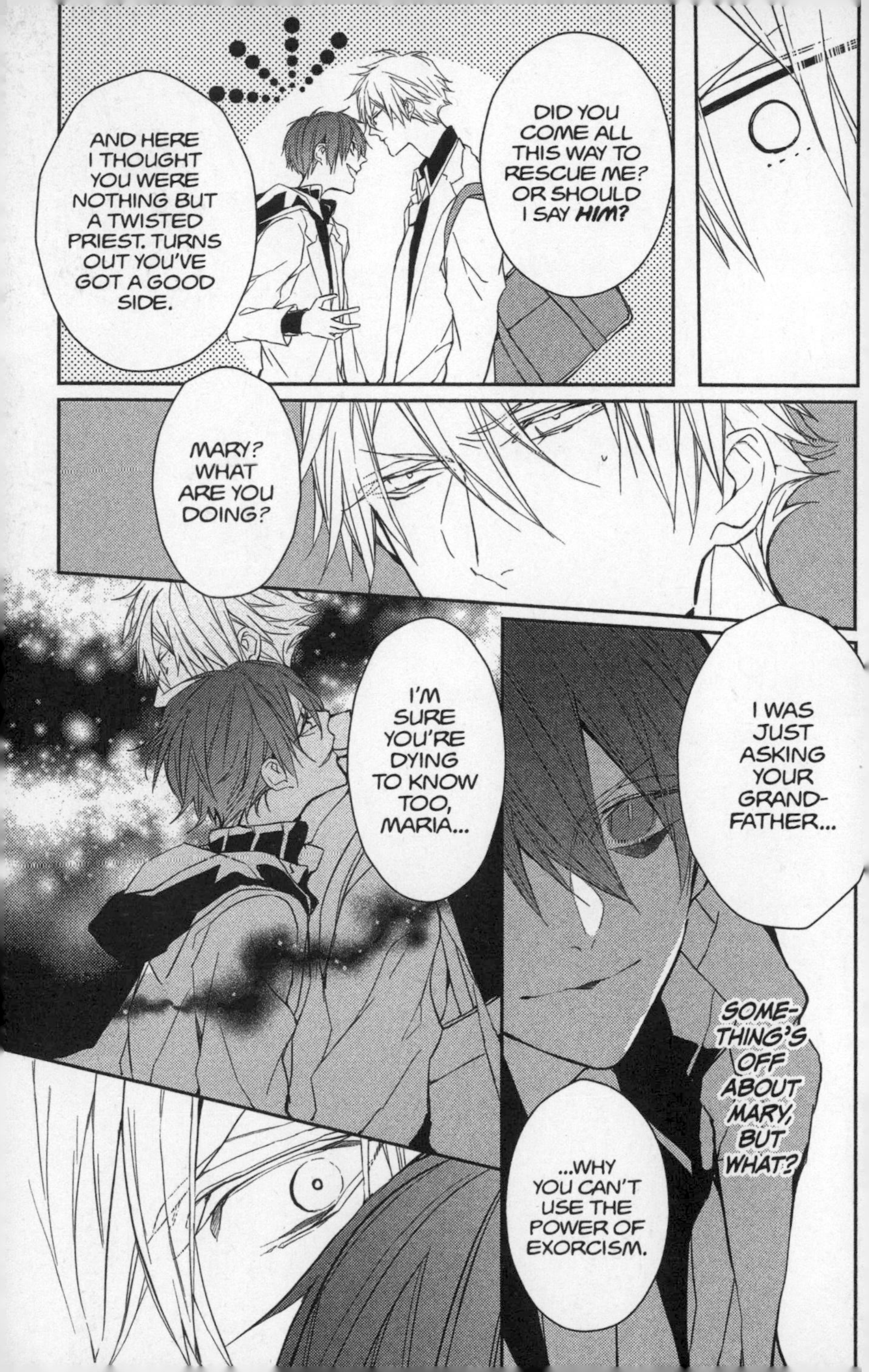
DID YOU COME ALL THIS WAY TO RESCUE ME? OR SHOULD I SAY *HIM*?
AND HERE I THOUGHT YOU WERE NOTHING BUT A TWISTED PRIEST. TURNS OUT YOU'VE GOT A GOOD SIDE.
MARY? WHAT ARE YOU DOING?
I WAS JUST ASKING YOUR GRAND-FATHER...
...WHY YOU CAN'T USE THE POWER OF EXORCISM.
I'M SURE YOU'RE DYING TO KNOW TOO, MARIA...
SOME-THING'S OFF ABOUT MARY, BUT WHAT?

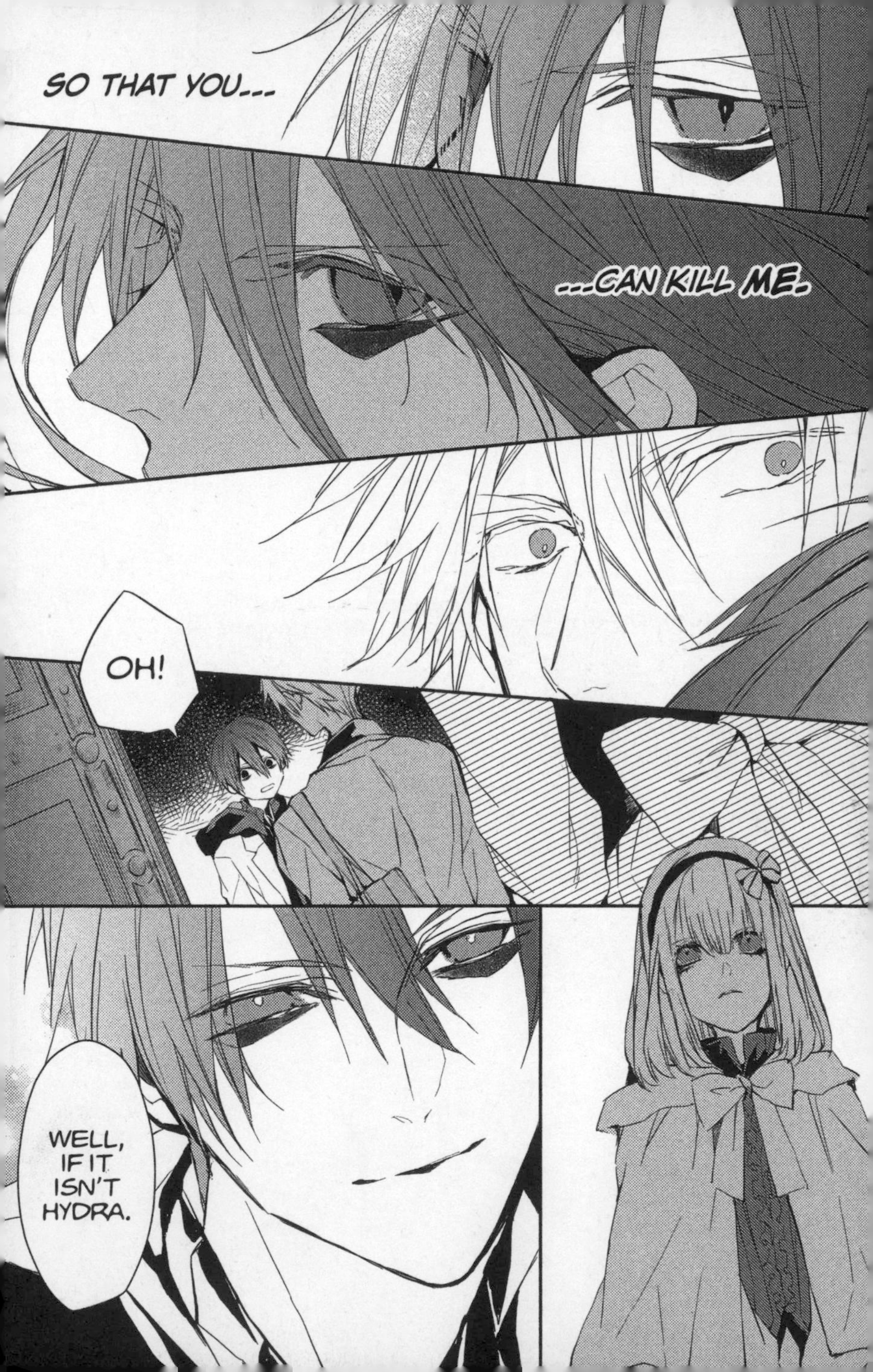
SO THAT YOU...
...CAN KILL ME.
OH!
WELL, IF IT ISN'T HYDRA.

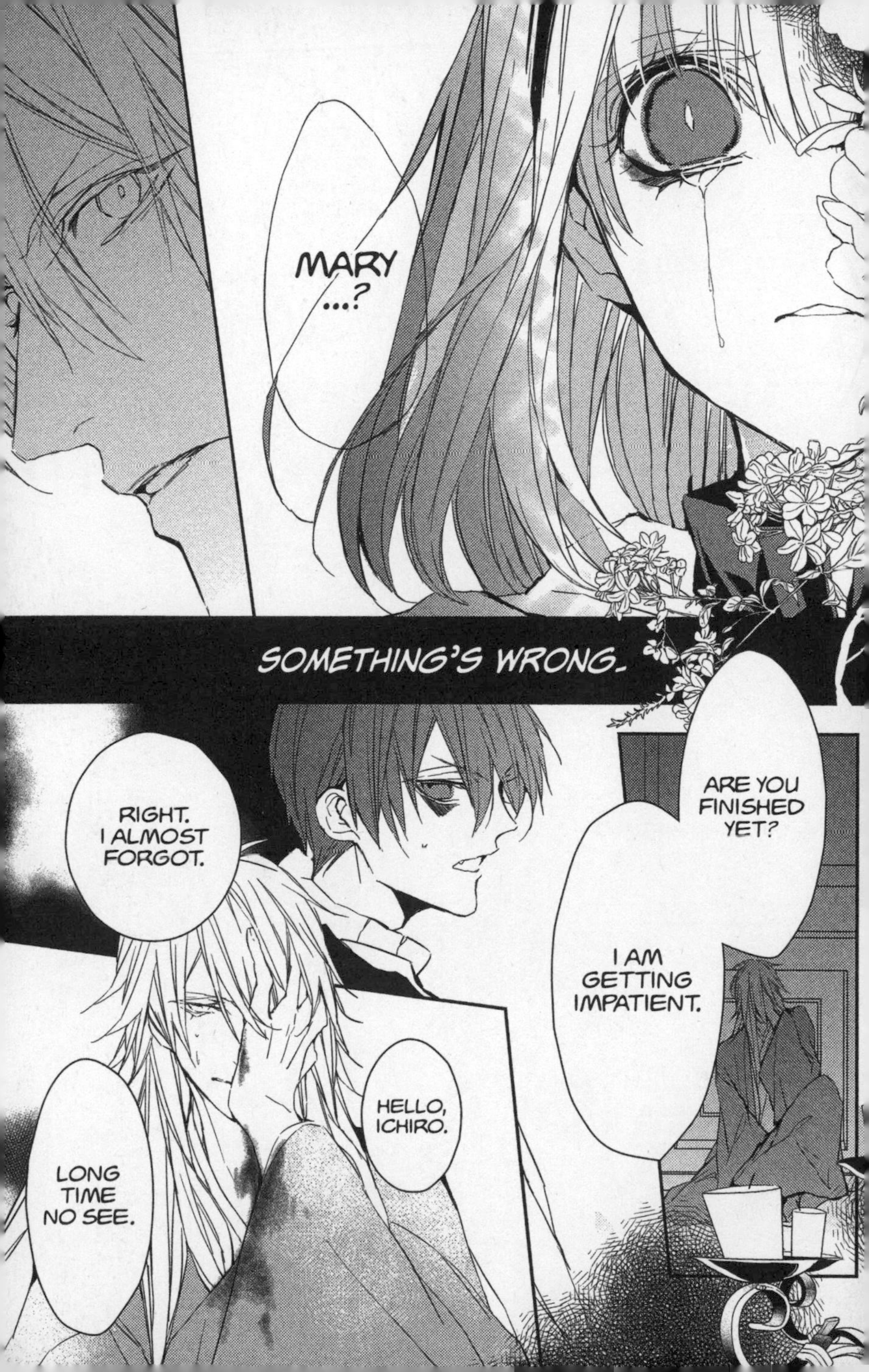
MARY ...?
SOMETHING'S WRONG...
ARE YOU FINISHED YET?
I AM GETTING IMPATIENT.
RIGHT. I ALMOST FORGOT.
HELLO, ICHIRO.
LONG TIME NO SEE.

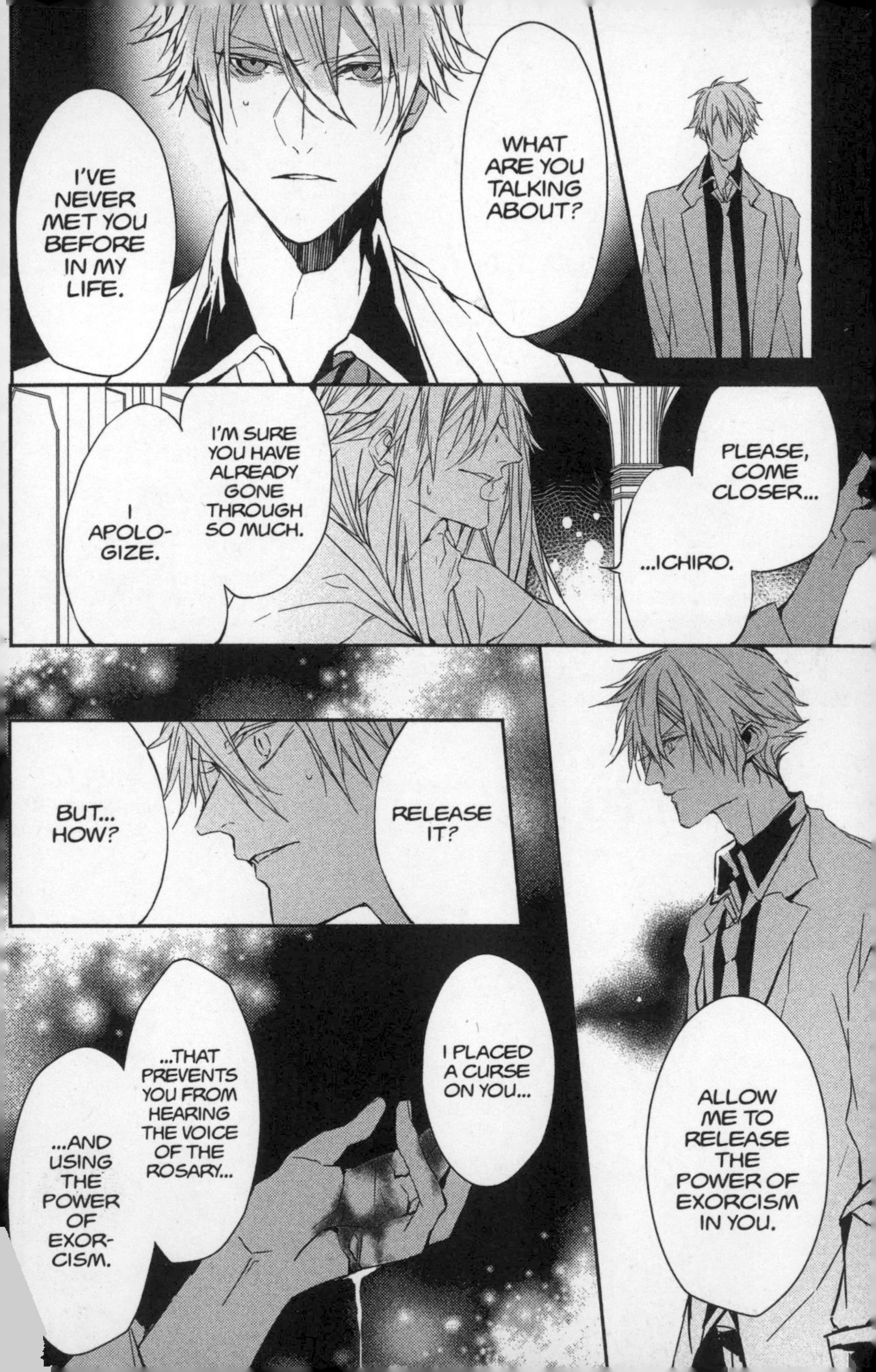
WHAT ARE YOU TALKING ABOUT?
I'VE NEVER MET YOU BEFORE IN MY LIFE.
PLEASE, COME CLOSER...
...ICHIRO.
I'M SURE YOU HAVE ALREADY GONE THROUGH SO MUCH.
I APOLOGIZE.
RELEASE IT?
BUT... HOW?
ALLOW ME TO RELEASE THE POWER OF EXORCISM IN YOU.
I PLACED A CURSE ON YOU...
...THAT PREVENTS YOU FROM HEARING THE VOICE OF THE ROSARY...
...AND USING THE POWER OF EXORCISM.

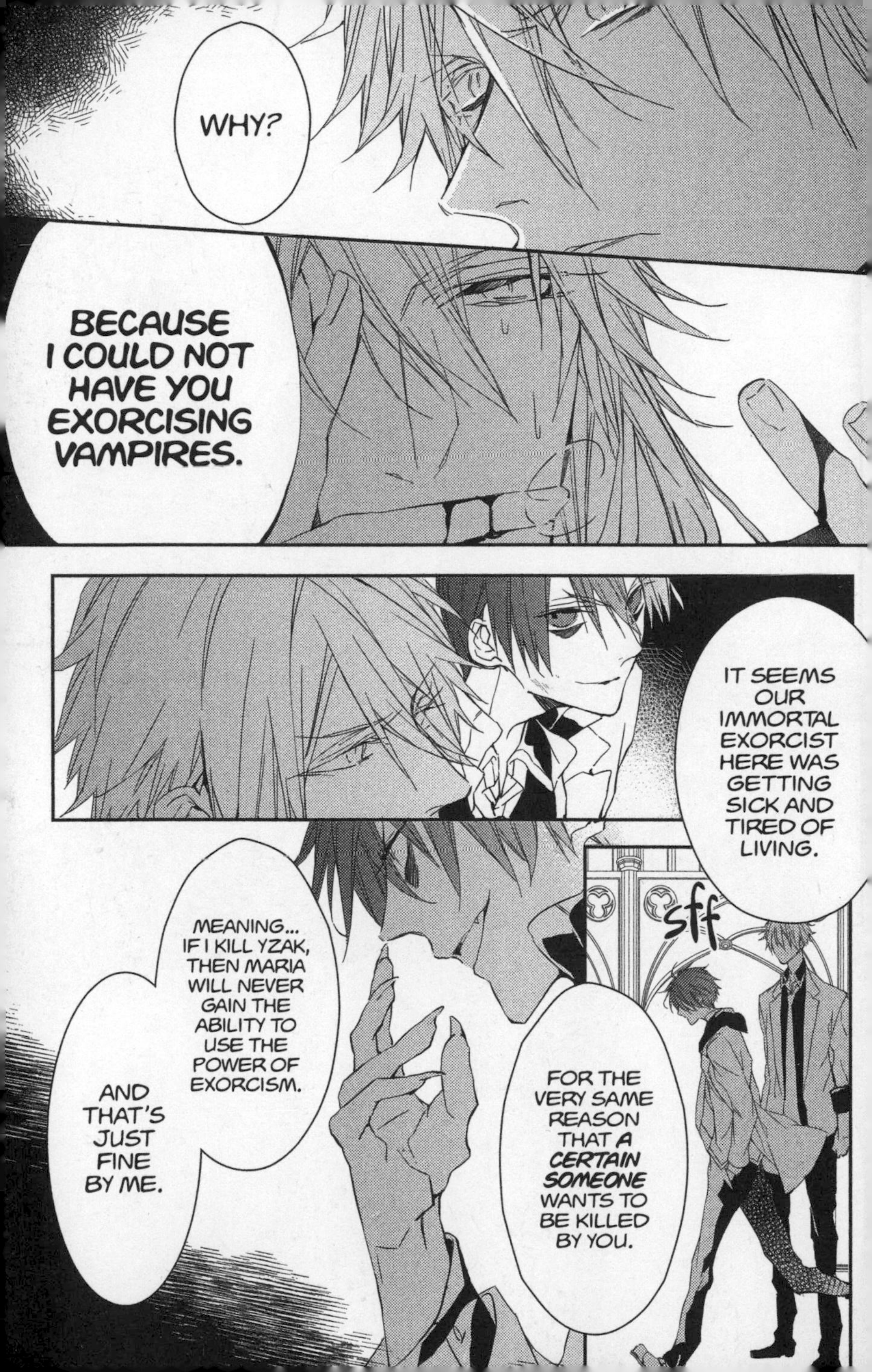
WHY?
BECAUSE I COULD NOT HAVE YOU EXORCISING VAMPIRES.
IT SEEMS OUR IMMORTAL EXORCIST HERE WAS GETTING SICK AND TIRED OF LIVING.
SFF
FOR THE VERY SAME REASON THAT ***A CERTAIN SOMEONE*** WANTS TO BE KILLED BY YOU.
MEANING... IF I KILL YZAK, THEN MARIA WILL NEVER GAIN THE ABILITY TO USE THE POWER OF EXORCISM.
AND THAT'S JUST FINE BY ME.

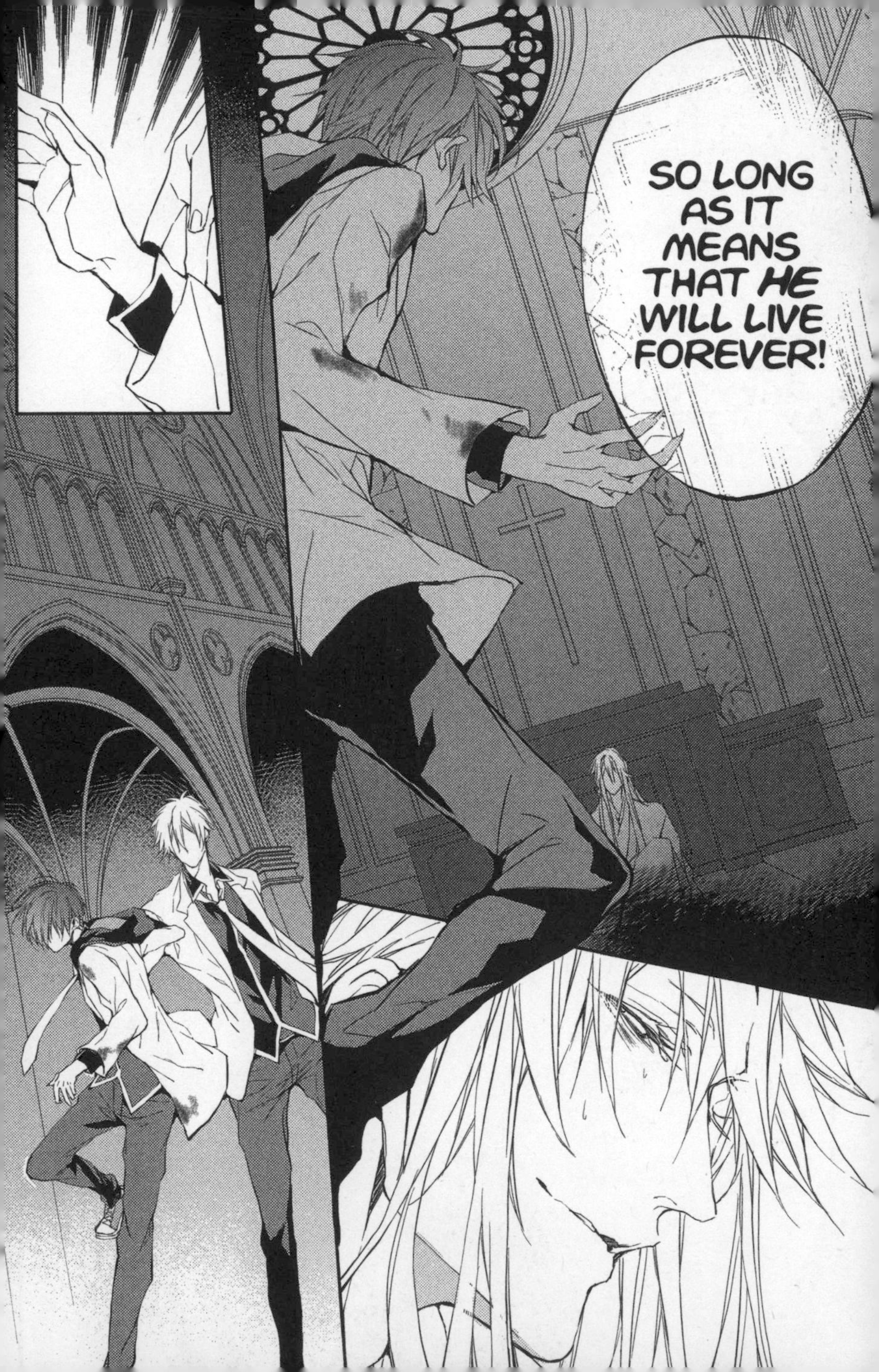
SO LONG AS IT MEANS THAT *HE* WILL LIVE FOREVER!

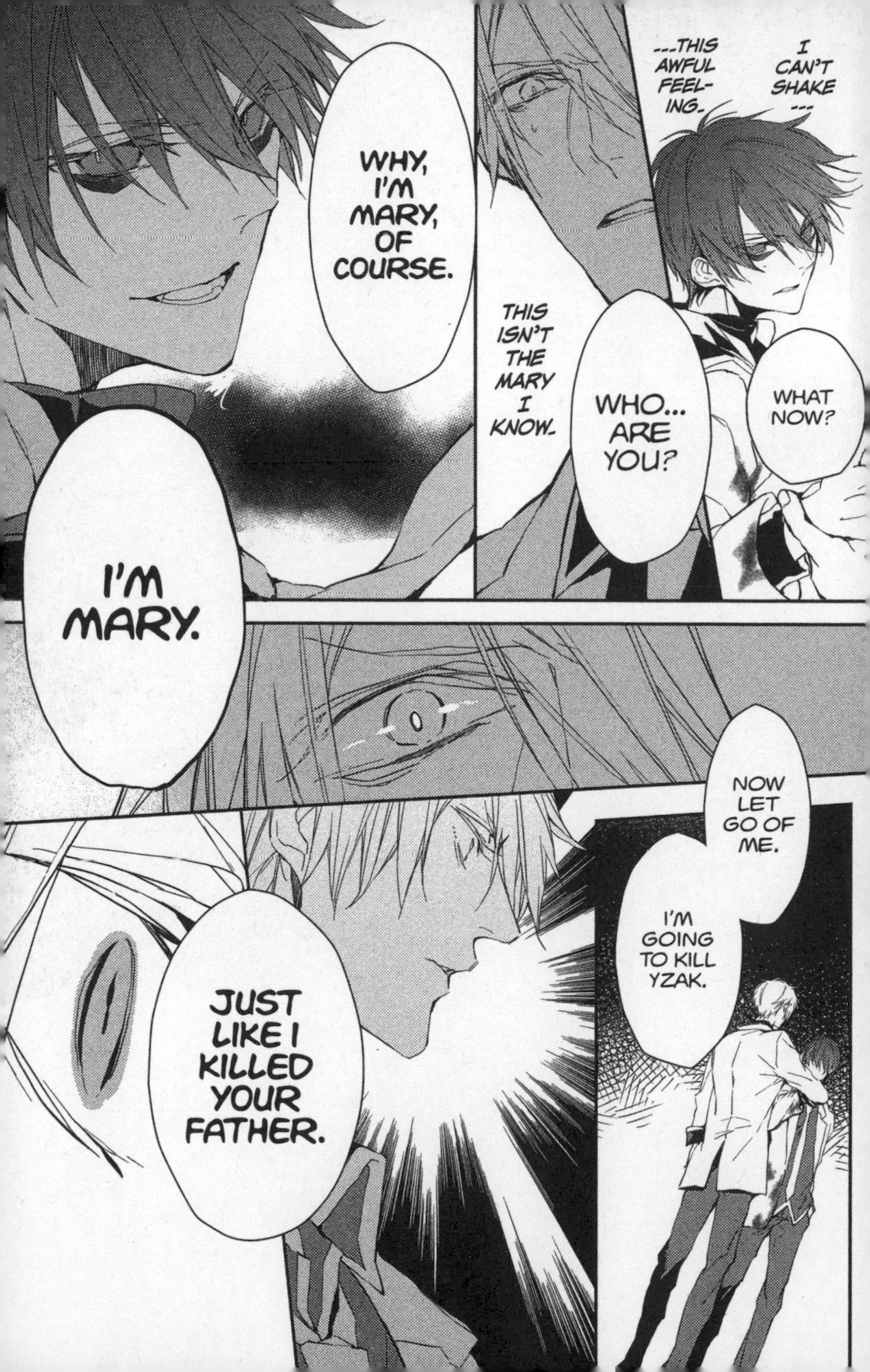
I CAN'T SHAKE ---
---THIS AWFUL FEEL-ING.
WHAT NOW?
WHO... ARE YOU?
THIS ISN'T THE MARY I KNOW.
WHY, I'M MARY, OF COURSE.
I'M MARY.
NOW LET GO OF ME.
I'M GOING TO KILL YZAK.
JUST LIKE I KILLED YOUR FATHER.

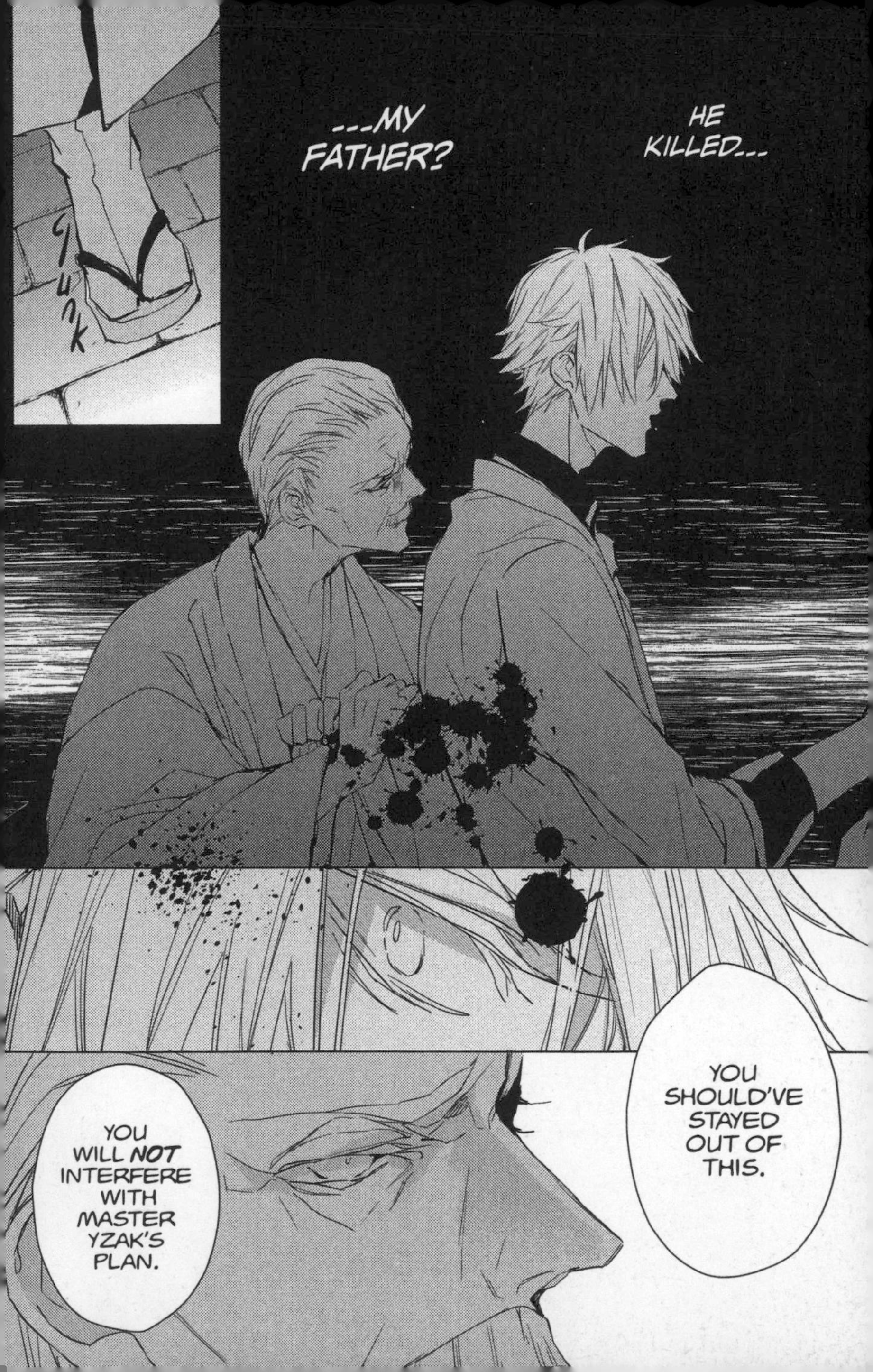
HE KILLED...
---MY FATHER?
GLUNK
YOU SHOULD'VE STAYED OUT OF THIS.
YOU WILL ***NOT*** INTERFERE WITH MASTER YZAK'S PLAN.

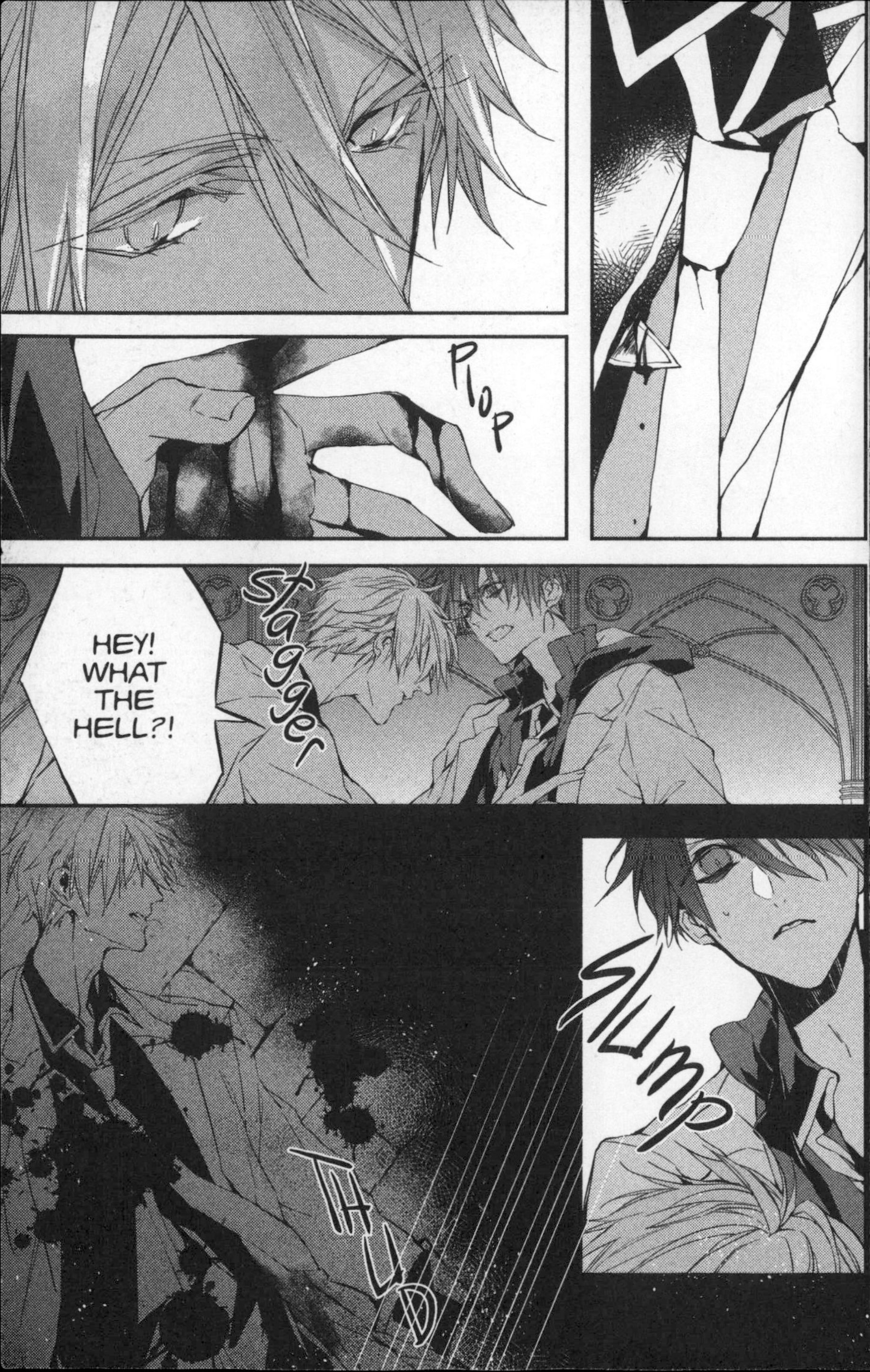
PLOP
stagger
HEY! WHAT THE HELL?!
SLUMP
THUD

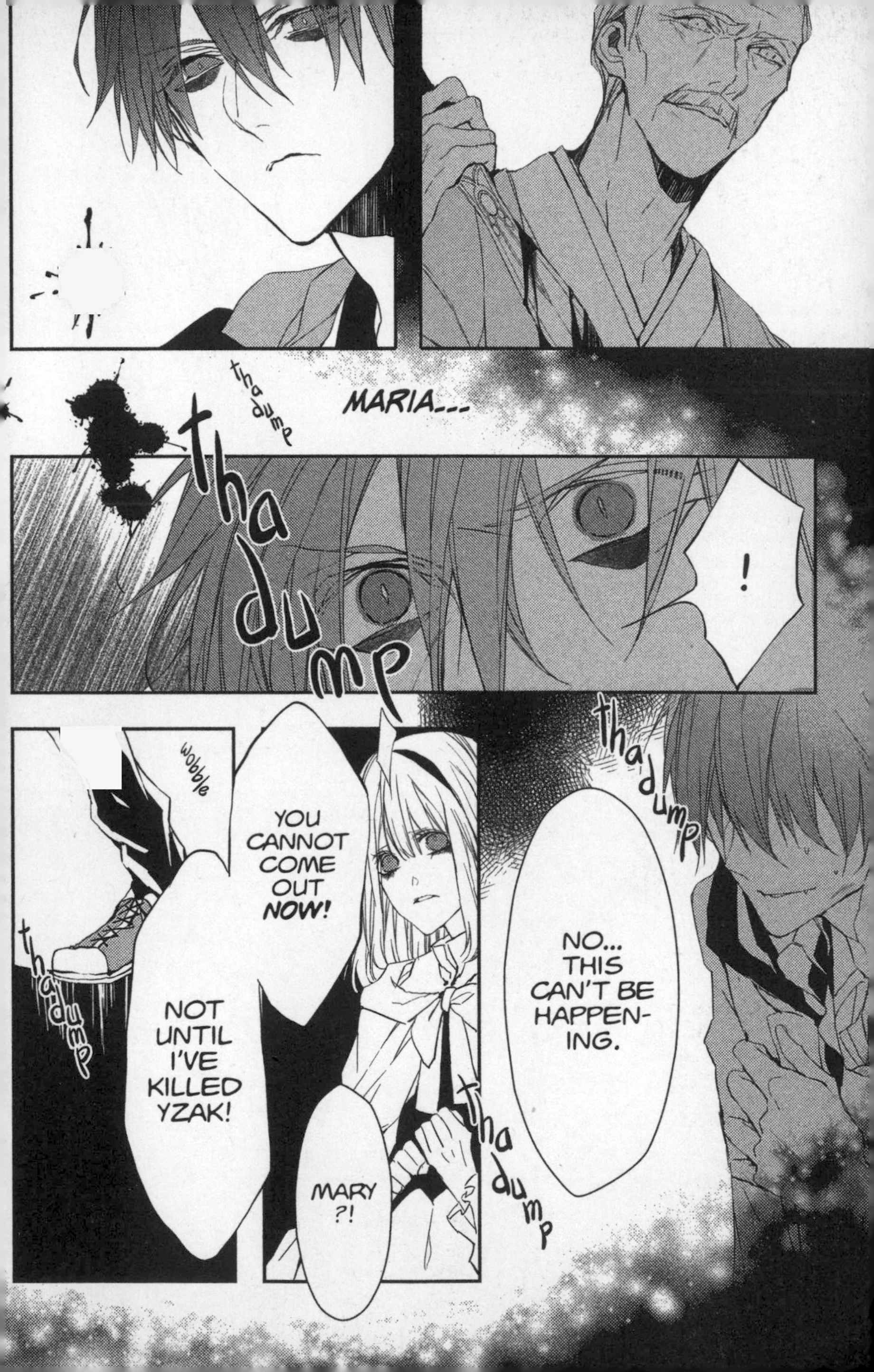
MARIA...
thadump
thadump
!
thadump
NO... THIS CAN'T BE HAPPEN-ING.
thadump
MARY ?!
YOU CANNOT COME OUT NOW!
NOT UNTIL I'VE KILLED YZAK!
wobble
thadump

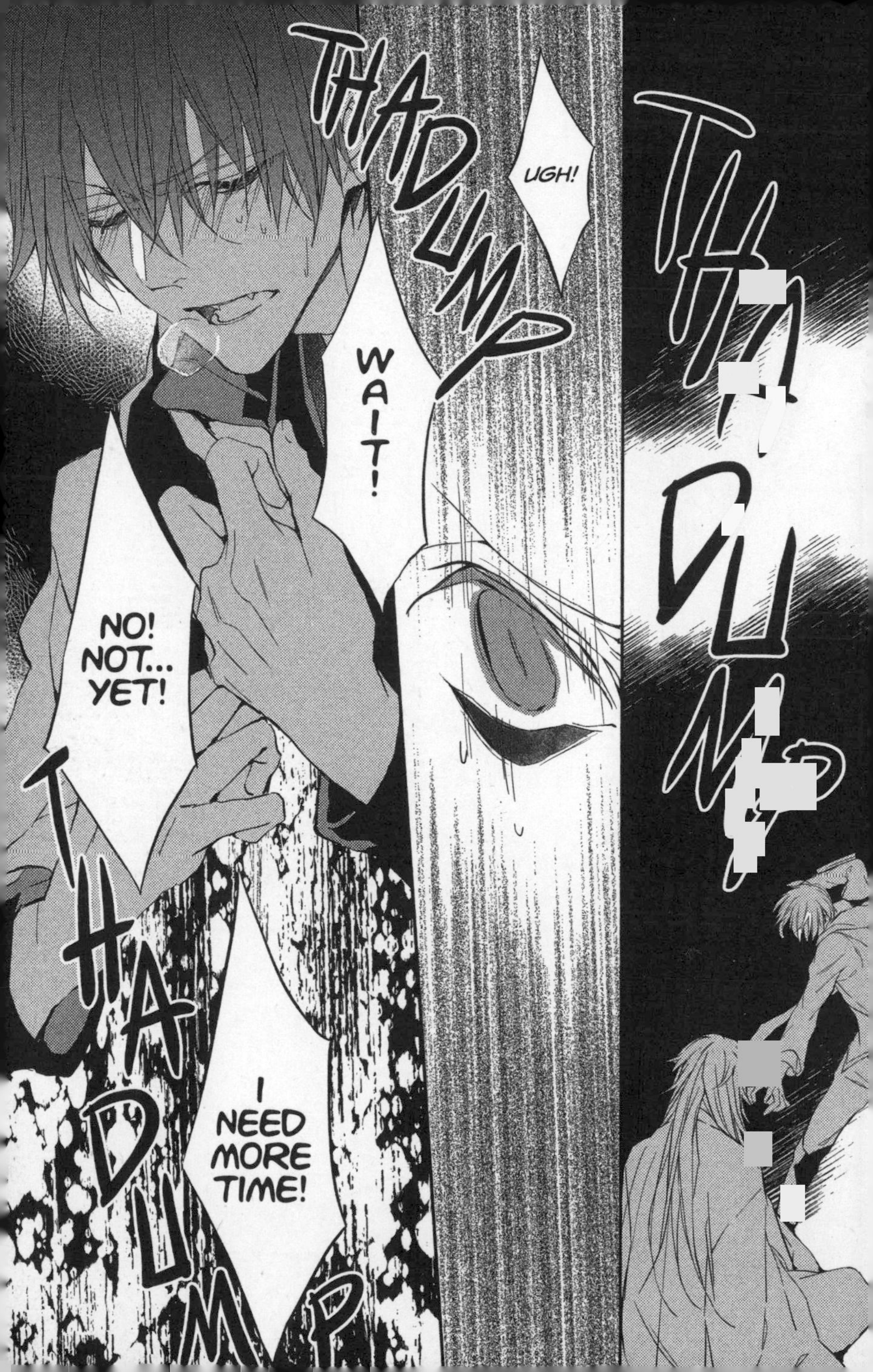
THADUMP
UGH!
THADUMP
WAIT!
NO! NOT... YET!
THADUMP
I NEED MORE TIME!

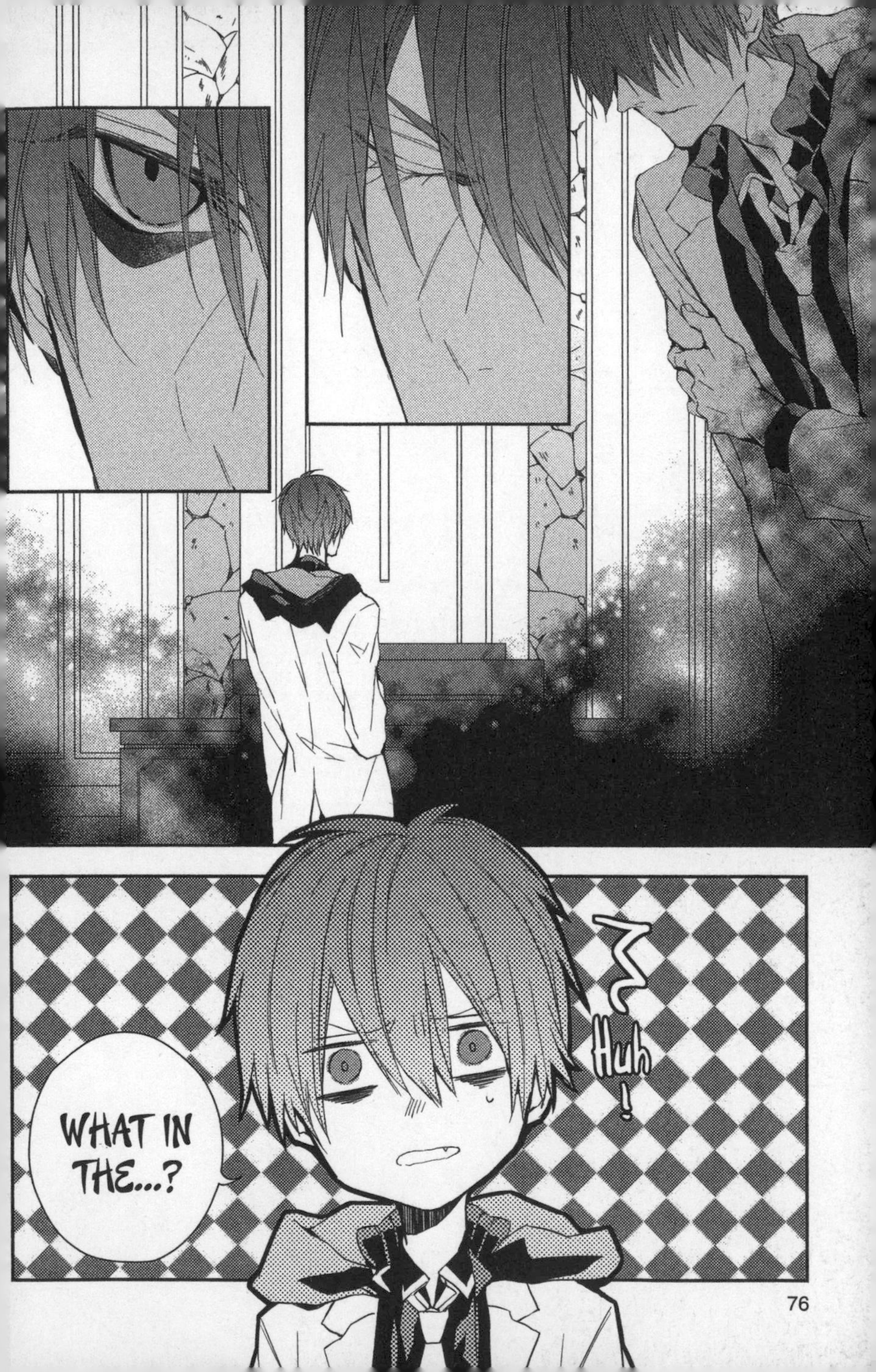
Huh!
WHAT IN THE...?

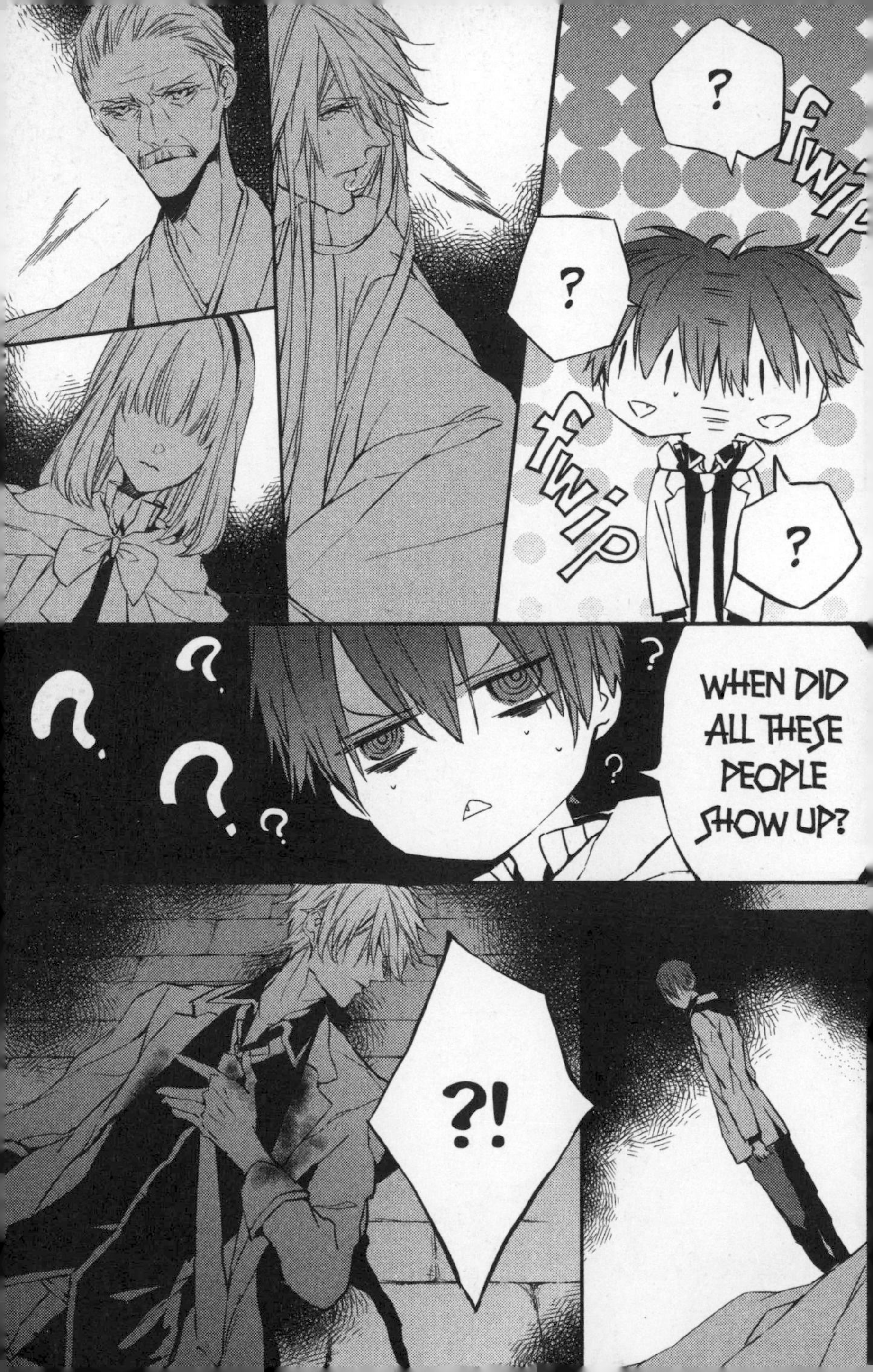
?
fwip
?
fwip
?
WHEN DID ALL THESE PEOPLE SHOW UP?
?!

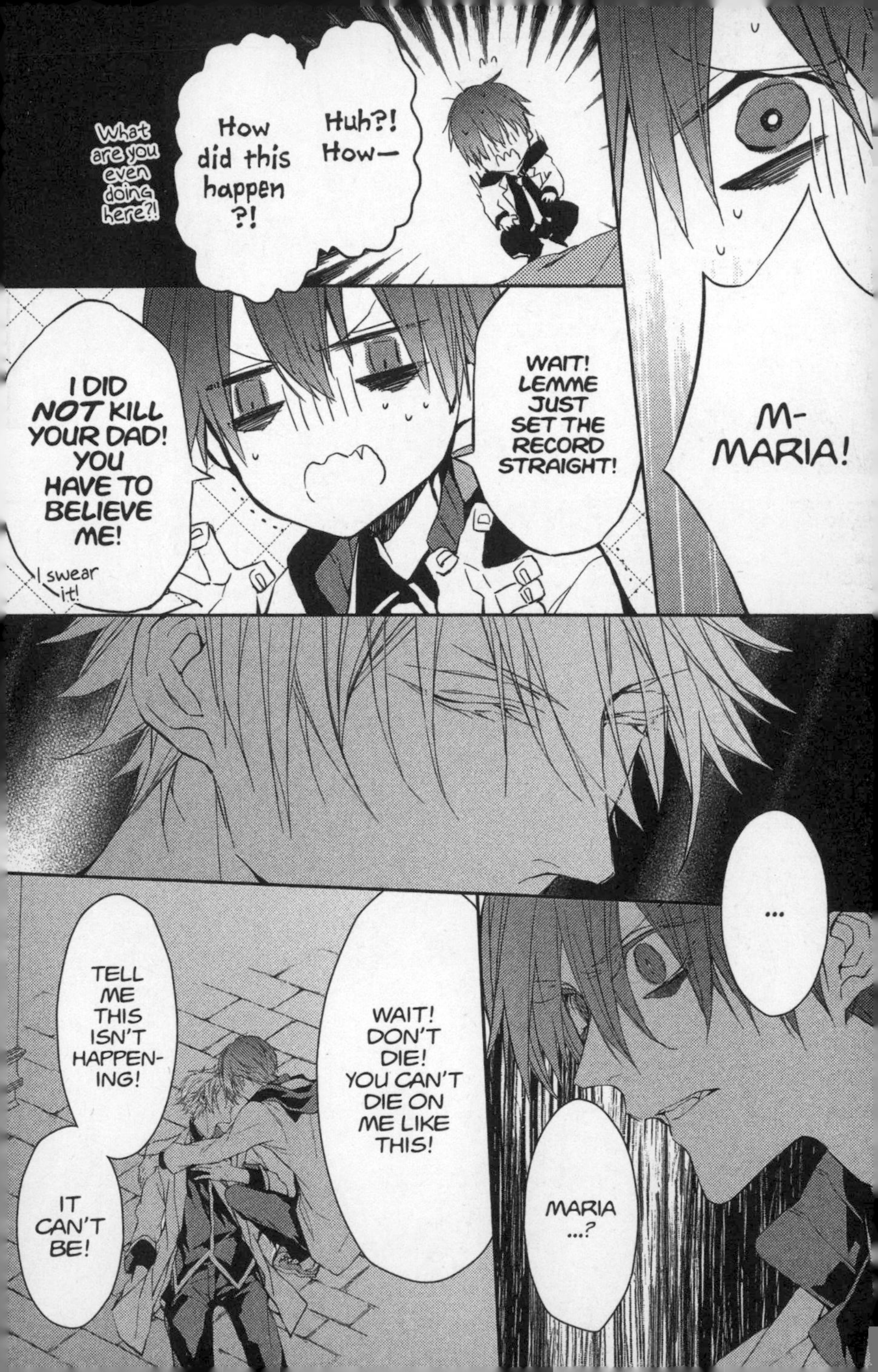
M-MARIA!
Huh?! How—
How did this happen ?!
What are you even doing here?!
WAIT! LEMME JUST SET THE RECORD STRAIGHT!
I DID **NOT** KILL YOUR DAD! YOU HAVE TO BELIEVE ME!
I swear it!
...
MARIA ...?
WAIT! DON'T DIE! YOU CAN'T DIE ON ME LIKE THIS!
TELL ME THIS ISN'T HAPPEN-ING!
IT CAN'T BE!

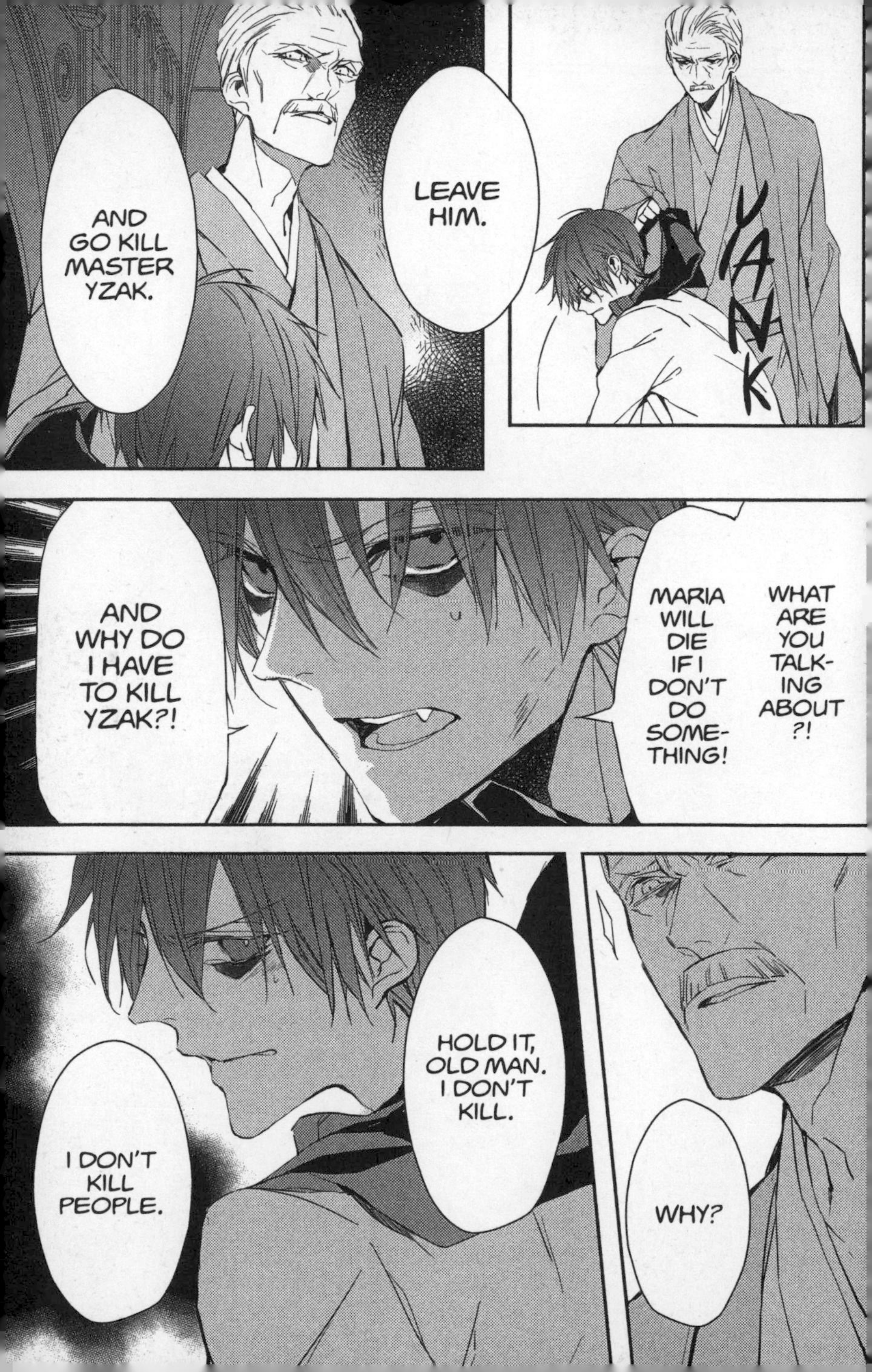
YANK
LEAVE HIM.
AND GO KILL MASTER YZAK.
WHAT ARE YOU TALKING ABOUT?!
MARIA WILL DIE IF I DON'T DO SOMETHING!
AND WHY DO I HAVE TO KILL YZAK?!
WHY?
HOLD IT, OLD MAN. I DON'T KILL.
I DON'T KILL PEOPLE.

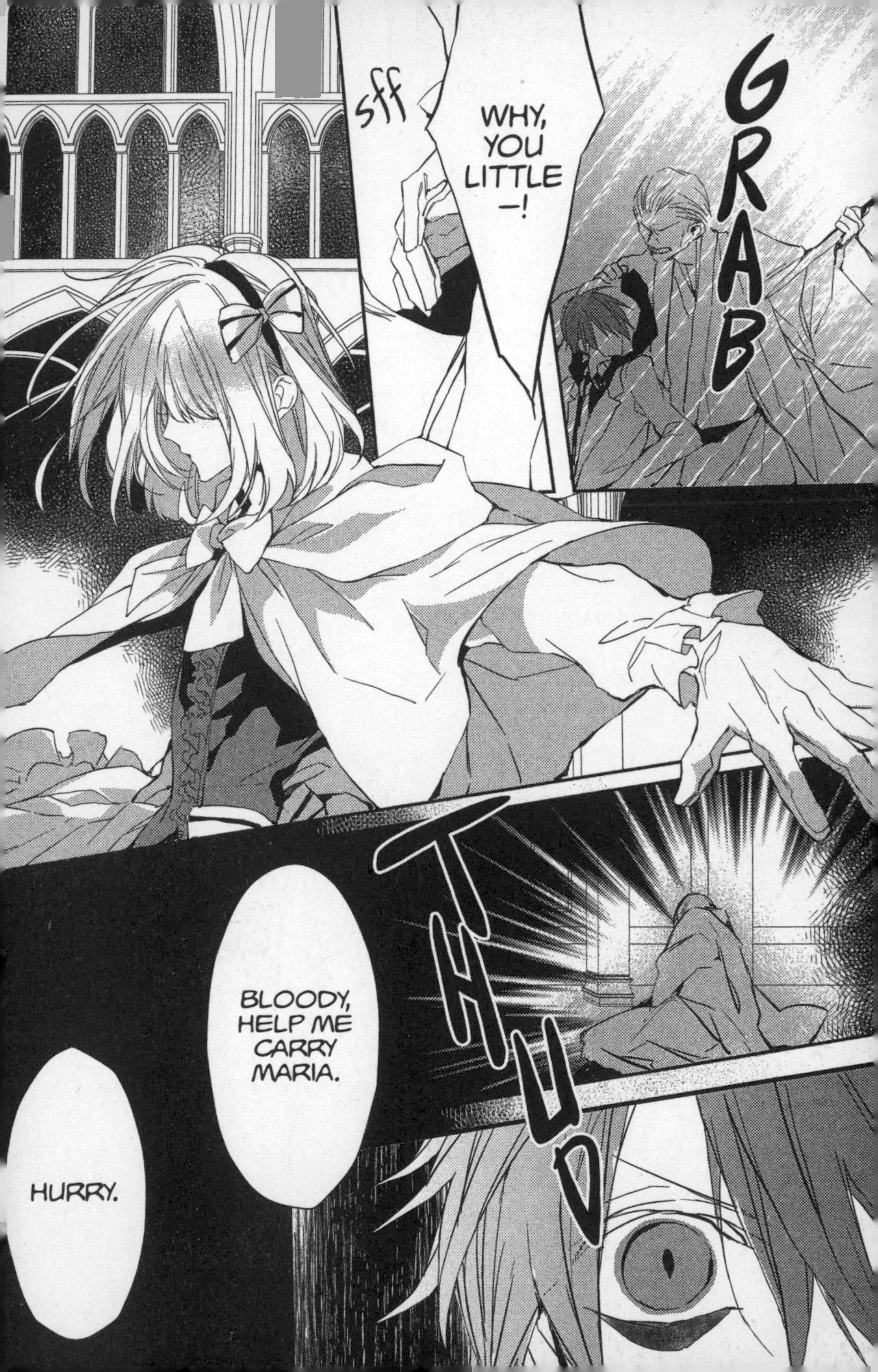
GRAB
WHY, YOU LITTLE —!
sff
THUD
BLOODY, HELP ME CARRY MARIA.
HURRY.

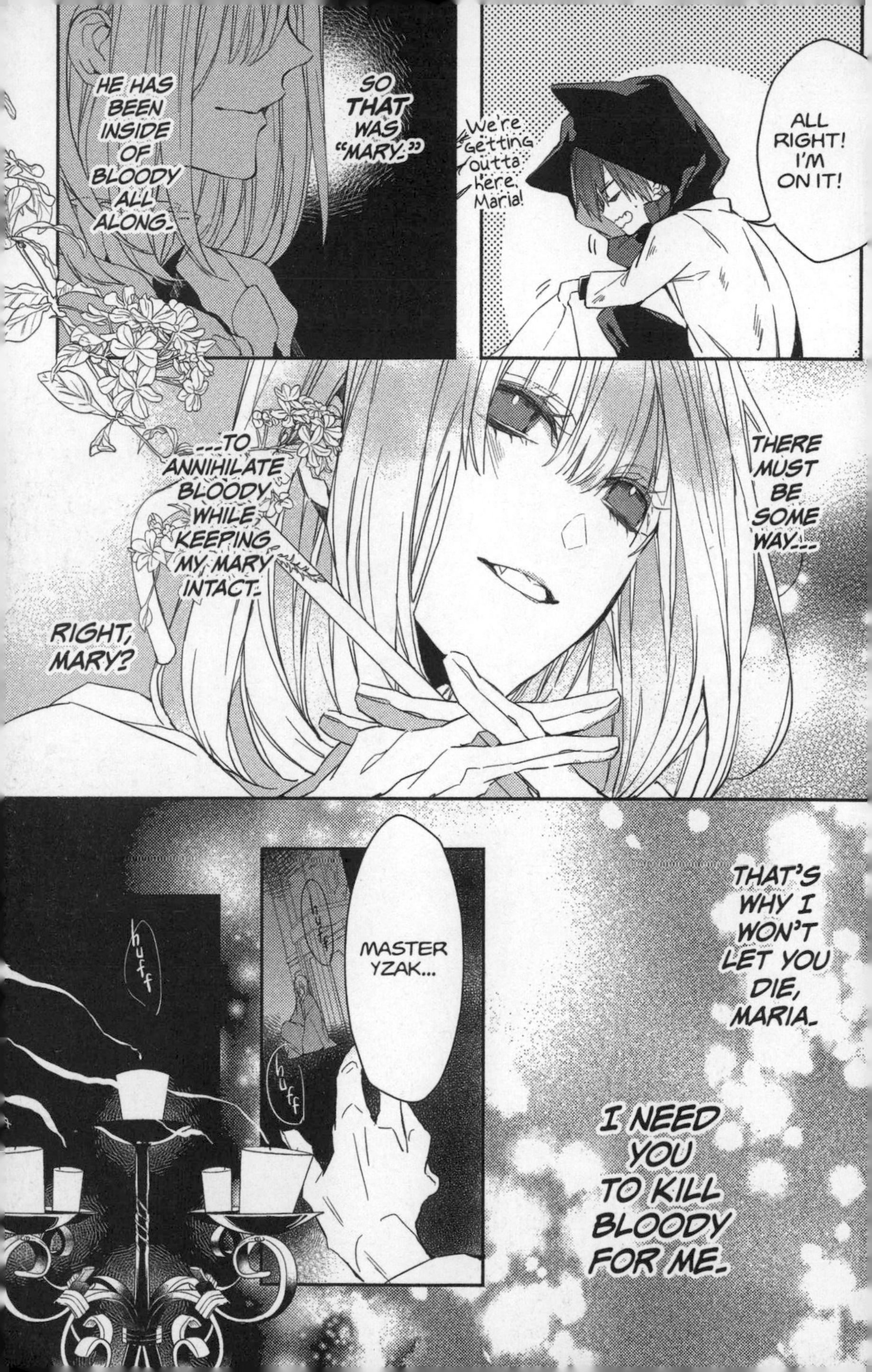
ALL RIGHT! I'M ON IT!
We're getting outta here, Maria!
SO THAT WAS "MARY."
HE HAS BEEN INSIDE OF BLOODY ALL ALONG.
THERE MUST BE SOME WAY...
...TO ANNIHILATE BLOODY WHILE KEEPING MY MARY INTACT.
RIGHT, MARY?
THAT'S WHY I WON'T LET YOU DIE, MARIA.
I NEED YOU TO KILL BLOODY FOR ME.
MASTER YZAK...
huff
huff
huff

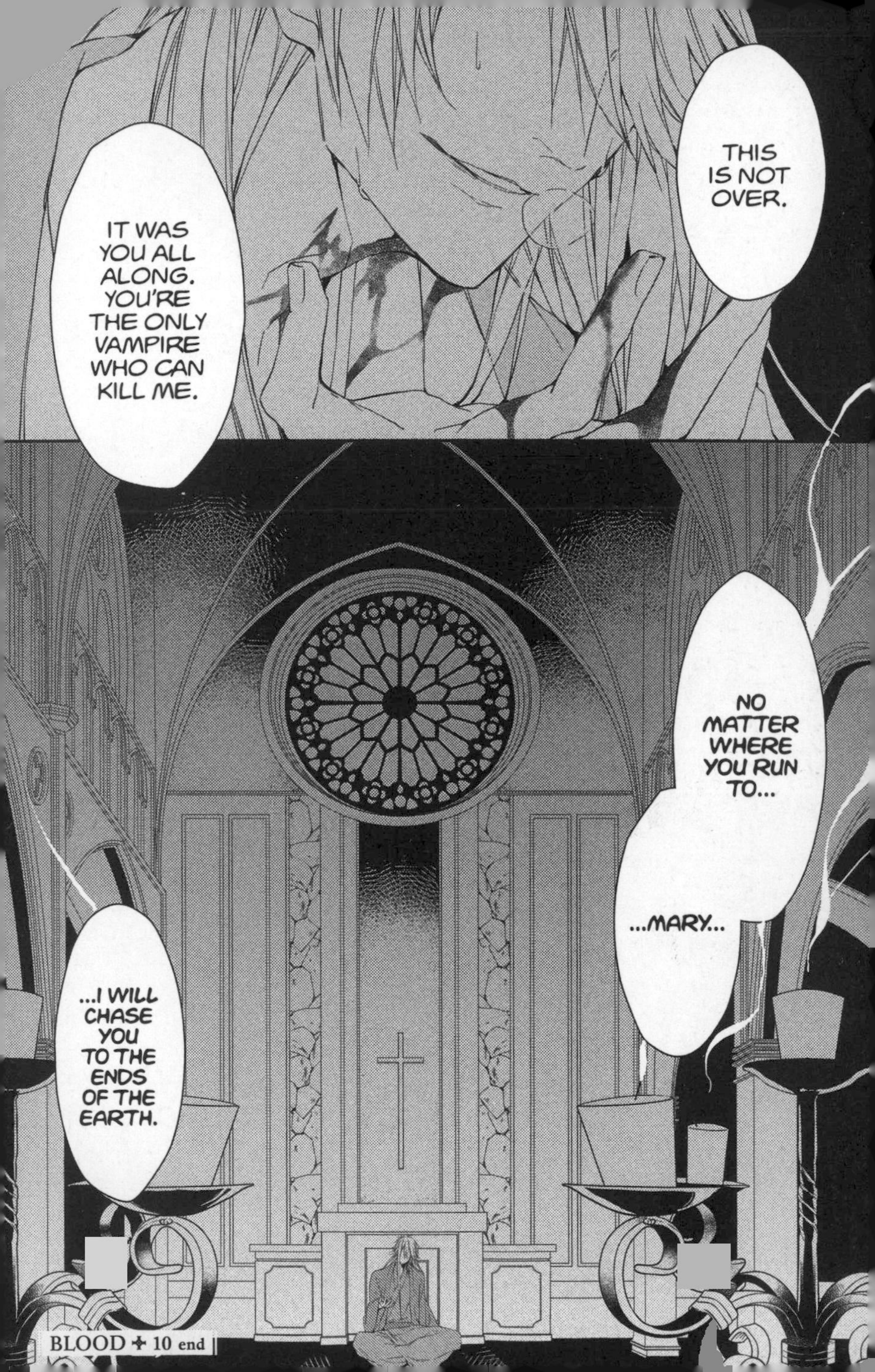
THIS IS NOT OVER.
IT WAS YOU ALL ALONG. YOU'RE THE ONLY VAMPIRE WHO CAN KILL ME.
NO MATTER WHERE YOU RUN TO...
...MARY...
...I WILL CHASE YOU TO THE ENDS OF THE EARTH.
BLOOD ✣ 10 end

Bloody+Mary

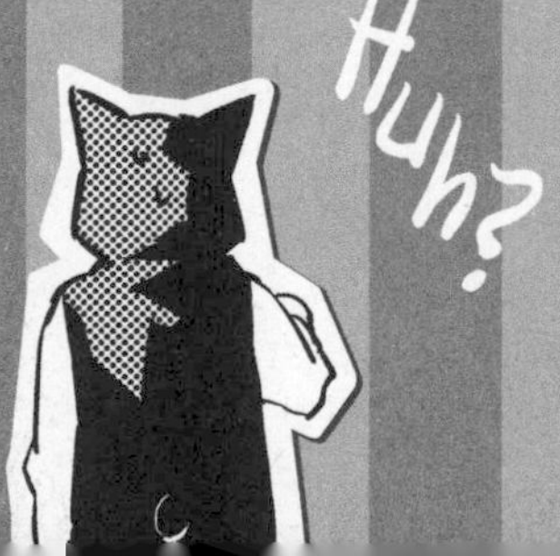
Huh?

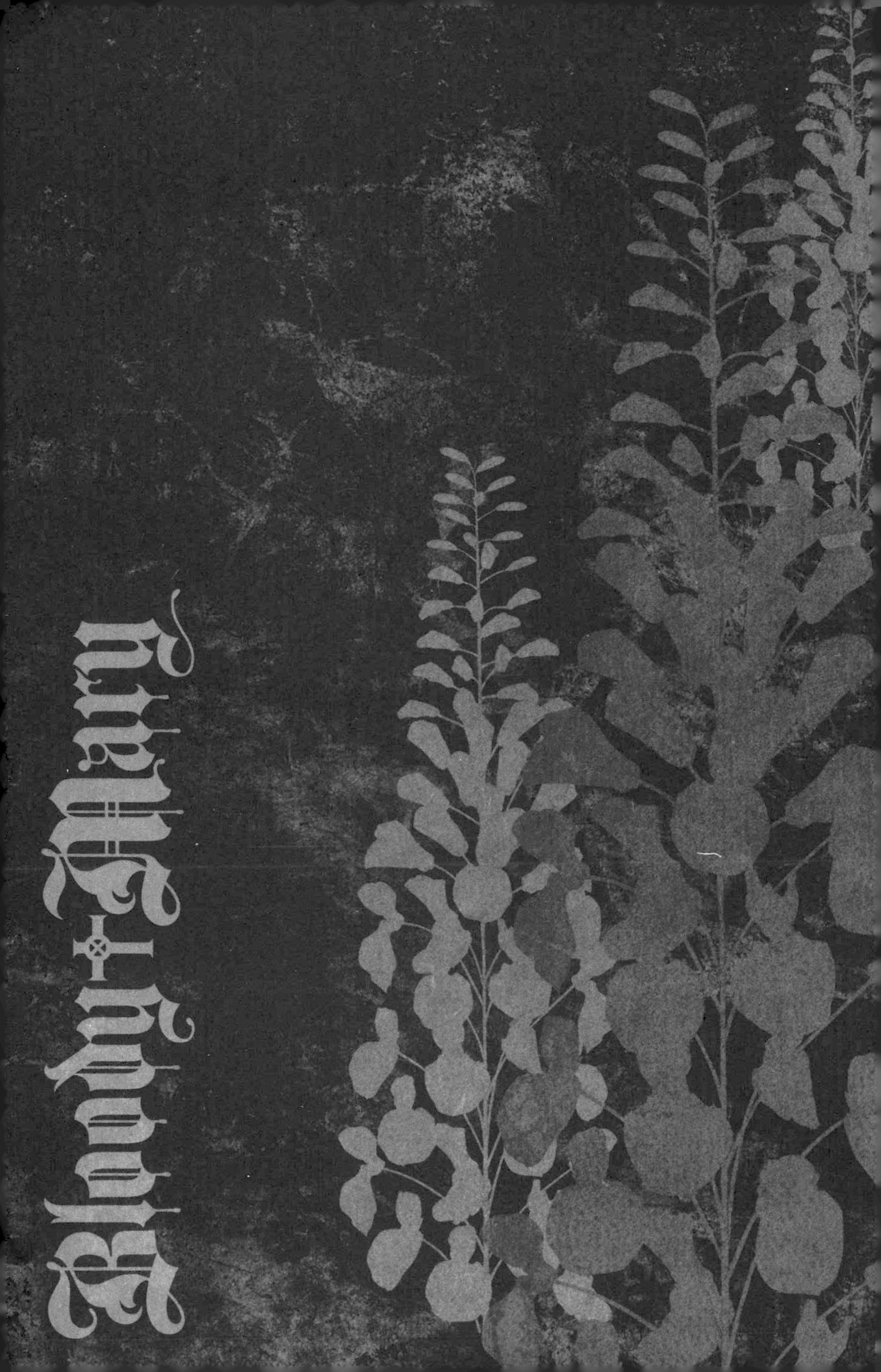
Bloody Mary

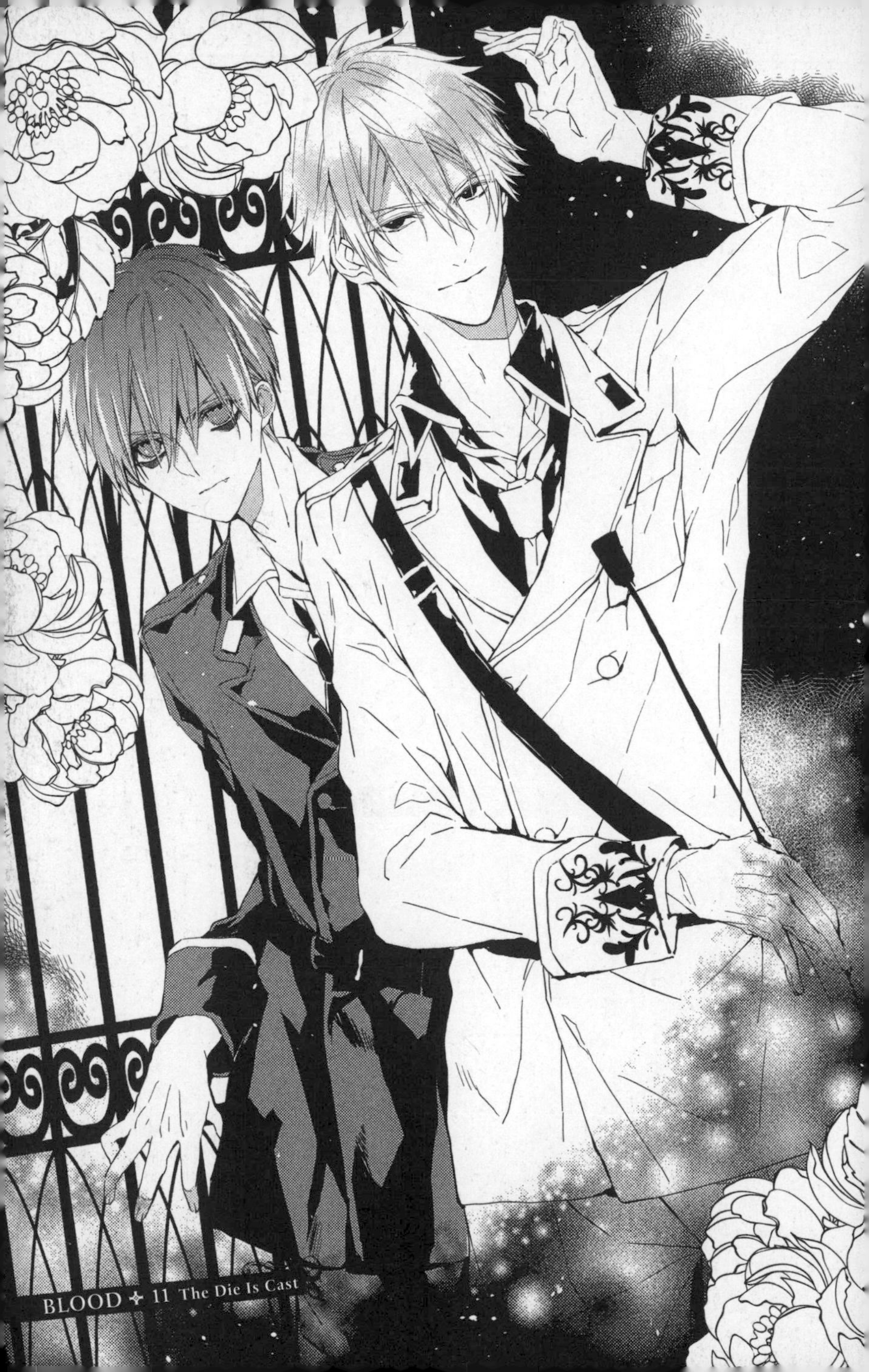
BLOOD ✧ 11 The Die Is Cast

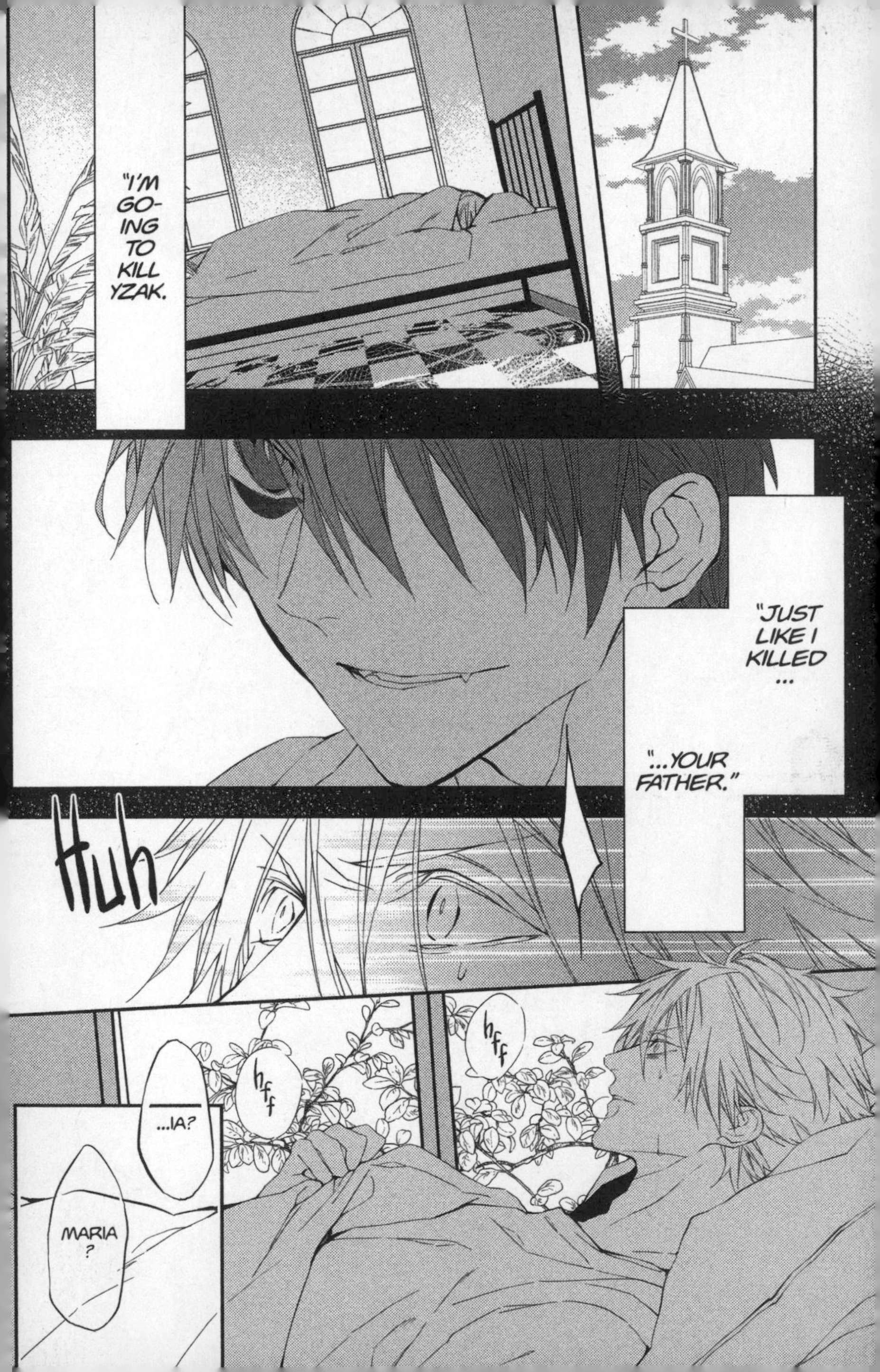
"I'M GO-ING TO KILL YZAK.
"JUST LIKE I KILLED ...
"...YOUR FATHER."
Huh
hff
hff
...IA?
MARIA ?

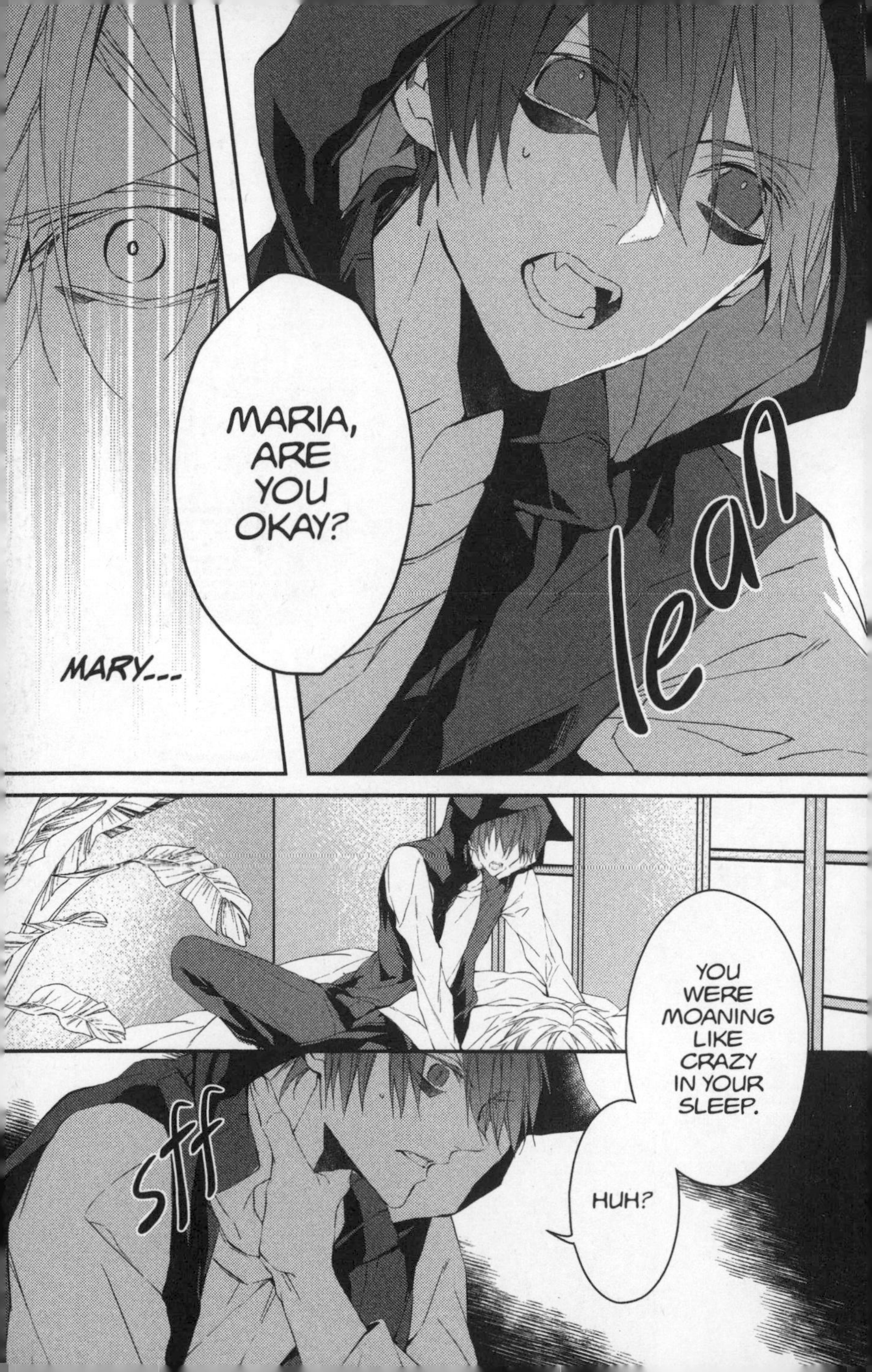
lean
MARIA, ARE YOU OKAY?
MARY...
YOU WERE MOANING LIKE CRAZY IN YOUR SLEEP.
HUH?
sff

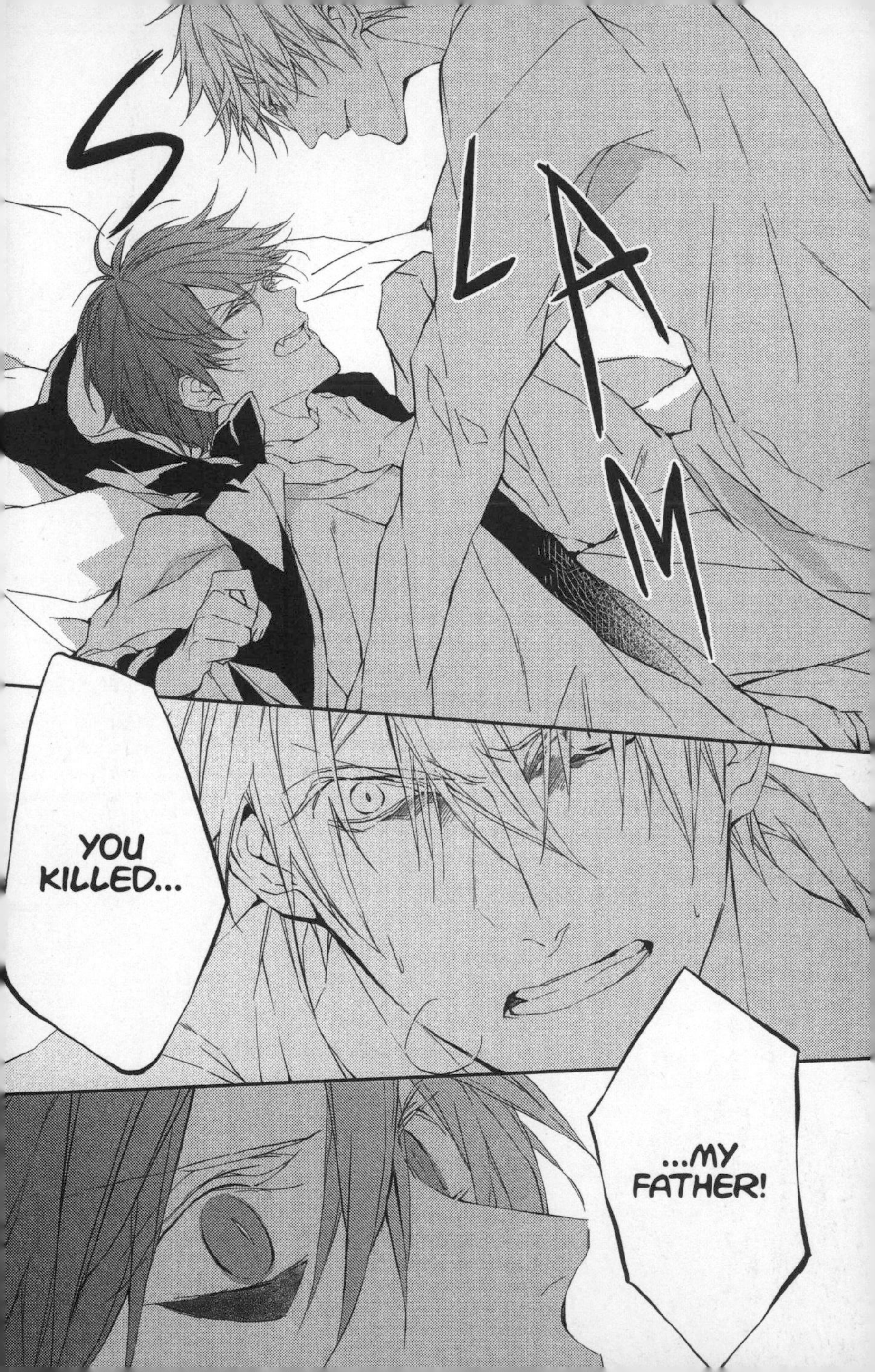
SLAM
YOU KILLED...
...MY FATHER!

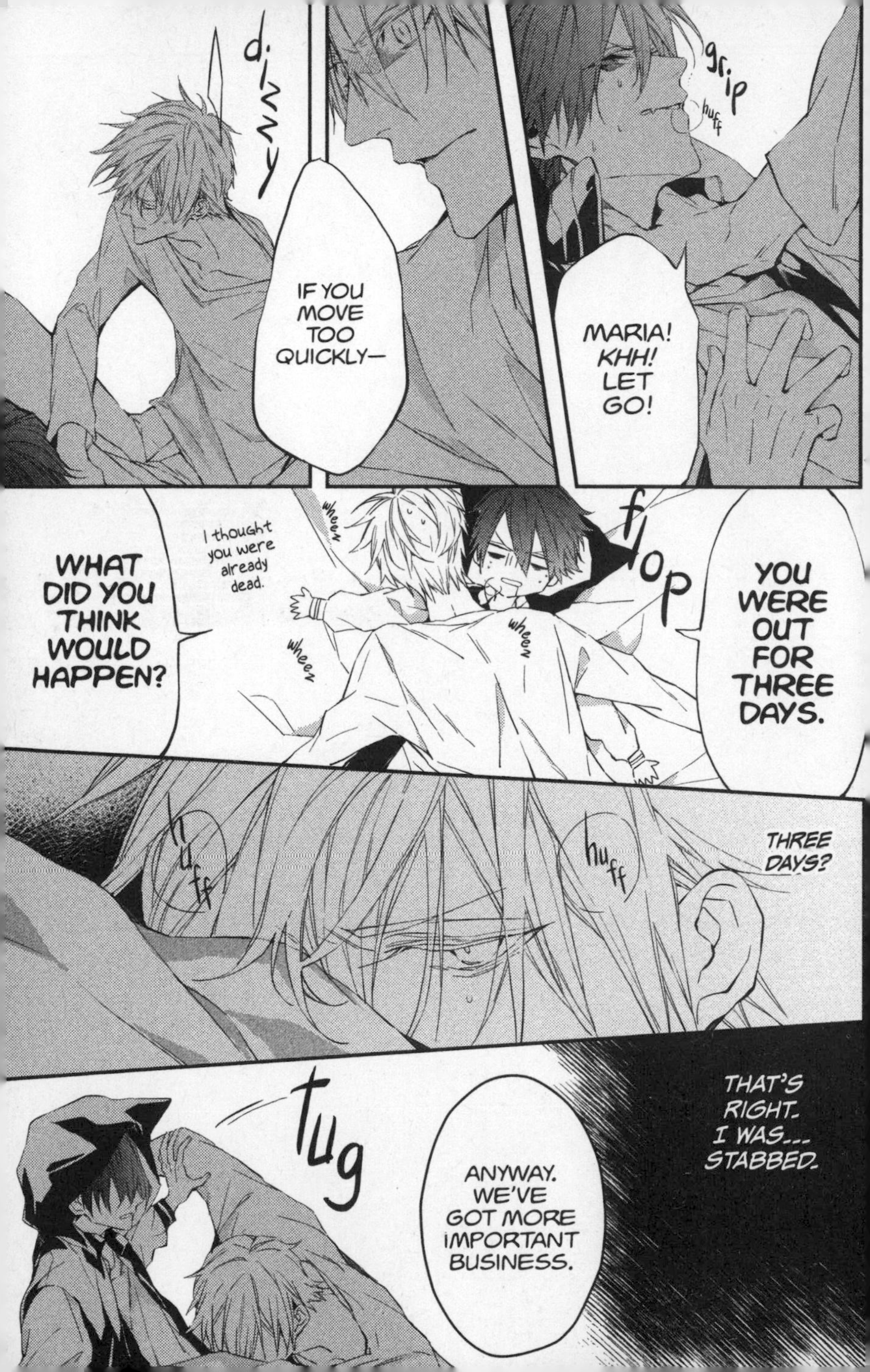
grip
huff
MARIA! KHH! LET GO!
IF YOU MOVE TOO QUICKLY—
dizzy
flop
YOU WERE OUT FOR THREE DAYS.
wheeze
wheeze
wheeze
I thought you were already dead.
WHAT DID YOU THINK WOULD HAPPEN?
THREE DAYS?
huff
huff
THAT'S RIGHT. I WAS... STABBED.
ANYWAY. WE'VE GOT MORE IMPORTANT BUSINESS.
tug

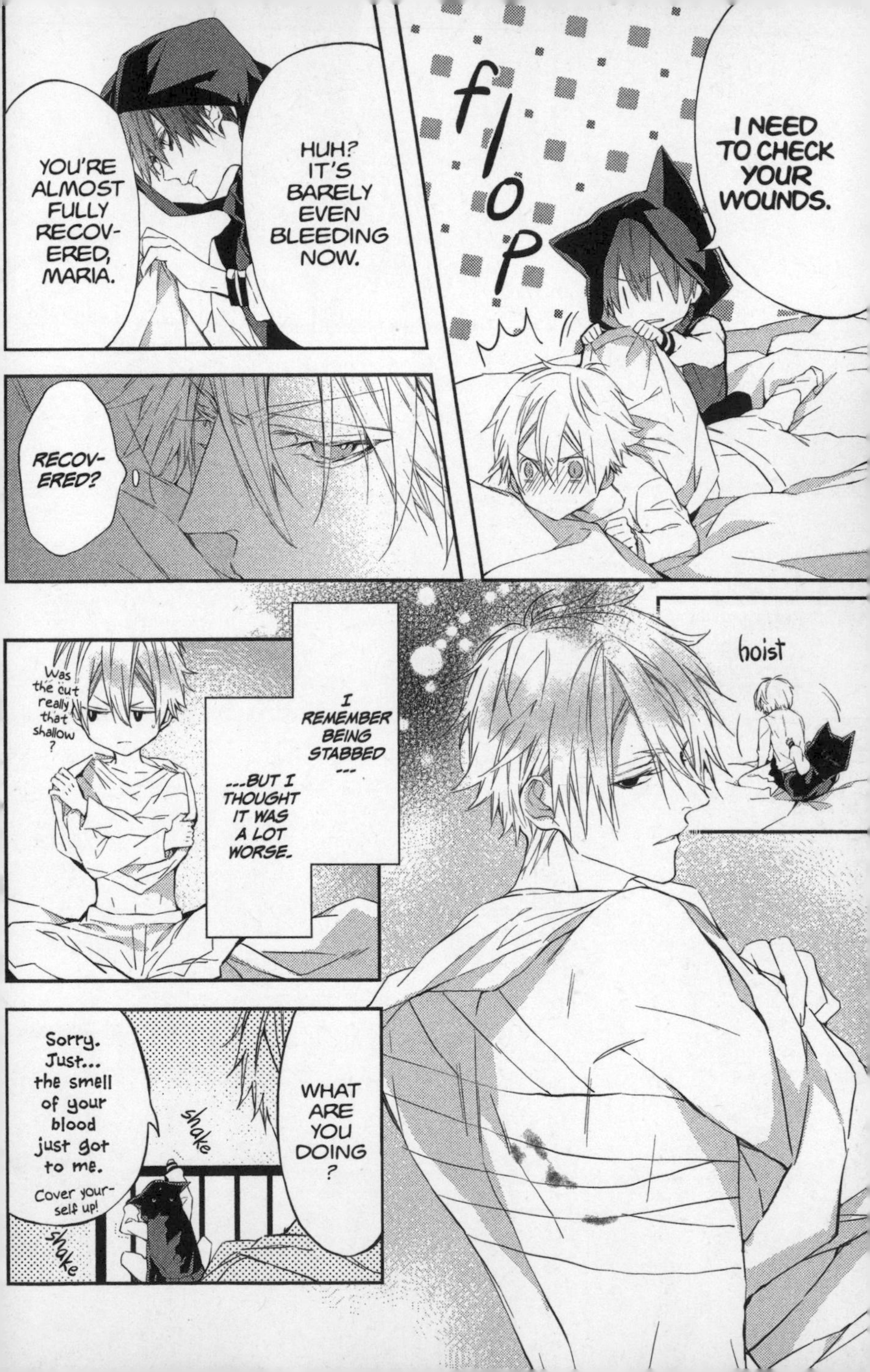
I NEED TO CHECK YOUR WOUNDS.
flop
HUH? IT'S BARELY EVEN BLEEDING NOW.
YOU'RE ALMOST FULLY RECOVERED, MARIA.
RECOVERED?
hoist
I REMEMBER BEING STABBED ---
---BUT I THOUGHT IT WAS A LOT WORSE.
Was the cut really that shallow?
WHAT ARE YOU DOING?
shake
Sorry. Just... the smell of your blood just got to me.
Cover yourself up!
shake

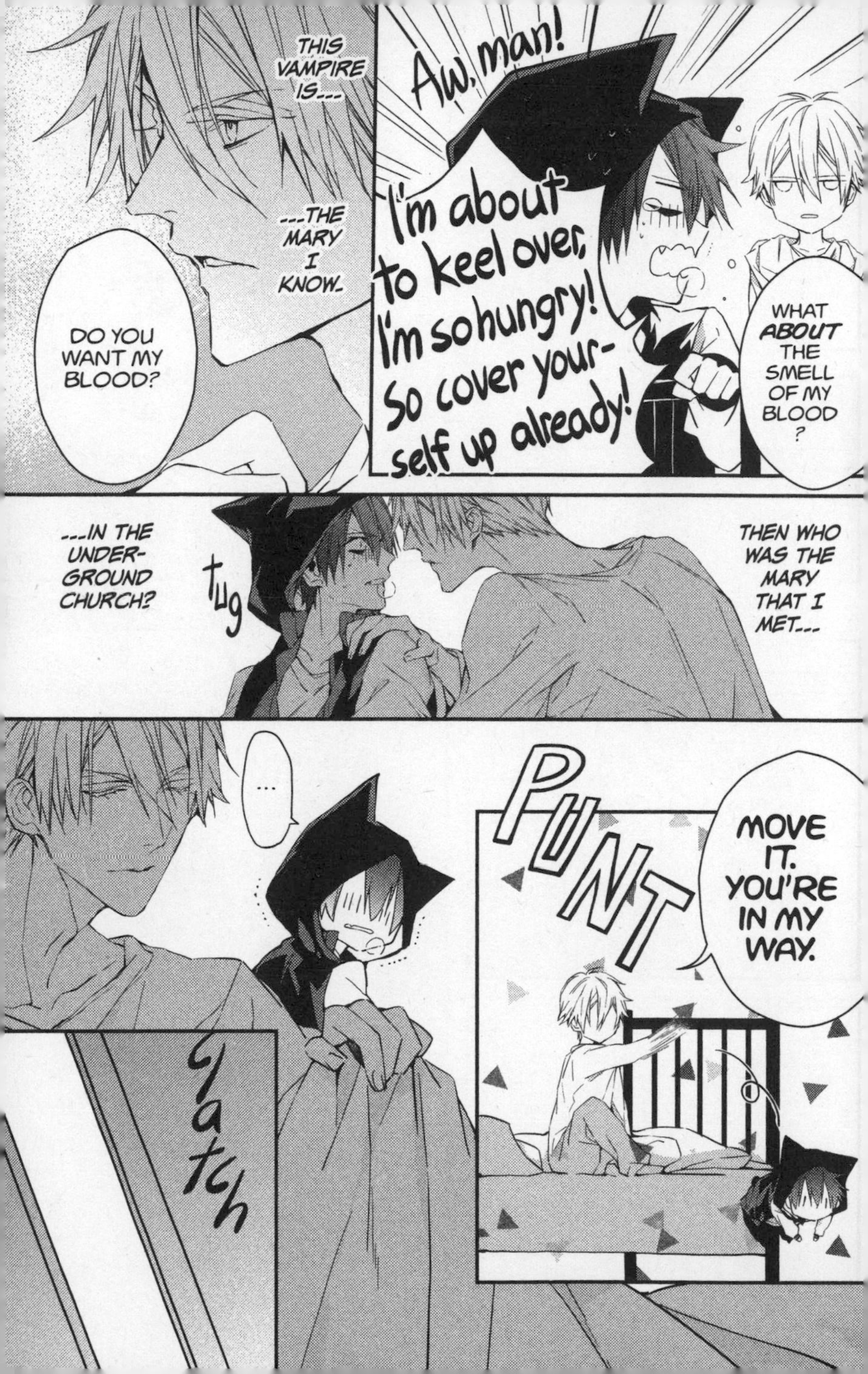
WHAT ABOUT THE SMELL OF MY BLOOD ?
Aw, man!
I'm about to keel over, I'm so hungry! So cover your-self up already!
THIS VAMPIRE IS---
---THE MARY I KNOW.
DO YOU WANT MY BLOOD?
THEN WHO WAS THE MARY THAT I MET---
tug
---IN THE UNDER-GROUND CHURCH?
MOVE IT. YOU'RE IN MY WAY.
PUNT
...
yatch

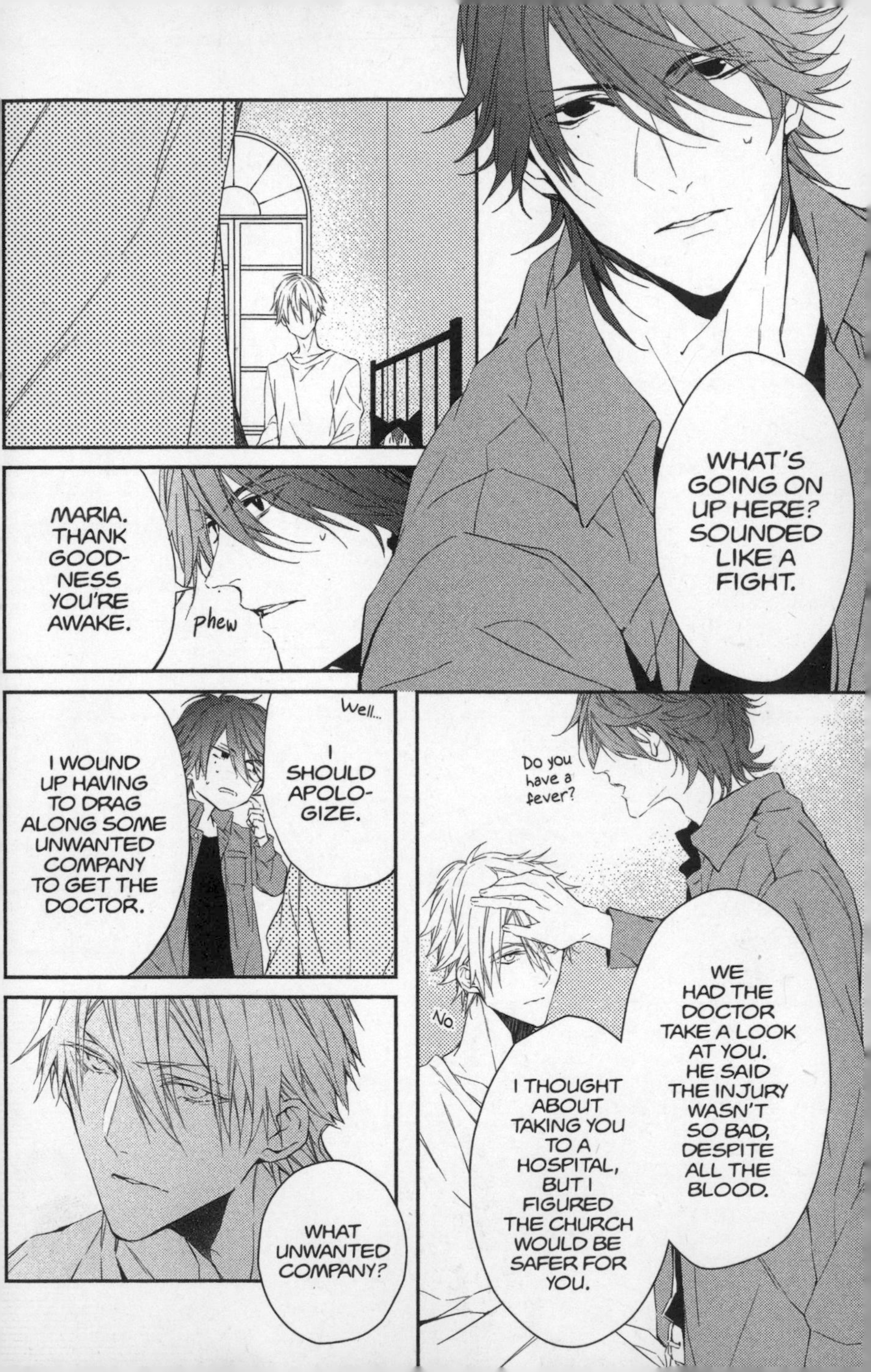
WHAT'S GOING ON UP HERE? SOUNDED LIKE A FIGHT.
phew
MARIA. THANK GOODNESS YOU'RE AWAKE.
Do you have a fever?
No.
WE HAD THE DOCTOR TAKE A LOOK AT YOU. HE SAID THE INJURY WASN'T SO BAD, DESPITE ALL THE BLOOD.
I THOUGHT ABOUT TAKING YOU TO A HOSPITAL, BUT I FIGURED THE CHURCH WOULD BE SAFER FOR YOU.
Well...
I SHOULD APOLOGIZE.
I WOUND UP HAVING TO DRAG ALONG SOME UNWANTED COMPANY TO GET THE DOCTOR.
WHAT UNWANTED COMPANY?

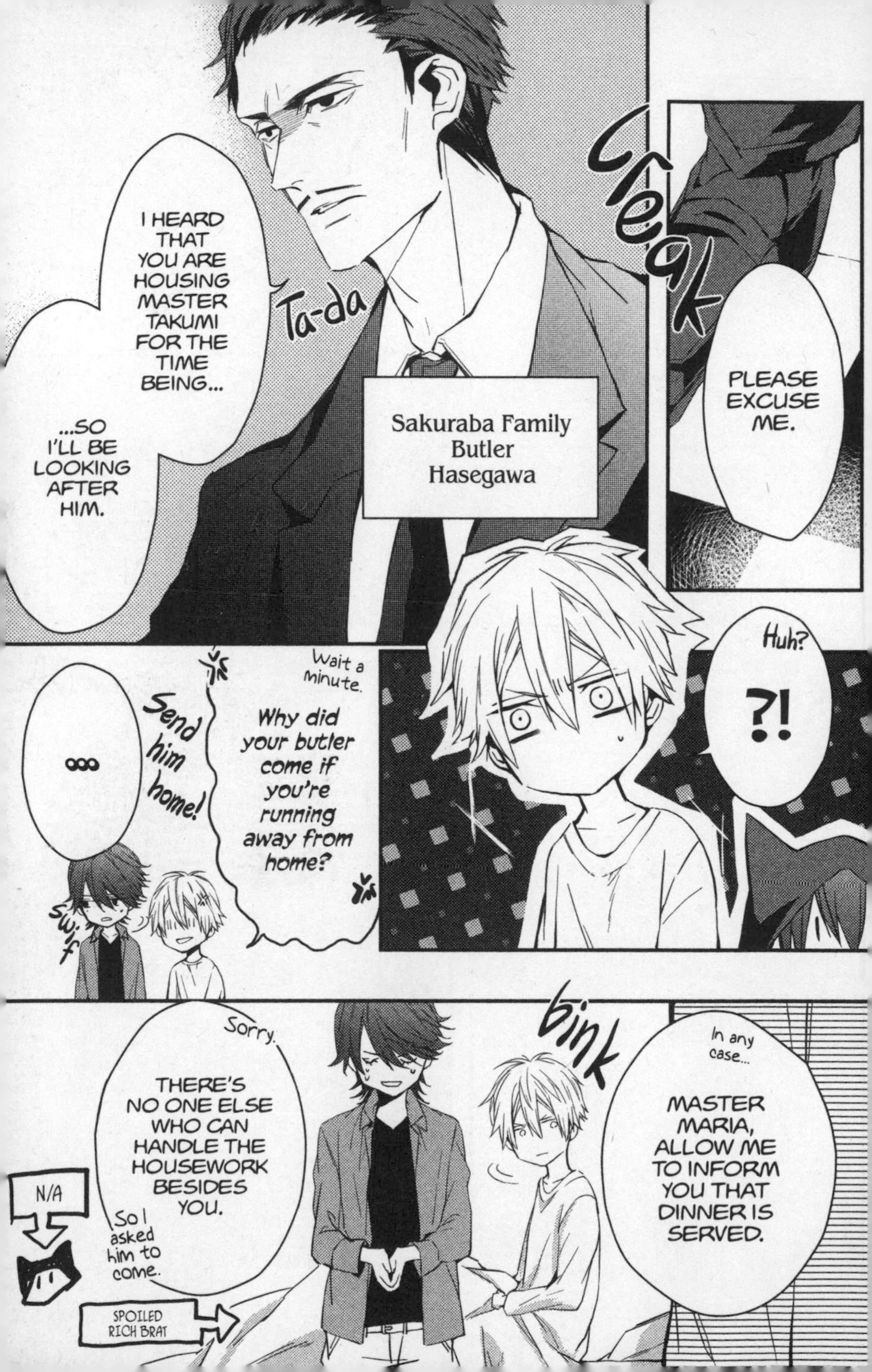
Creak
PLEASE EXCUSE ME.
Ta-da
I HEARD THAT YOU ARE HOUSING MASTER TAKUMI FOR THE TIME BEING...
...SO I'LL BE LOOKING AFTER HIM.
Sakuraba Family Butler Hasegawa
Huh?
?!
Wait a minute.
Why did your butler come if you're running away from home?
Send him home!
...
Swif
In any case...
MASTER MARIA, ALLOW ME TO INFORM YOU THAT DINNER IS SERVED.
bink
Sorry.
THERE'S NO ONE ELSE WHO CAN HANDLE THE HOUSEWORK BESIDES YOU.
So I asked him to come.
N/A
SPOILED RICH BRAT

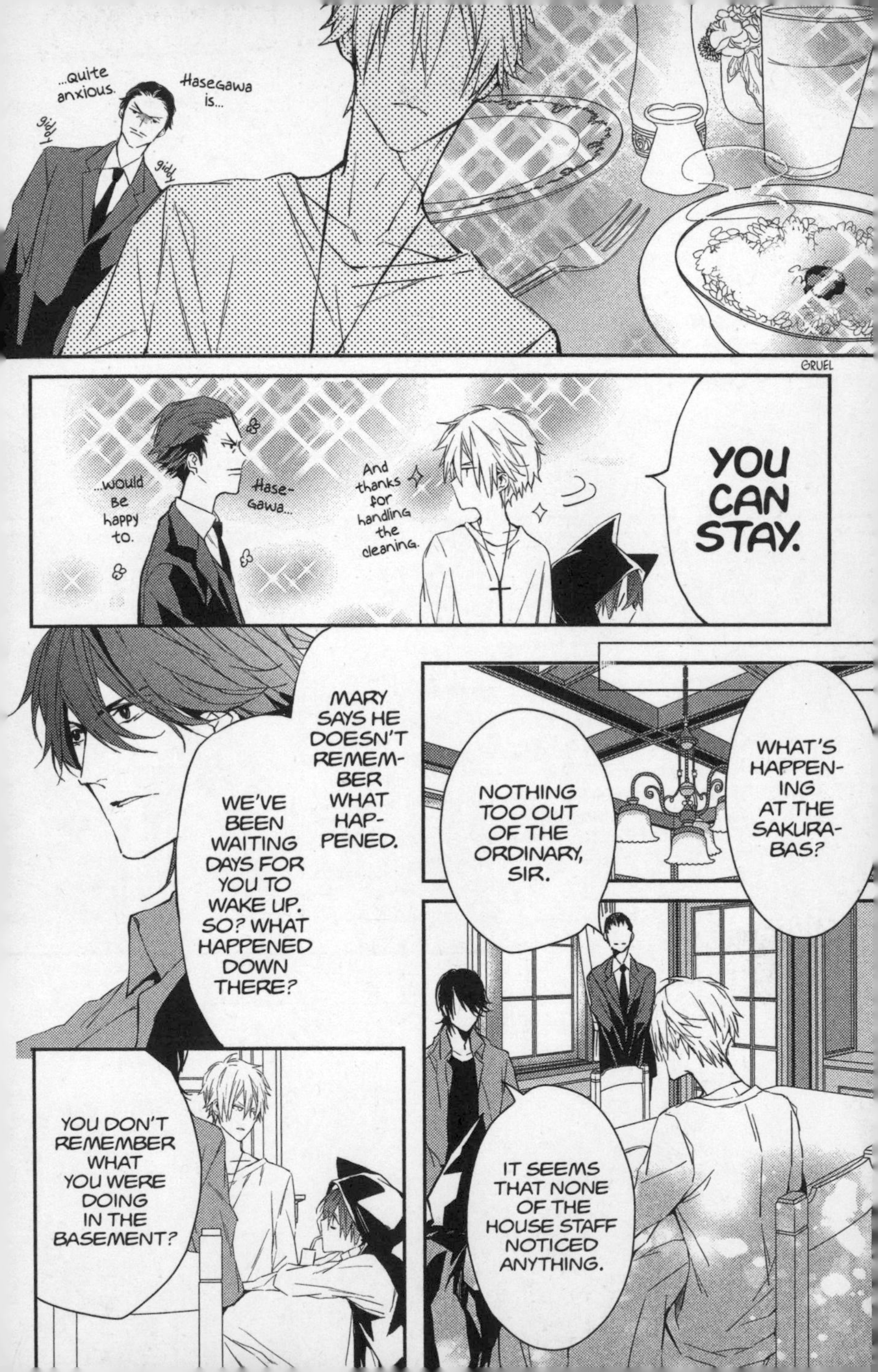
Hasegawa is...
...Quite anxious.
giddy
giddy
GRUEL
YOU CAN STAY.
And thanks for handling the cleaning.
Hase-gawa...
...would be happy to.
WHAT'S HAPPEN-ING AT THE SAKURA-BAS?
NOTHING TOO OUT OF THE ORDINARY, SIR.
IT SEEMS THAT NONE OF THE HOUSE STAFF NOTICED ANYTHING.
MARY SAYS HE DOESN'T REMEM-BER WHAT HAP-PENED.
WE'VE BEEN WAITING DAYS FOR YOU TO WAKE UP. SO? WHAT HAPPENED DOWN THERE?
YOU DON'T REMEMBER WHAT YOU WERE DOING IN THE BASEMENT?

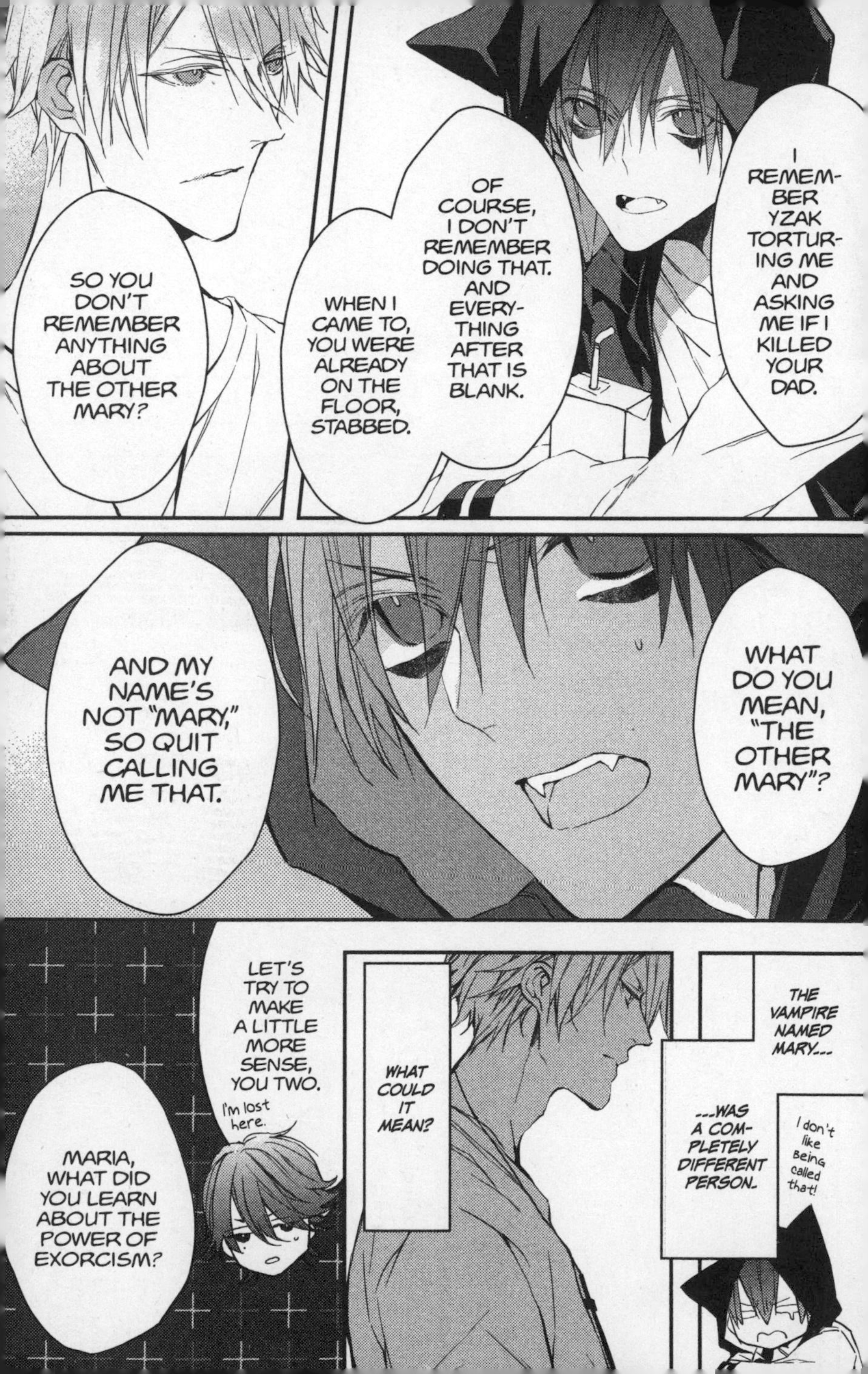
I REMEMBER YZAK TORTURING ME AND ASKING ME IF I KILLED YOUR DAD.
OF COURSE, I DON'T REMEMBER DOING THAT. AND EVERYTHING AFTER THAT IS BLANK.
WHEN I CAME TO, YOU WERE ALREADY ON THE FLOOR, STABBED.
SO YOU DON'T REMEMBER ANYTHING ABOUT THE OTHER MARY?
WHAT DO YOU MEAN, "THE OTHER MARY"?
AND MY NAME'S NOT "MARY," SO QUIT CALLING ME THAT.
THE VAMPIRE NAMED MARY...
...WAS A COMPLETELY DIFFERENT PERSON.
I don't like Being called that!
WHAT COULD IT MEAN?
LET'S TRY TO MAKE A LITTLE MORE SENSE, YOU TWO.
I'm lost here.
MARIA, WHAT DID YOU LEARN ABOUT THE POWER OF EXORCISM?

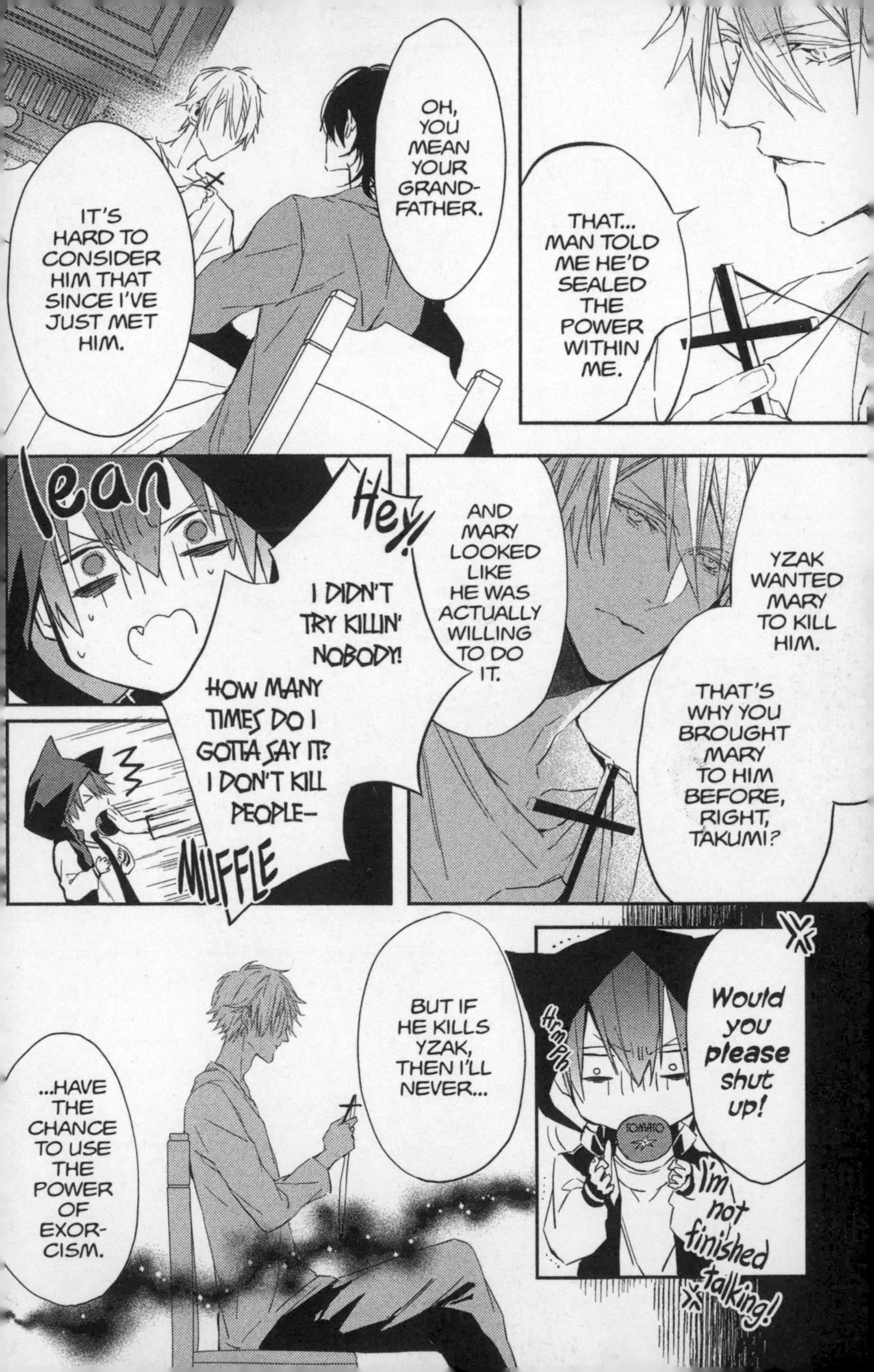
THAT... MAN TOLD ME HE'D SEALED THE POWER WITHIN ME.
OH, YOU MEAN YOUR GRAND-FATHER.
IT'S HARD TO CONSIDER HIM THAT SINCE I'VE JUST MET HIM.
YZAK WANTED MARY TO KILL HIM.
THAT'S WHY YOU BROUGHT MARY TO HIM BEFORE, RIGHT, TAKUMI?
AND MARY LOOKED LIKE HE WAS ACTUALLY WILLING TO DO IT.
Hey!
lean
I DIDN'T TRY KILLIN' NOBODY!
HOW MANY TIMES DO I GOTTA SAY IT? I DON'T KILL PEOPLE–
MUFFLE
Would you please shut up!
Hrmph
I'm not finished talking!
TOMATO
BUT IF HE KILLS YZAK, THEN I'LL NEVER...
...HAVE THE CHANCE TO USE THE POWER OF EXOR-CISM.

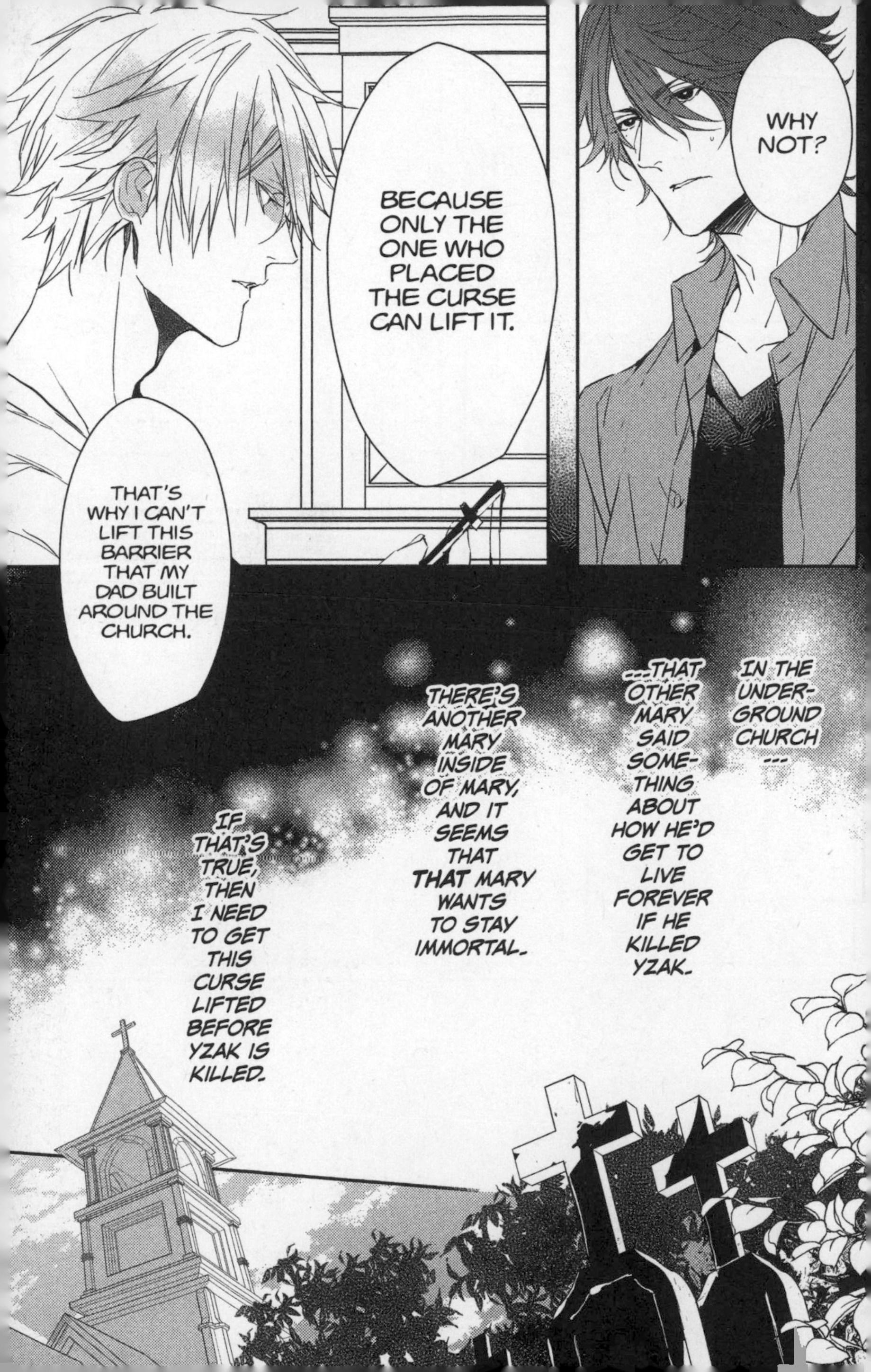
WHY NOT?
BECAUSE ONLY THE ONE WHO PLACED THE CURSE CAN LIFT IT.
THAT'S WHY I CAN'T LIFT THIS BARRIER THAT MY DAD BUILT AROUND THE CHURCH.
IN THE UNDER-GROUND CHURCH---
---THAT OTHER MARY SAID SOME-THING ABOUT HOW HE'D GET TO LIVE FOREVER IF HE KILLED YZAK.
THERE'S ANOTHER MARY INSIDE OF MARY, AND IT SEEMS THAT THAT MARY WANTS TO STAY IMMORTAL.
IF THAT'S TRUE, THEN I NEED TO GET THIS CURSE LIFTED BEFORE YZAK IS KILLED.

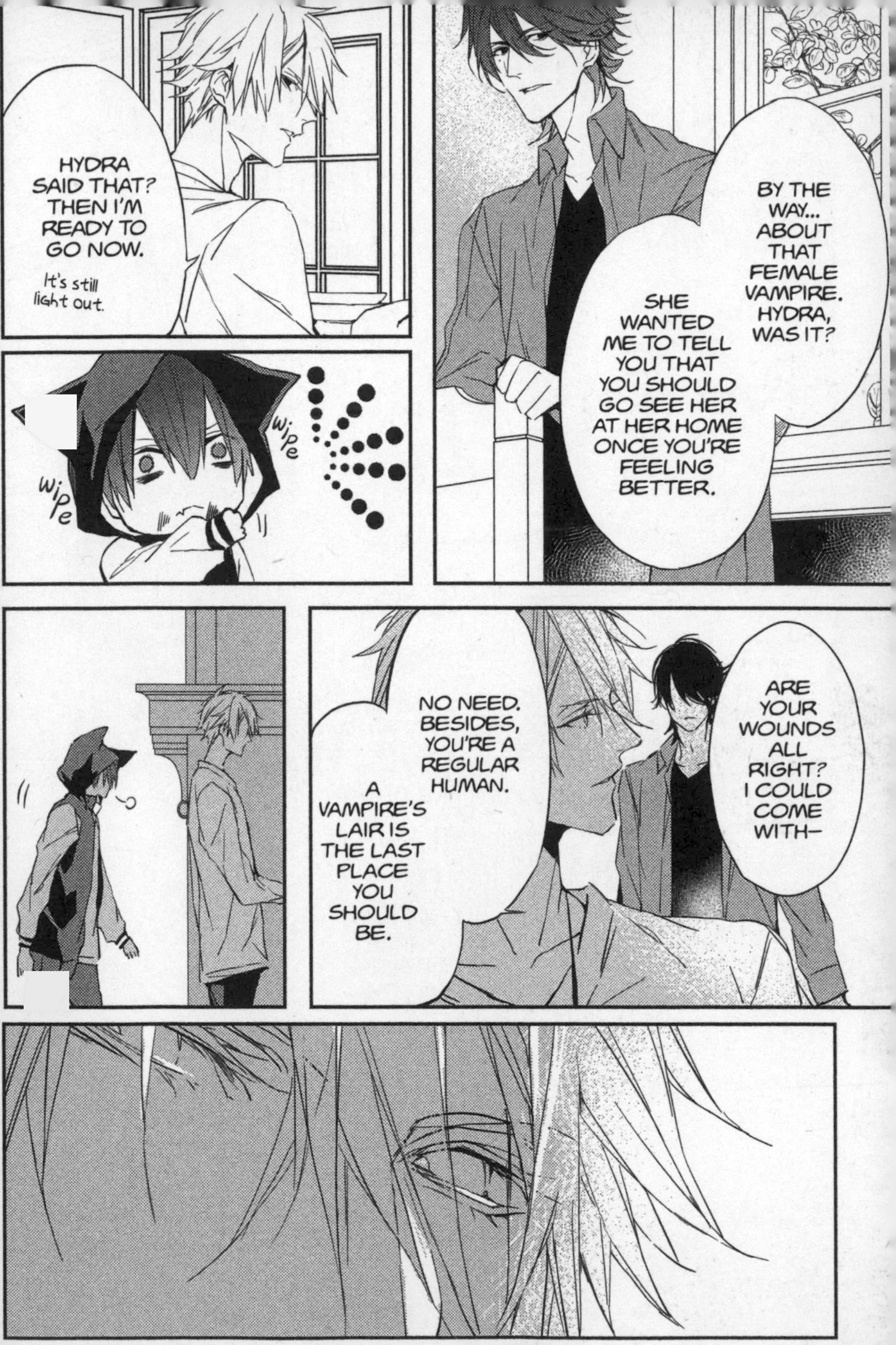
BY THE WAY... ABOUT THAT FEMALE VAMPIRE. HYDRA, WAS IT?
SHE WANTED ME TO TELL YOU THAT YOU SHOULD GO SEE HER AT HER HOME ONCE YOU'RE FEELING BETTER.
HYDRA SAID THAT? THEN I'M READY TO GO NOW.
It's still light out.
wipe
wipe
ARE YOUR WOUNDS ALL RIGHT? I COULD COME WITH—
NO NEED. BESIDES, YOU'RE A REGULAR HUMAN.
A VAMPIRE'S LAIR IS THE LAST PLACE YOU SHOULD BE.

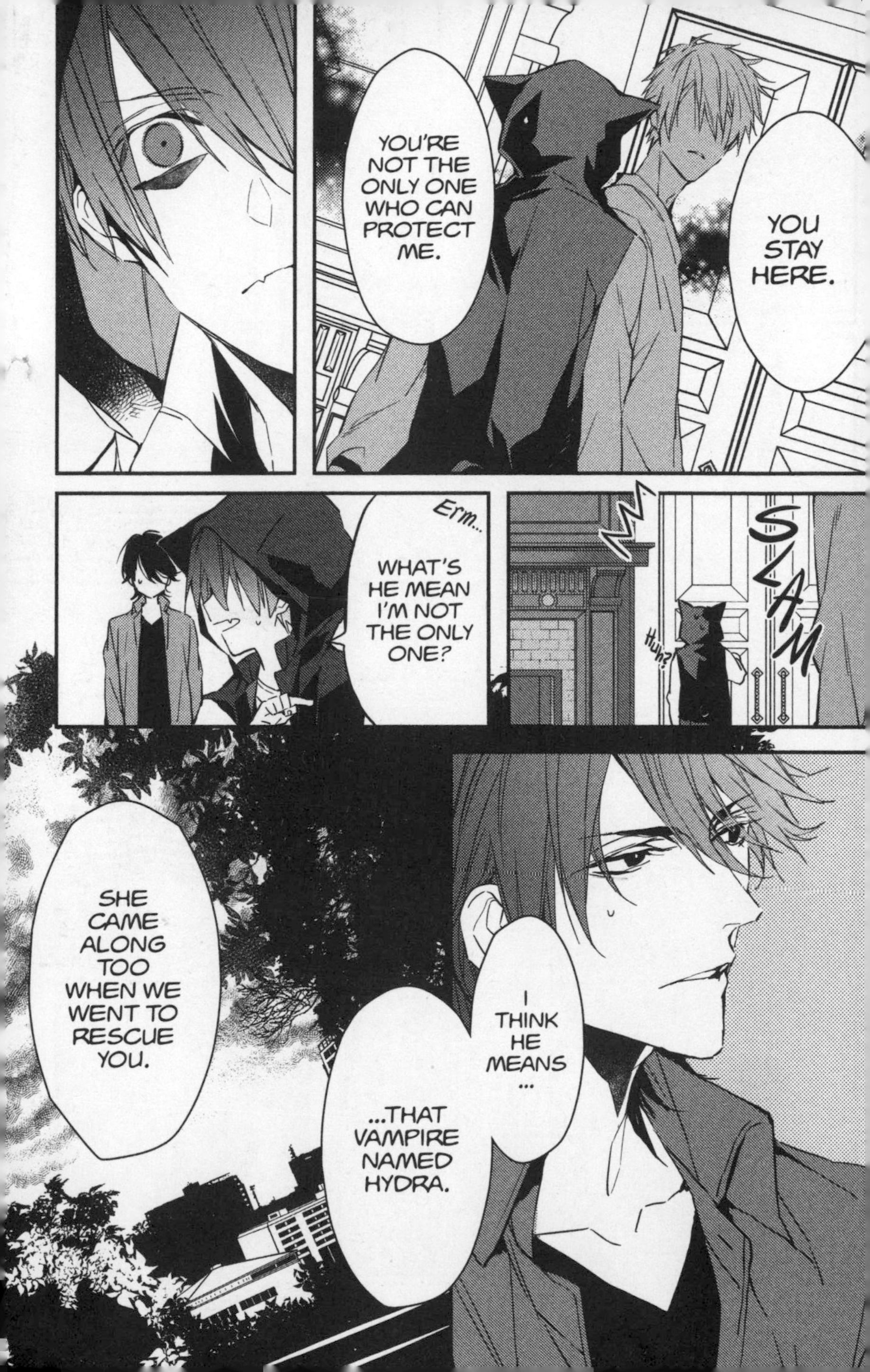
YOU STAY HERE.
YOU'RE NOT THE ONLY ONE WHO CAN PROTECT ME.
SLAM
Huh?
Erm...
WHAT'S HE MEAN I'M NOT THE ONLY ONE?
I THINK HE MEANS...
...THAT VAMPIRE NAMED HYDRA.
SHE CAME ALONG TOO WHEN WE WENT TO RESCUE YOU.

MASTER MARIA, WE'VE BEEN EXPECTING YOU.

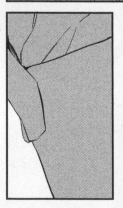

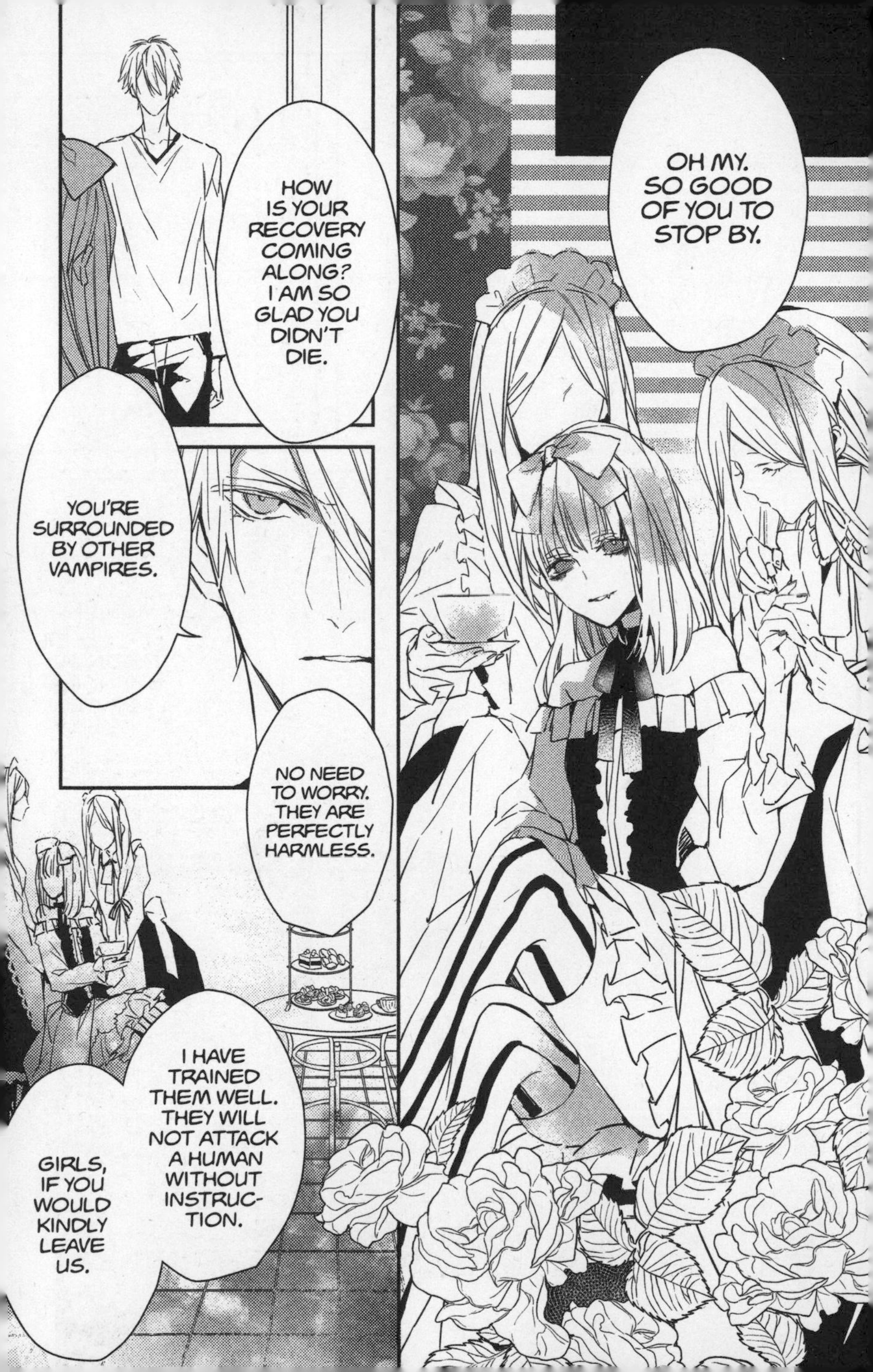
OH MY. SO GOOD OF YOU TO STOP BY.
HOW IS YOUR RECOVERY COMING ALONG? I AM SO GLAD YOU DIDN'T DIE.
YOU'RE SURROUNDED BY OTHER VAMPIRES.
NO NEED TO WORRY. THEY ARE PERFECTLY HARMLESS.
I HAVE TRAINED THEM WELL. THEY WILL NOT ATTACK A HUMAN WITHOUT INSTRUC-TION.
GIRLS, IF YOU WOULD KINDLY LEAVE US.

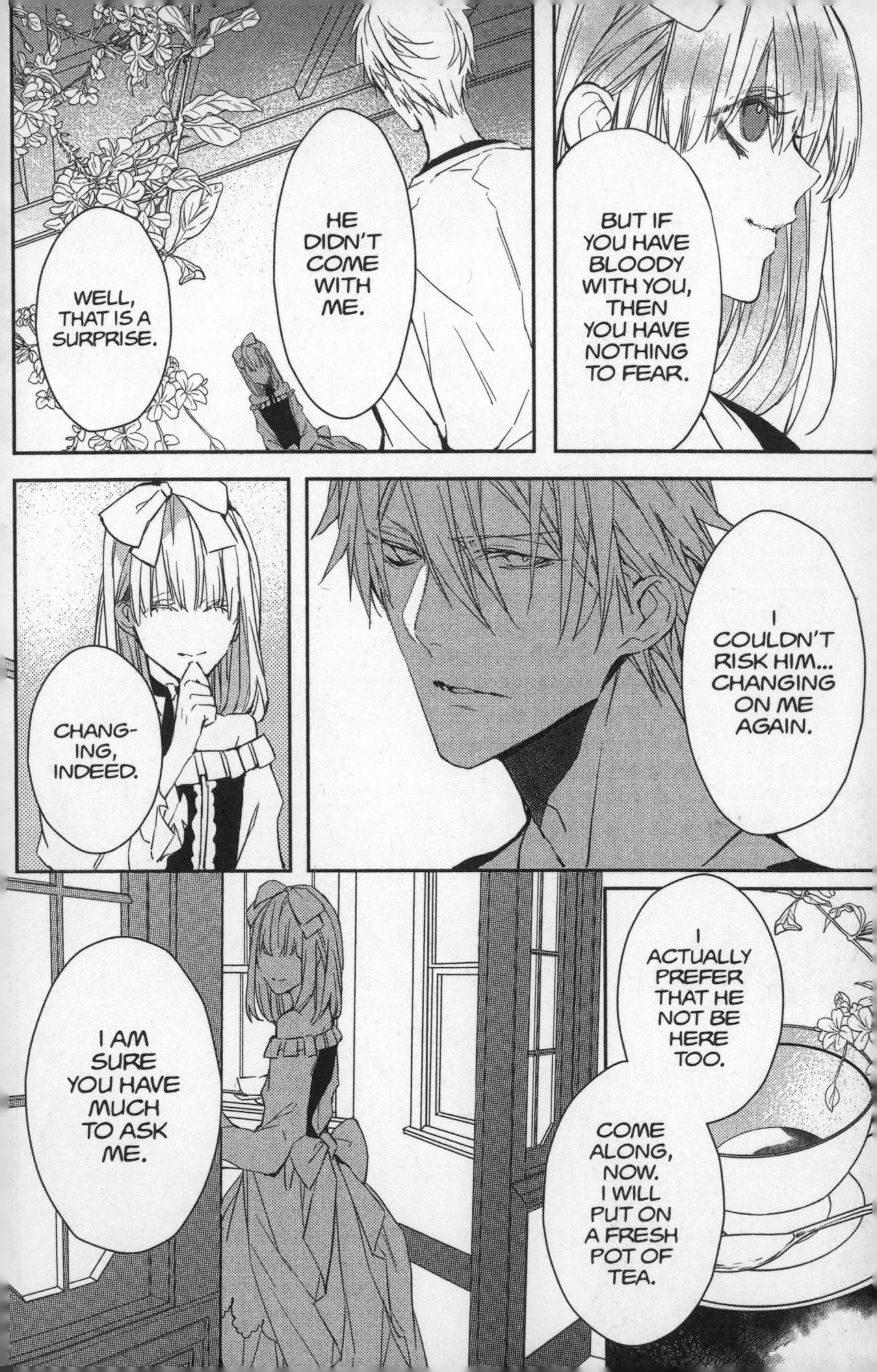
BUT IF YOU HAVE BLOODY WITH YOU, THEN YOU HAVE NOTHING TO FEAR.
HE DIDN'T COME WITH ME.
WELL, THAT IS A SURPRISE.
I COULDN'T RISK HIM... CHANGING ON ME AGAIN.
CHANG-ING, INDEED.
I ACTUALLY PREFER THAT HE NOT BE HERE TOO.
COME ALONG, NOW. I WILL PUT ON A FRESH POT OF TEA.
I AM SURE YOU HAVE MUCH TO ASK ME.

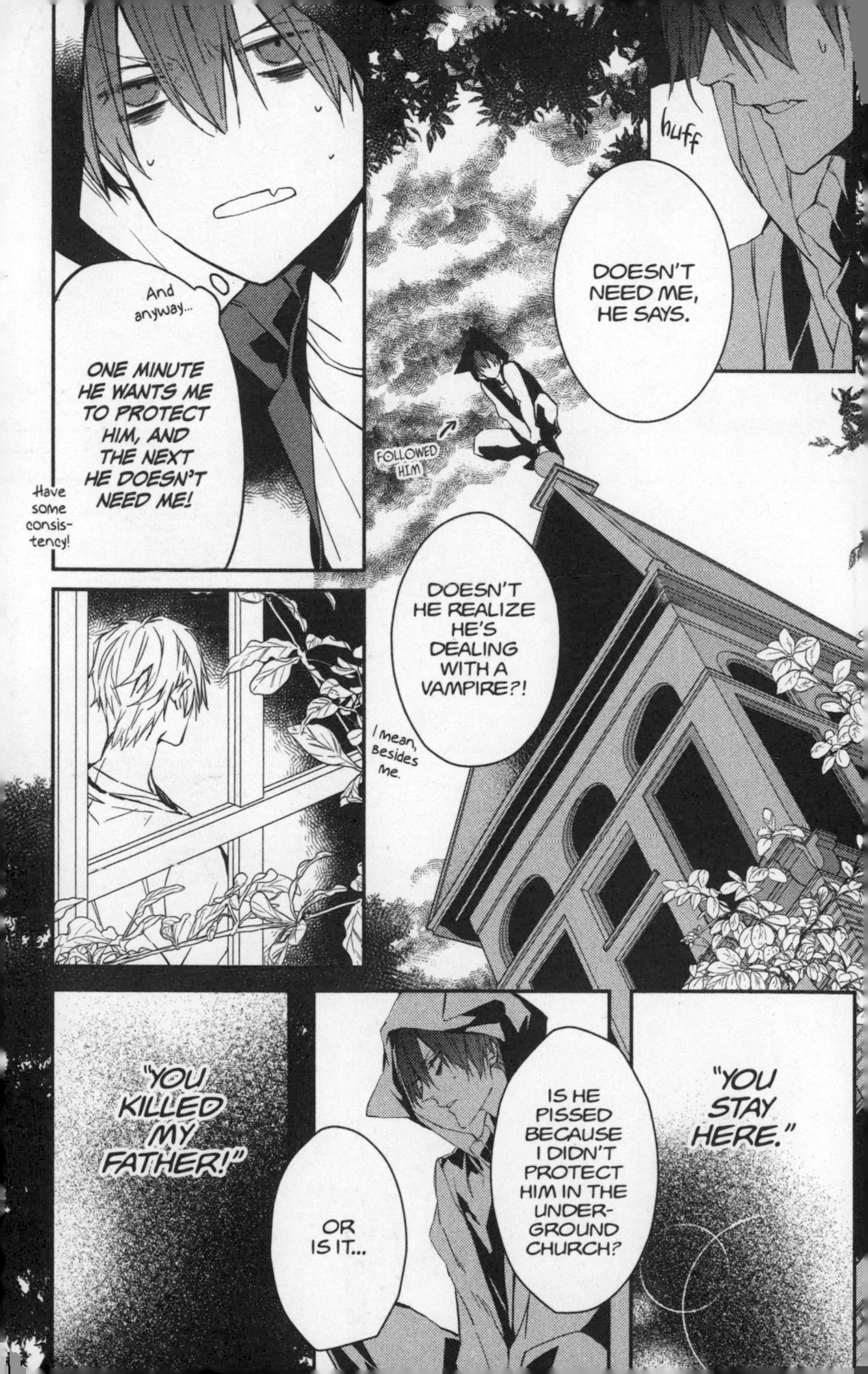
huff
DOESN'T NEED ME, HE SAYS.
FOLLOWED HIM
And anyway...
ONE MINUTE HE WANTS ME TO PROTECT HIM, AND THE NEXT HE DOESN'T NEED ME!
Have some consis-tency!
DOESN'T HE REALIZE HE'S DEALING WITH A VAMPIRE?!
I mean, Besides me.
"YOU STAY HERE."
IS HE PISSED BECAUSE I DIDN'T PROTECT HIM IN THE UNDER-GROUND CHURCH?
OR IS IT...
"YOU KILLED MY FATHER!"

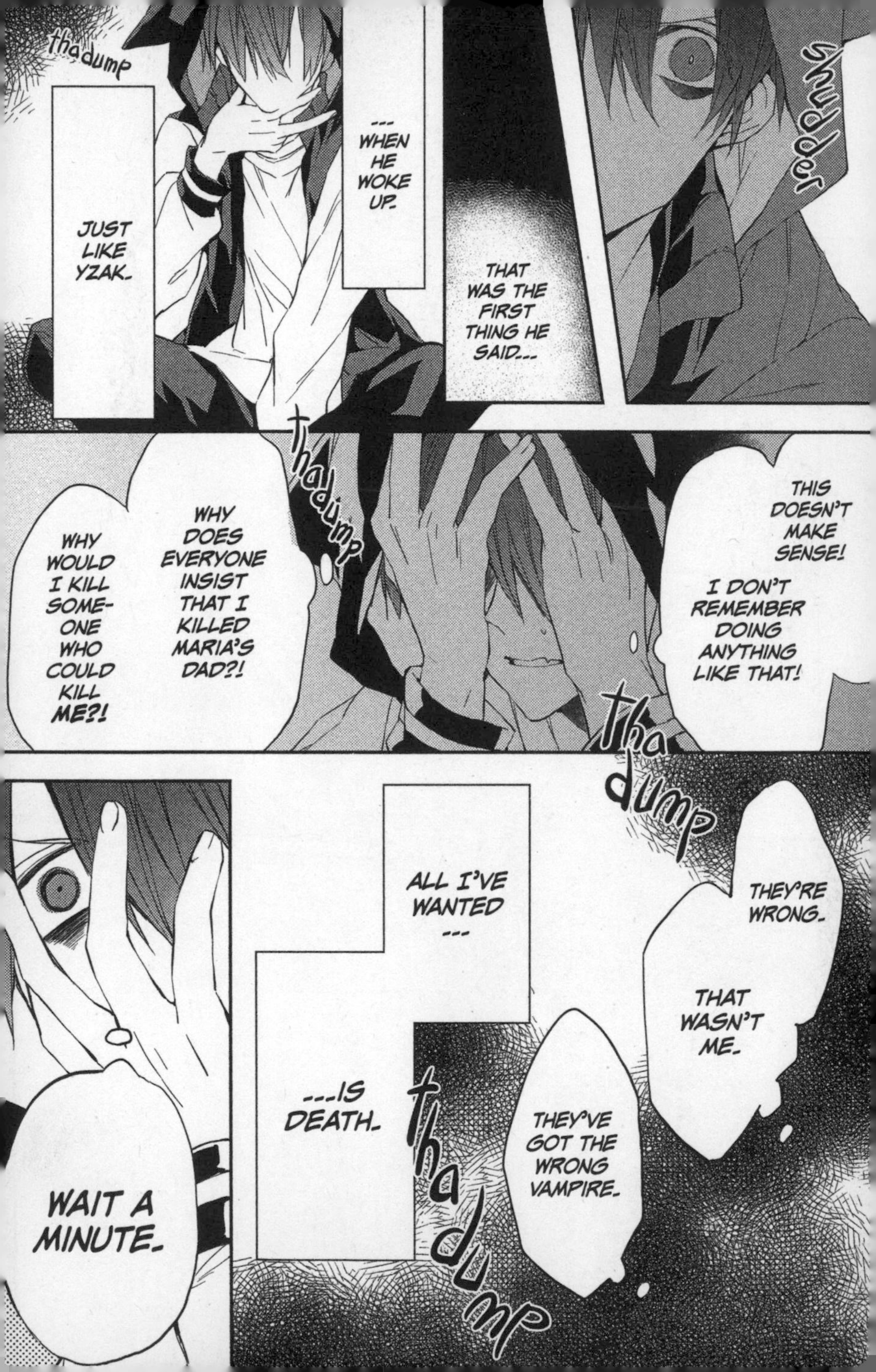
shudder
THAT WAS THE FIRST THING HE SAID...
...WHEN HE WOKE UP.
JUST LIKE YZAK.
thadump
THIS DOESN'T MAKE SENSE!
I DON'T REMEMBER DOING ANYTHING LIKE THAT!
thadump
thadump
WHY DOES EVERYONE INSIST THAT I KILLED MARIA'S DAD?!
WHY WOULD I KILL SOMEONE WHO COULD KILL ME?!
thadump
THEY'RE WRONG.
THAT WASN'T ME.
THEY'VE GOT THE WRONG VAMPIRE.
thadump
ALL I'VE WANTED ...
...IS DEATH.
WAIT A MINUTE.

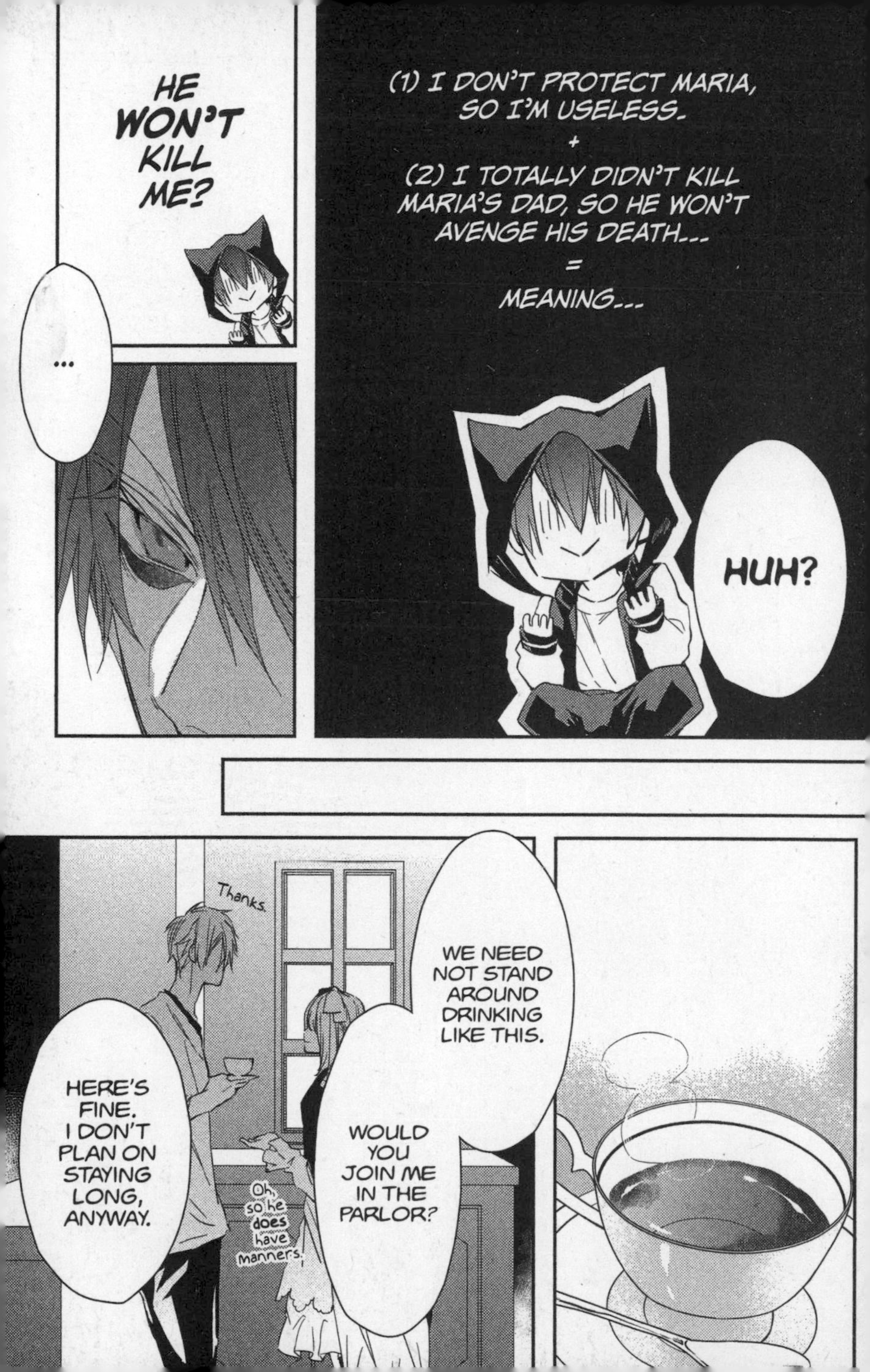
(1) I DON'T PROTECT MARIA, SO I'M USELESS.
+
(2) I TOTALLY DIDN'T KILL MARIA'S DAD, SO HE WON'T AVENGE HIS DEATH...
=
MEANING...
HUH?
HE WON'T KILL ME?
...
WE NEED NOT STAND AROUND DRINKING LIKE THIS.
WOULD YOU JOIN ME IN THE PARLOR?
Thanks.
HERE'S FINE. I DON'T PLAN ON STAYING LONG, ANYWAY.
Oh, so he does have manners.

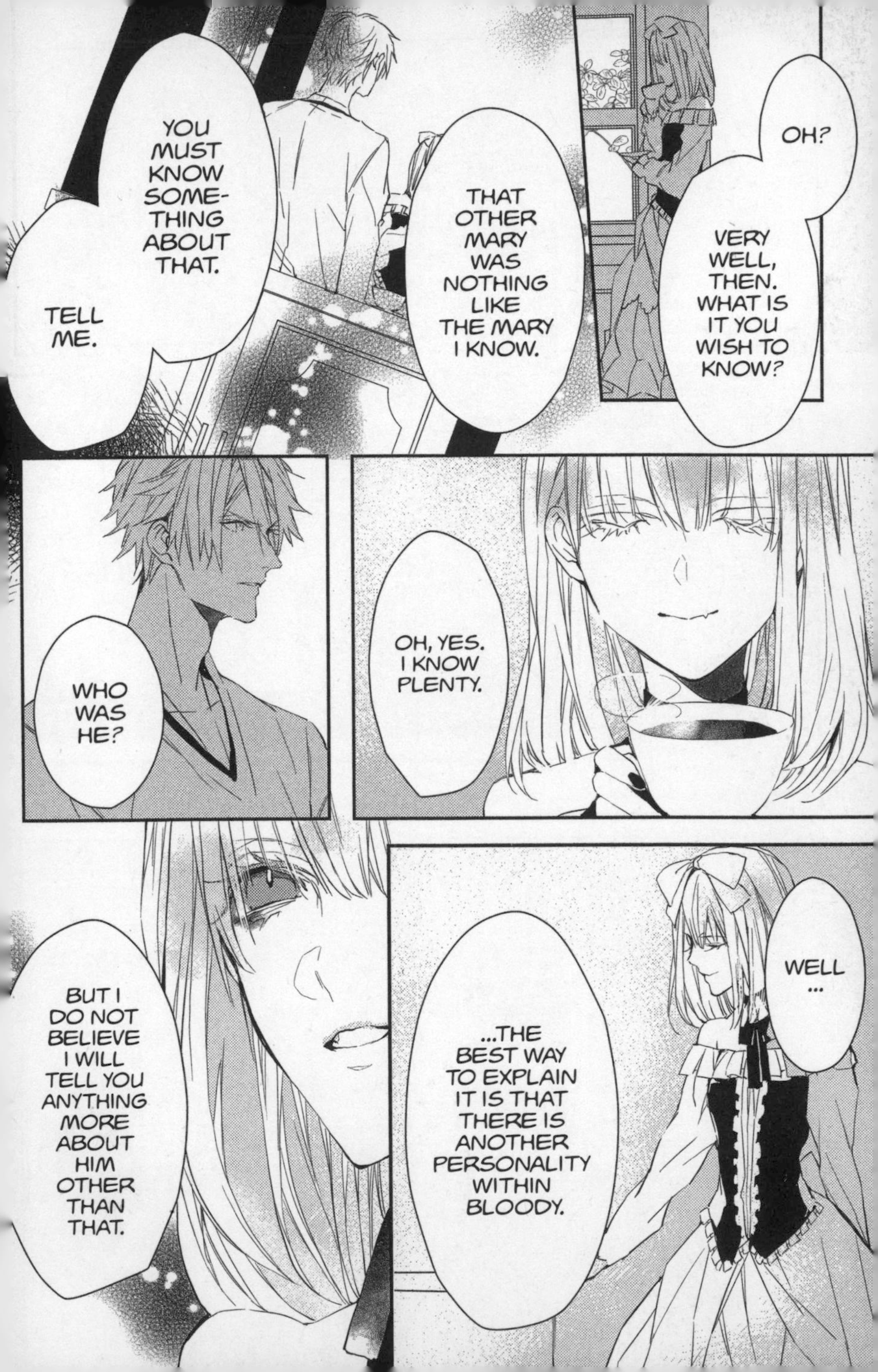
OH?
VERY WELL, THEN. WHAT IS IT YOU WISH TO KNOW?
THAT OTHER MARY WAS NOTHING LIKE THE MARY I KNOW.
YOU MUST KNOW SOME-THING ABOUT THAT.
TELL ME.
OH, YES. I KNOW PLENTY.
WHO WAS HE?
WELL ...
...THE BEST WAY TO EXPLAIN IT IS THAT THERE IS ANOTHER PERSONALITY WITHIN BLOODY.
BUT I DO NOT BELIEVE I WILL TELL YOU ANYTHING MORE ABOUT HIM OTHER THAN THAT.

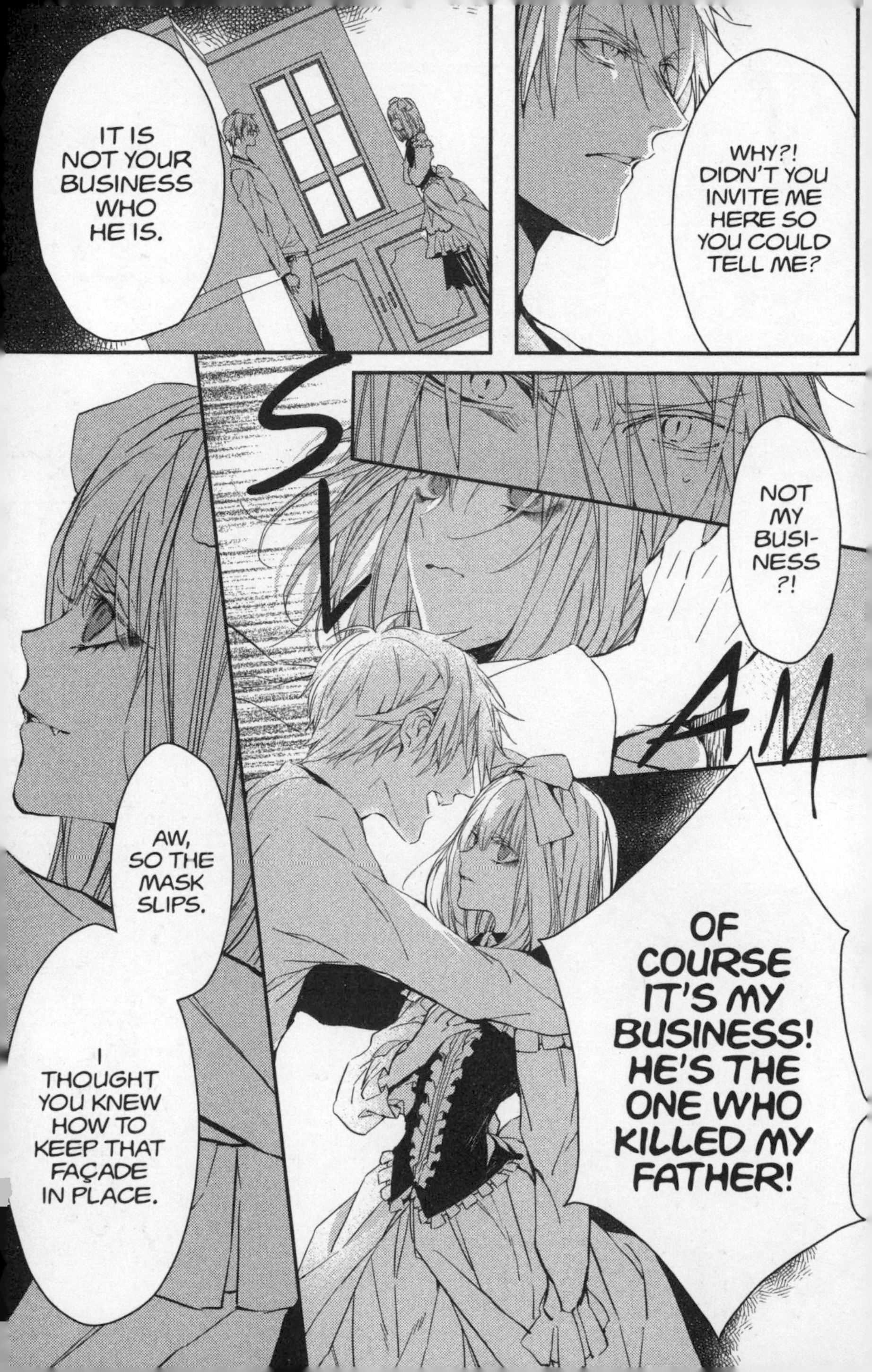
WHY?! DIDN'T YOU INVITE ME HERE SO YOU COULD TELL ME?
IT IS NOT YOUR BUSINESS WHO HE IS.
NOT MY BUSINESS?!
SLAM
OF COURSE IT'S MY BUSINESS! HE'S THE ONE WHO KILLED MY FATHER!
AW, SO THE MASK SLIPS.
I THOUGHT YOU KNEW HOW TO KEEP THAT FAÇADE IN PLACE.

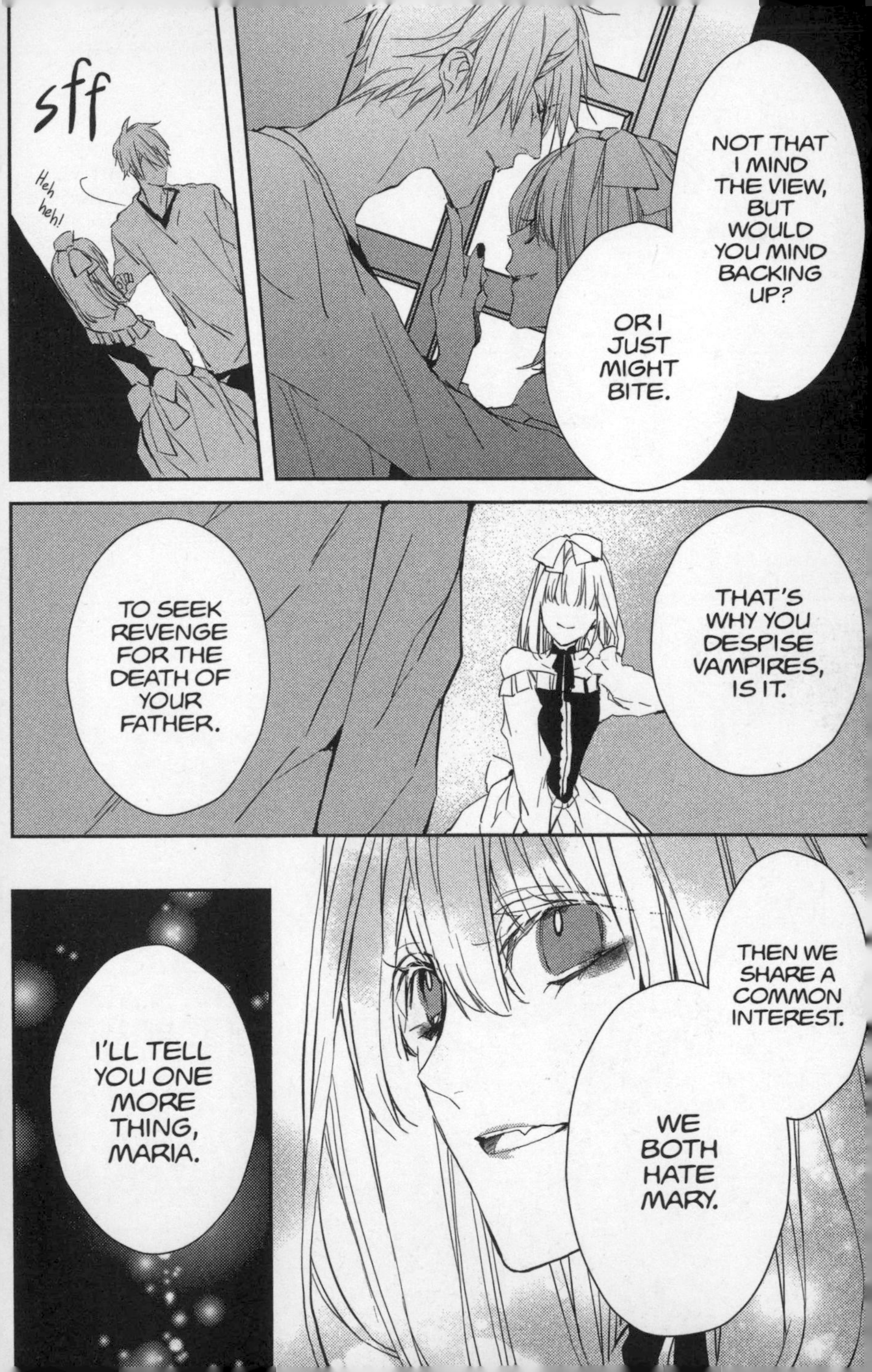
NOT THAT I MIND THE VIEW, BUT WOULD YOU MIND BACKING UP?
OR I JUST MIGHT BITE.
sff
Heh heh!
THAT'S WHY YOU DESPISE VAMPIRES, IS IT.
TO SEEK REVENGE FOR THE DEATH OF YOUR FATHER.
THEN WE SHARE A COMMON INTEREST.
WE BOTH HATE MARY.
I'LL TELL YOU ONE MORE THING, MARIA.

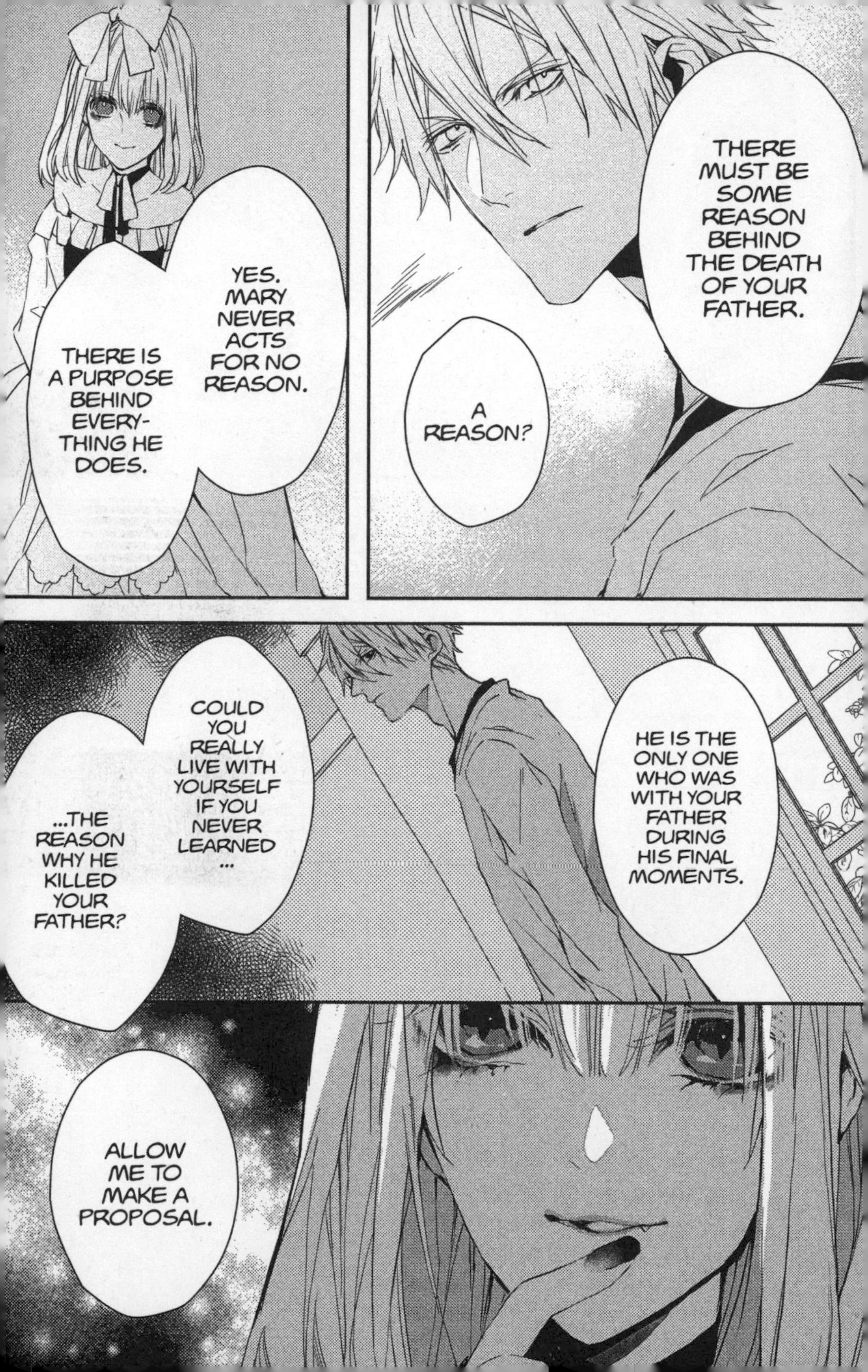
THERE MUST BE SOME REASON BEHIND THE DEATH OF YOUR FATHER.
A REASON?
YES. MARY NEVER ACTS FOR NO REASON.
THERE IS A PURPOSE BEHIND EVERY-THING HE DOES.
HE IS THE ONLY ONE WHO WAS WITH YOUR FATHER DURING HIS FINAL MOMENTS.
COULD YOU REALLY LIVE WITH YOURSELF IF YOU NEVER LEARNED...
...THE REASON WHY HE KILLED YOUR FATHER?
ALLOW ME TO MAKE A PROPOSAL.

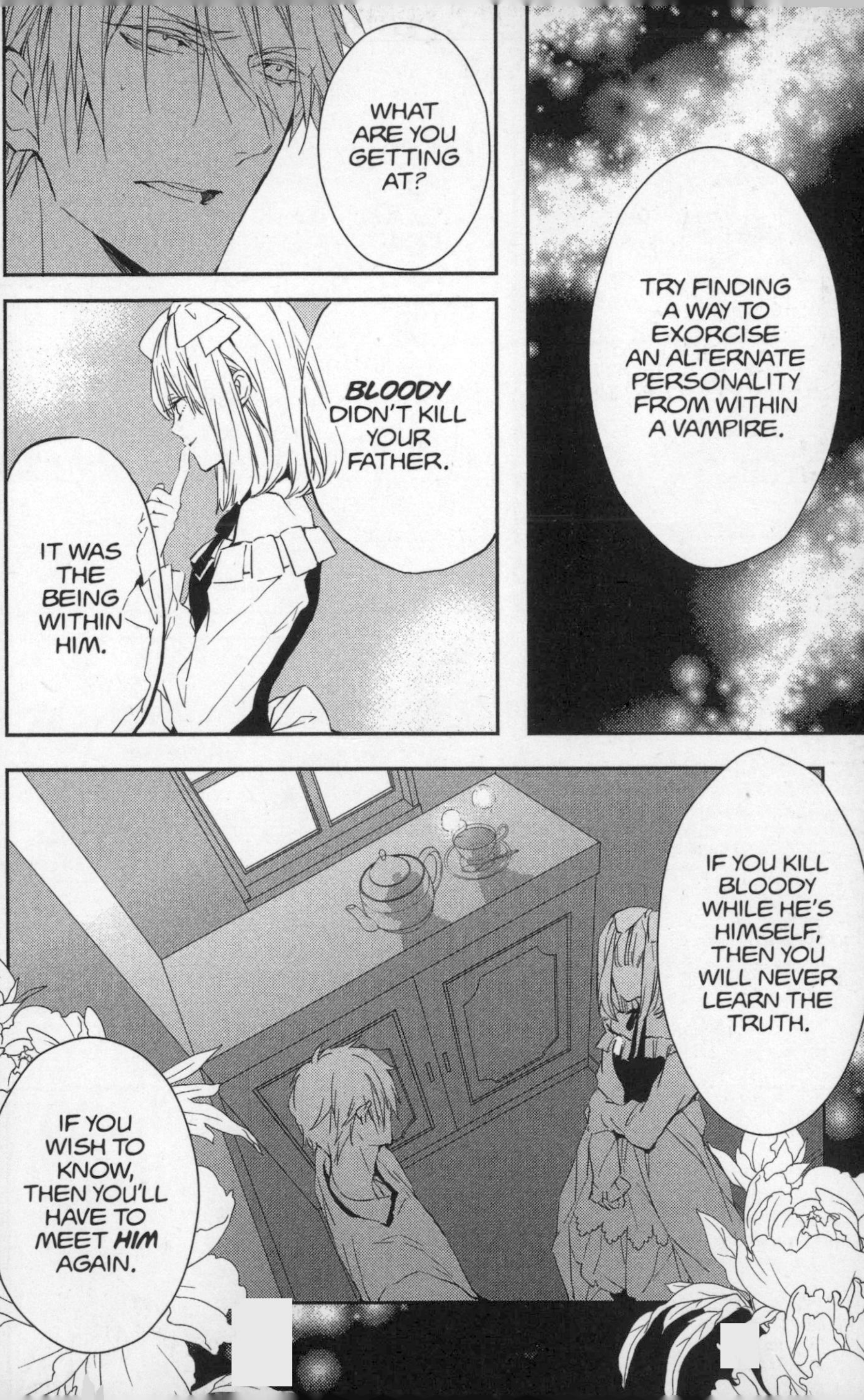
TRY FINDING A WAY TO EXORCISE AN ALTERNATE PERSONALITY FROM WITHIN A VAMPIRE.
WHAT ARE YOU GETTING AT?
BLOODY DIDN'T KILL YOUR FATHER.
IT WAS THE BEING WITHIN HIM.
IF YOU KILL BLOODY WHILE HE'S HIMSELF, THEN YOU WILL NEVER LEARN THE TRUTH.
IF YOU WISH TO KNOW, THEN YOU'LL HAVE TO MEET **HIM** AGAIN.

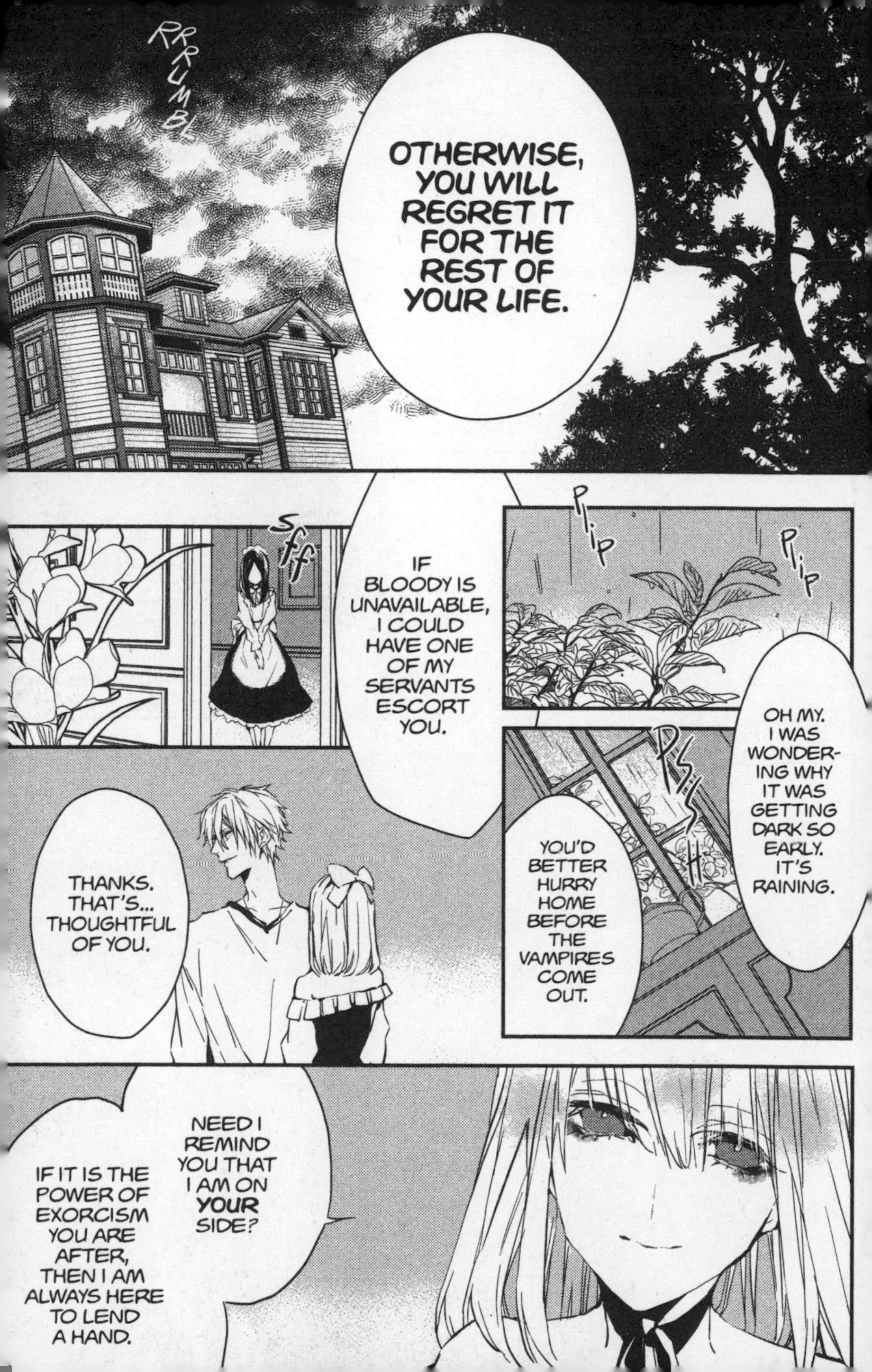
RRRUMBL
OTHERWISE, YOU WILL REGRET IT FOR THE REST OF YOUR LIFE.
Plip
Plip
OH MY. I WAS WONDERING WHY IT WAS GETTING DARK SO EARLY. IT'S RAINING.
PSSH
YOU'D BETTER HURRY HOME BEFORE THE VAMPIRES COME OUT.
IF BLOODY IS UNAVAILABLE, I COULD HAVE ONE OF MY SERVANTS ESCORT YOU.
Sff
THANKS. THAT'S... THOUGHTFUL OF YOU.
NEED I REMIND YOU THAT I AM ON **YOUR** SIDE?
IF IT IS THE POWER OF EXORCISM YOU ARE AFTER, THEN I AM ALWAYS HERE TO LEND A HAND.

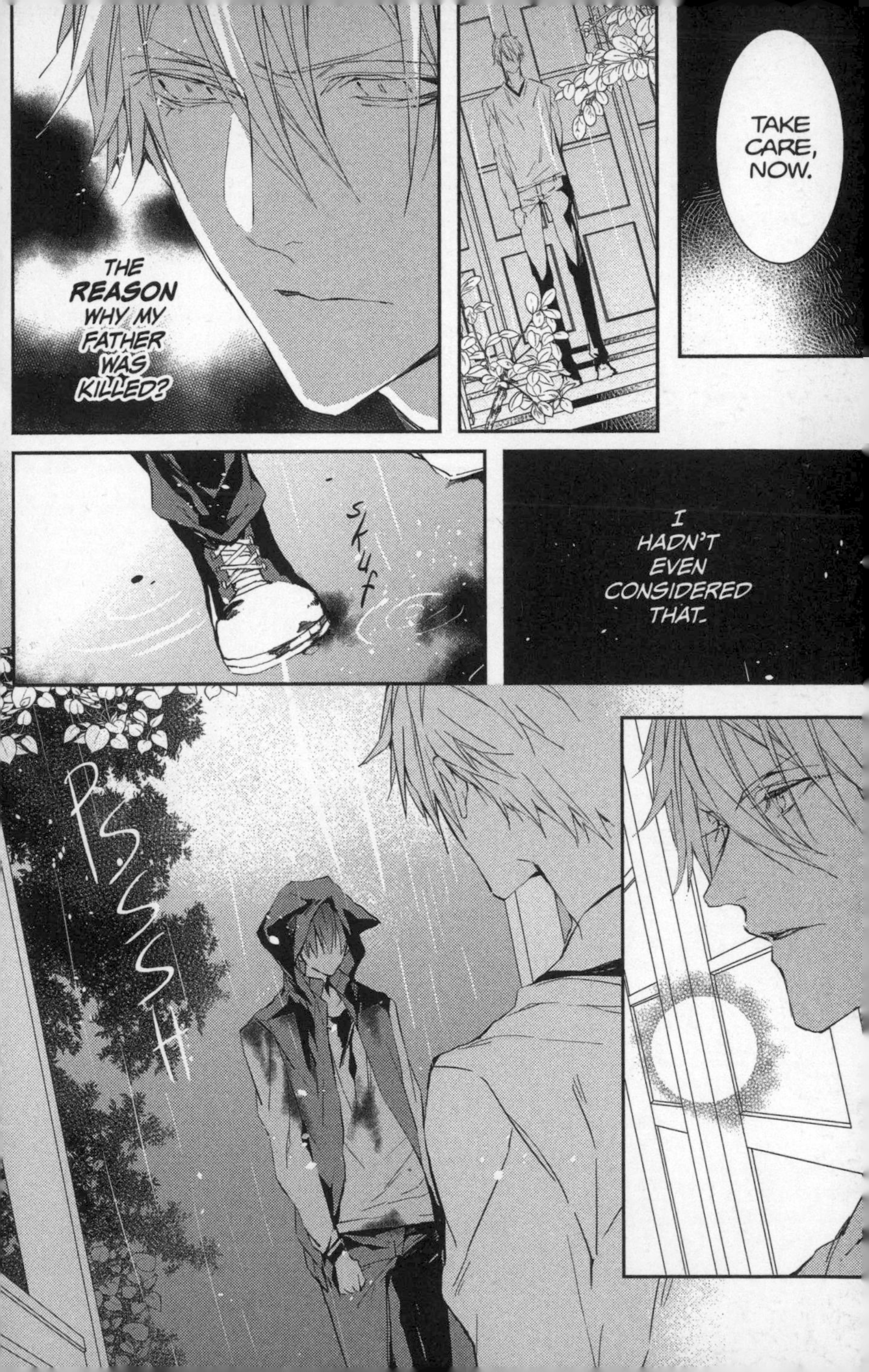
TAKE CARE, NOW.
THE REASON WHY MY FATHER WAS KILLED?
I HADN'T EVEN CONSIDERED THAT.
SKUF
PSSSH

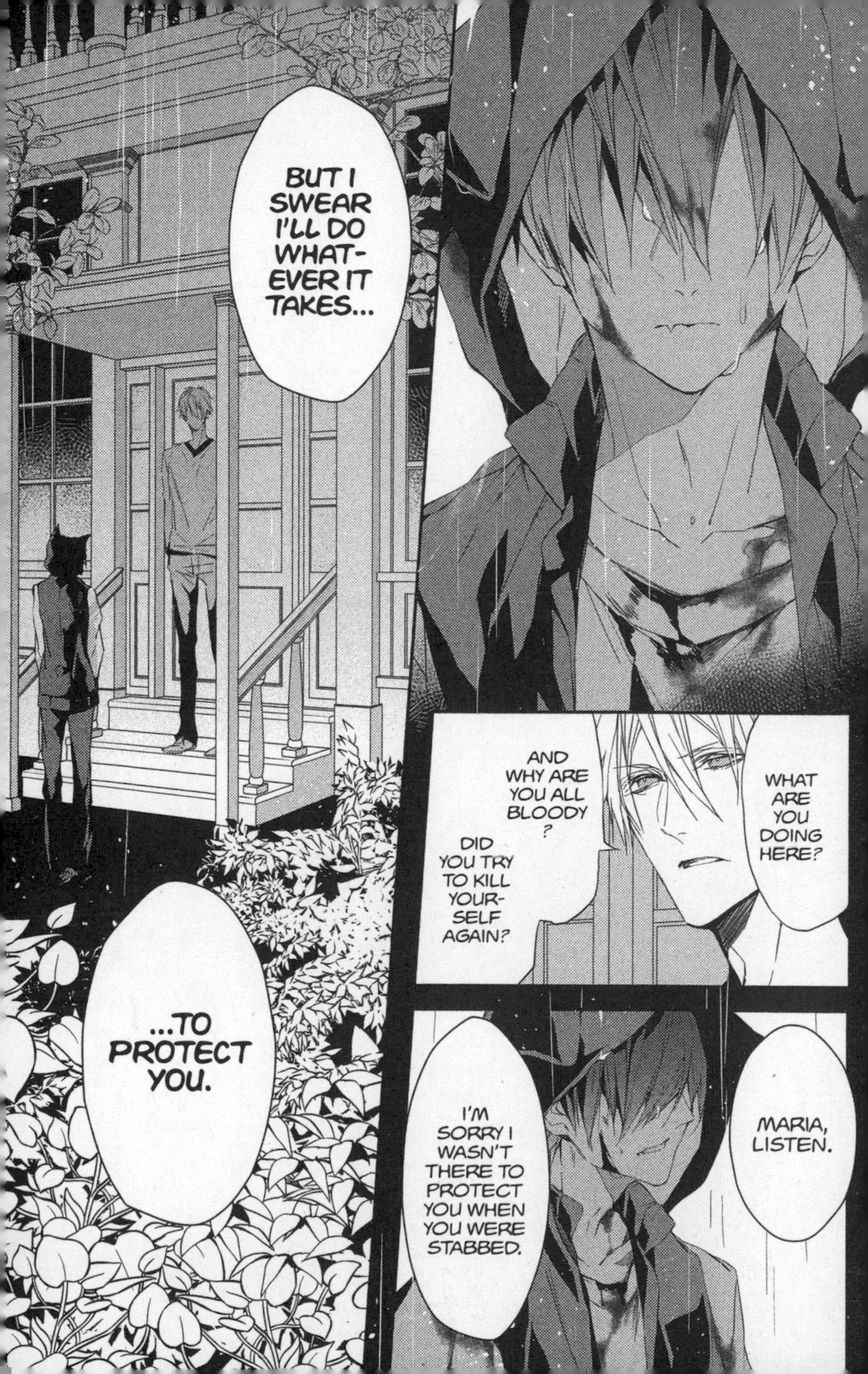
WHAT ARE YOU DOING HERE?
AND WHY ARE YOU ALL BLOODY?
DID YOU TRY TO KILL YOUR-SELF AGAIN?
MARIA, LISTEN.
I'M SORRY I WASN'T THERE TO PROTECT YOU WHEN YOU WERE STABBED.
BUT I SWEAR I'LL DO WHAT-EVER IT TAKES...
...TO PROTECT YOU.

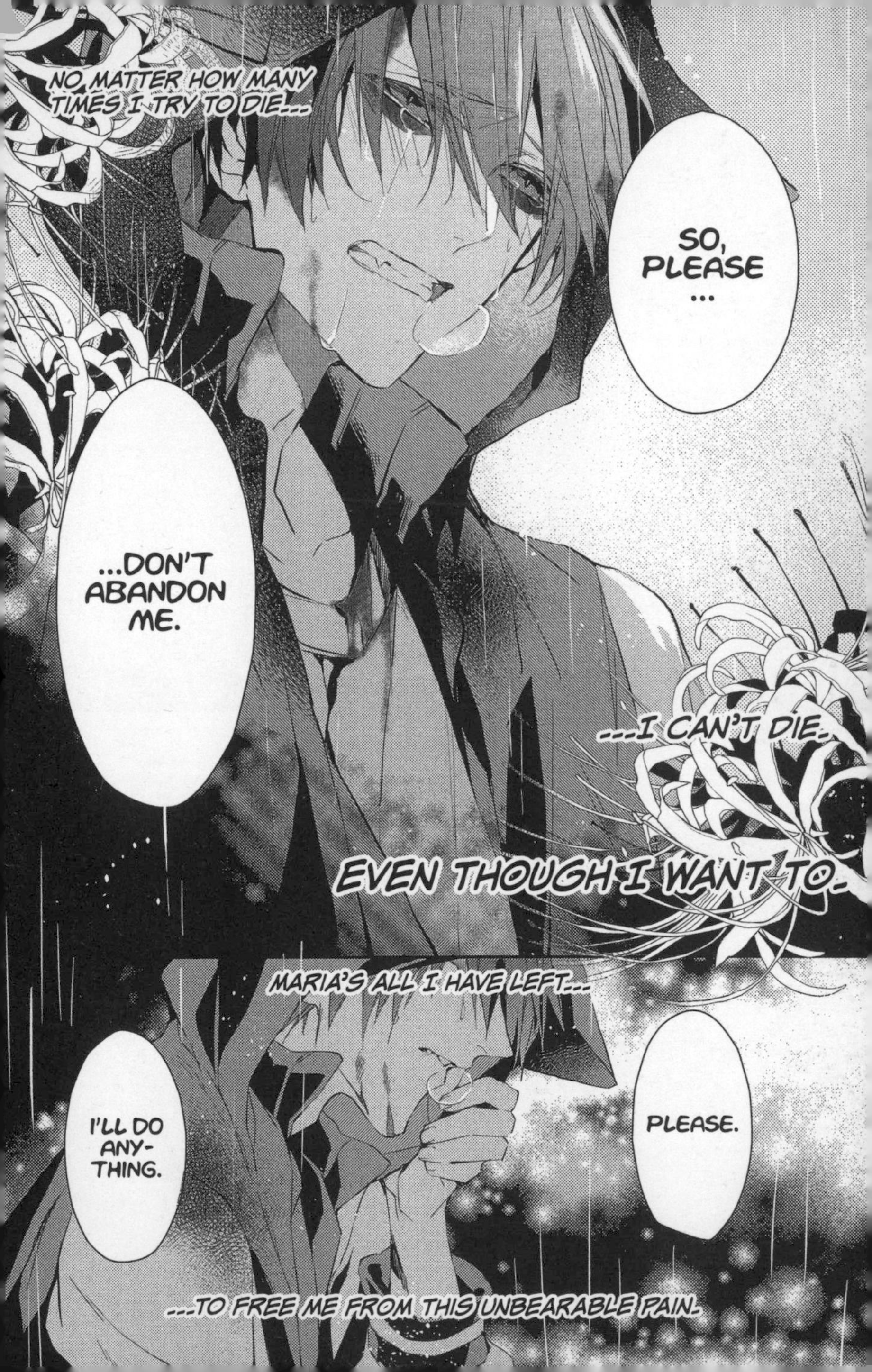
SO, PLEASE ...
NO MATTER HOW MANY TIMES I TRY TO DIE...
...DON'T ABANDON ME.
...I CAN'T DIE.
EVEN THOUGH I WANT TO.
MARIA'S ALL I HAVE LEFT...
PLEASE.
I'LL DO ANY-THING.
...TO FREE ME FROM THIS UNBEARABLE PAIN.

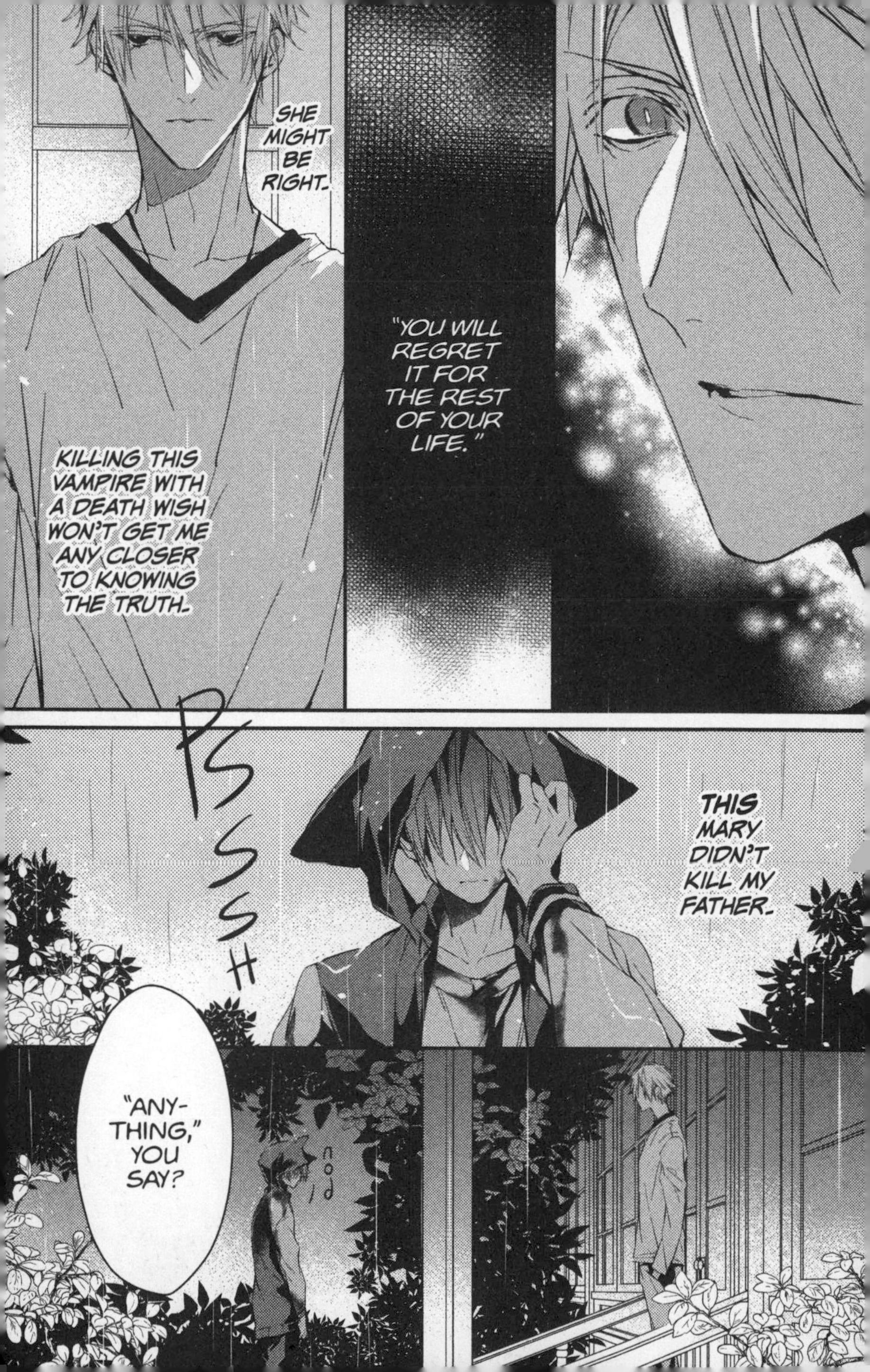
"YOU WILL REGRET IT FOR THE REST OF YOUR LIFE."
SHE MIGHT BE RIGHT.
KILLING THIS VAMPIRE WITH A DEATH WISH WON'T GET ME ANY CLOSER TO KNOWING THE TRUTH.
THIS MARY DIDN'T KILL MY FATHER.
PSSSH
nod
"ANY-THING," YOU SAY?

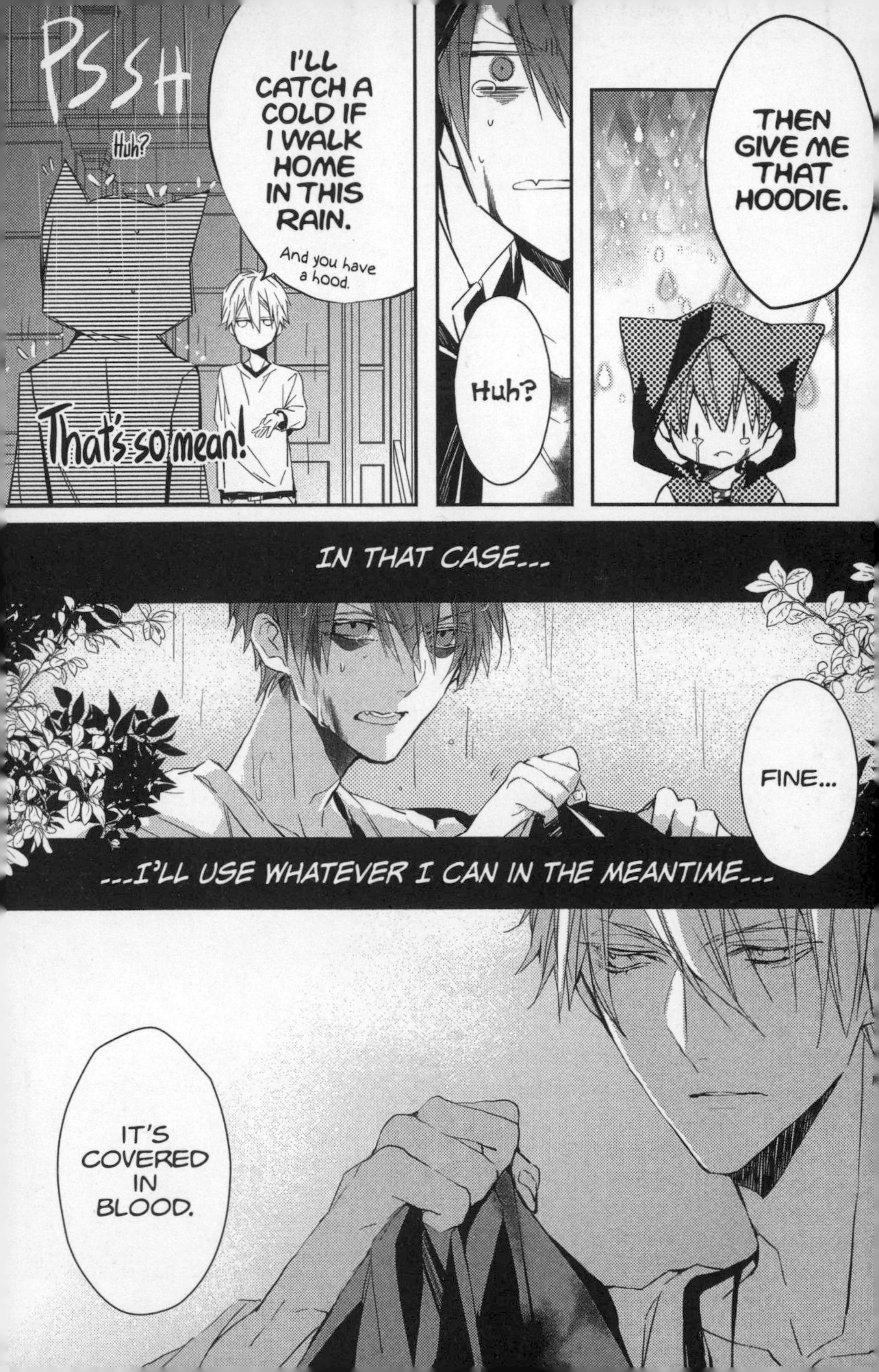
THEN GIVE ME THAT HOODIE.
Huh?
PSSH
Huh?
I'LL CATCH A COLD IF I WALK HOME IN THIS RAIN.
And you have a hood.
That's so mean!
IN THAT CASE...
FINE...
...I'LL USE WHATEVER I CAN IN THE MEANTIME...
IT'S COVERED IN BLOOD.

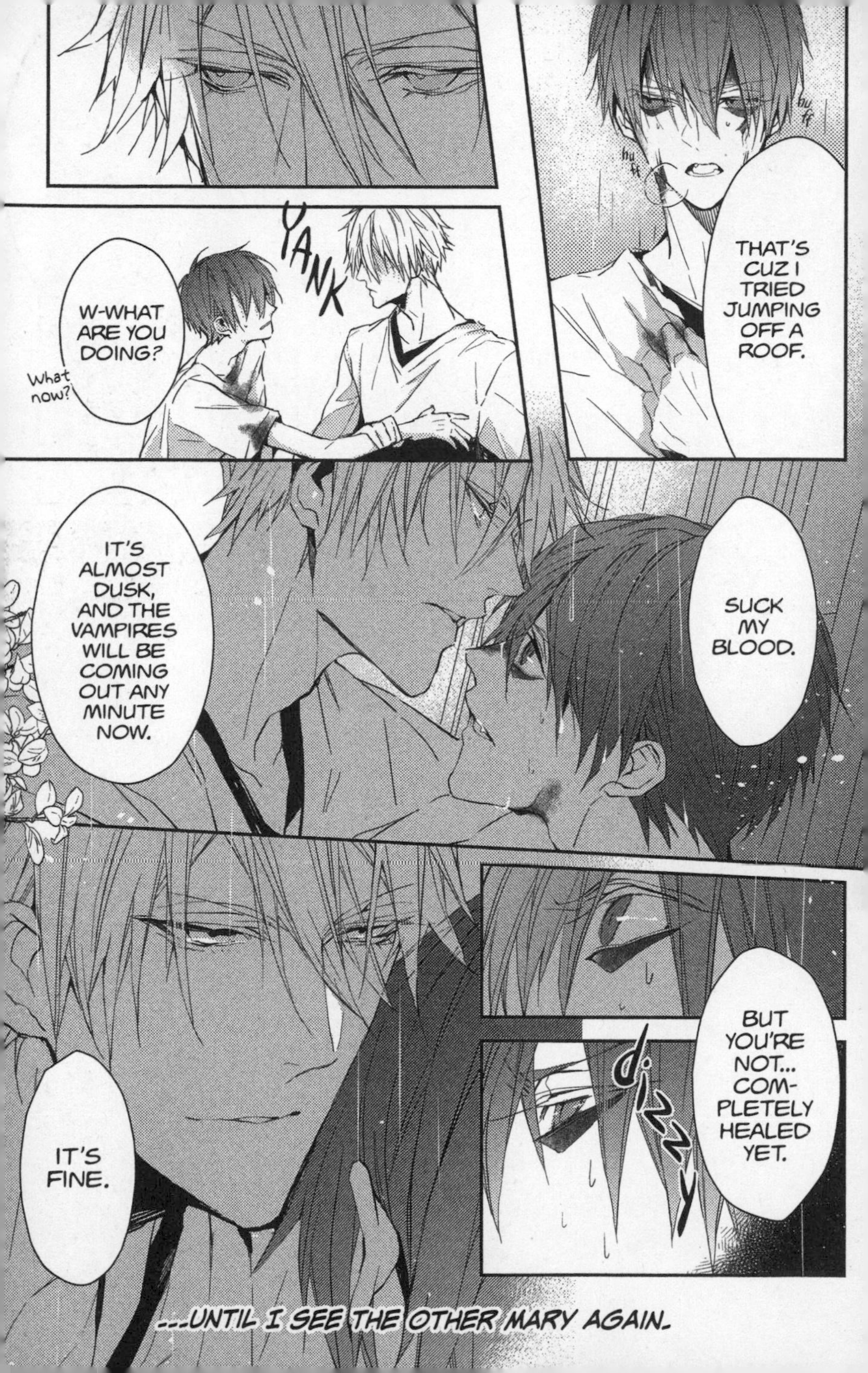
huff
huff
THAT'S CUZ I TRIED JUMPING OFF A ROOF.
YANK
W-WHAT ARE YOU DOING?
What now?
SUCK MY BLOOD.
IT'S ALMOST DUSK, AND THE VAMPIRES WILL BE COMING OUT ANY MINUTE NOW.
BUT YOU'RE NOT... COM-PLETELY HEALED YET.
dizzy
IT'S FINE.
...UNTIL I SEE THE OTHER MARY AGAIN.

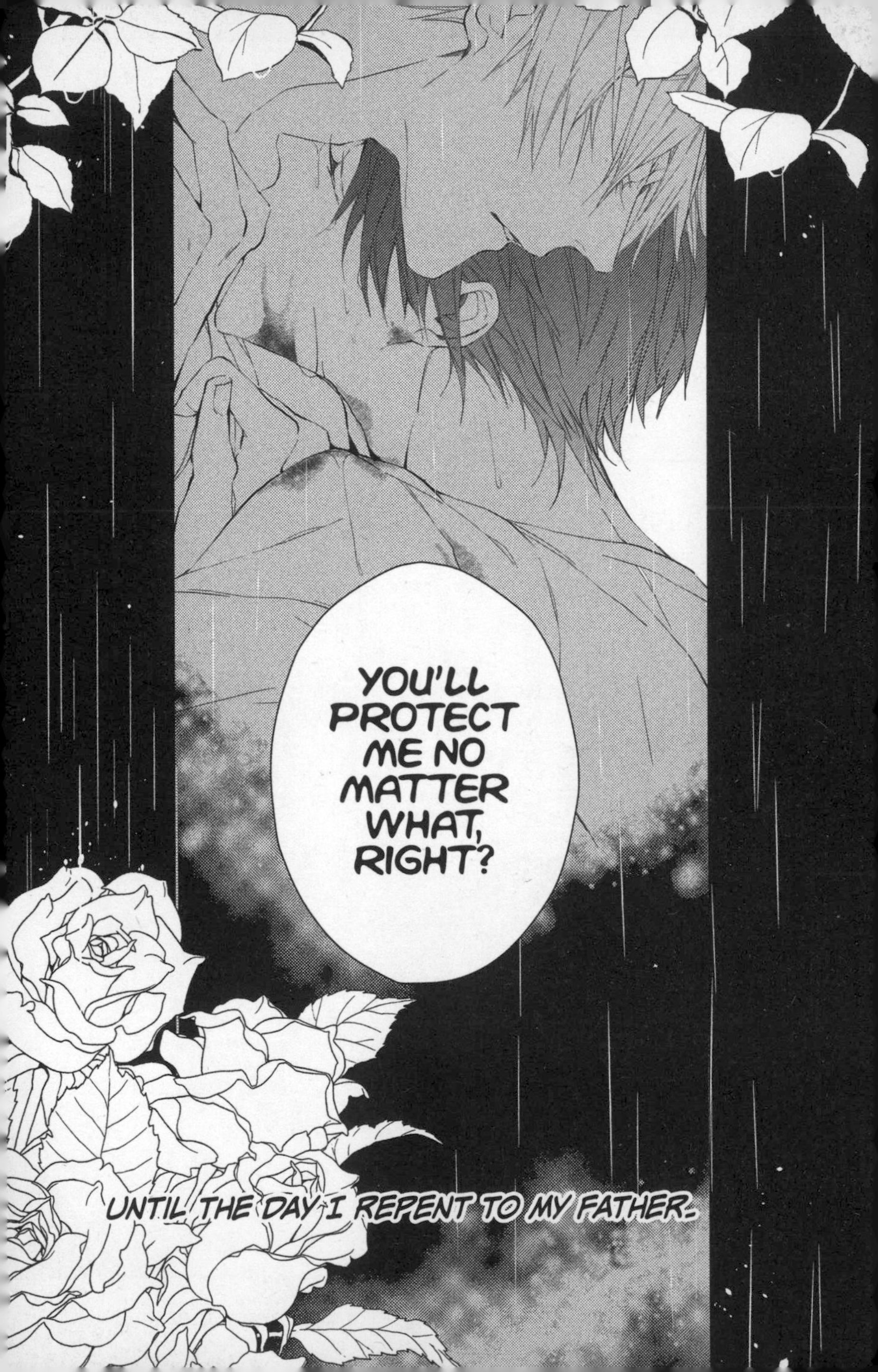
YOU'LL PROTECT ME NO MATTER WHAT, RIGHT?
UNTIL THE DAY I REPENT TO MY FATHER.

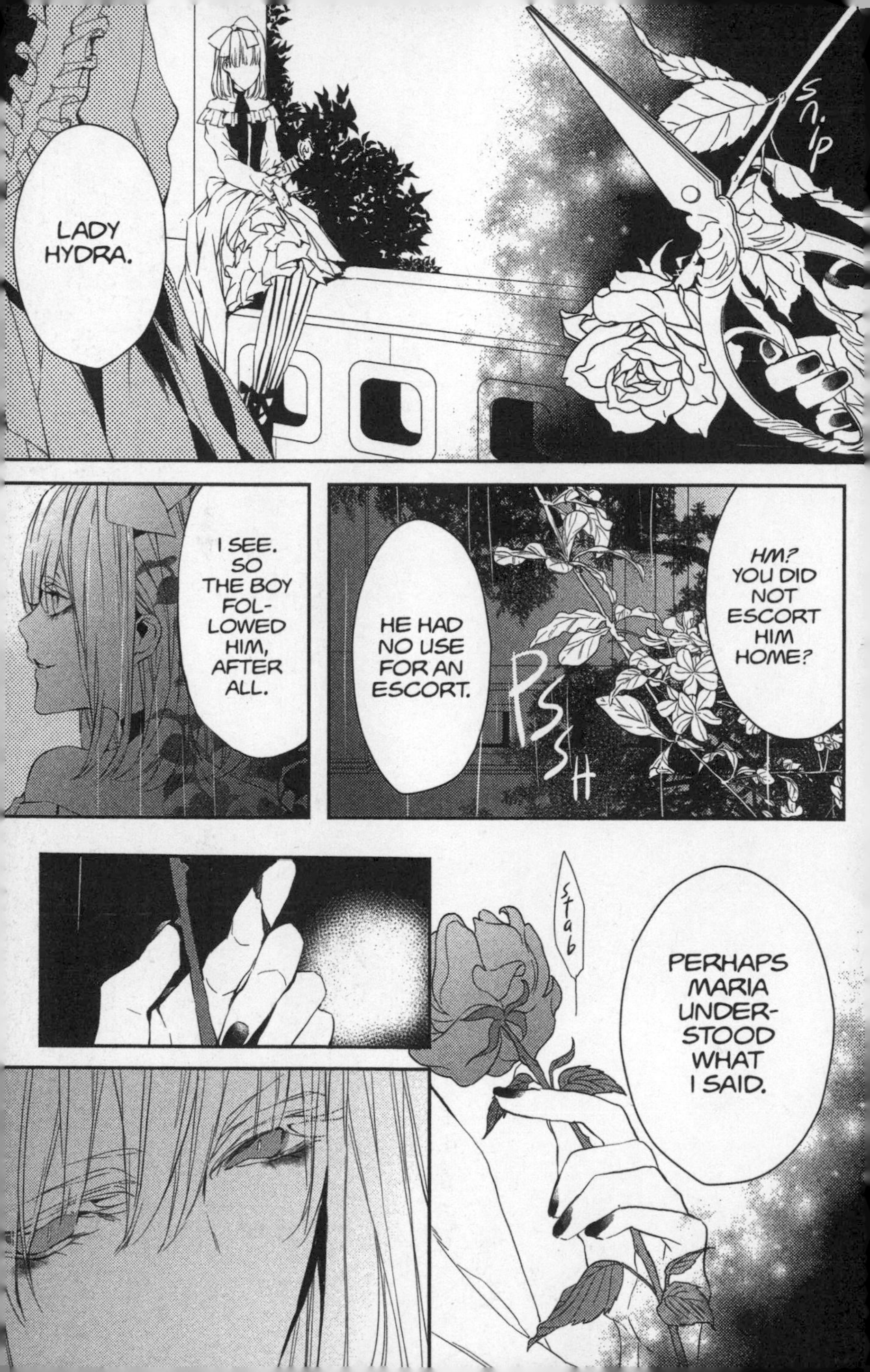
snip
LADY HYDRA.
HM? YOU DID NOT ESCORT HIM HOME?
PSSH
HE HAD NO USE FOR AN ESCORT.
I SEE. SO THE BOY FOL-LOWED HIM, AFTER ALL.
stab
PERHAPS MARIA UNDER-STOOD WHAT I SAID.

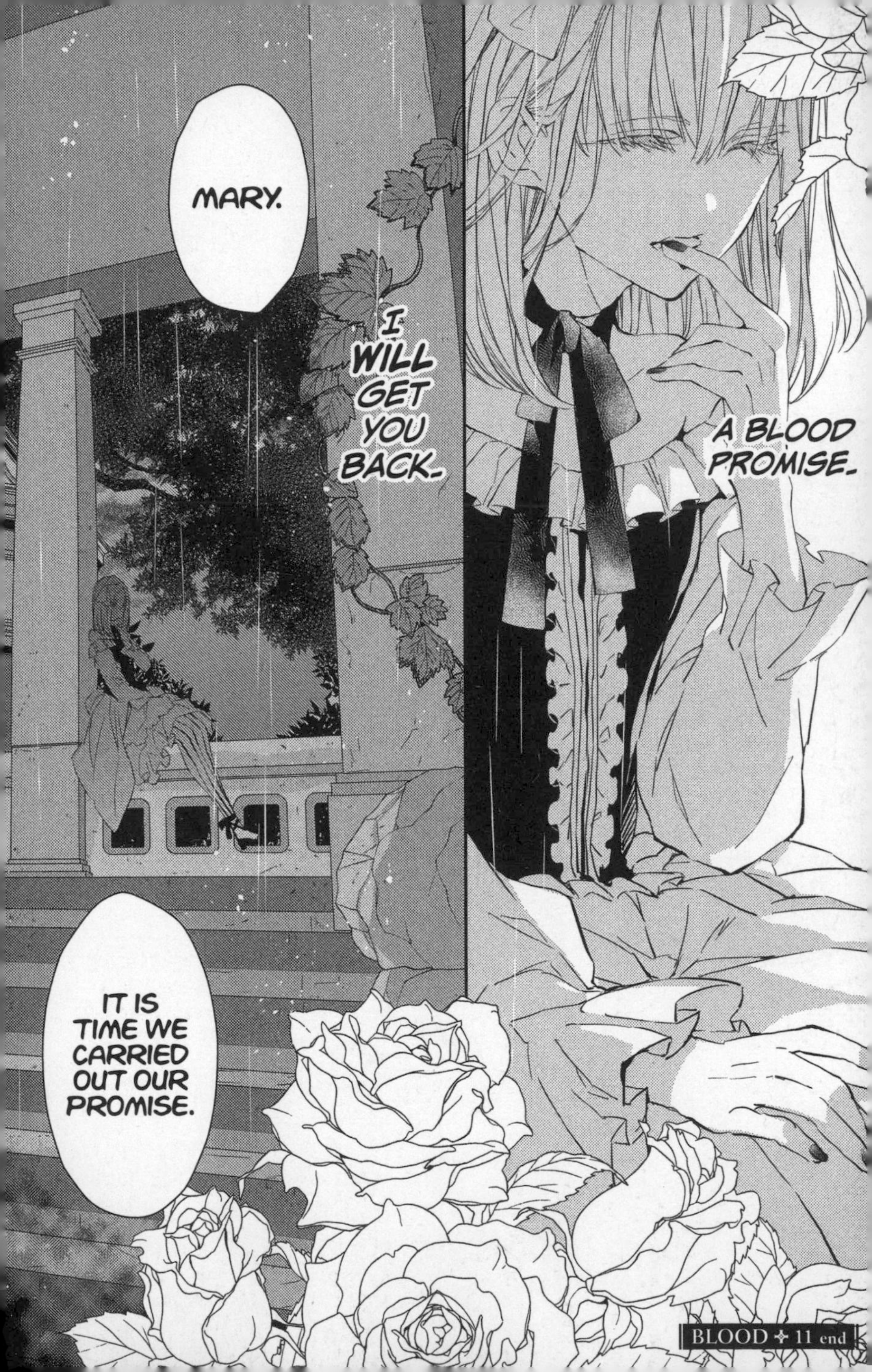
A BLOOD PROMISE...
MARY.
I WILL GET YOU BACK...
IT IS TIME WE CARRIED OUT OUR PROMISE.
BLOOD ✧ 11 end

Bloody†Mary

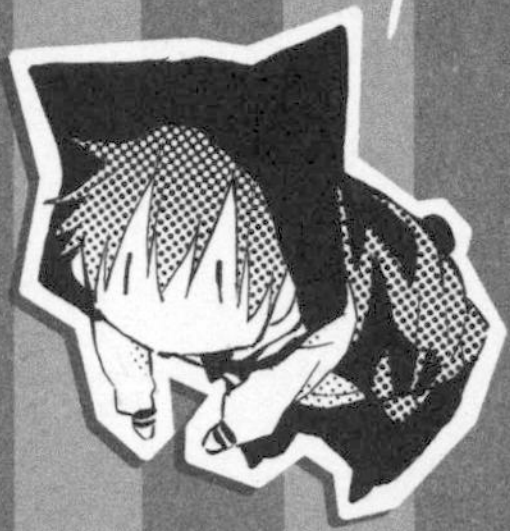

Bloody+Mary

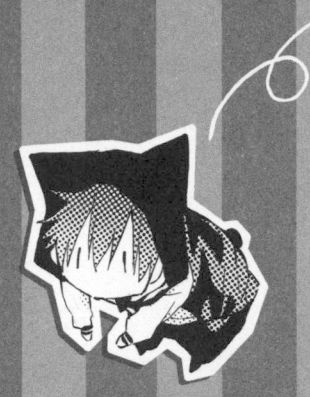

BLOOD ✧ 12 Premonition of a New Beginning

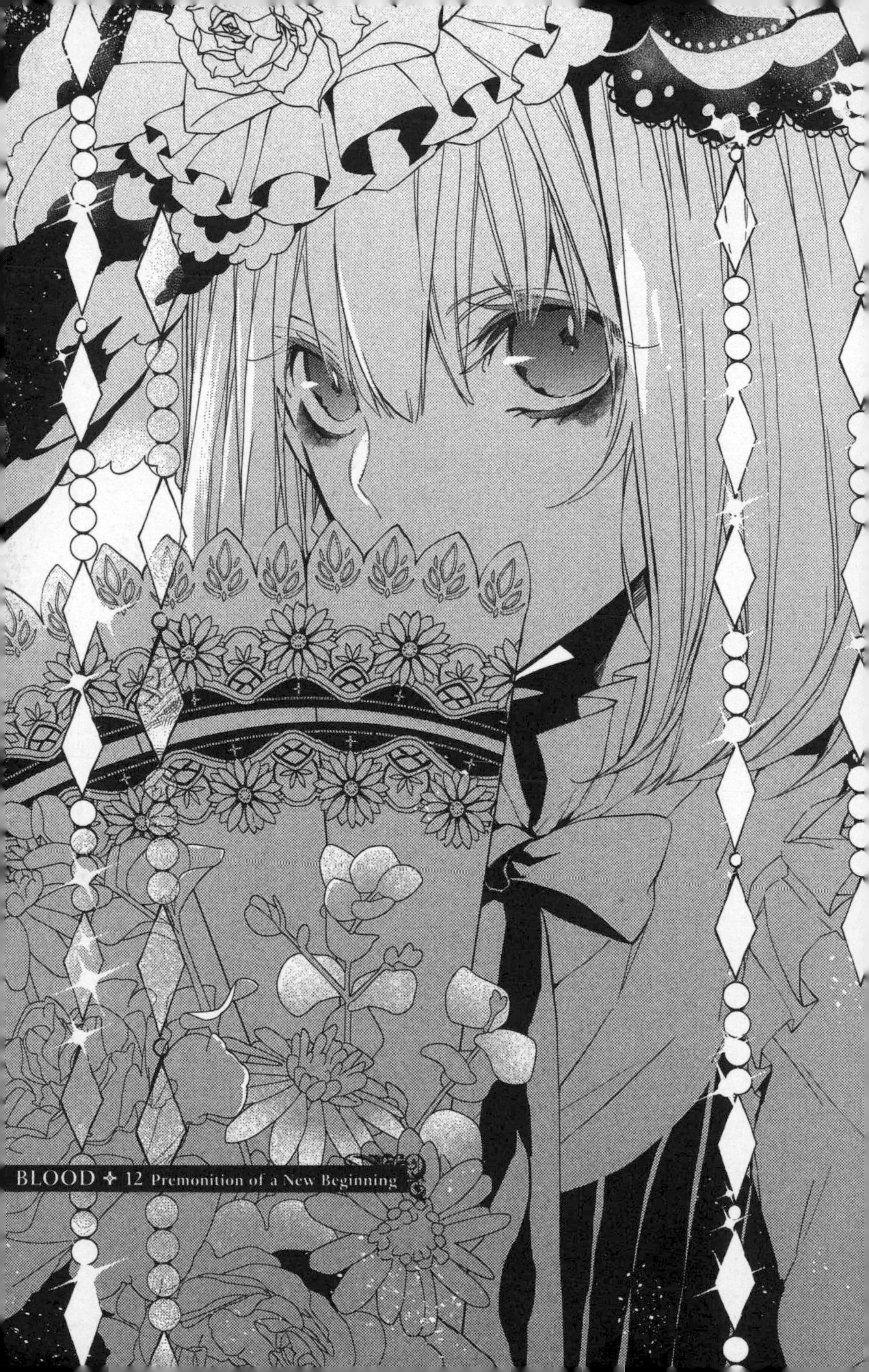

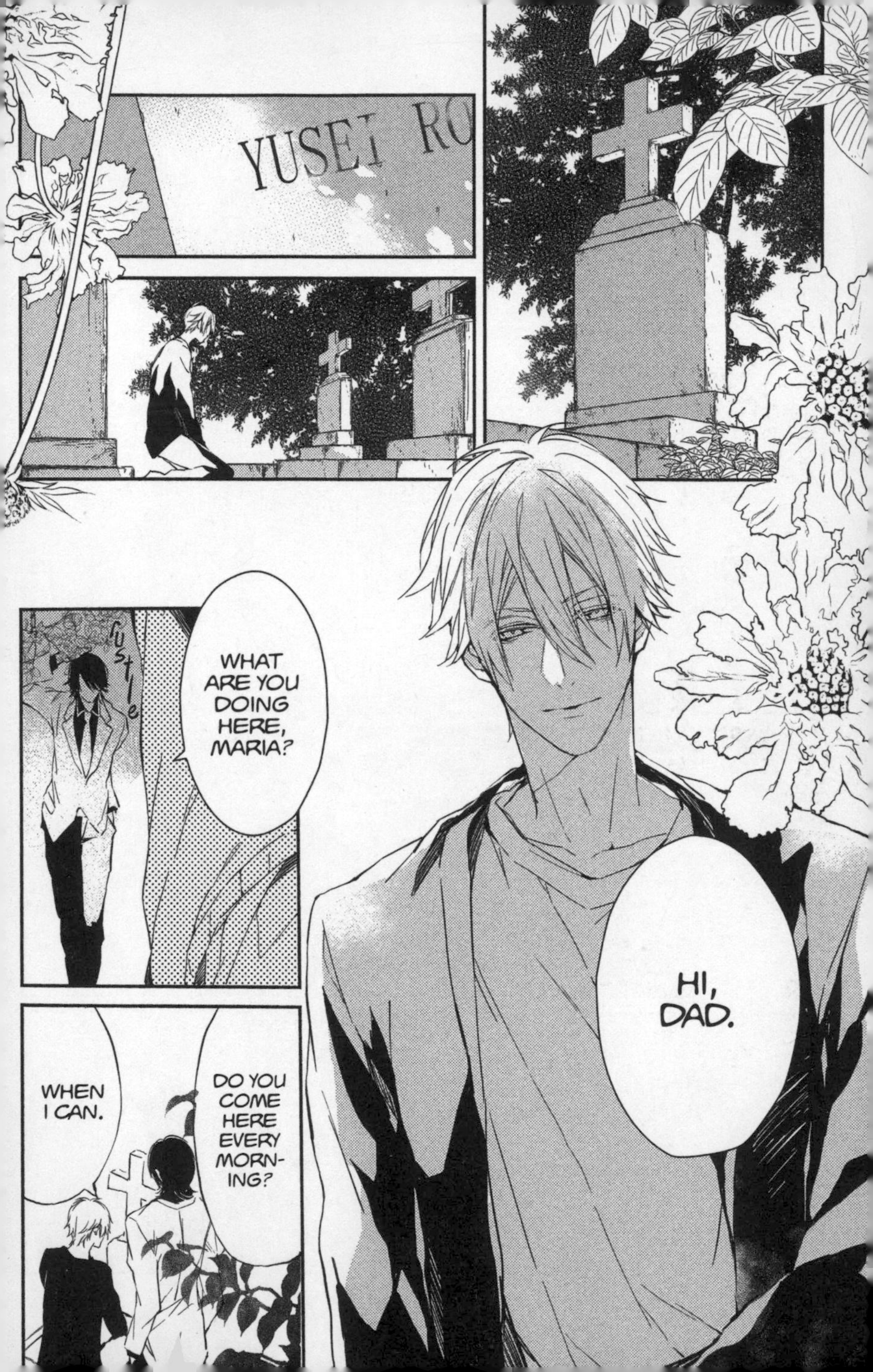
YUSEI RO
HI, DAD.
rustle
WHAT ARE YOU DOING HERE, MARIA?
DO YOU COME HERE EVERY MORN-ING?
WHEN I CAN.

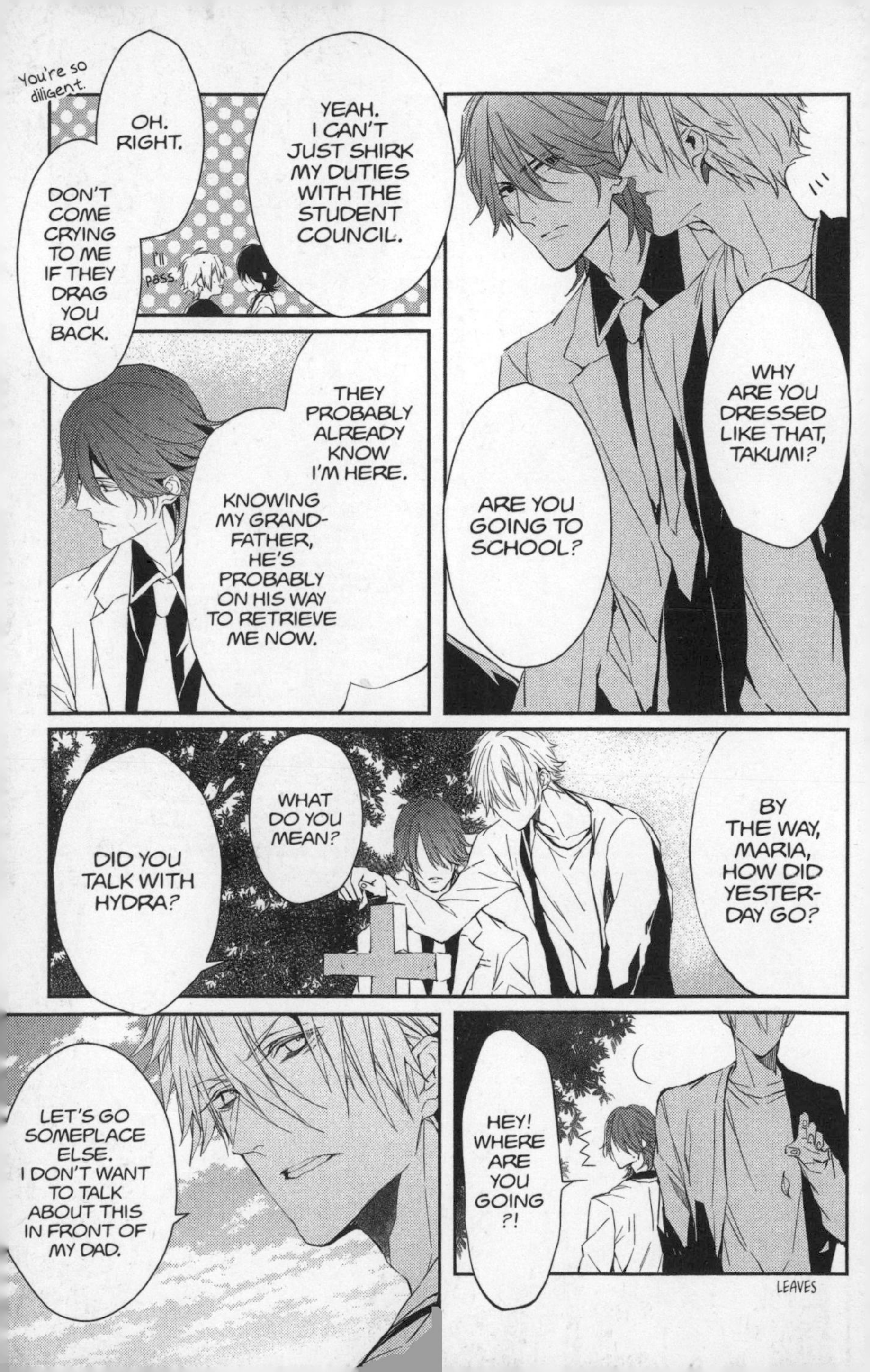
WHY ARE YOU DRESSED LIKE THAT, TAKUMI?
ARE YOU GOING TO SCHOOL?
YEAH. I CAN'T JUST SHIRK MY DUTIES WITH THE STUDENT COUNCIL.
OH. RIGHT.
DON'T COME CRYING TO ME IF THEY DRAG YOU BACK.
I'll pass.
You're so diligent.
THEY PROBABLY ALREADY KNOW I'M HERE.
KNOWING MY GRAND-FATHER, HE'S PROBABLY ON HIS WAY TO RETRIEVE ME NOW.
BY THE WAY, MARIA, HOW DID YESTER-DAY GO?
WHAT DO YOU MEAN?
DID YOU TALK WITH HYDRA?
HEY! WHERE ARE YOU GOING ?!
LEAVES
LET'S GO SOMEPLACE ELSE. I DON'T WANT TO TALK ABOUT THIS IN FRONT OF MY DAD.

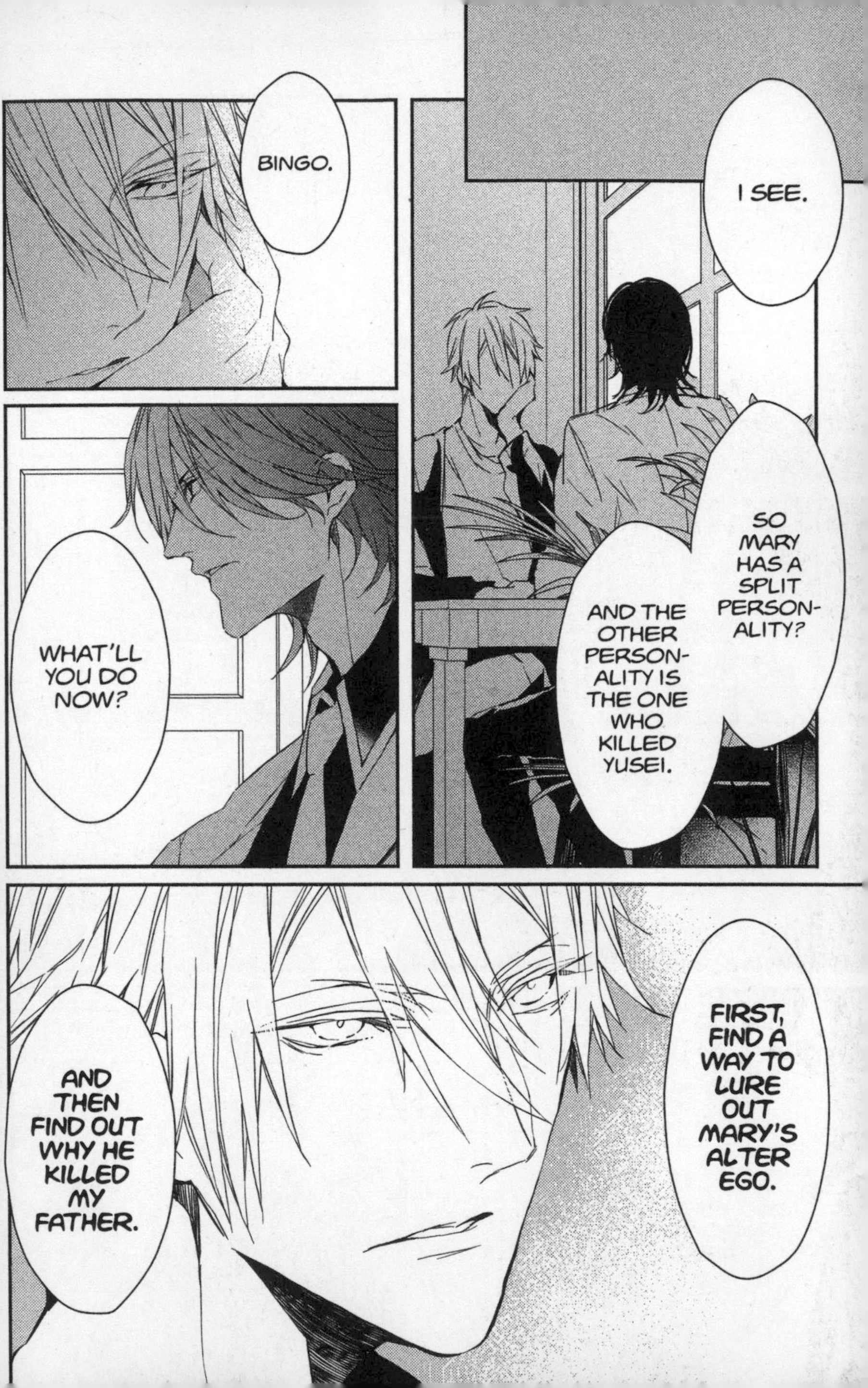
I SEE.
SO MARY HAS A SPLIT PERSON-ALITY?
AND THE OTHER PERSON-ALITY IS THE ONE WHO KILLED YUSEI.
BINGO.
WHAT'LL YOU DO NOW?
FIRST, FIND A WAY TO LURE OUT MARY'S ALTER EGO.
AND THEN FIND OUT WHY HE KILLED MY FATHER.

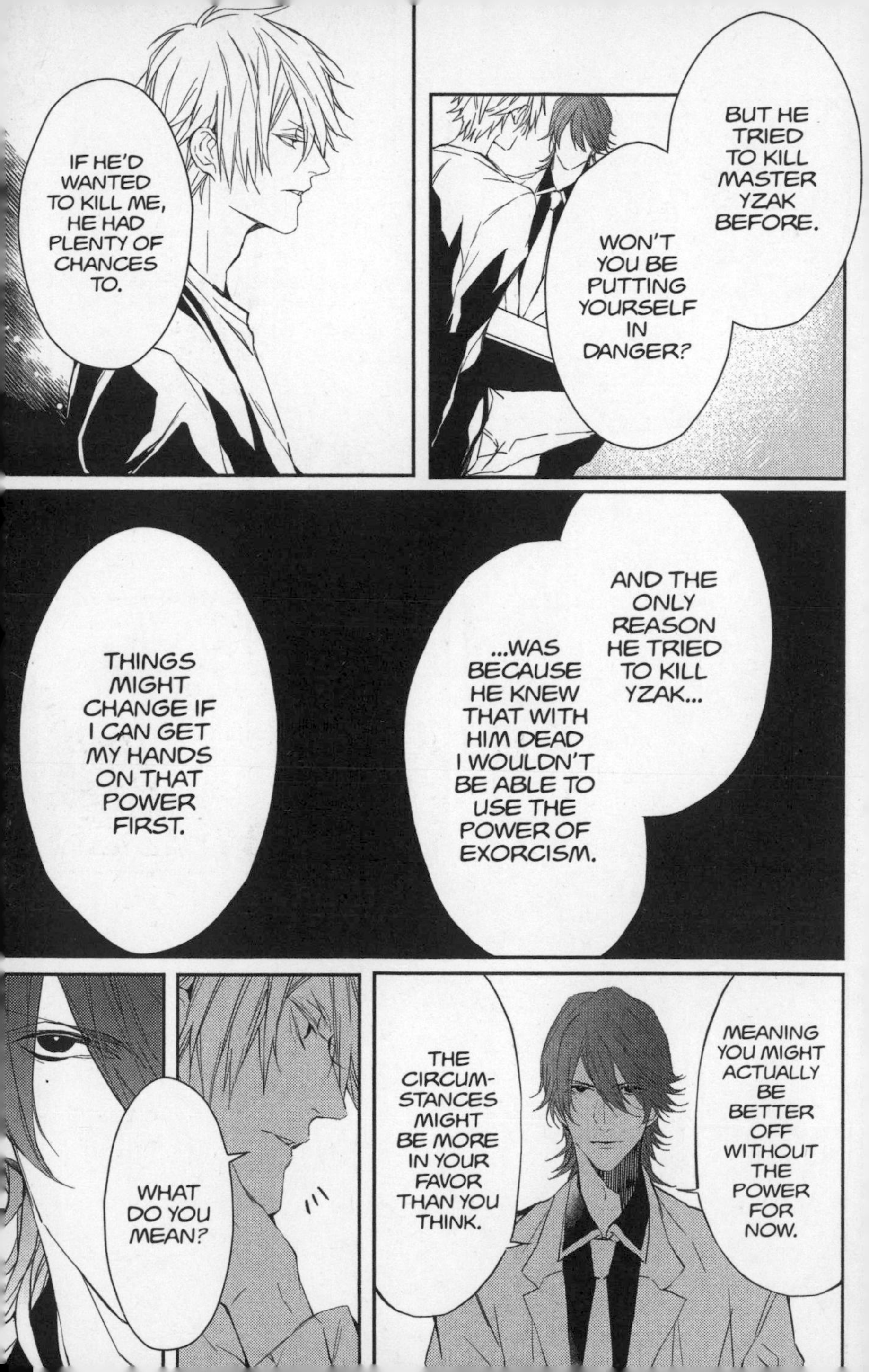
BUT HE TRIED TO KILL MASTER YZAK BEFORE.
WON'T YOU BE PUTTING YOURSELF IN DANGER?
IF HE'D WANTED TO KILL ME, HE HAD PLENTY OF CHANCES TO.
AND THE ONLY REASON HE TRIED TO KILL YZAK...
...WAS BECAUSE HE KNEW THAT WITH HIM DEAD I WOULDN'T BE ABLE TO USE THE POWER OF EXORCISM.
THINGS MIGHT CHANGE IF I CAN GET MY HANDS ON THAT POWER FIRST.
MEANING YOU MIGHT ACTUALLY BE BETTER OFF WITHOUT THE POWER FOR NOW.
THE CIRCUM-STANCES MIGHT BE MORE IN YOUR FAVOR THAN YOU THINK.
WHAT DO YOU MEAN?

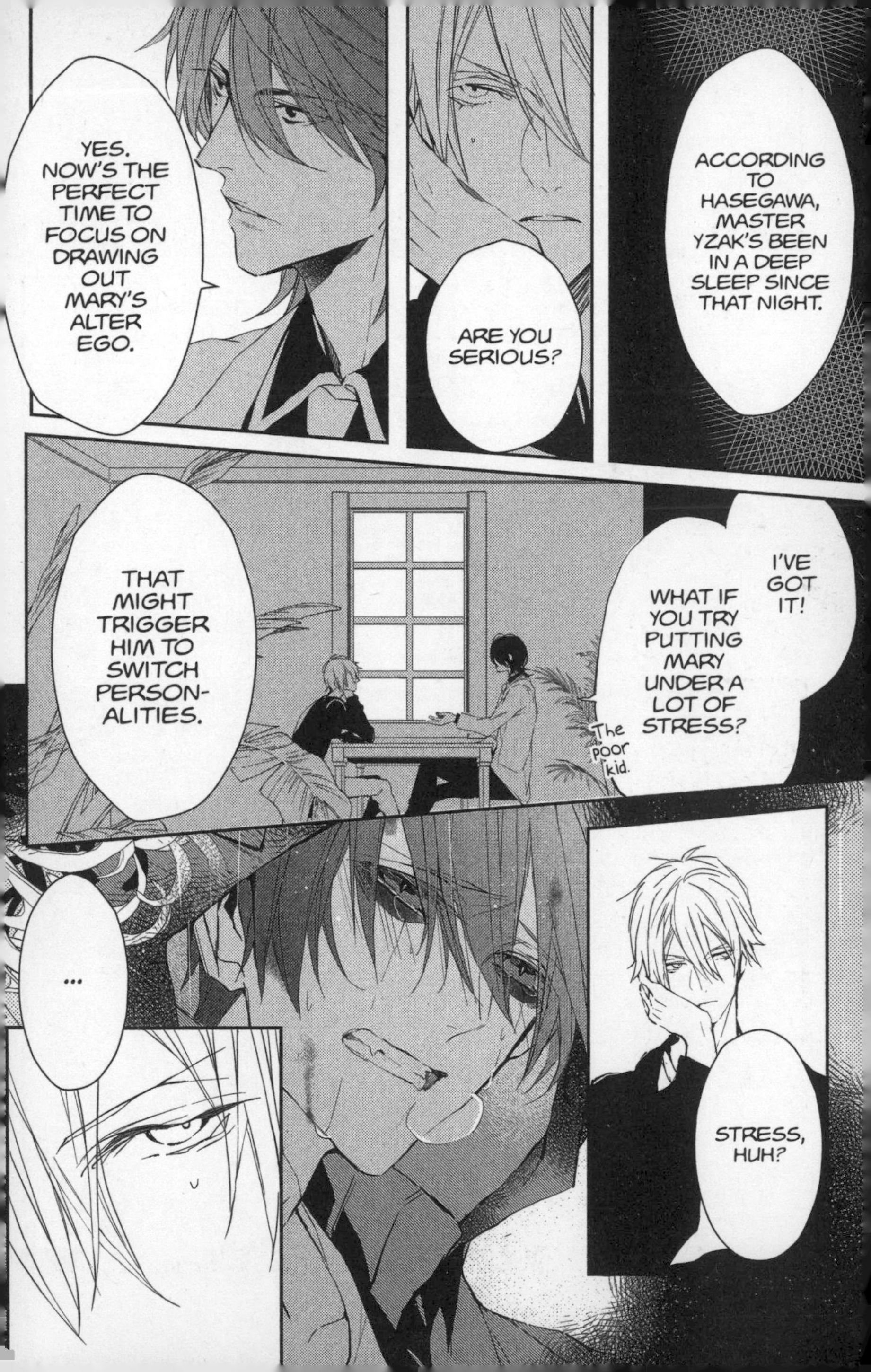
ACCORDING TO HASEGAWA, MASTER YZAK'S BEEN IN A DEEP SLEEP SINCE THAT NIGHT.
ARE YOU SERIOUS?
YES. NOW'S THE PERFECT TIME TO FOCUS ON DRAWING OUT MARY'S ALTER EGO.
I'VE GOT IT!
WHAT IF YOU TRY PUTTING MARY UNDER A LOT OF STRESS?
The poor kid.
THAT MIGHT TRIGGER HIM TO SWITCH PERSON-ALITIES.
STRESS, HUH?
...

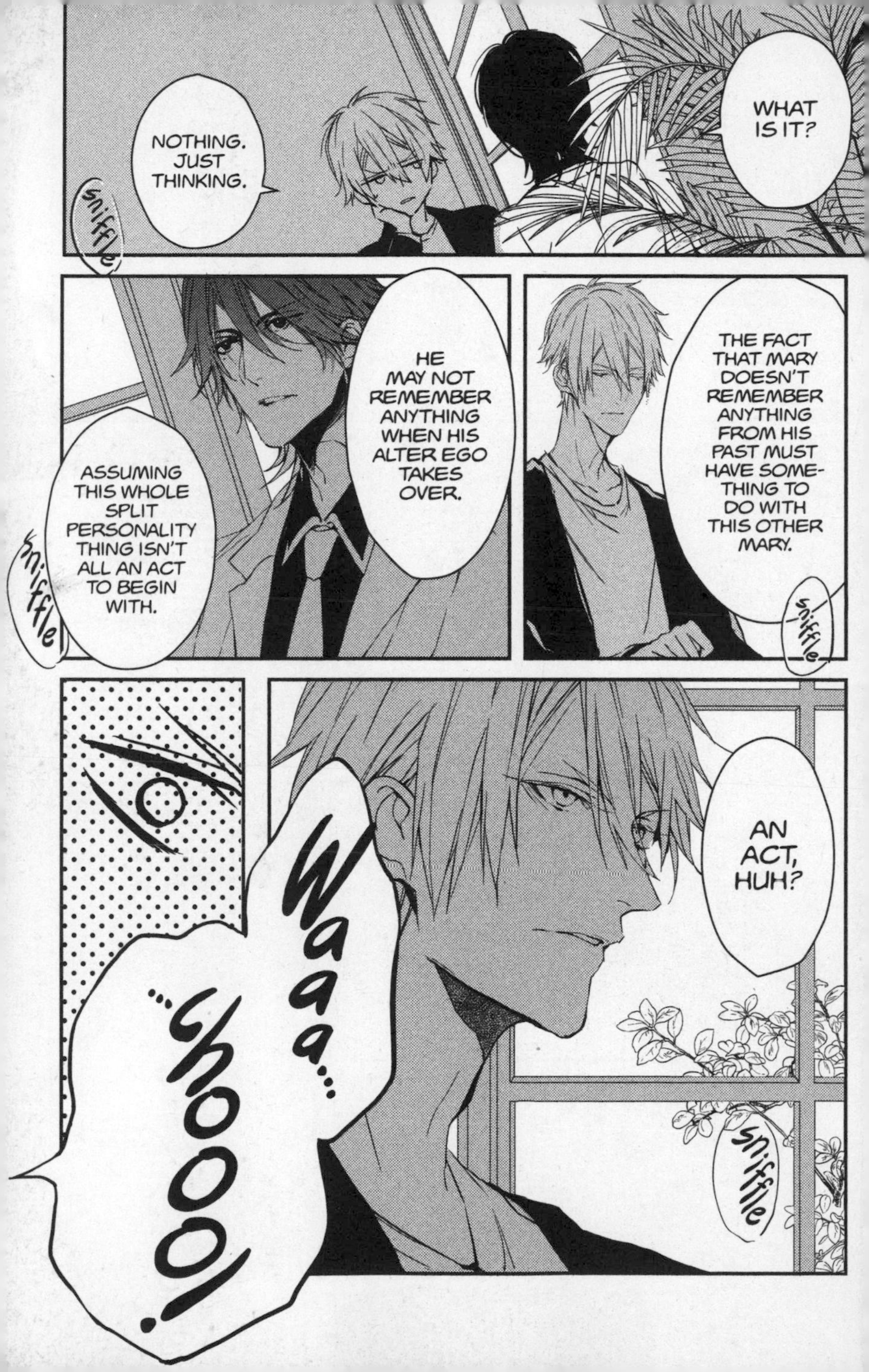
WHAT IS IT?
NOTHING. JUST THINKING.
sniffle
THE FACT THAT MARY DOESN'T REMEMBER ANYTHING FROM HIS PAST MUST HAVE SOME-THING TO DO WITH THIS OTHER MARY.
sniffle
HE MAY NOT REMEMBER ANYTHING WHEN HIS ALTER EGO TAKES OVER.
ASSUMING THIS WHOLE SPLIT PERSONALITY THING ISN'T ALL AN ACT TO BEGIN WITH.
sniffle
AN ACT, HUH?
sniffle
Waaa... ...chooo!

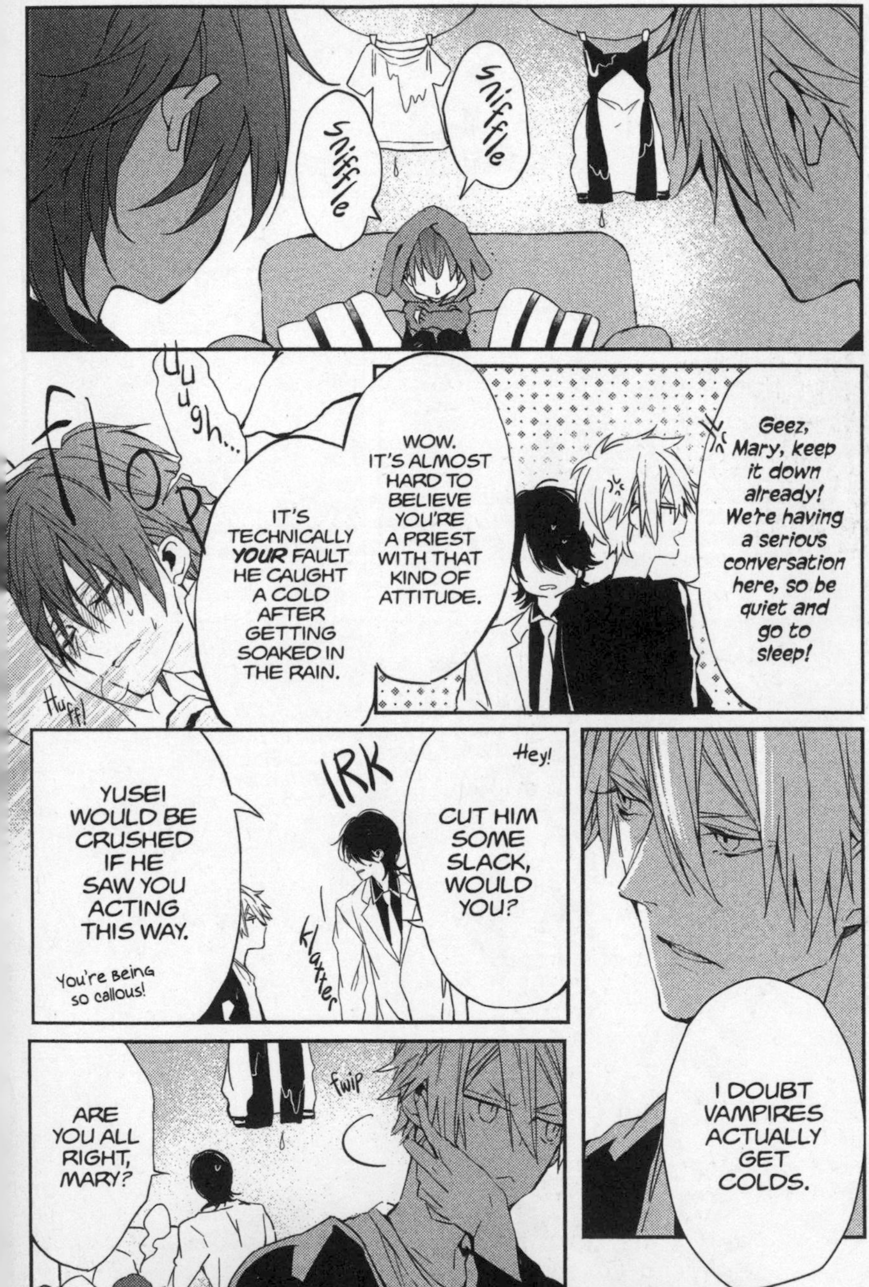
sniffle
sniffle
Geez, Mary, keep it down already! We're having a serious conversation here, so be quiet and go to sleep!
WOW. IT'S ALMOST HARD TO BELIEVE YOU'RE A PRIEST WITH THAT KIND OF ATTITUDE.
IT'S TECHNICALLY YOUR FAULT HE CAUGHT A COLD AFTER GETTING SOAKED IN THE RAIN.
Uugh...
FLOP
Huff!
I DOUBT VAMPIRES ACTUALLY GET COLDS.
Hey!
CUT HIM SOME SLACK, WOULD YOU?
IRK
klatter
YUSEI WOULD BE CRUSHED IF HE SAW YOU ACTING THIS WAY.
You're being so callous!
fwip
ARE YOU ALL RIGHT, MARY?

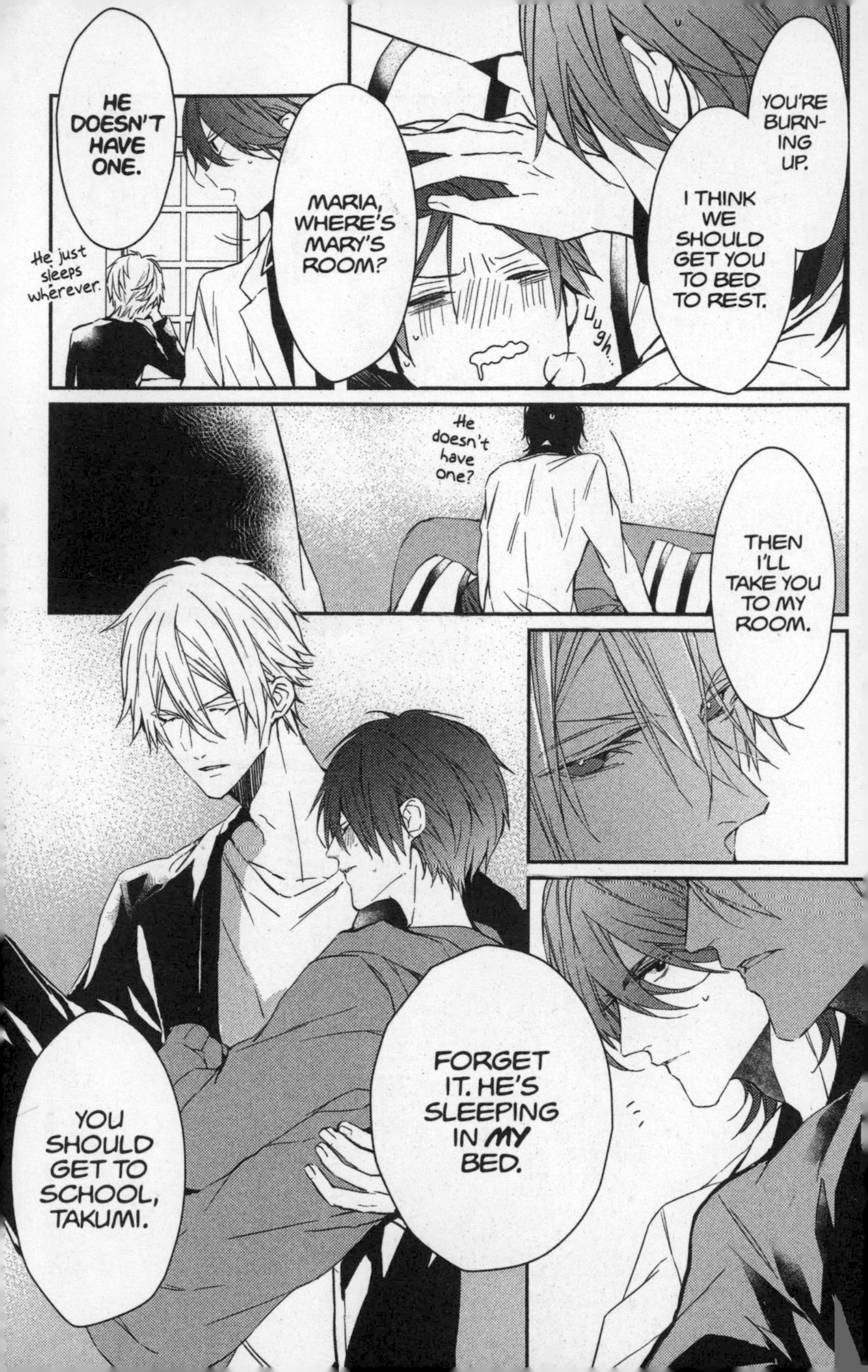
YOU'RE BURNING UP.
I THINK WE SHOULD GET YOU TO BED TO REST.
Uugh...
MARIA, WHERE'S MARY'S ROOM?
HE DOESN'T HAVE ONE.
He just sleeps wherever.
THEN I'LL TAKE YOU TO MY ROOM.
He doesn't have one?
FORGET IT. HE'S SLEEPING IN *MY* BED.
YOU SHOULD GET TO SCHOOL, TAKUMI.

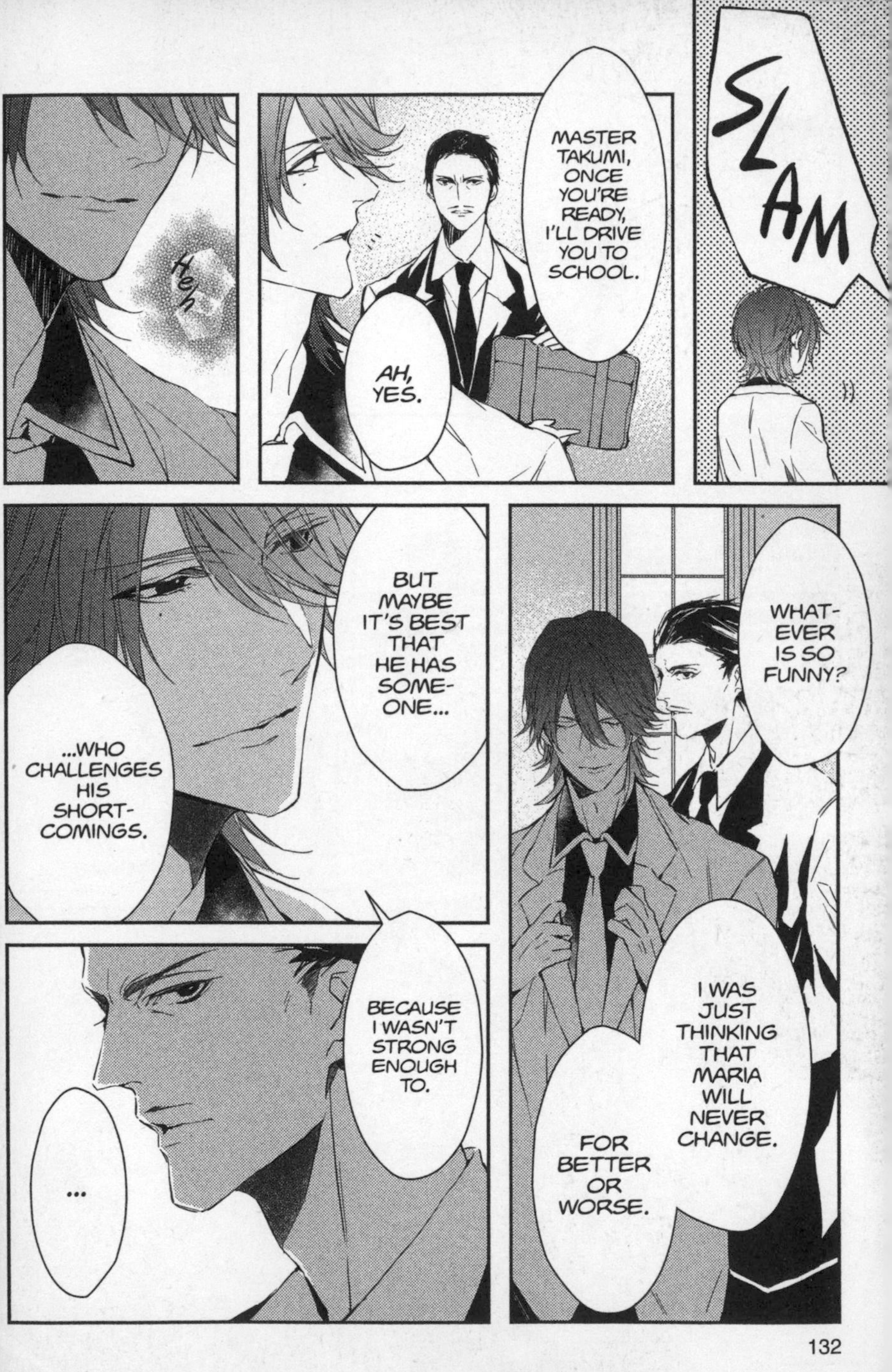
SLAM
MASTER TAKUMI, ONCE YOU'RE READY, I'LL DRIVE YOU TO SCHOOL.
AH, YES.
Heh
WHAT-EVER IS SO FUNNY?
I WAS JUST THINKING THAT MARIA WILL NEVER CHANGE.
FOR BETTER OR WORSE.
BUT MAYBE IT'S BEST THAT HE HAS SOME-ONE...
...WHO CHALLENGES HIS SHORT-COMINGS.
BECAUSE I WASN'T STRONG ENOUGH TO.
...

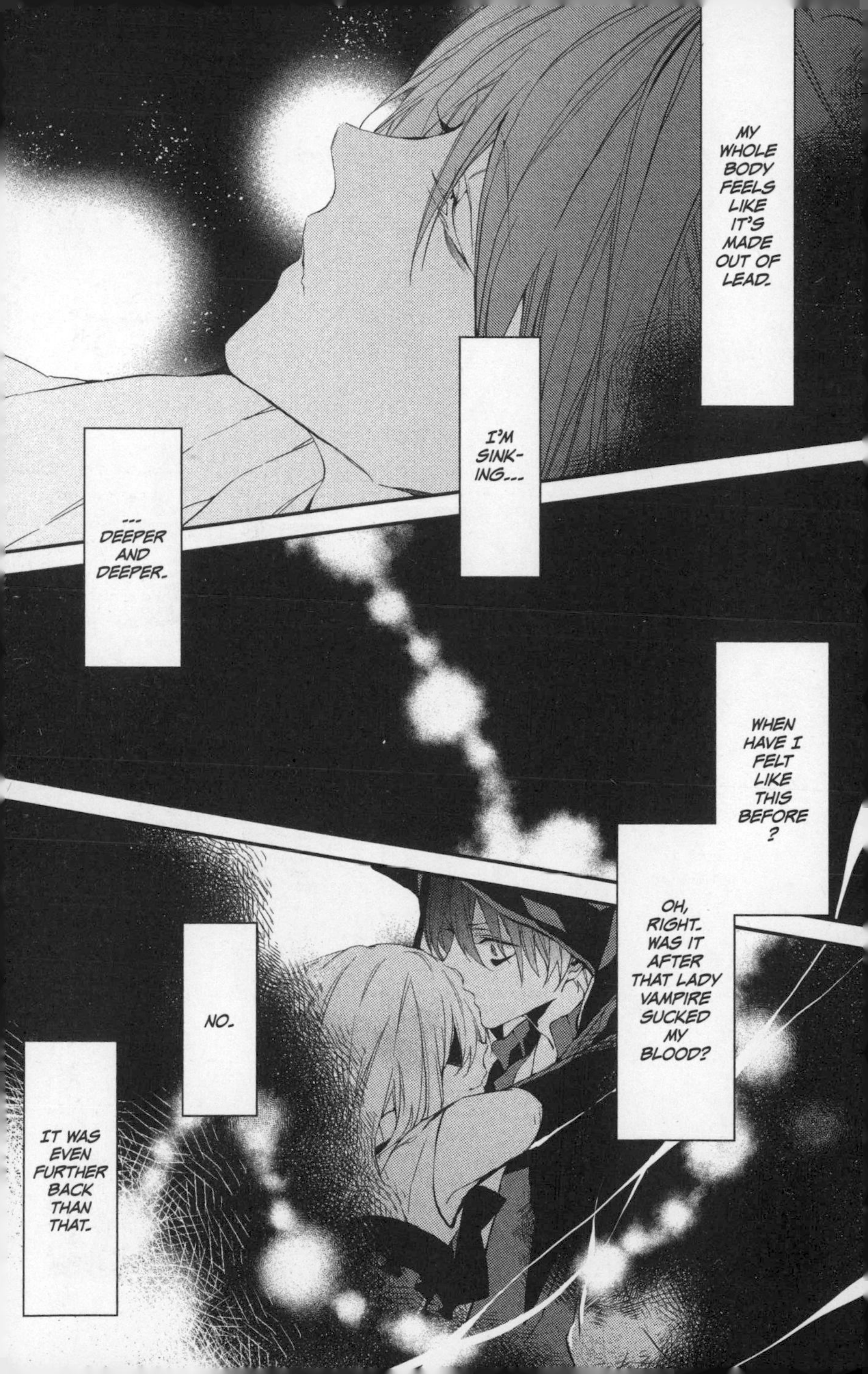
MY WHOLE BODY FEELS LIKE IT'S MADE OUT OF LEAD.
I'M SINK-ING...
...DEEPER AND DEEPER.
WHEN HAVE I FELT LIKE THIS BEFORE?
OH, RIGHT. WAS IT AFTER THAT LADY VAMPIRE SUCKED MY BLOOD?
NO.
IT WAS EVEN FURTHER BACK THAN THAT.

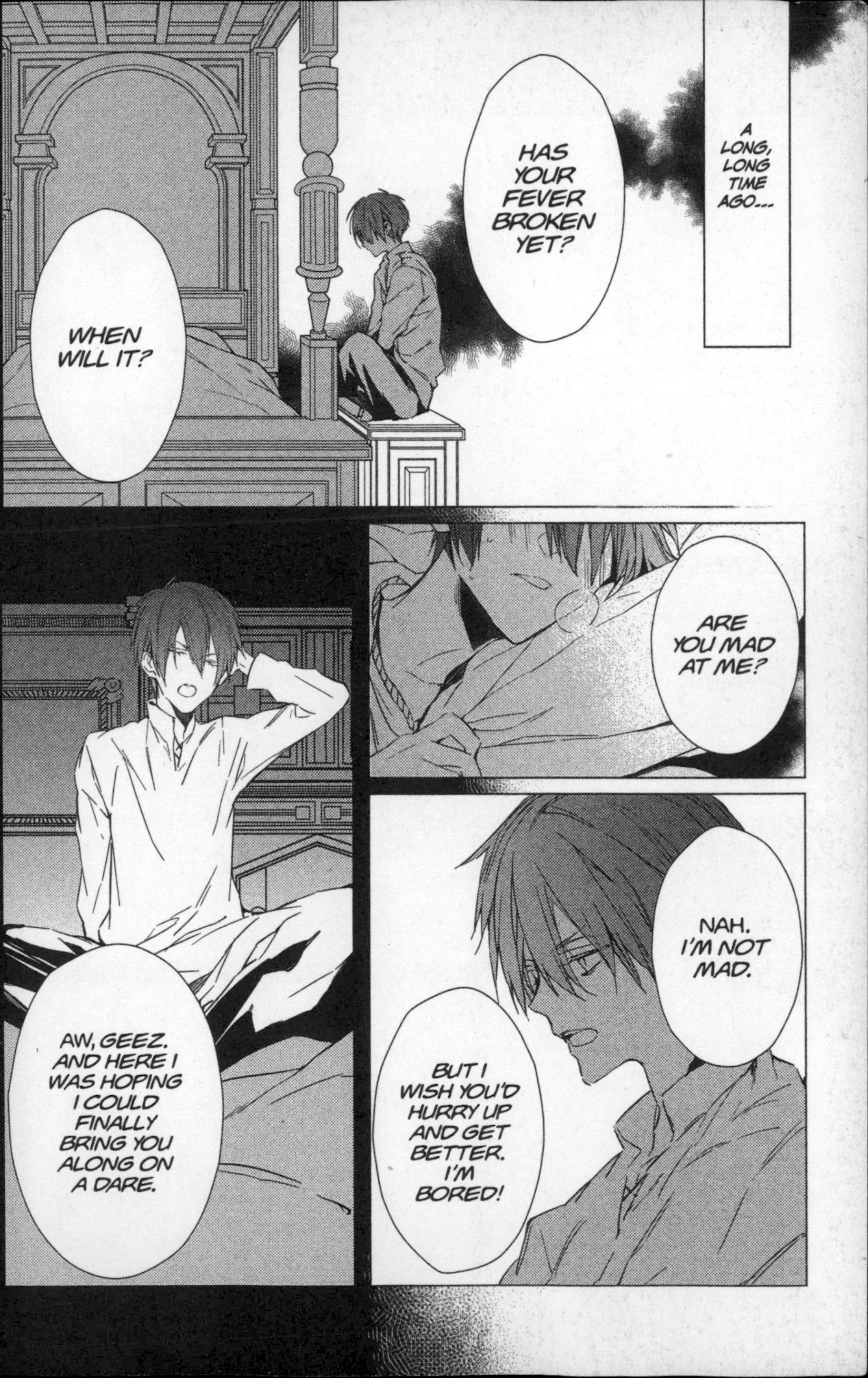
A LONG, LONG TIME AGO...
HAS YOUR FEVER BROKEN YET?
WHEN WILL IT?
ARE YOU MAD AT ME?
NAH. I'M NOT MAD.
BUT I WISH YOU'D HURRY UP AND GET BETTER. I'M BORED!
AW, GEEZ. AND HERE I WAS HOPING I COULD FINALLY BRING YOU ALONG ON A DARE.

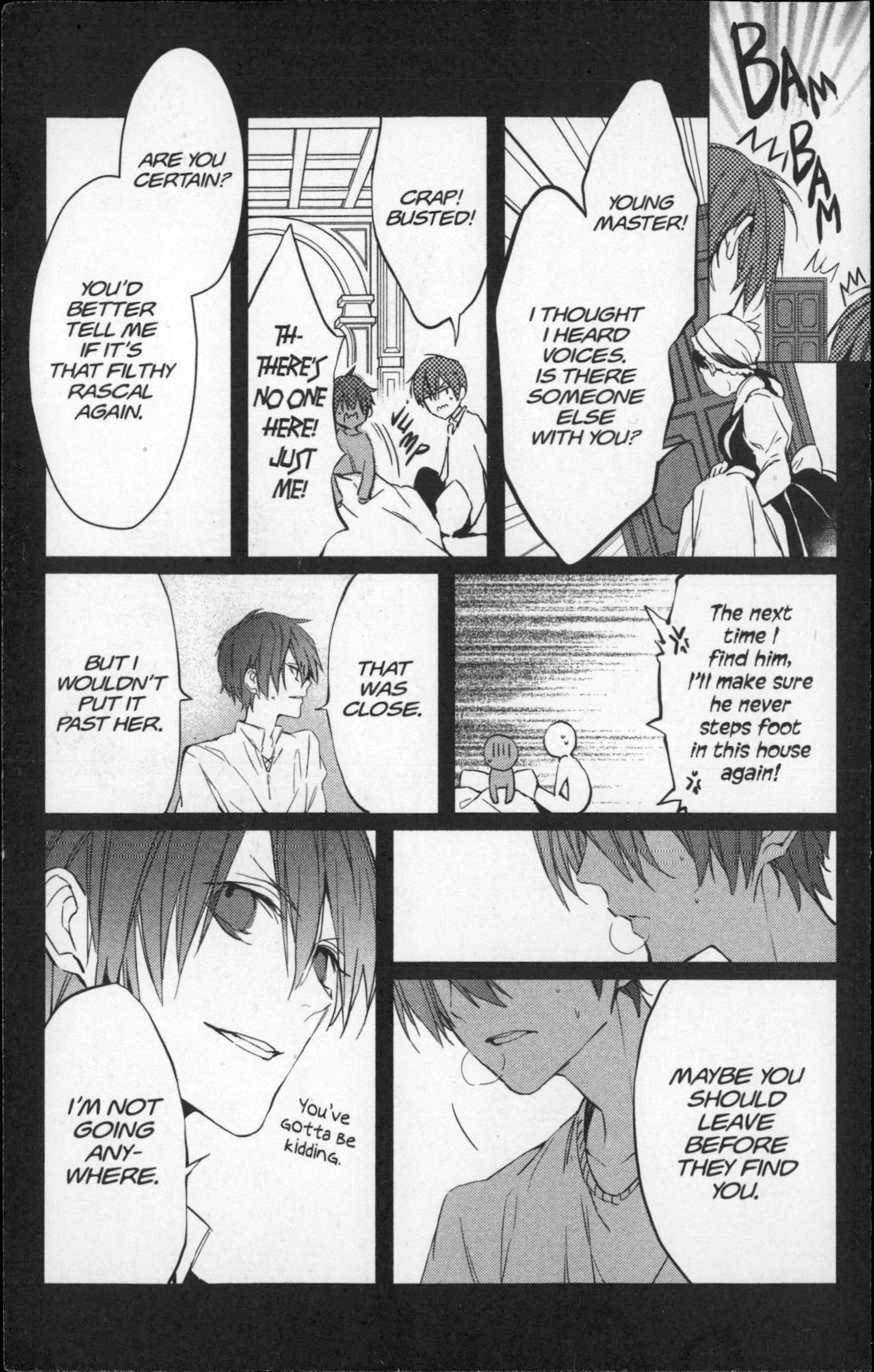
BAM BAM BAM
YOUNG MASTER!
I THOUGHT I HEARD VOICES. IS THERE SOMEONE ELSE WITH YOU?
CRAP! BUSTED!
JUMP
TH-THERE'S NO ONE HERE! JUST ME!
ARE YOU CERTAIN?
YOU'D BETTER TELL ME IF IT'S THAT FILTHY RASCAL AGAIN.
The next time I find him, I'll make sure he never steps foot in this house again!
THAT WAS CLOSE.
BUT I WOULDN'T PUT IT PAST HER.
MAYBE YOU SHOULD LEAVE BEFORE THEY FIND YOU.
I'M NOT GOING ANY-WHERE.
You've gotta be kidding.

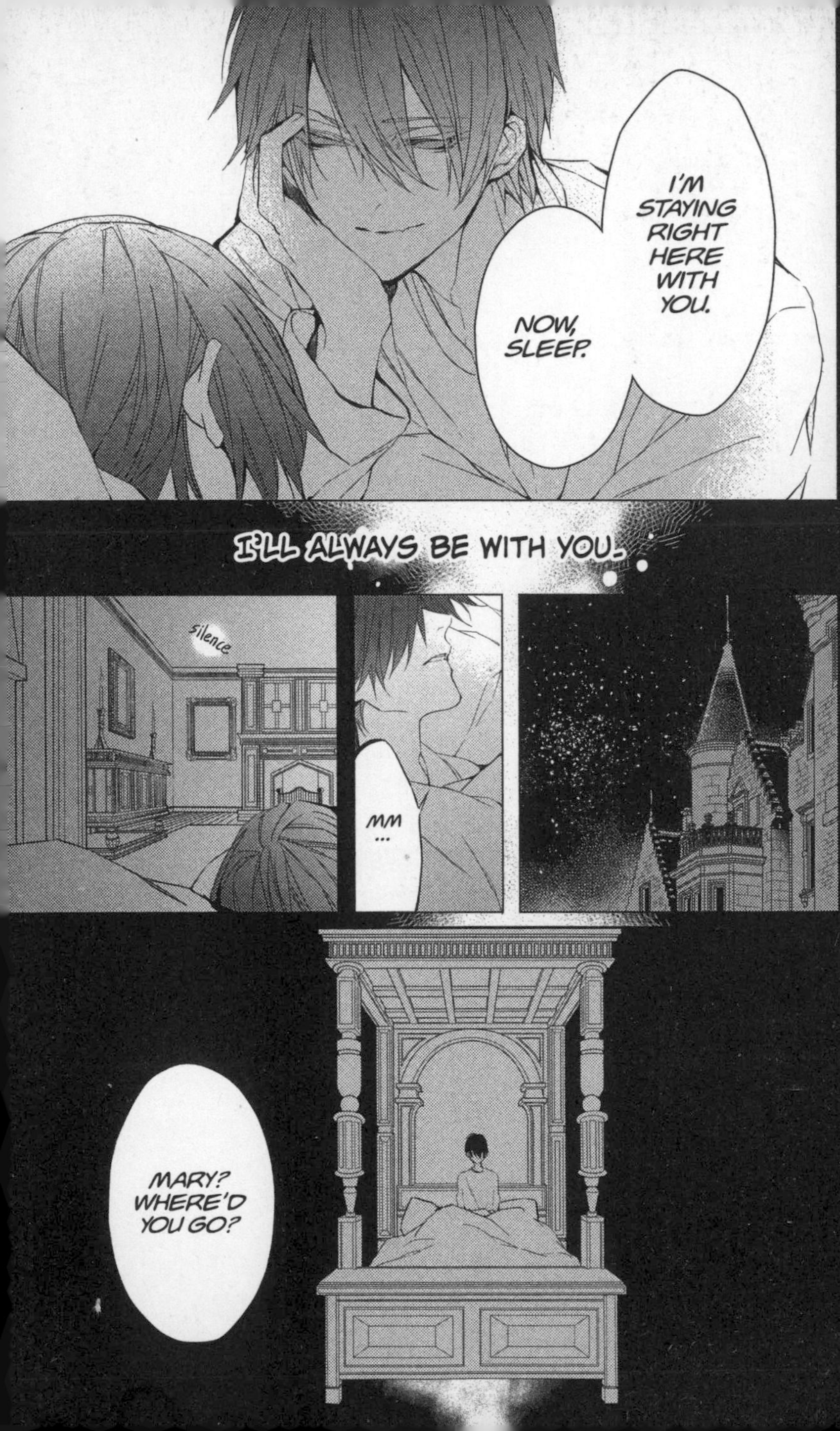
I'M STAYING RIGHT HERE WITH YOU.
NOW, SLEEP.
I'LL ALWAYS BE WITH YOU.
MM ...
silence
MARY? WHERE'D YOU GO?

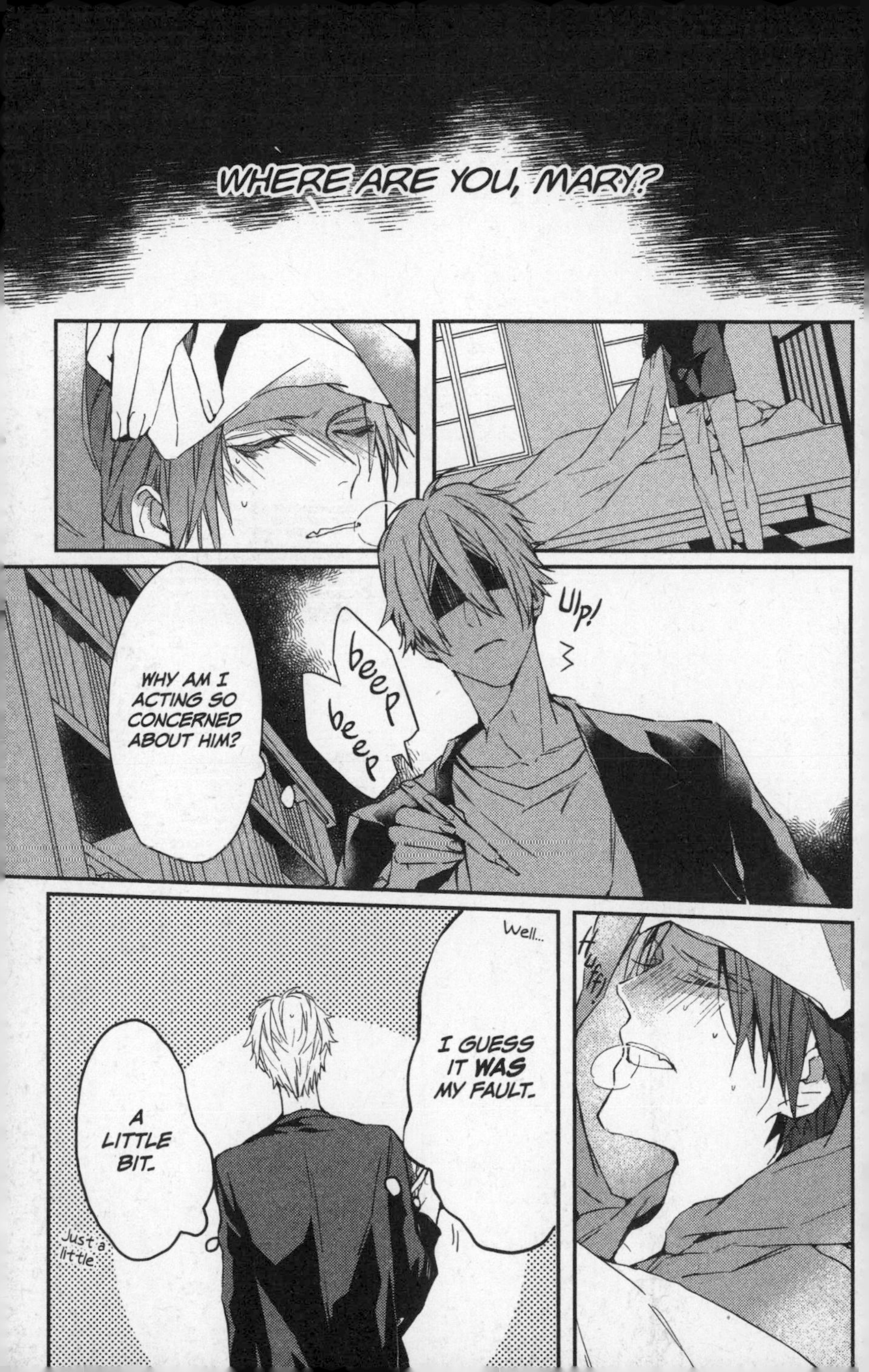
WHERE ARE YOU, MARY?
Ulp!
beep beep
WHY AM I ACTING SO CONCERNED ABOUT HIM?
Huff
Well...
I GUESS IT WAS MY FAULT.
A LITTLE BIT.
Just a little.

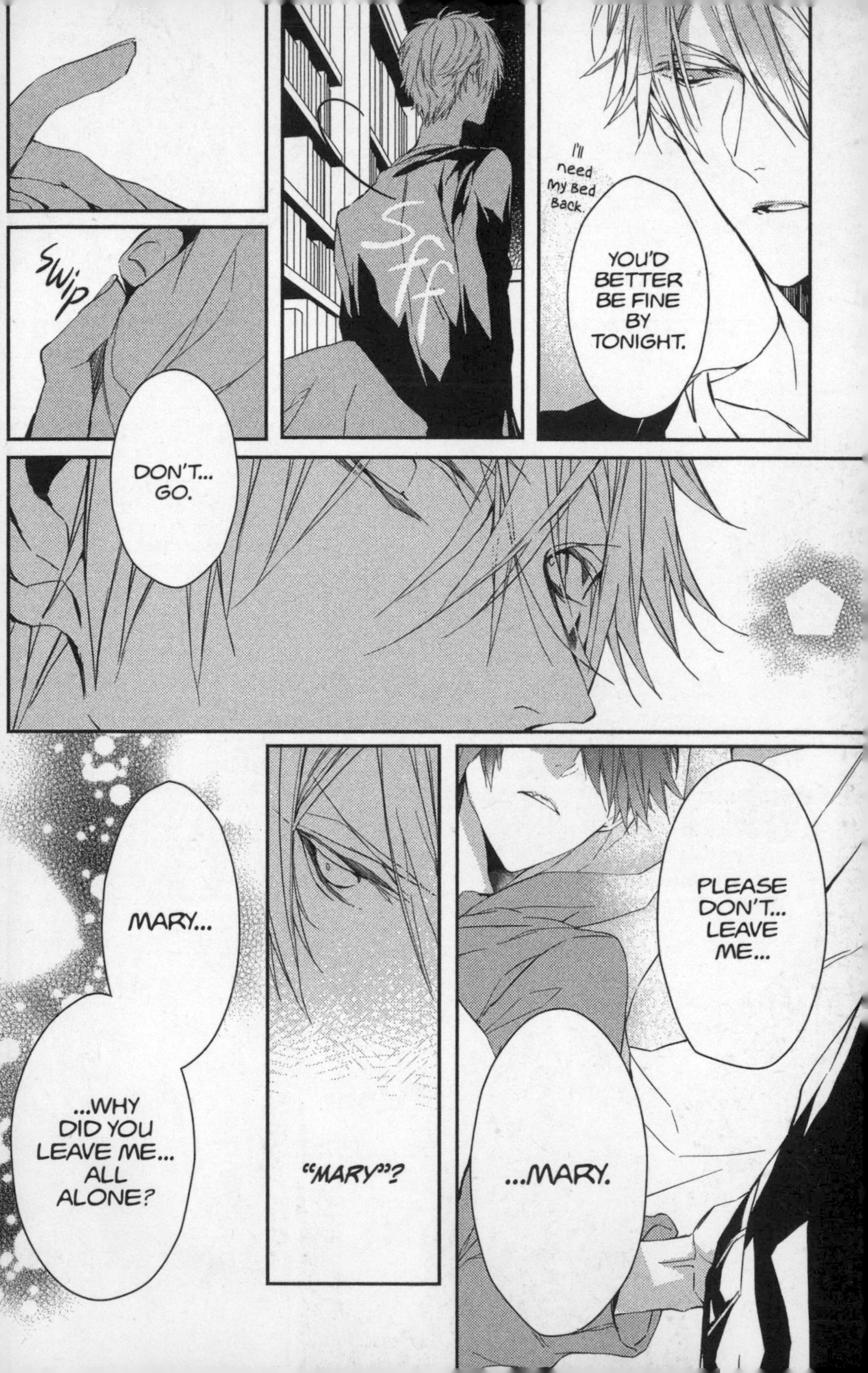
YOU'D BETTER BE FINE BY TONIGHT.
I'll need My Bed Back.
Sff
Swip
DON'T... GO.
PLEASE DON'T... LEAVE ME...
...MARY.
"MARY"?
MARY...
...WHY DID YOU LEAVE ME... ALL ALONE?

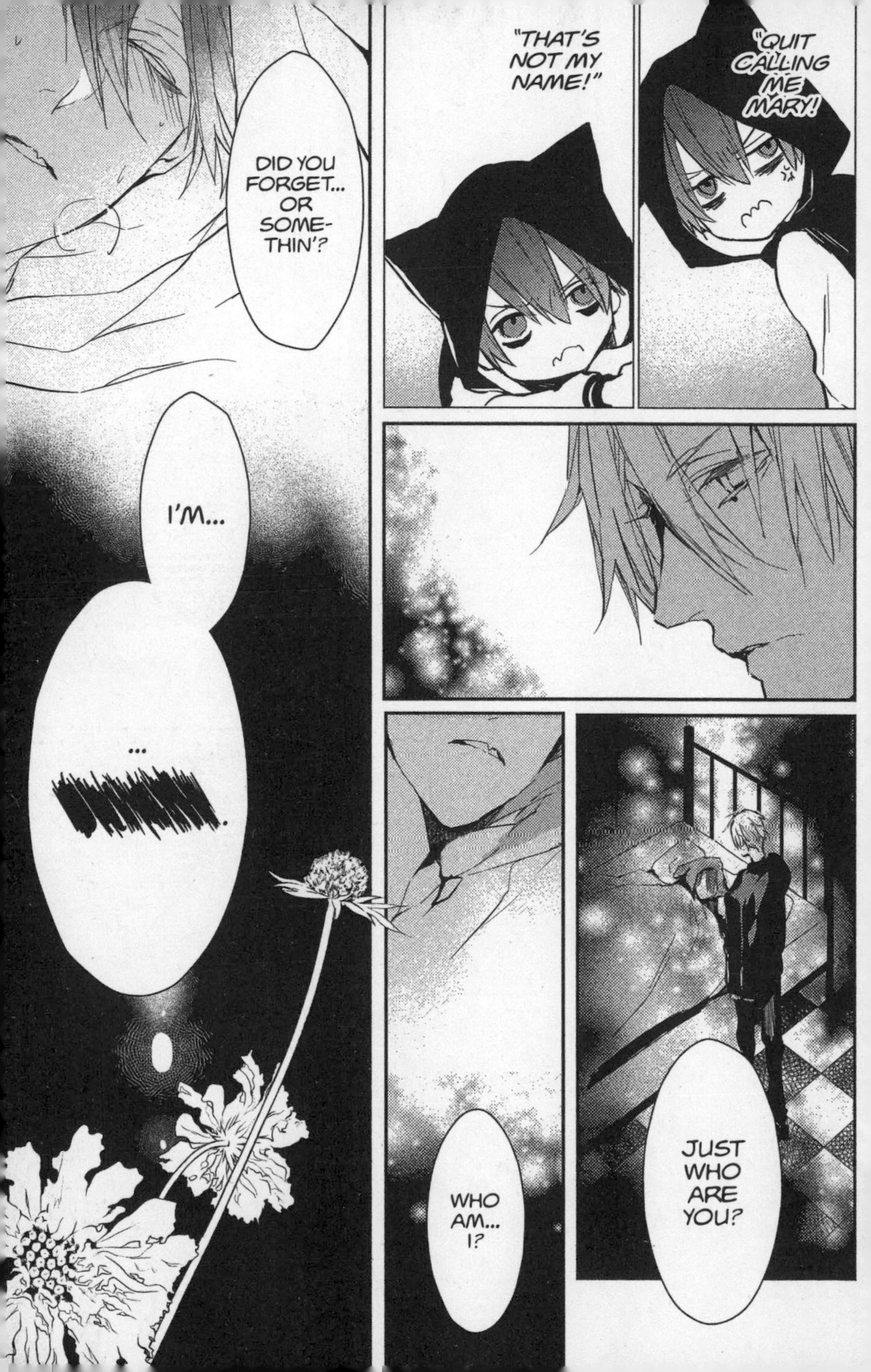
"QUIT CALLING ME MARY!
"THAT'S NOT MY NAME!"
JUST WHO ARE YOU?
WHO AM... I?
DID YOU FORGET... OR SOME-THIN'?
I'M...
... [redacted].

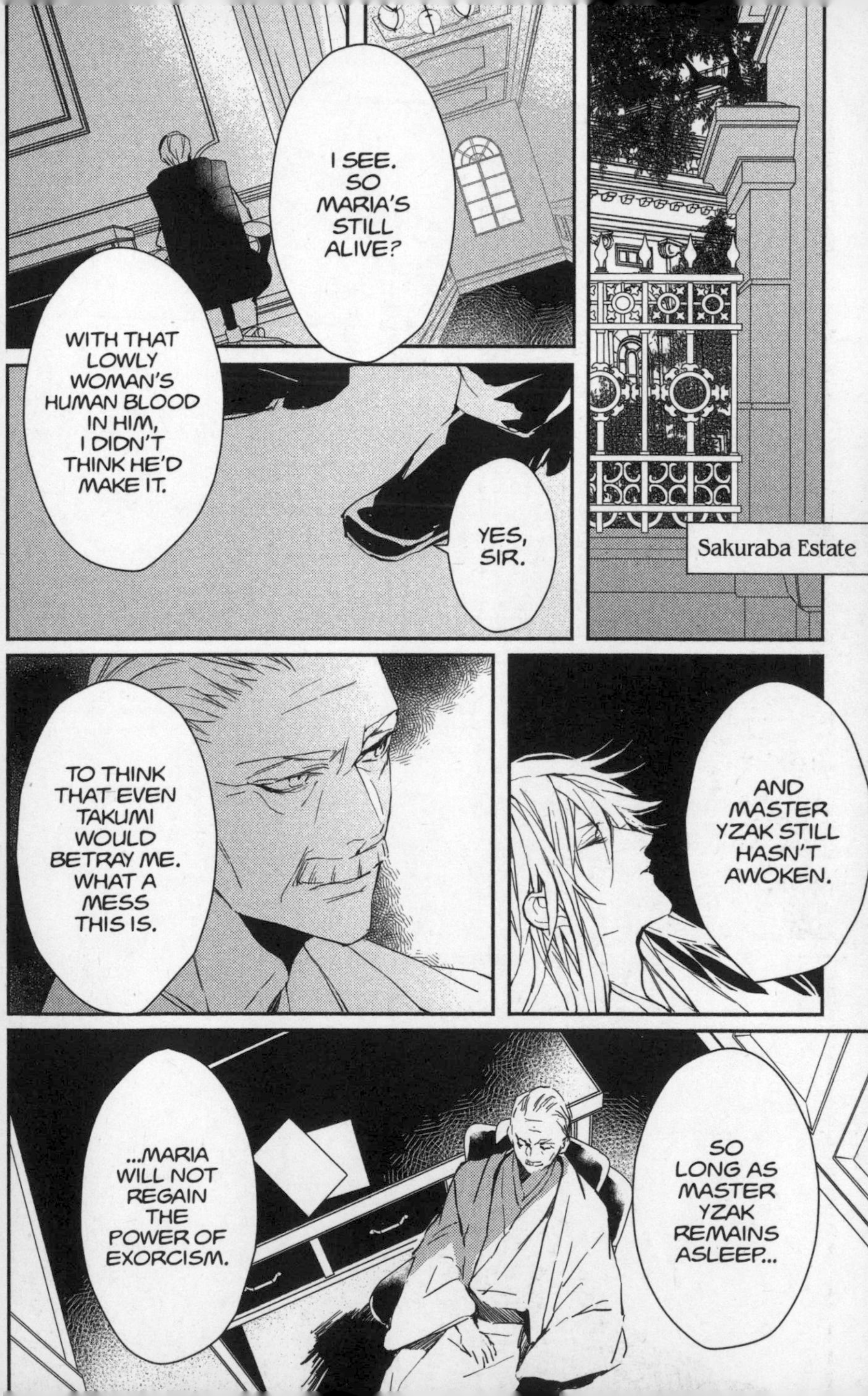
Sakuraba Estate
I SEE. SO MARIA'S STILL ALIVE?
WITH THAT LOWLY WOMAN'S HUMAN BLOOD IN HIM, I DIDN'T THINK HE'D MAKE IT.
YES, SIR.
AND MASTER YZAK STILL HASN'T AWOKEN.
TO THINK THAT EVEN TAKUMI WOULD BETRAY ME. WHAT A MESS THIS IS.
SO LONG AS MASTER YZAK REMAINS ASLEEP...
...MARIA WILL NOT REGAIN THE POWER OF EXORCISM.

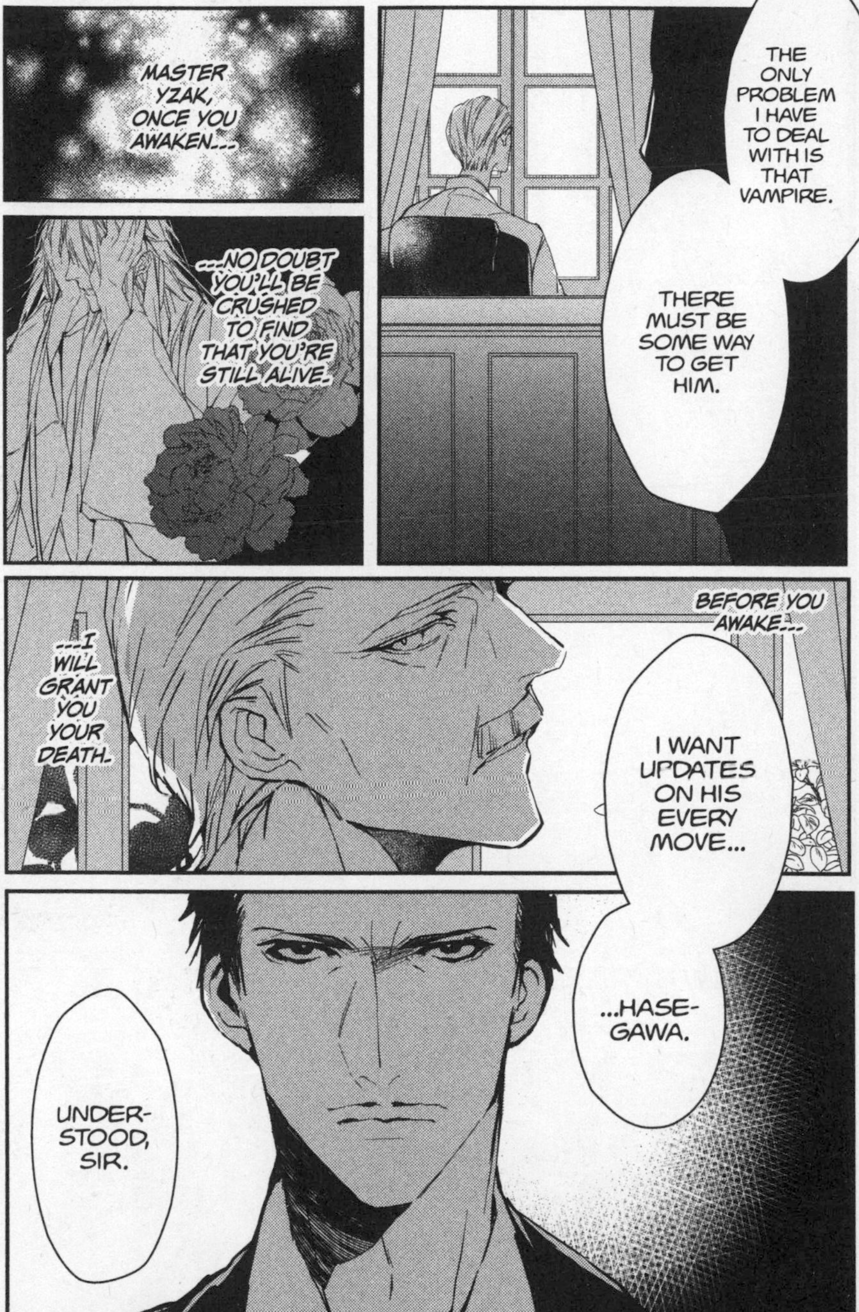
THE ONLY PROBLEM I HAVE TO DEAL WITH IS THAT VAMPIRE.
THERE MUST BE SOME WAY TO GET HIM.
MASTER YZAK, ONCE YOU AWAKEN...
...NO DOUBT YOU'LL BE CRUSHED TO FIND THAT YOU'RE STILL ALIVE.
BEFORE YOU AWAKE...
I WANT UPDATES ON HIS EVERY MOVE...
...I WILL GRANT YOU YOUR DEATH.
...HASE-GAWA.
UNDER-STOOD, SIR.

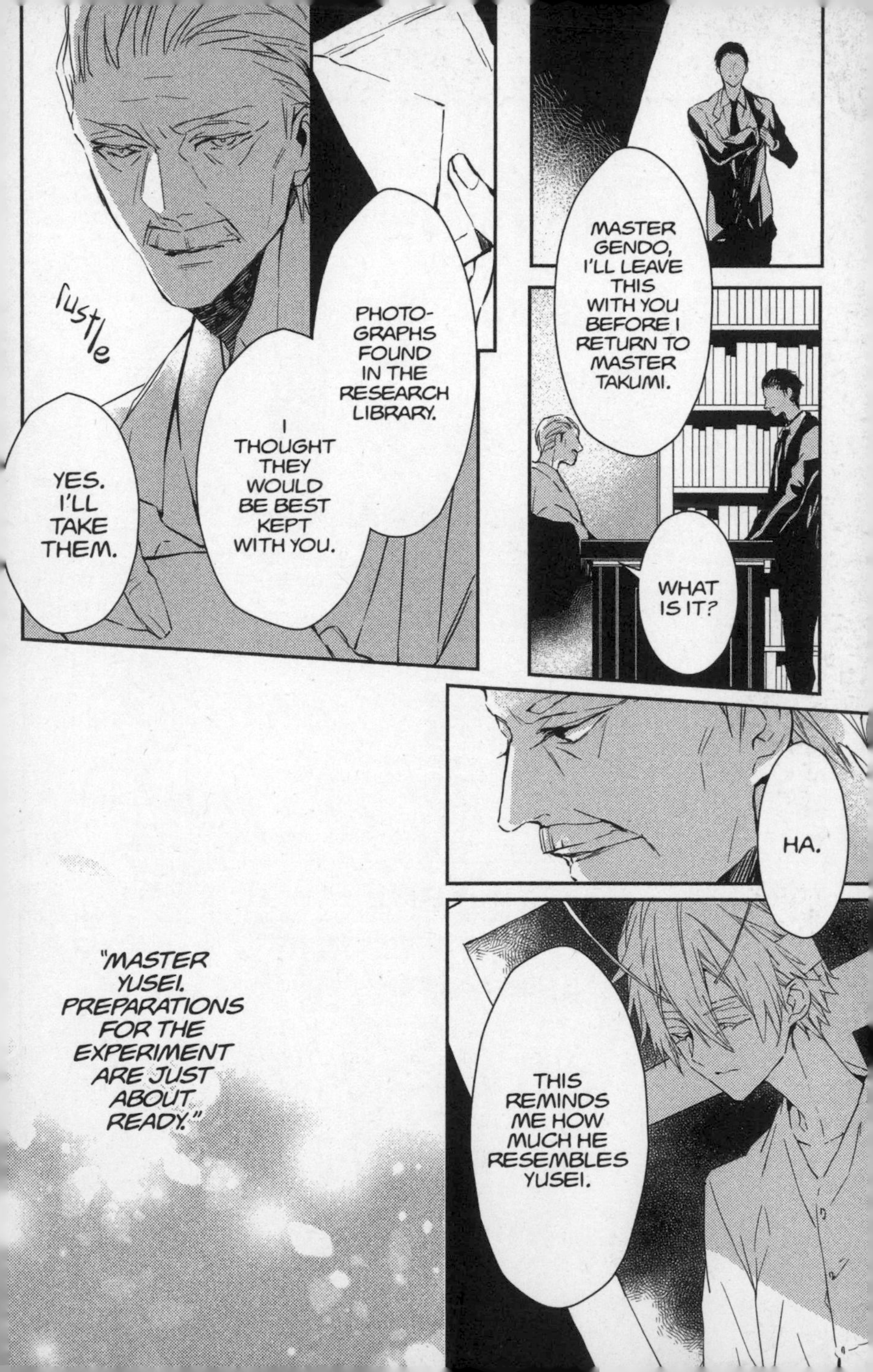
MASTER GENDO, I'LL LEAVE THIS WITH YOU BEFORE I RETURN TO MASTER TAKUMI.
WHAT IS IT?
PHOTO-GRAPHS FOUND IN THE RESEARCH LIBRARY.
I THOUGHT THEY WOULD BE BEST KEPT WITH YOU.
rustle
YES. I'LL TAKE THEM.
HA.
THIS REMINDS ME HOW MUCH HE RESEMBLES YUSEI.
"MASTER YUSEI. PREPARATIONS FOR THE EXPERIMENT ARE JUST ABOUT READY."

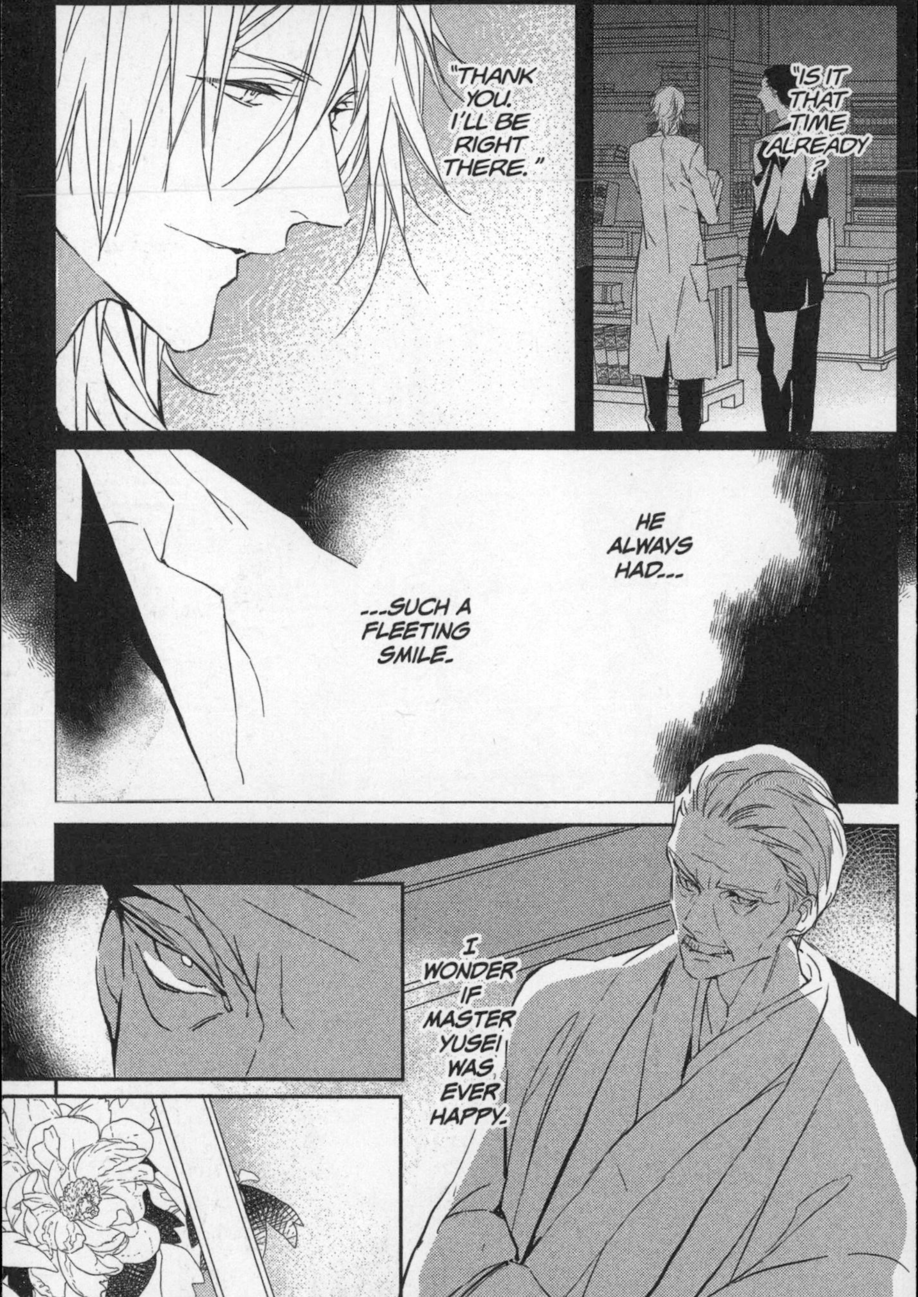
"IS IT THAT TIME ALREADY?
"THANK YOU. I'LL BE RIGHT THERE."
HE ALWAYS HAD...
...SUCH A FLEETING SMILE.
I WONDER IF MASTER YUSEI WAS EVER HAPPY.

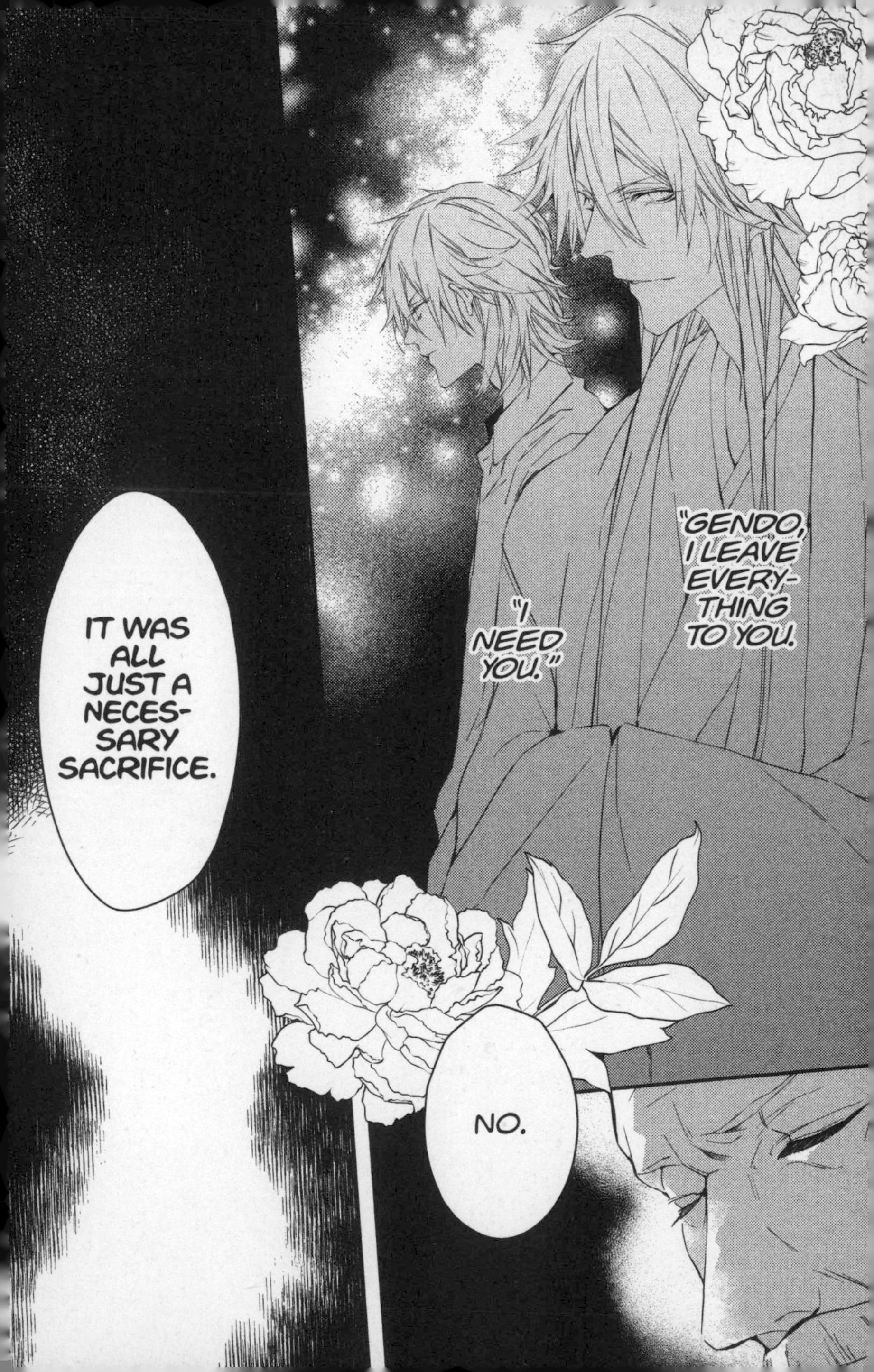
"GENDO, I LEAVE EVERY-THING TO YOU.
"I NEED YOU."
NO.
IT WAS ALL JUST A NECES-SARY SACRIFICE.

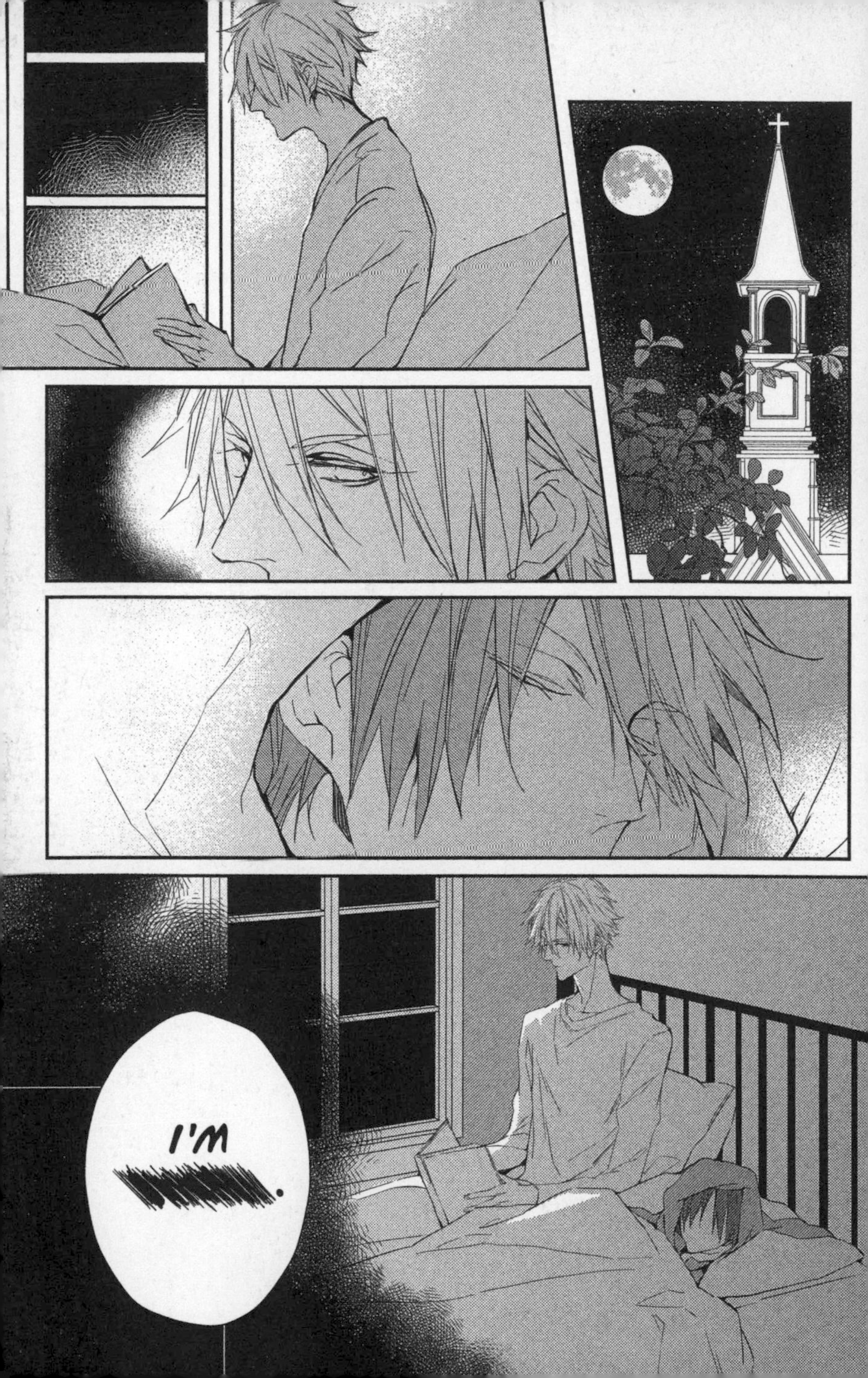
I'M [redacted].

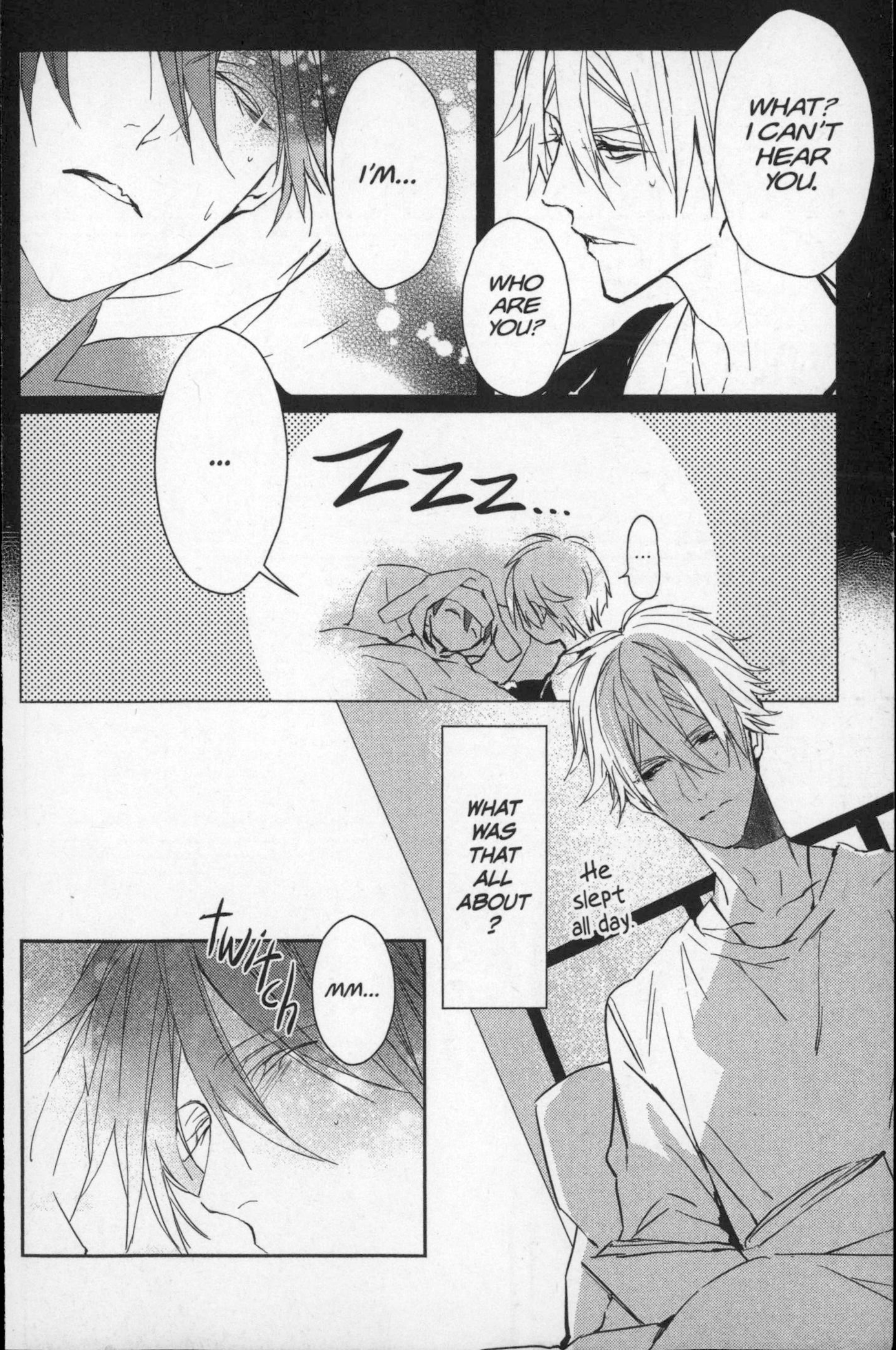
WHAT? I CAN'T HEAR YOU.
WHO ARE YOU?
I'M...
...
ZZZ...
...
He slept all day.
WHAT WAS THAT ALL ABOUT?
mm...
twitch

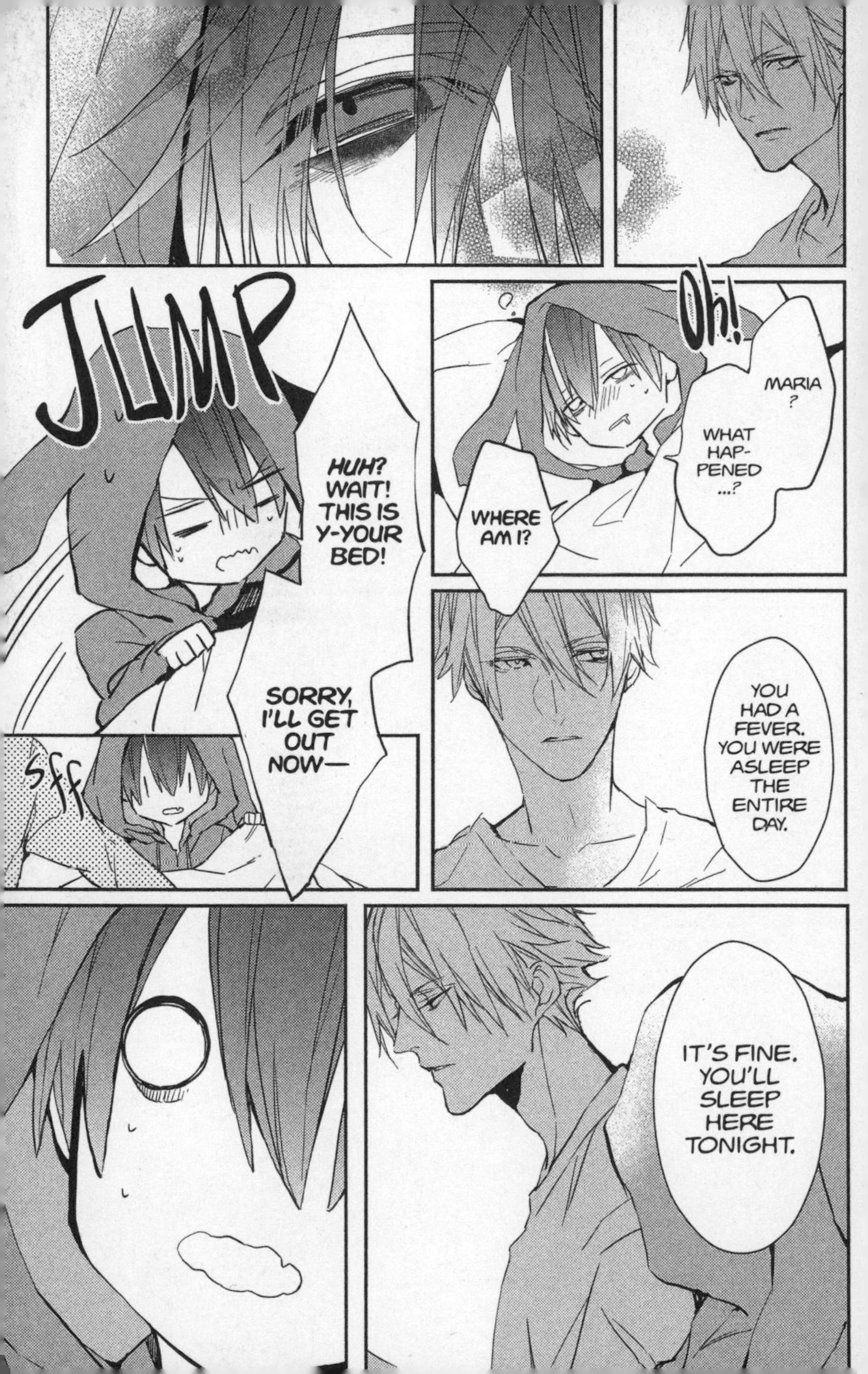
Oh!
MARIA?
WHAT HAP-PENED ...?
WHERE AM I?
YOU HAD A FEVER. YOU WERE ASLEEP THE ENTIRE DAY.
JUMP
HUH? WAIT! THIS IS Y-YOUR BED!
SORRY, I'LL GET OUT NOW—
Sff
IT'S FINE. YOU'LL SLEEP HERE TONIGHT.

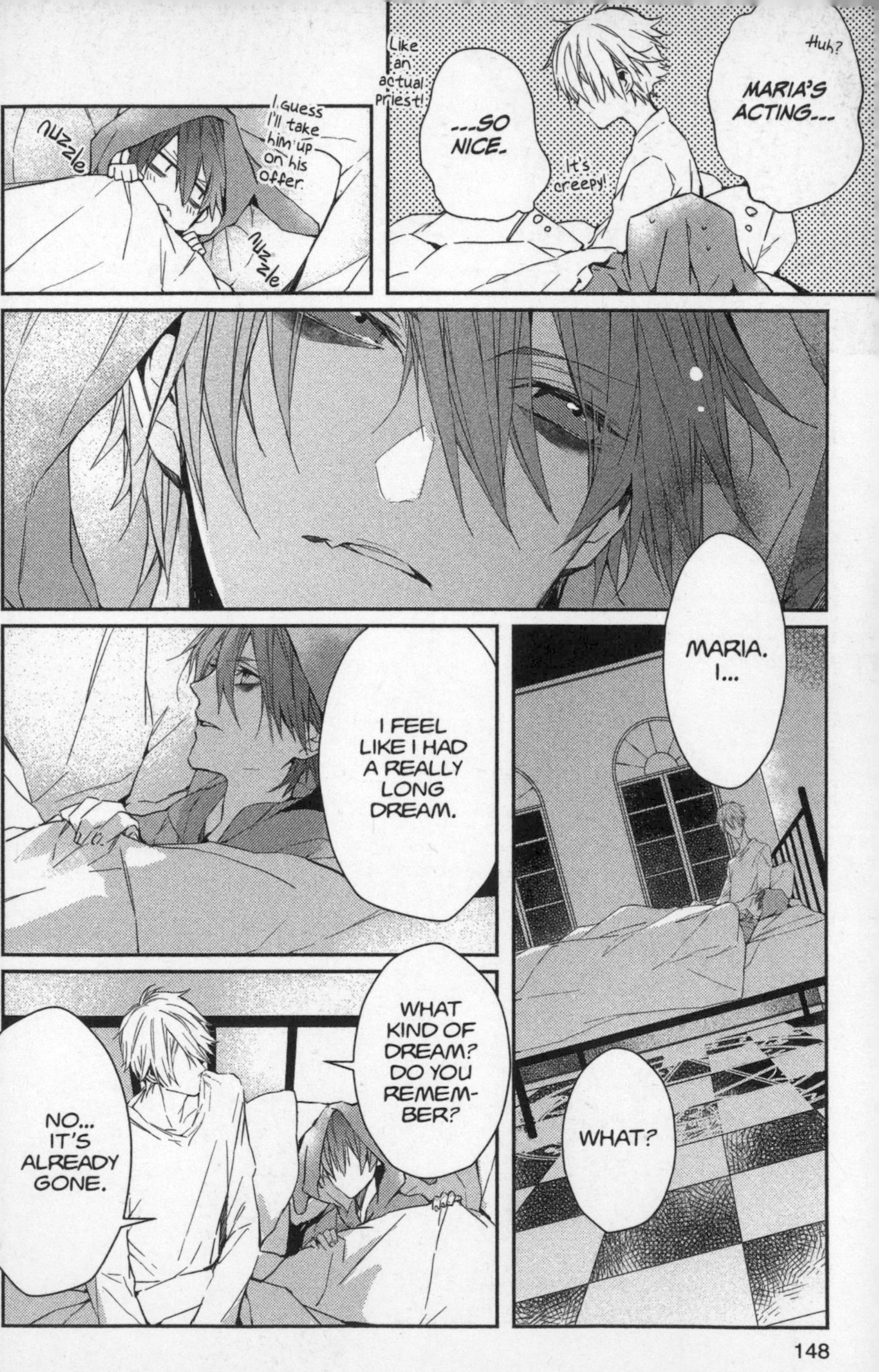
Huh?
MARIA'S ACTING...
---SO NICE.
Like an actual priest!
It's creepy!
nuzzle
I guess I'll take him up on his offer.
nuzzle
MARIA. I...
WHAT?
I FEEL LIKE I HAD A REALLY LONG DREAM.
WHAT KIND OF DREAM? DO YOU REMEMBER?
NO... IT'S ALREADY GONE.

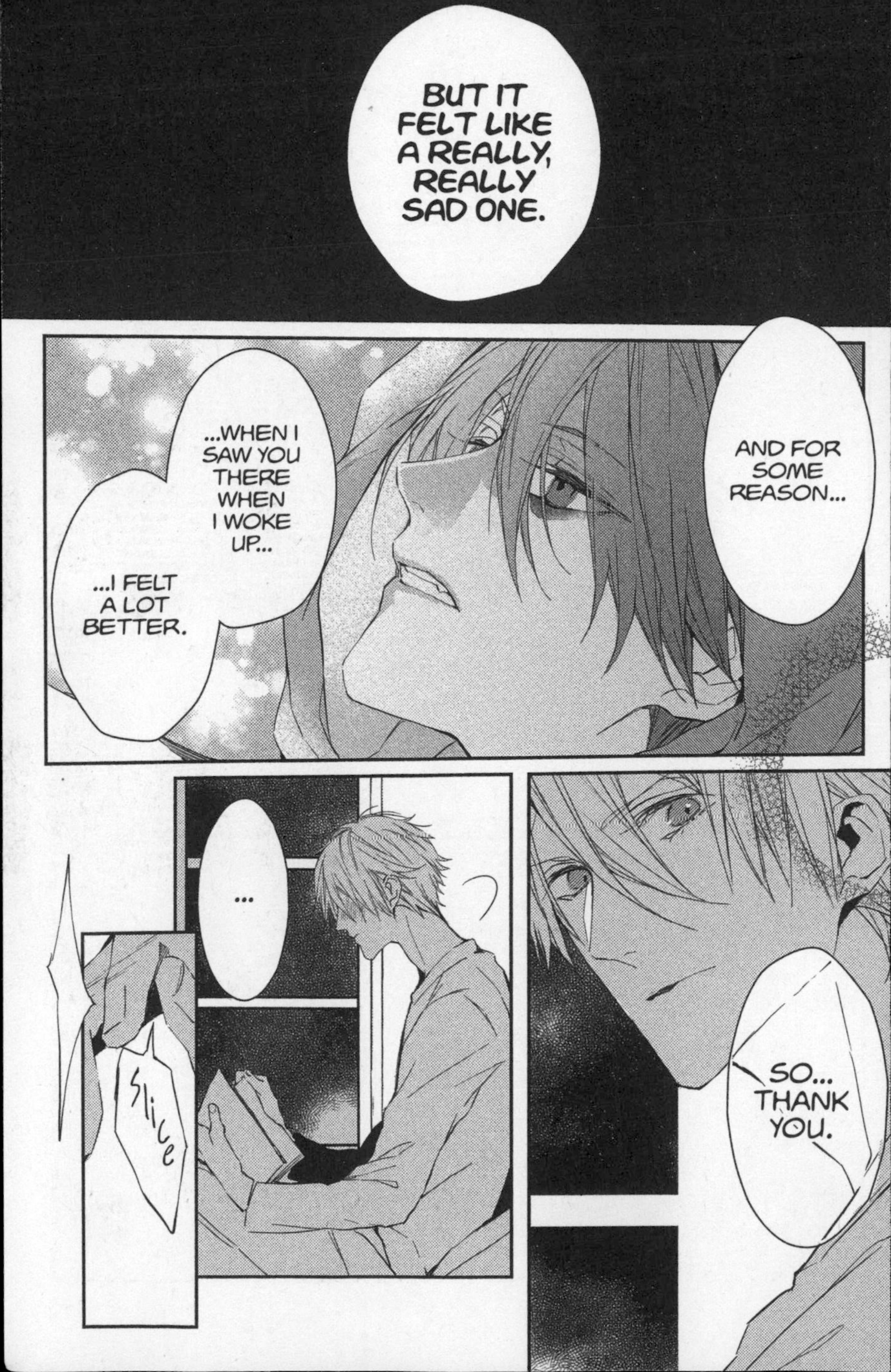
BUT IT FELT LIKE A REALLY, REALLY SAD ONE.
AND FOR SOME REASON...
...WHEN I SAW YOU THERE WHEN I WOKE UP...
...I FELT A LOT BETTER.
SO... THANK YOU.
...
Slice

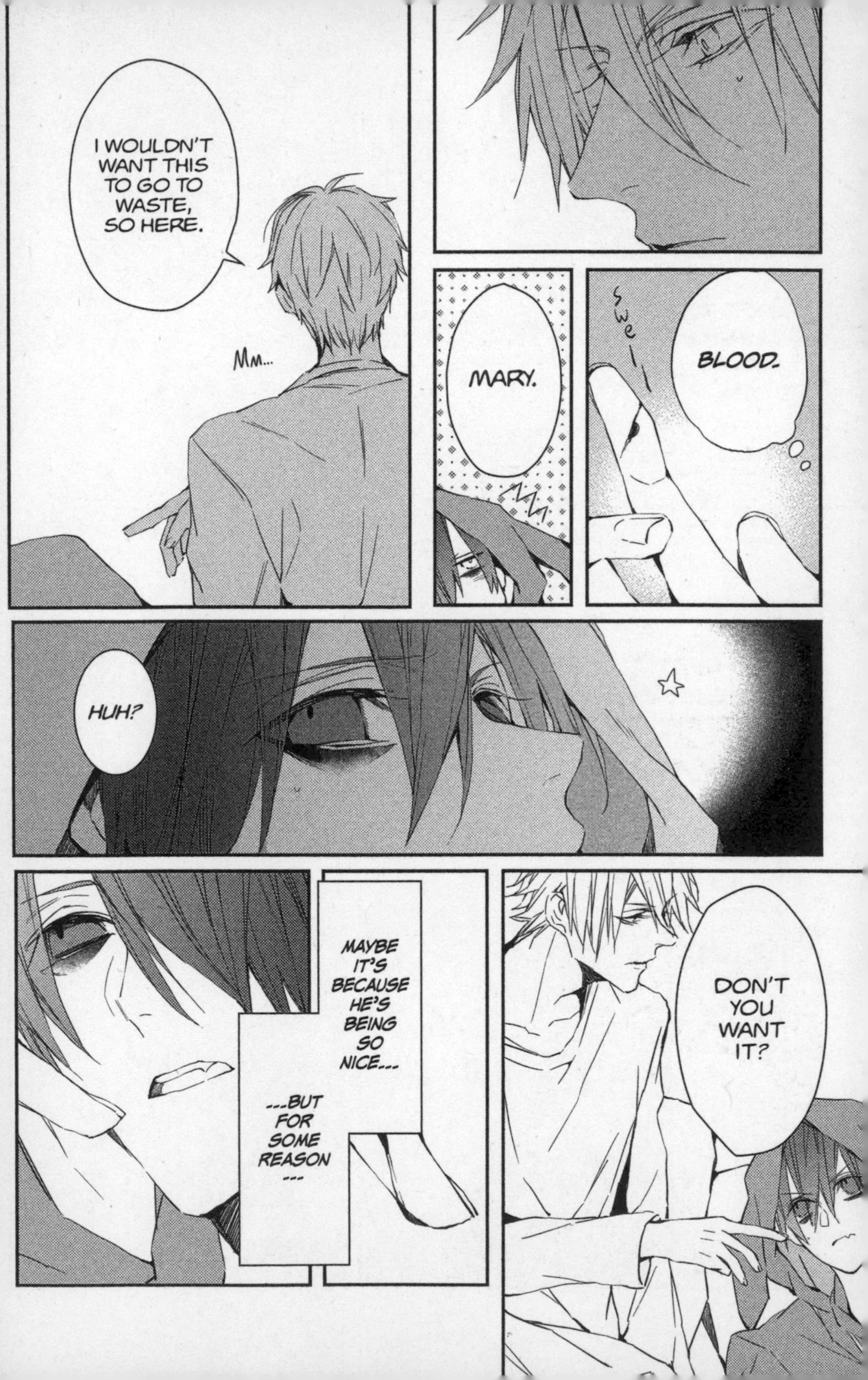
BLOOD.
swe
MARY.
I WOULDN'T WANT THIS TO GO TO WASTE, SO HERE.
Mm...
HUH?
DON'T YOU WANT IT?
MAYBE IT'S BECAUSE HE'S BEING SO NICE...
...BUT FOR SOME REASON
...

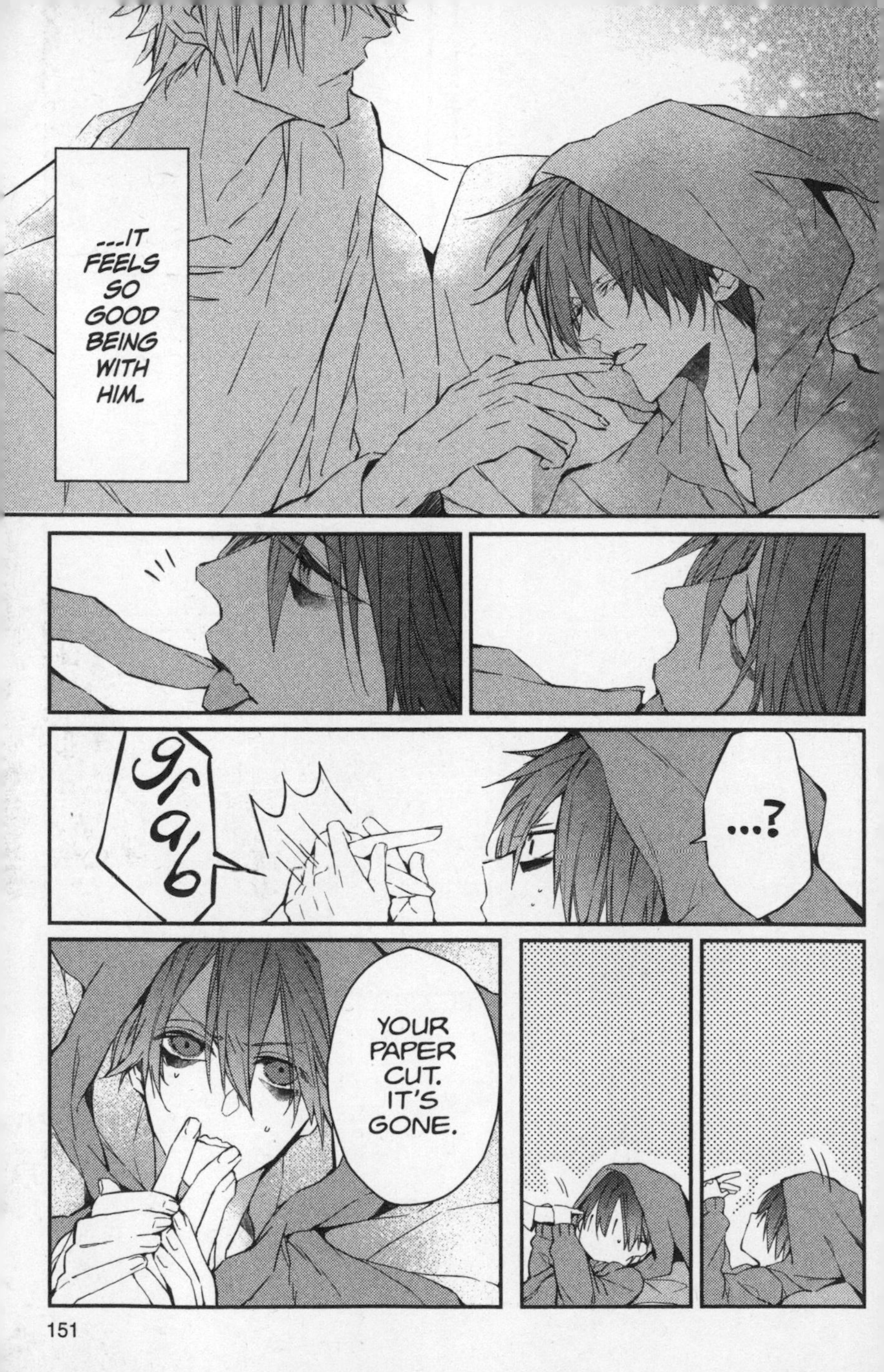
...IT FEELS SO GOOD BEING WITH HIM...
...?
grab
YOUR PAPER CUT. IT'S GONE.

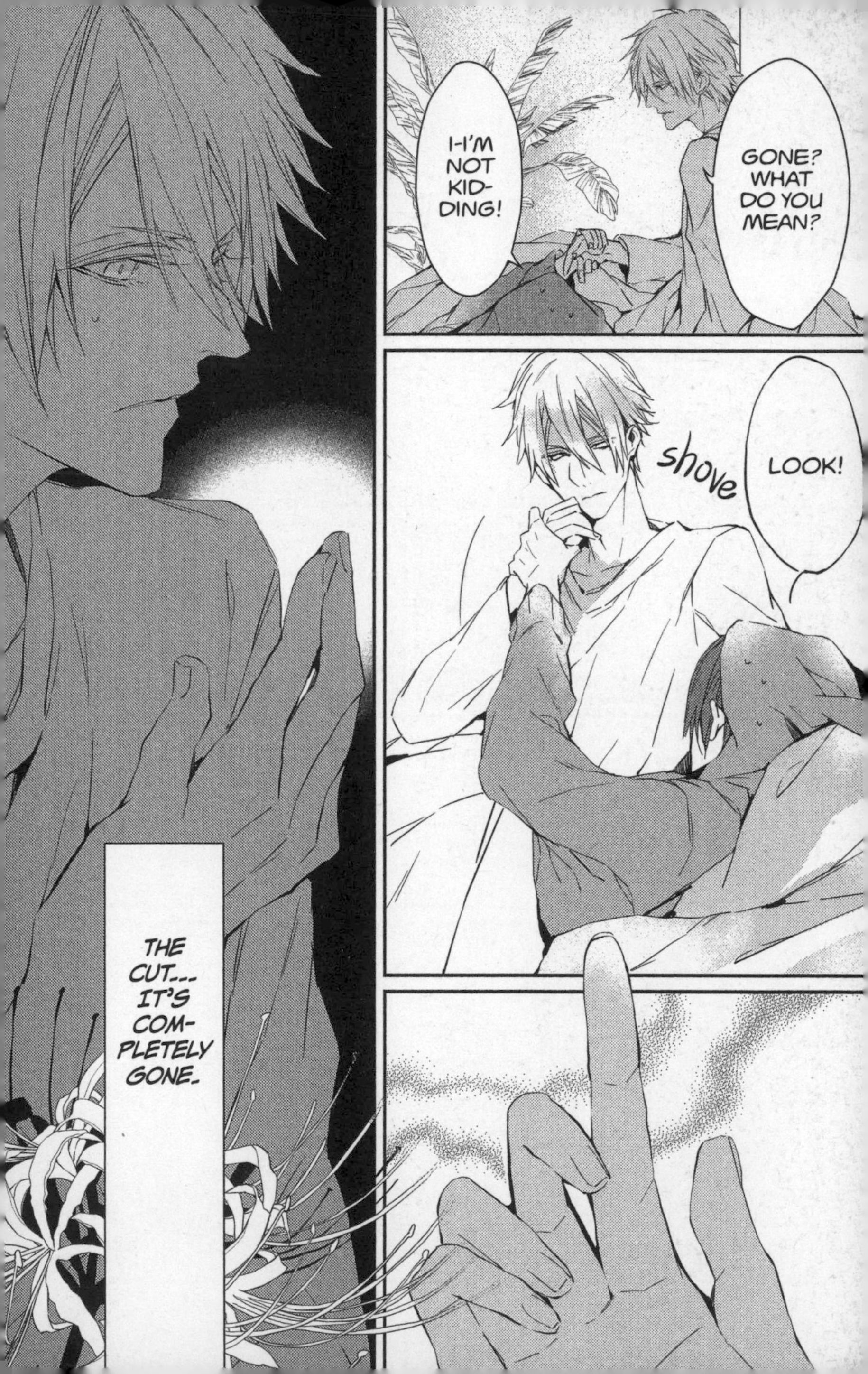
GONE? WHAT DO YOU MEAN?
I-I'M NOT KID-DING!
LOOK!
shove
THE CUT... IT'S COM-PLETELY GONE.

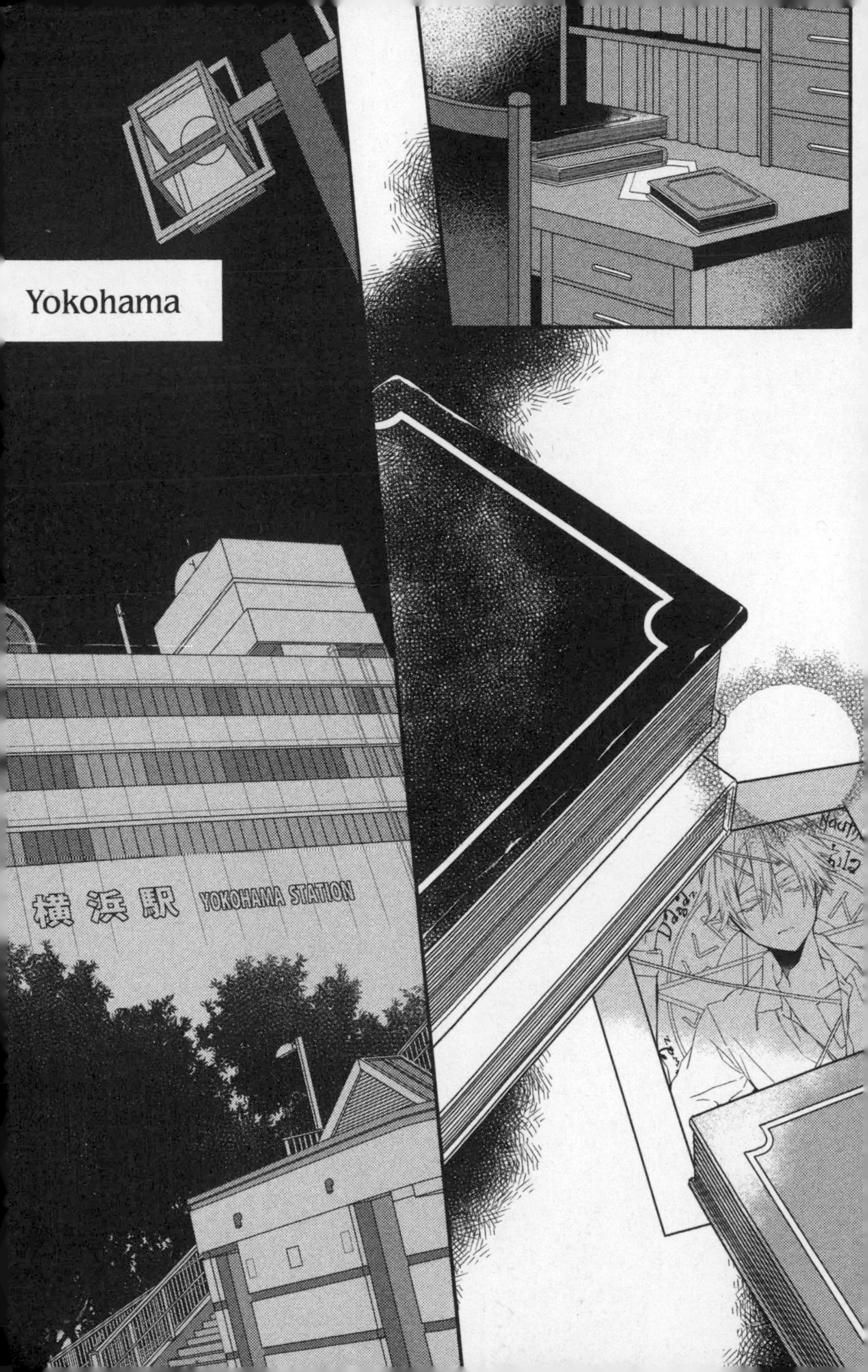
Yokohama
横浜駅 YOKOHAMA STATION

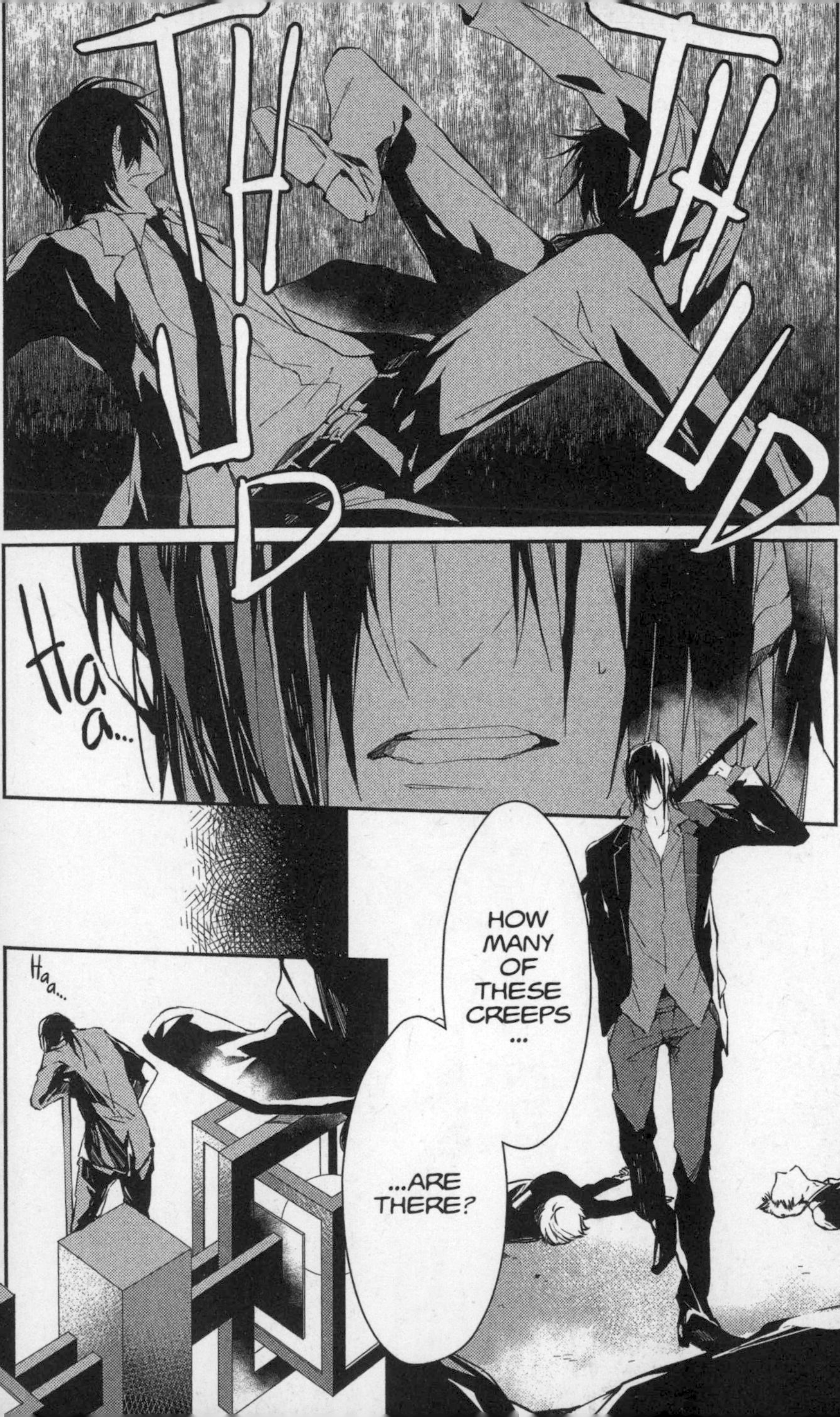
THUD
THUD
Haa...
HOW MANY OF THESE CREEPS...
...ARE THERE?
Haa...

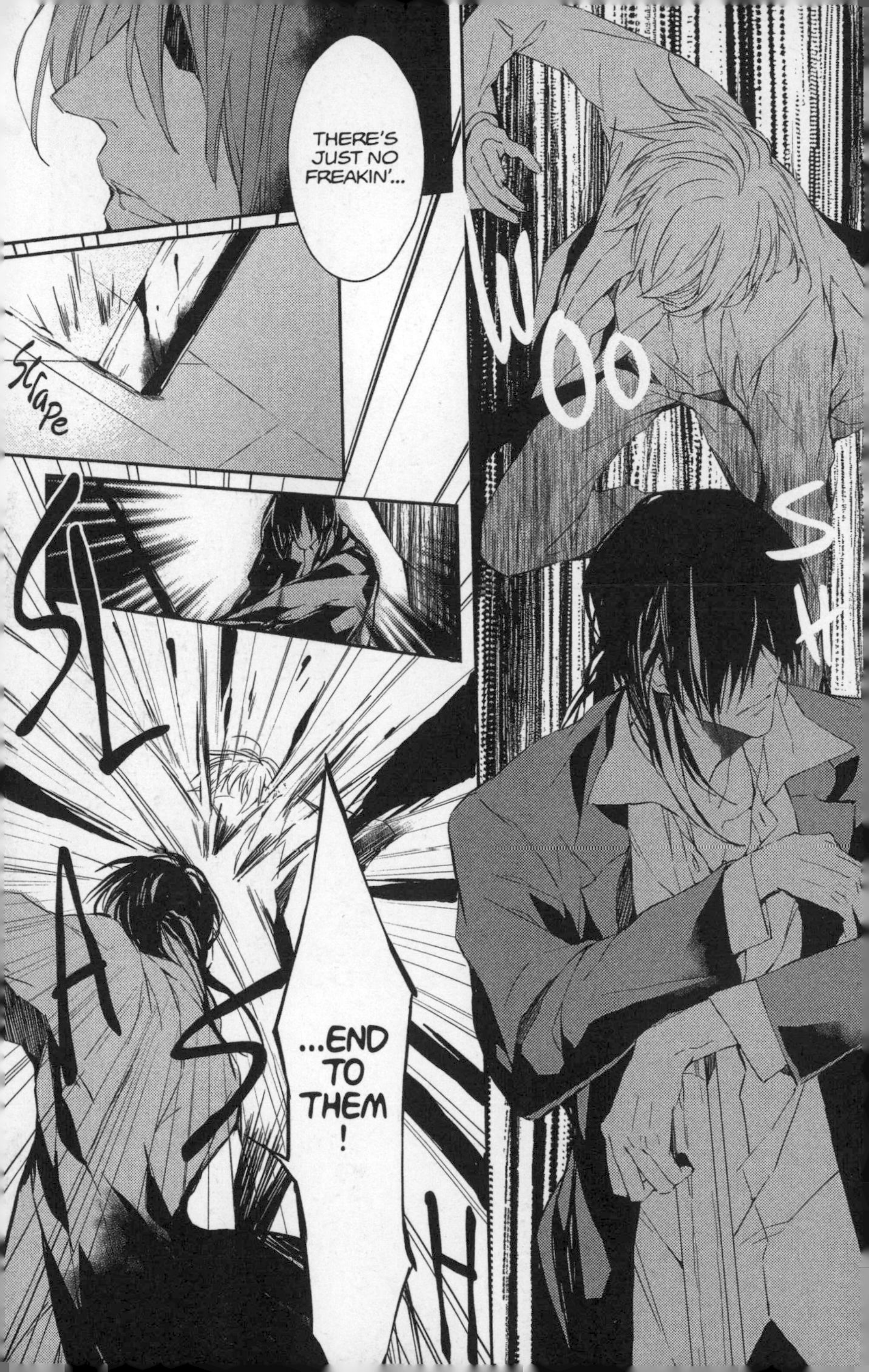
WOOSH
THERE'S JUST NO FREAKIN'...
scrape
SLASH
...END TO THEM!

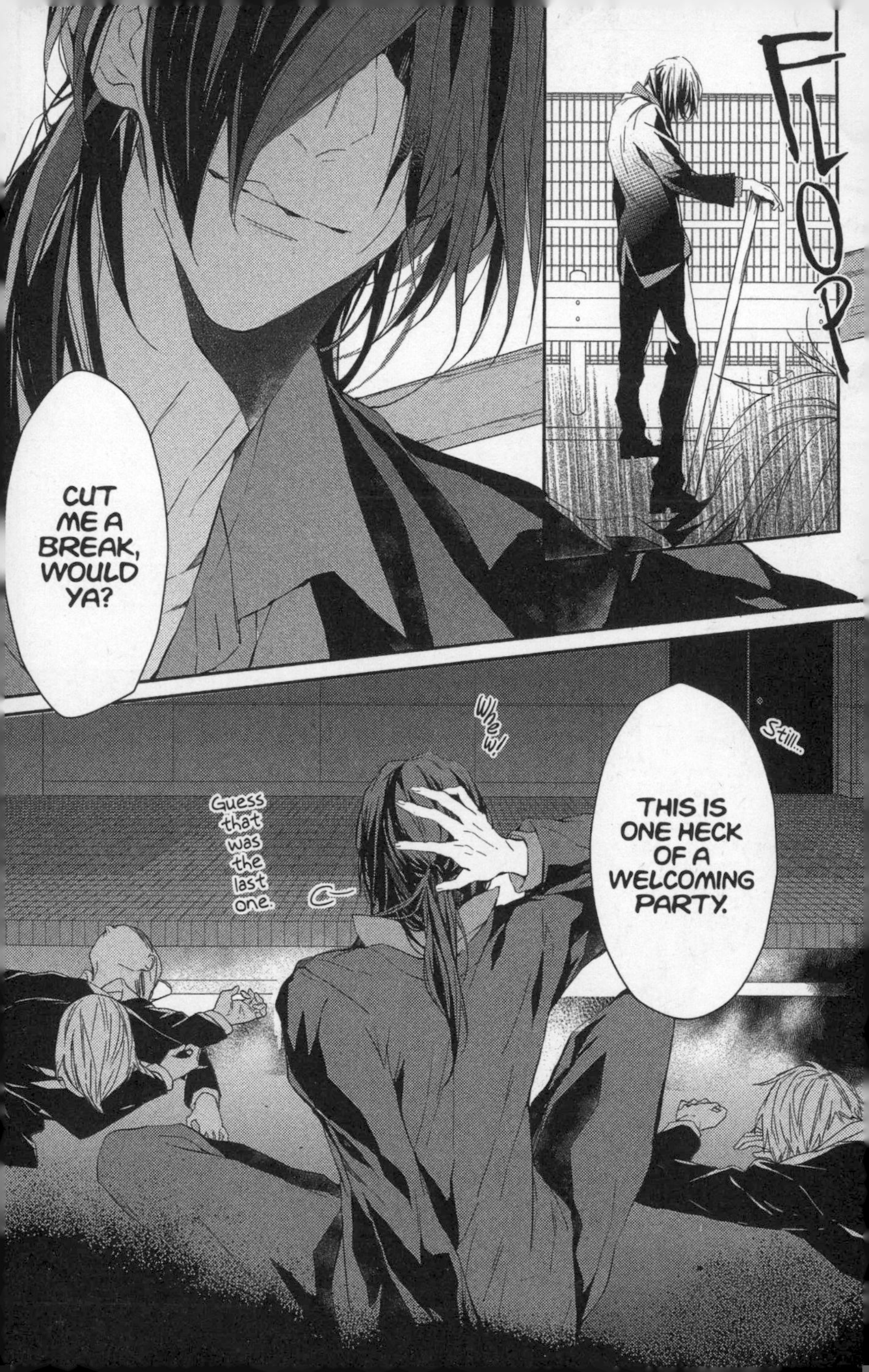
FLOP
CUT ME A BREAK, WOULD YA?
Still...
THIS IS ONE HECK OF A WELCOMING PARTY.
Whew!
Guess that was the last one.

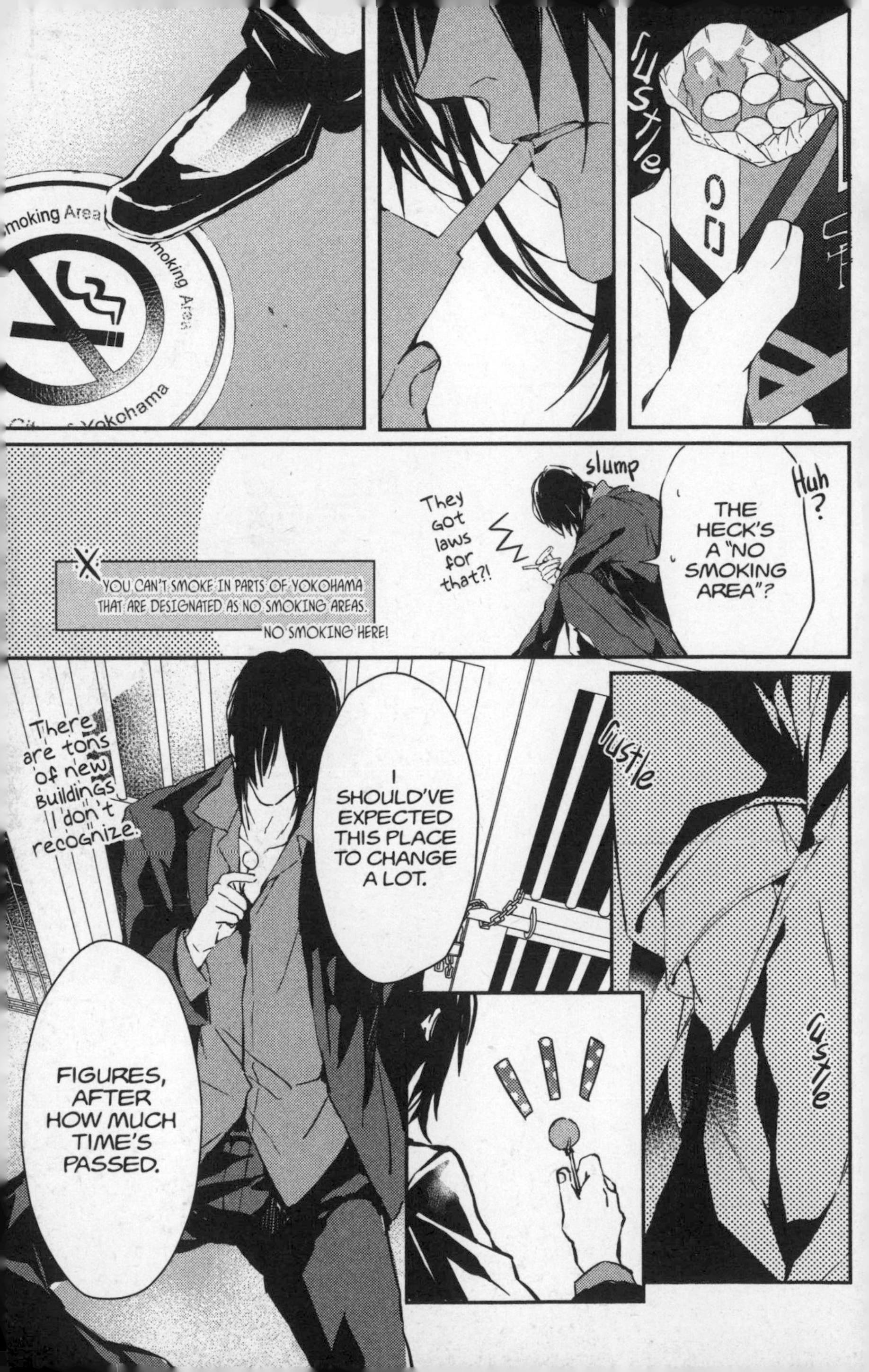
Rustle
Huh?
THE HECK'S A "NO SMOKING AREA"?
slump
They got laws for that?!
※YOU CAN'T SMOKE IN PARTS OF YOKOHAMA THAT ARE DESIGNATED AS NO SMOKING AREAS.
NO SMOKING HERE!
Smoking Area
City of Yokohama
Rustle
Rustle
I SHOULD'VE EXPECTED THIS PLACE TO CHANGE A LOT.
There are tons of new buildings I don't recognize.
FIGURES, AFTER HOW MUCH TIME'S PASSED.

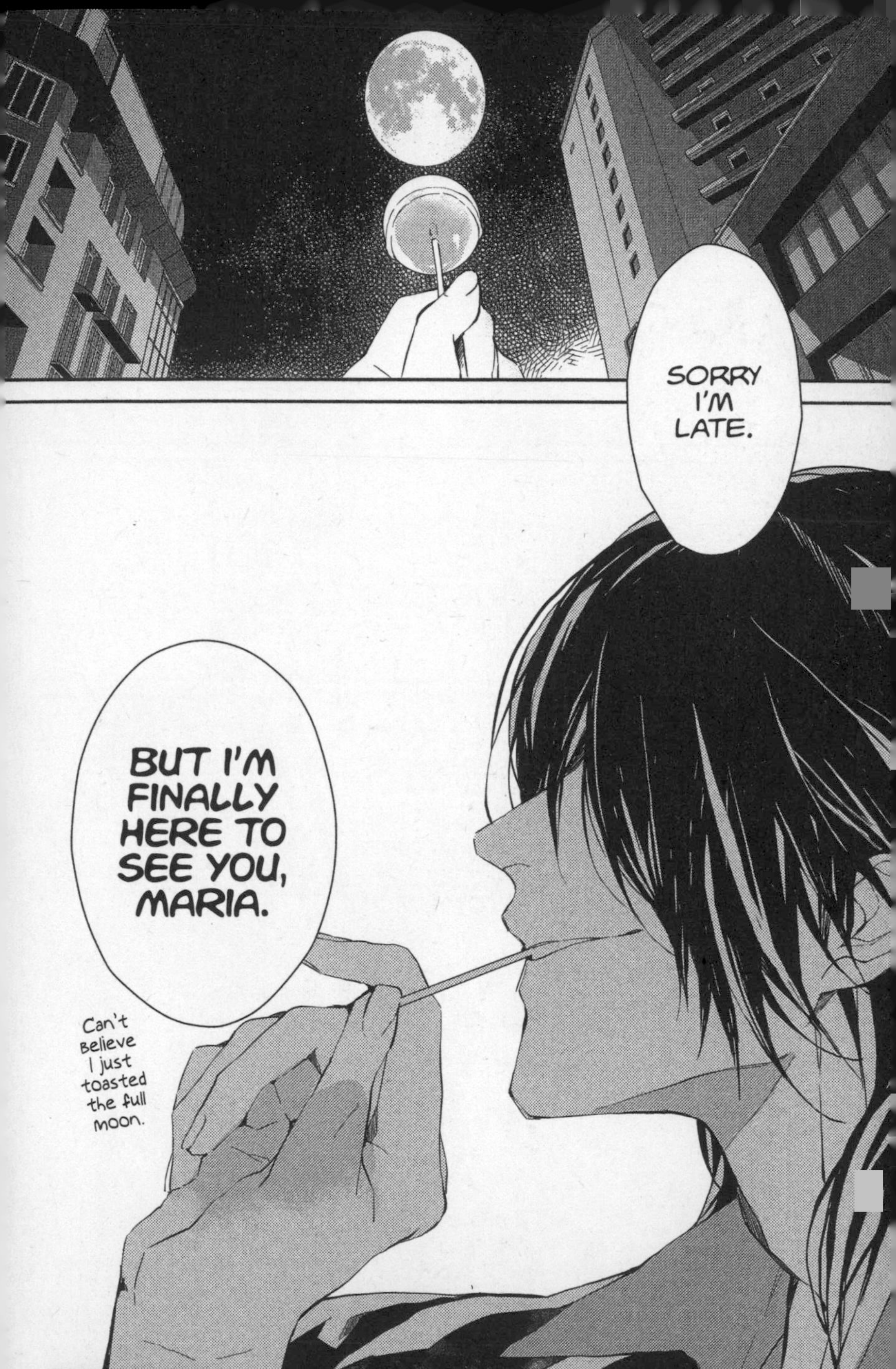
SORRY I'M LATE.
BUT I'M FINALLY HERE TO SEE YOU, MARIA.
Can't Believe I just toasted the full moon.

BLOOD ✦ 12 end

Bloody+Mary

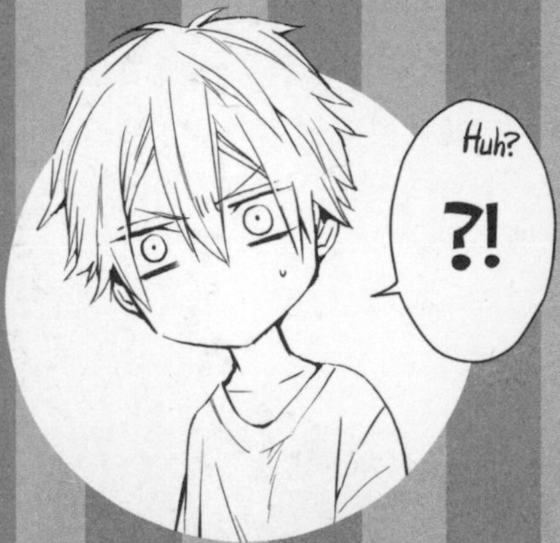
Huh?
?!

Postscript

◆ Thank you for picking up *Bloody Mary* volume three! This is the first time a series I've made has ever reached (three) volumes, so I'm pretty excited! Thank you so much to everyone who's stuck with me for the ride.

◆ When I first started this series, I'd just gotten a cat (named Hana). That's from a certain magical girl anime. And it's already been one year since she's started living with me. She's always showing off, but she's really cute. She doesn't answer to "Hana," but say "dinner" and she'll come running!

◆ Of all the questions I'm asked, the most common one is what manga software I use. I use Manga Studio EX! The color work is done in Photoshop CC, with some help from Clips Studio! There's still a lot I don't know about digital art, so I still get excited when I discover something that I didn't know how to do before. For example, it was only during chapter 12 that I finally learned how to move the frame lines... (easily)

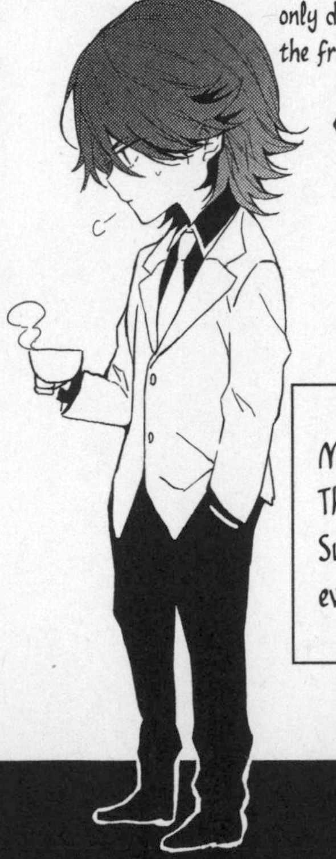

◆ In the next volume, I think we'll learn about Yusei's past (Maria's father). We've still got a while to go, so I hope you stick with me in the next volume!

SPECIAL THANKS

Mihoru, H-saka, H-gawa, M-fuchi, T-mizu, Ezaki, The Madam, T-ko, the production team/Haruo, Sumida, M-ika, M-naga, Editor S, the designers, everyone who supported me...and the readers!

akaza samamiya

Born November 7, Cancer, blood type B.
I could never make up my mind
about what Mary wears underneath
his hoodie, but I finally figured it
out in this volume!

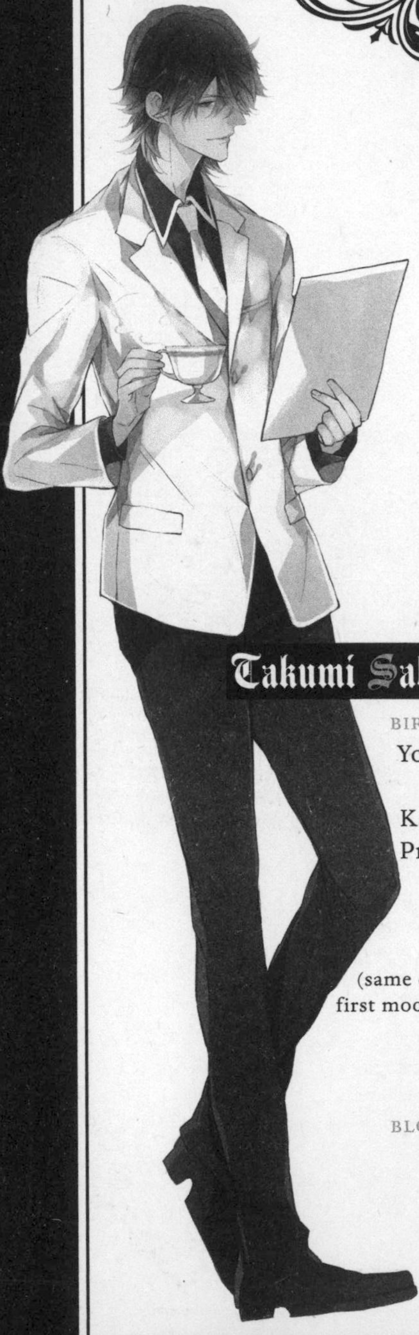

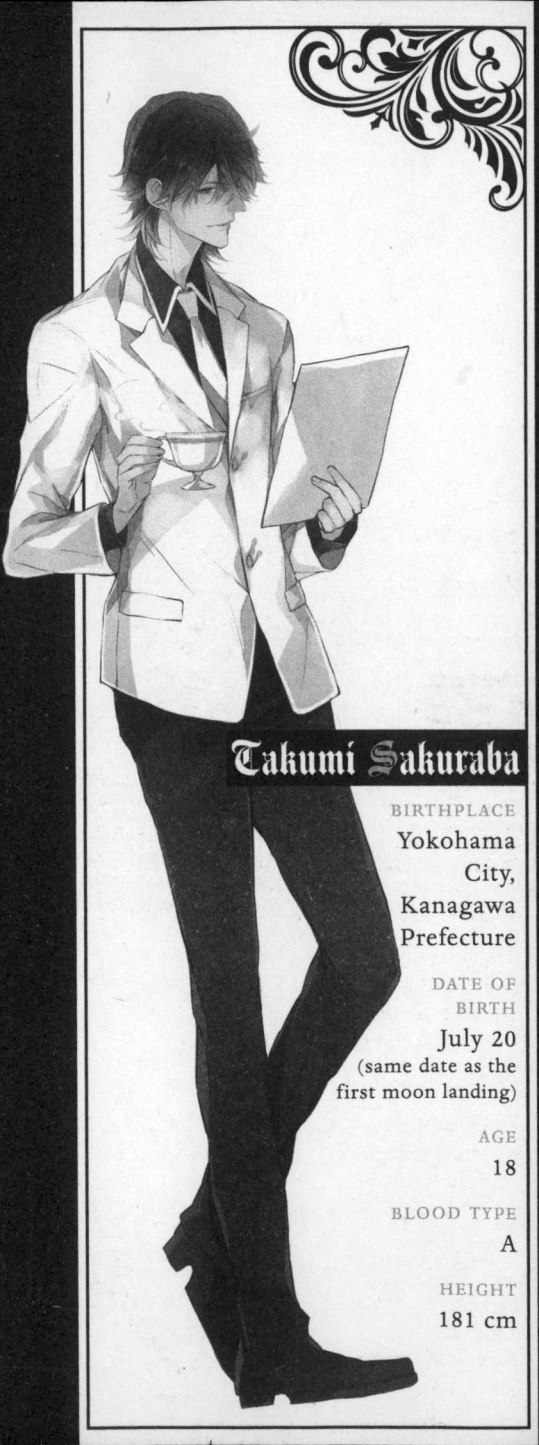

Takumi Sakuraba

BIRTHPLACE
Yokohama City, Kanagawa Prefecture

DATE OF BIRTH
July 20 (same date as the first moon landing)

AGE
18

BLOOD TYPE
A

HEIGHT
181 cm

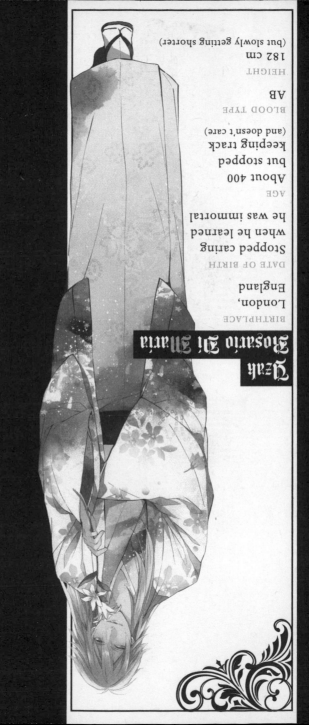

Yzak Ziosario Zij Jlaria

BIRTHPLACE
London, England

DATE OF BIRTH
Stopped caring when he learned he was immortal

AGE
About 400 but stopped keeping track (and doesn't care)

BLOOD TYPE
AB

HEIGHT
182 cm (but slowly getting shorter)

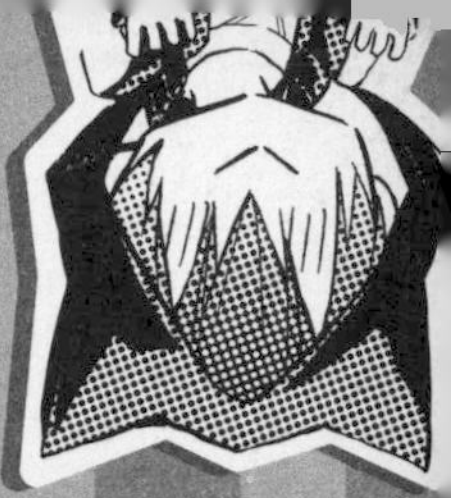

I-Mary

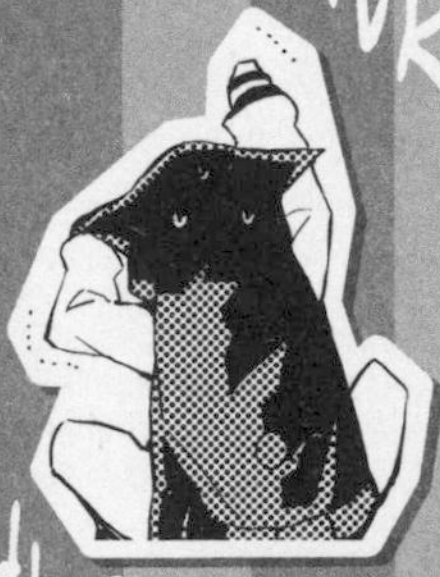
SHIVR
SHIVR

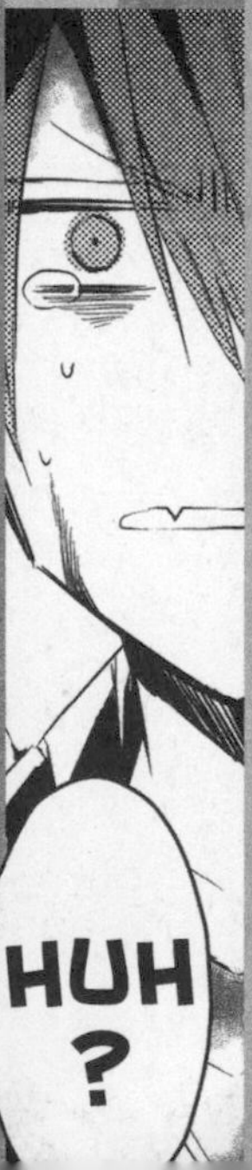
HUH ?

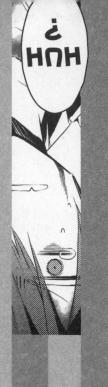

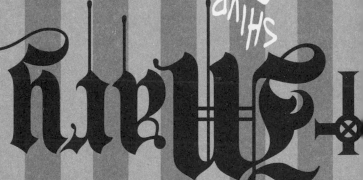

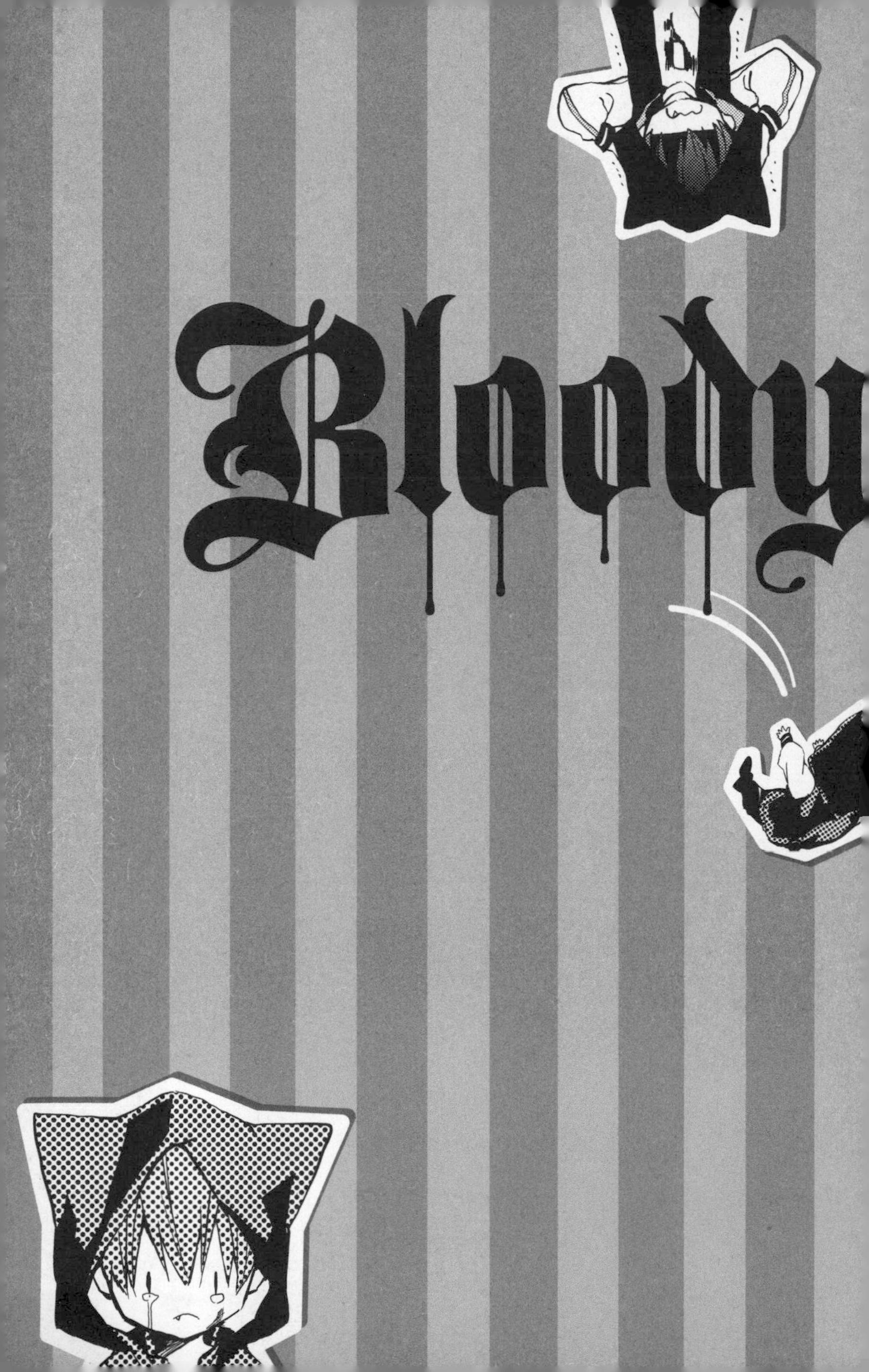
Bloody

Bloody Mary

Volume 3
Shojo Beat Edition

story and art by Akaza Samamiya

translation Katherine Schilling
touch-up art & lettering Sabrina Heep
design Fawn Lau
editor Erica Yee

BLOODY MARY Volume 3
© Akaza SAMAMIYA 2014
Edited by KADOKAWA SHOTEN
First published in Japan in 2014 by KADOKAWA
CORPORATION, Tokyo.
English translation rights arranged with KADOKAWA
CORPORATION, Tokyo.

Printed in the U.S.A.

Published by VIZ Media, LLC
P.O. Box 77010
San Francisco, CA 94107

10 9 8 7 6 5 4 3 2 1
First printing, June 2016

www.viz.com   www.shojobeat.com